RWBY

THE OFFICIAL MANGA

VOLUME

3

STORY AND ART

BUNTA KINAMI

BASED ON THE ROOSTER TEETH SERIES CREATED BY MONTY OUM

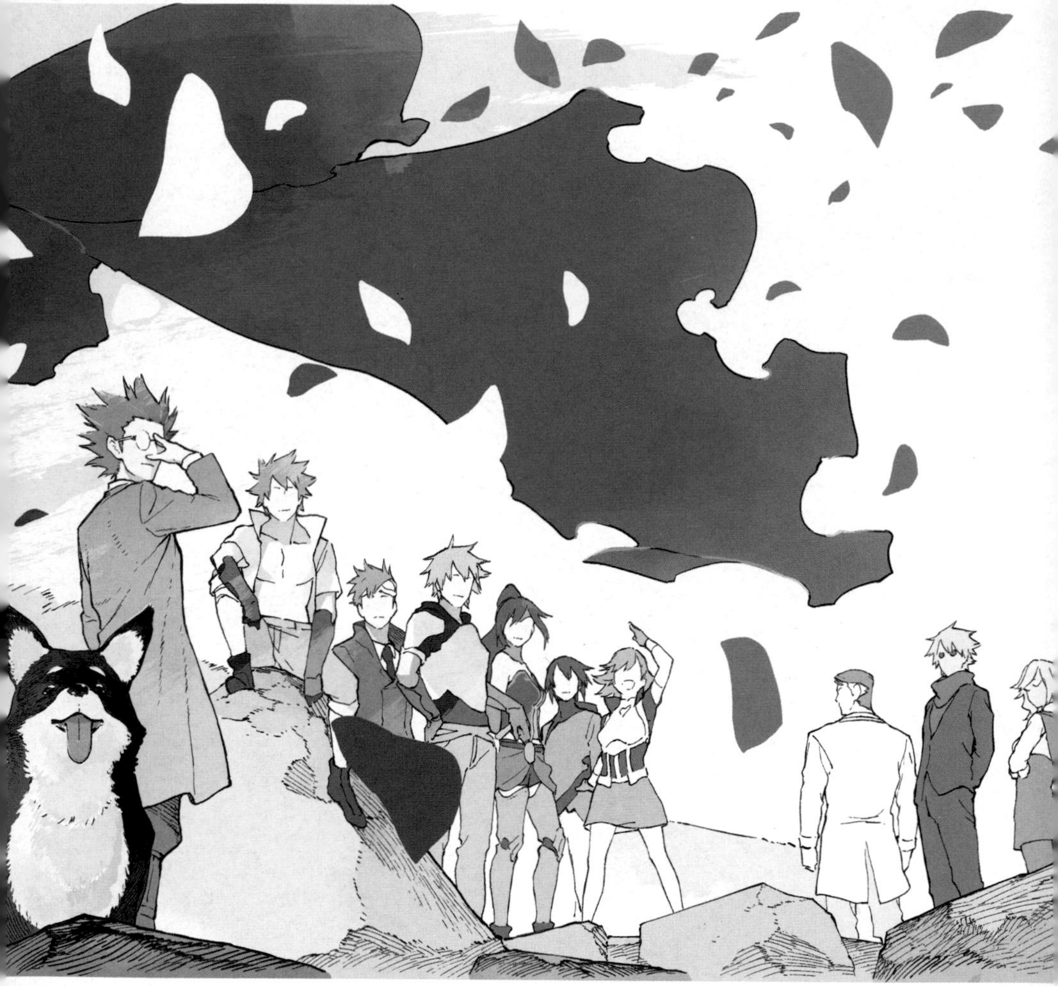

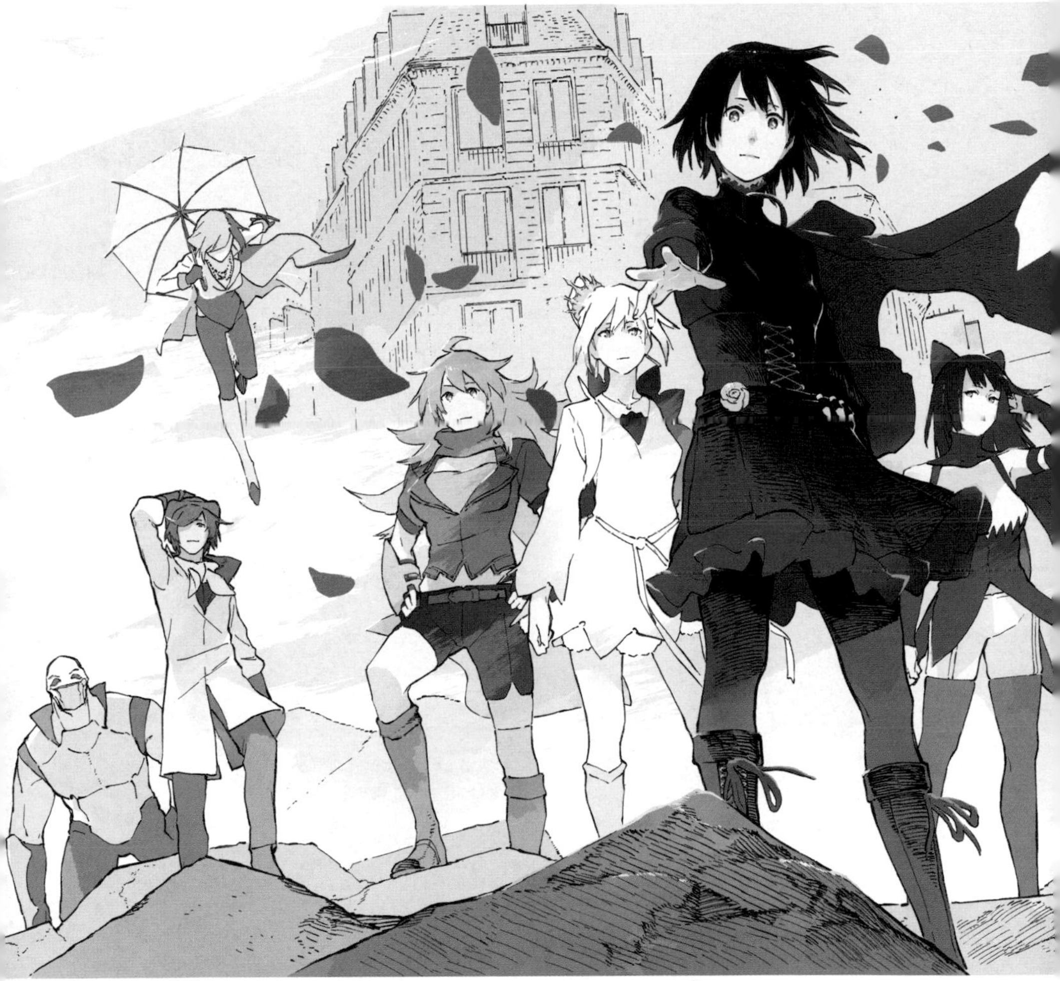

CONTENTS

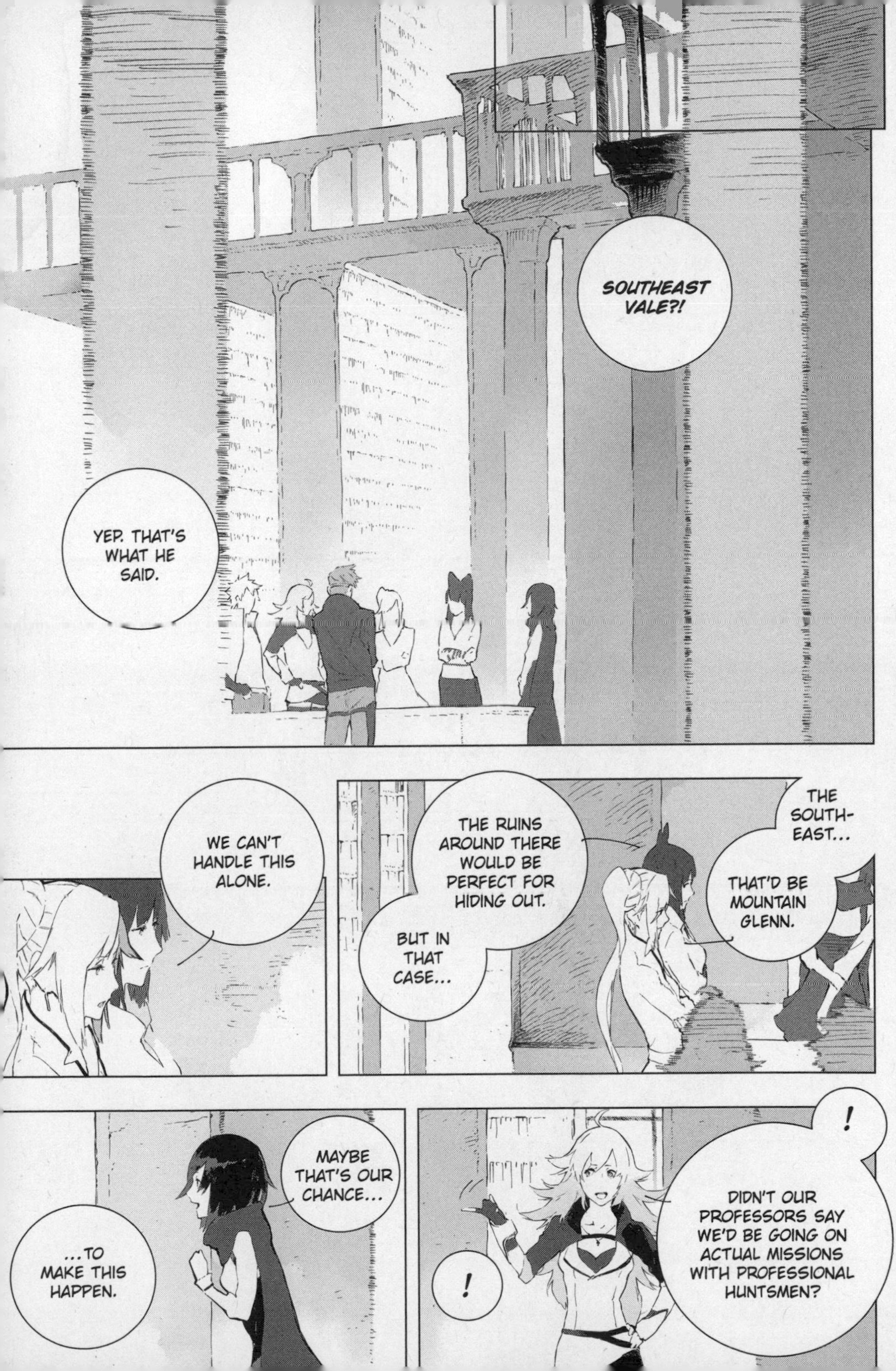
SOUTHEAST VALE?!
YEP. THAT'S WHAT HE SAID.
THE SOUTH-EAST...
THAT'D BE MOUNTAIN GLENN.
THE RUINS AROUND THERE WOULD BE PERFECT FOR HIDING OUT.
BUT IN THAT CASE...
WE CAN'T HANDLE THIS ALONE.
!
DIDN'T OUR PROFESSORS SAY WE'D BE GOING ON ACTUAL MISSIONS WITH PROFESSIONAL HUNTSMEN?
!
MAYBE THAT'S OUR CHANCE...
...TO MAKE THIS HAPPEN.

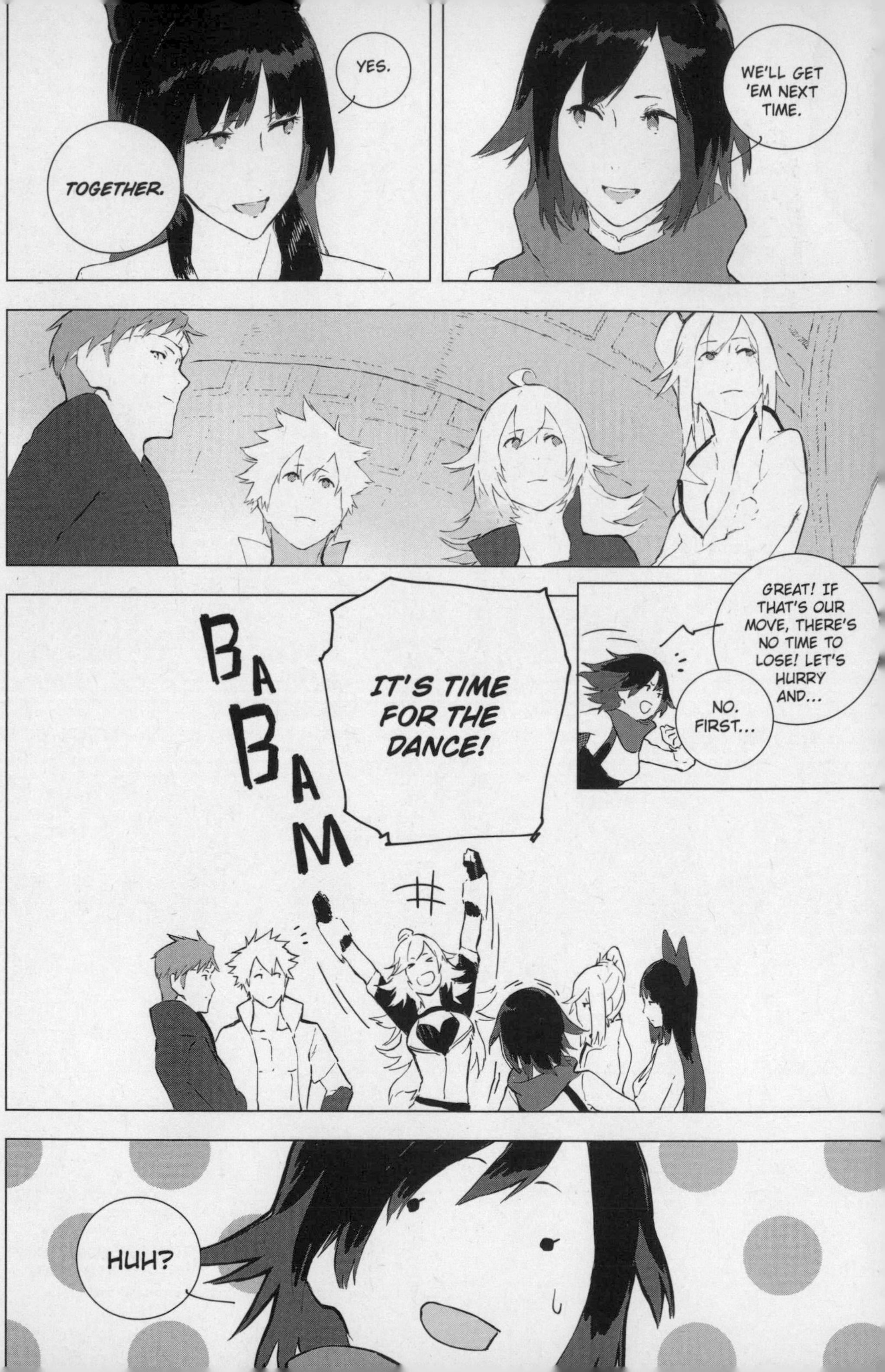
WE'LL GET 'EM NEXT TIME.
YES.
TOGETHER.
GREAT! IF THAT'S OUR MOVE, THERE'S NO TIME TO LOSE! LET'S HURRY AND...
NO. FIRST...
BABAM
IT'S TIME FOR THE DANCE!
HUH?

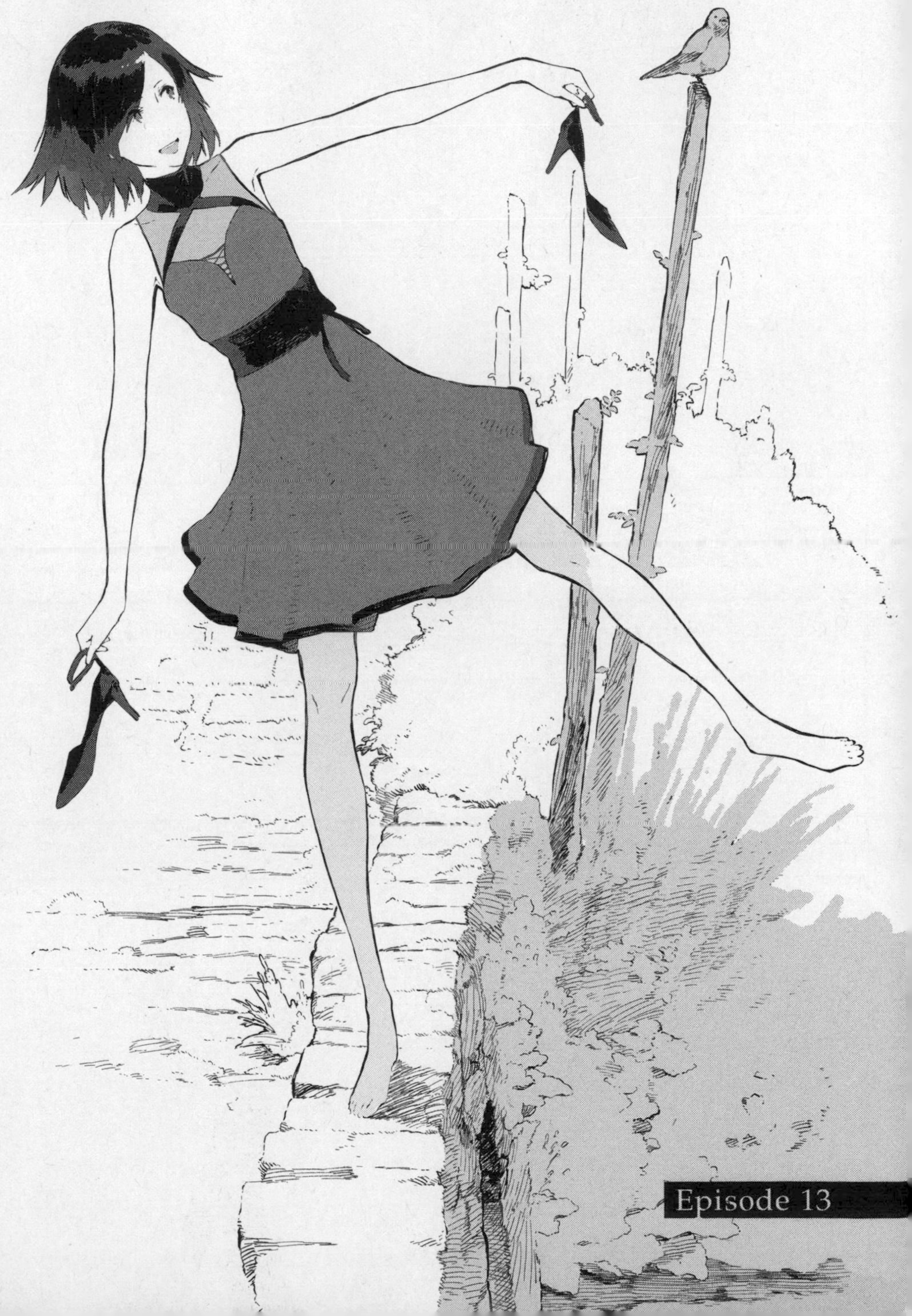
Episode 13

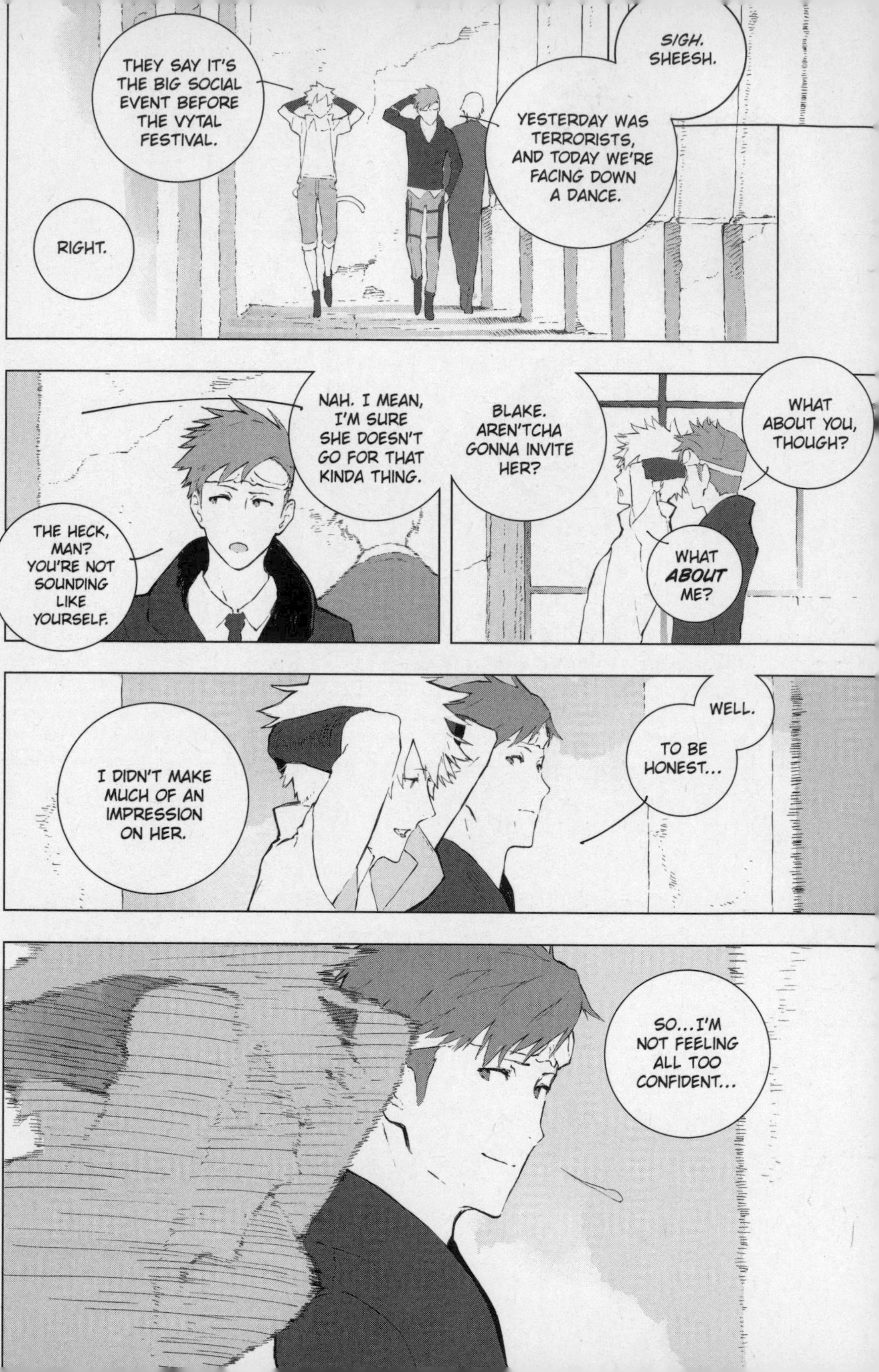
SIGH. SHEESH.
YESTERDAY WAS TERRORISTS, AND TODAY WE'RE FACING DOWN A DANCE.
THEY SAY IT'S THE BIG SOCIAL EVENT BEFORE THE VYTAL FESTIVAL.
RIGHT.
WHAT ABOUT YOU, THOUGH?
WHAT ***ABOUT*** ME?
BLAKE. AREN'TCHA GONNA INVITE HER?
NAH. I MEAN, I'M SURE SHE DOESN'T GO FOR THAT KINDA THING.
THE HECK, MAN? YOU'RE NOT SOUNDING LIKE YOURSELF.
WELL.
TO BE HONEST...
I DIDN'T MAKE MUCH OF AN IMPRESSION ON HER.
SO...I'M NOT FEELING ALL TOO CONFIDENT...

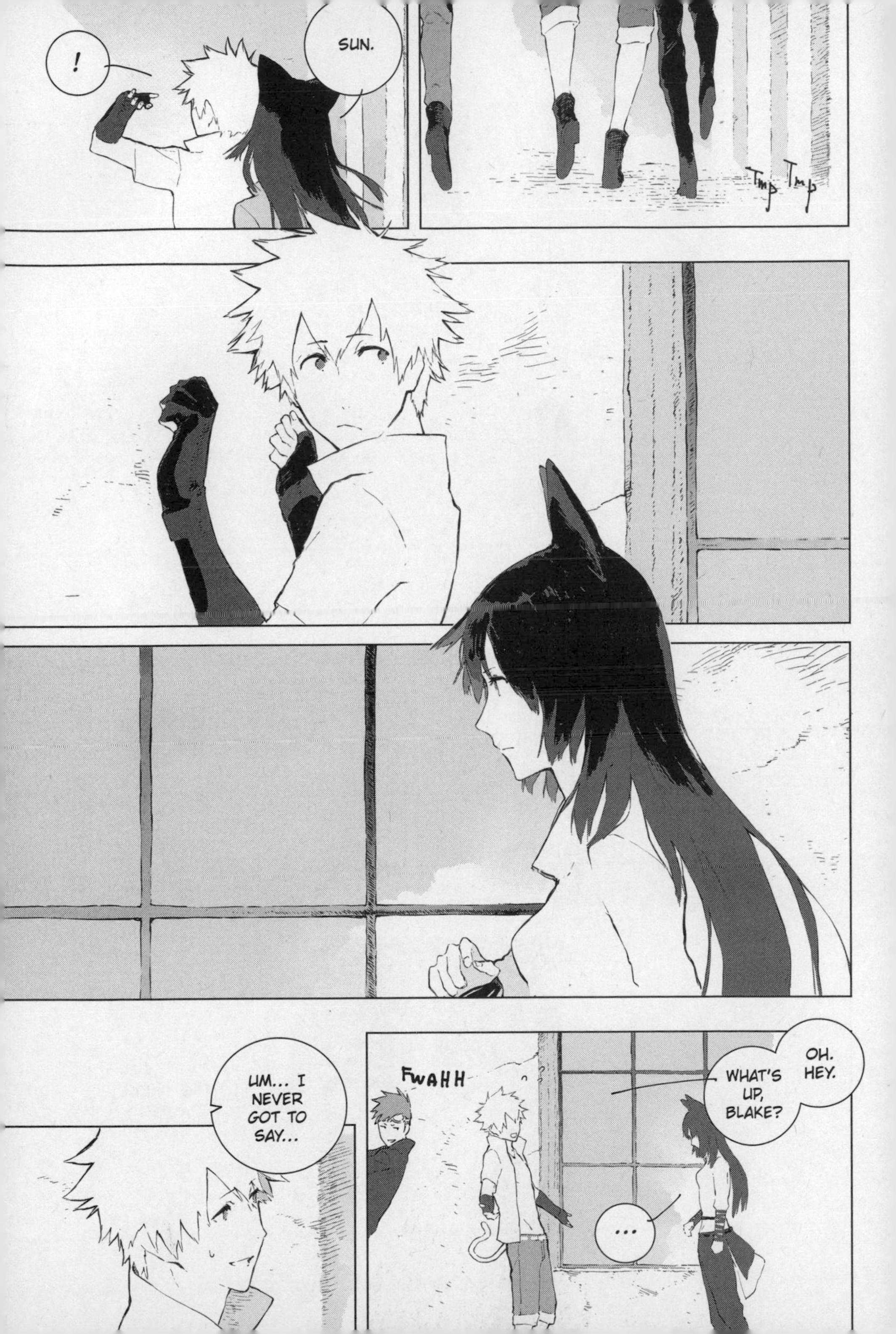
Tmp Tmp
SUN.
!
OH. HEY.
WHAT'S UP, BLAKE?
FWAHH
...
UM... I NEVER GOT TO SAY...

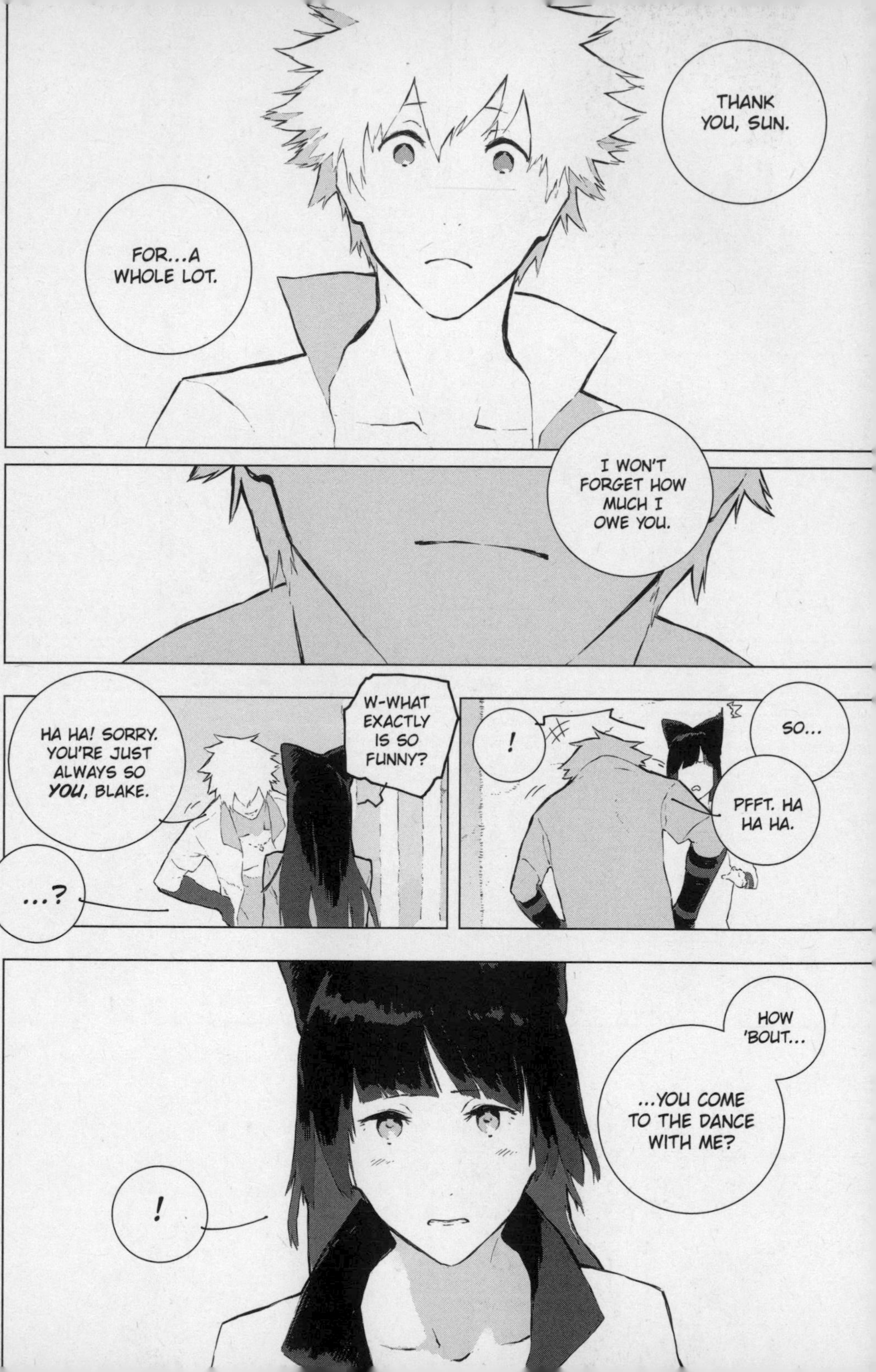
THANK YOU, SUN.
FOR...A WHOLE LOT.
I WON'T FORGET HOW MUCH I OWE YOU.
SO...
!
PFFT. HA HA HA.
W-WHAT EXACTLY IS SO FUNNY?
HA HA! SORRY. YOU'RE JUST ALWAYS SO *YOU*, BLAKE.
...?
HOW 'BOUT...
...YOU COME TO THE DANCE WITH ME?
!

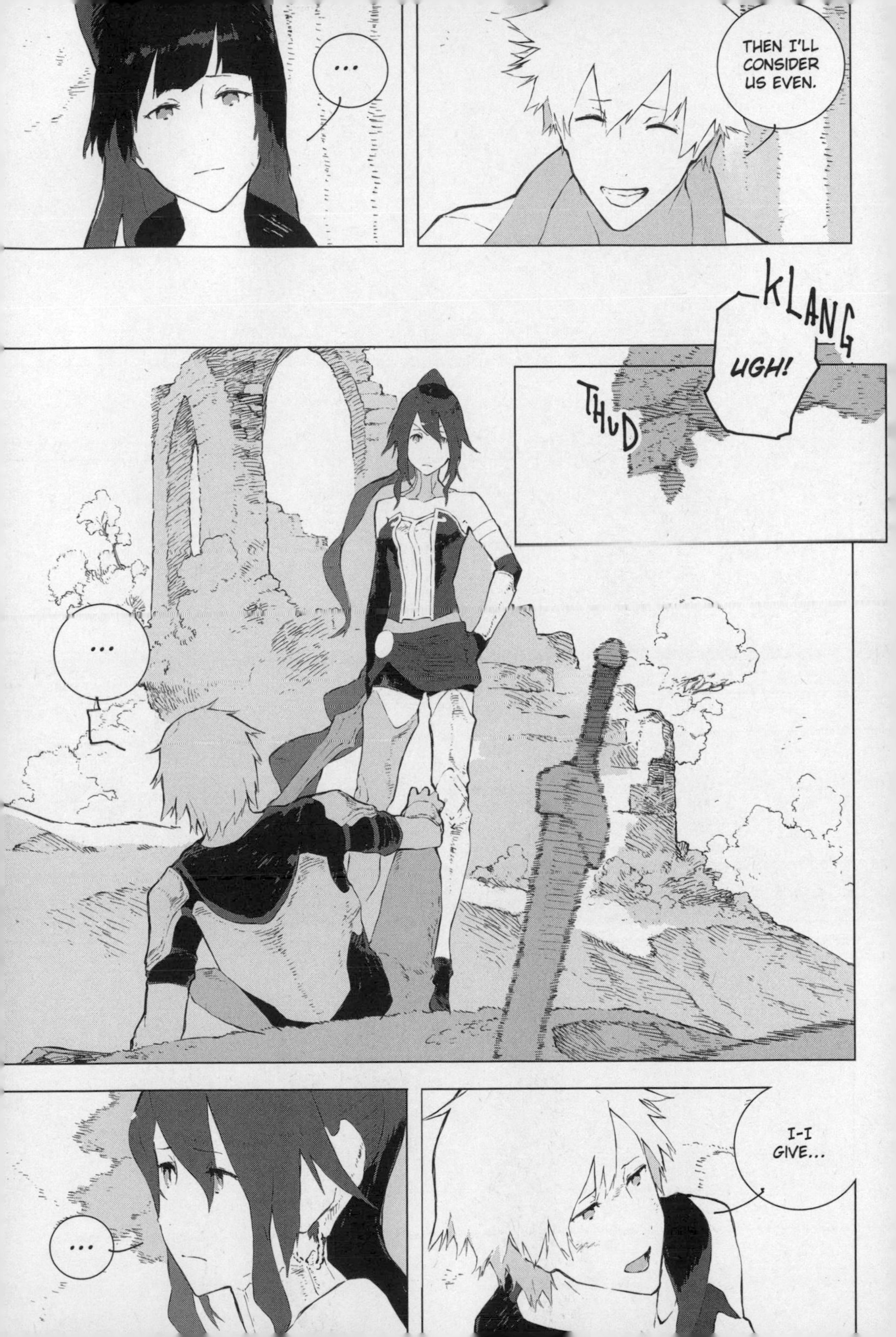
THEN I'LL CONSIDER US EVEN.
...
KLANG
UGH!
THUD
...
I-I GIVE...
...

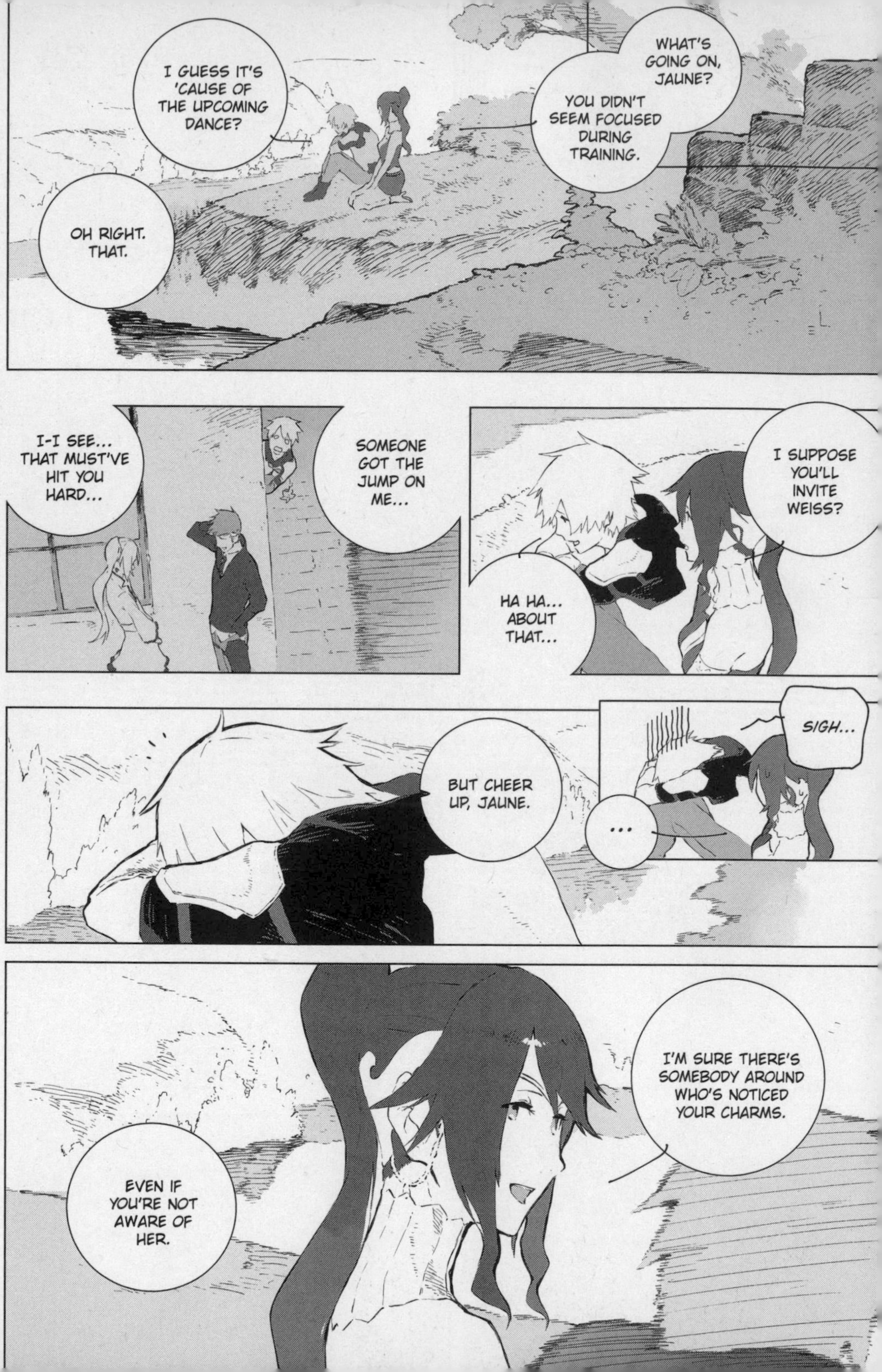
WHAT'S GOING ON, JAUNE?
YOU DIDN'T SEEM FOCUSED DURING TRAINING.
I GUESS IT'S 'CAUSE OF THE UPCOMING DANCE?
OH RIGHT. THAT.
I SUPPOSE YOU'LL INVITE WEISS?
HA HA... ABOUT THAT...
SOMEONE GOT THE JUMP ON ME...
I-I SEE... THAT MUST'VE HIT YOU HARD...
SIGH...
...
BUT CHEER UP, JAUNE.
I'M SURE THERE'S SOMEBODY AROUND WHO'S NOTICED YOUR CHARMS.
EVEN IF YOU'RE NOT AWARE OF HER.

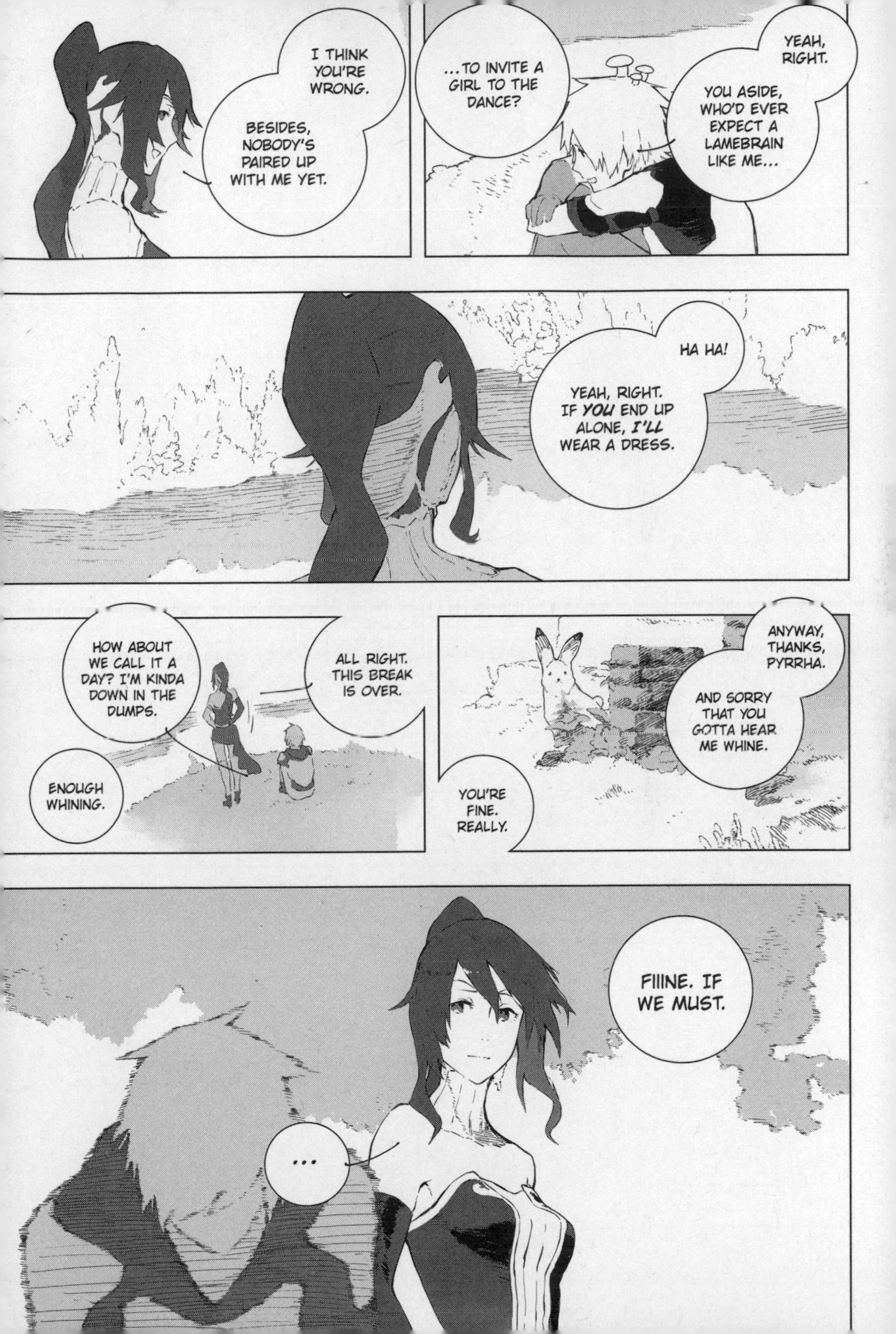
YEAH, RIGHT.
YOU ASIDE, WHO'D EVER EXPECT A LAMEBRAIN LIKE ME...
...TO INVITE A GIRL TO THE DANCE?
I THINK YOU'RE WRONG.
BESIDES, NOBODY'S PAIRED UP WITH ME YET.
HA HA!
YEAH, RIGHT. IF *YOU* END UP ALONE, *I'LL* WEAR A DRESS.
ANYWAY, THANKS, PYRRHA.
AND SORRY THAT YOU GOTTA HEAR ME WHINE.
YOU'RE FINE. REALLY.
ALL RIGHT. THIS BREAK IS OVER.
HOW ABOUT WE CALL IT A DAY? I'M KINDA DOWN IN THE DUMPS.
ENOUGH WHINING.
FIIINE. IF WE MUST.
...

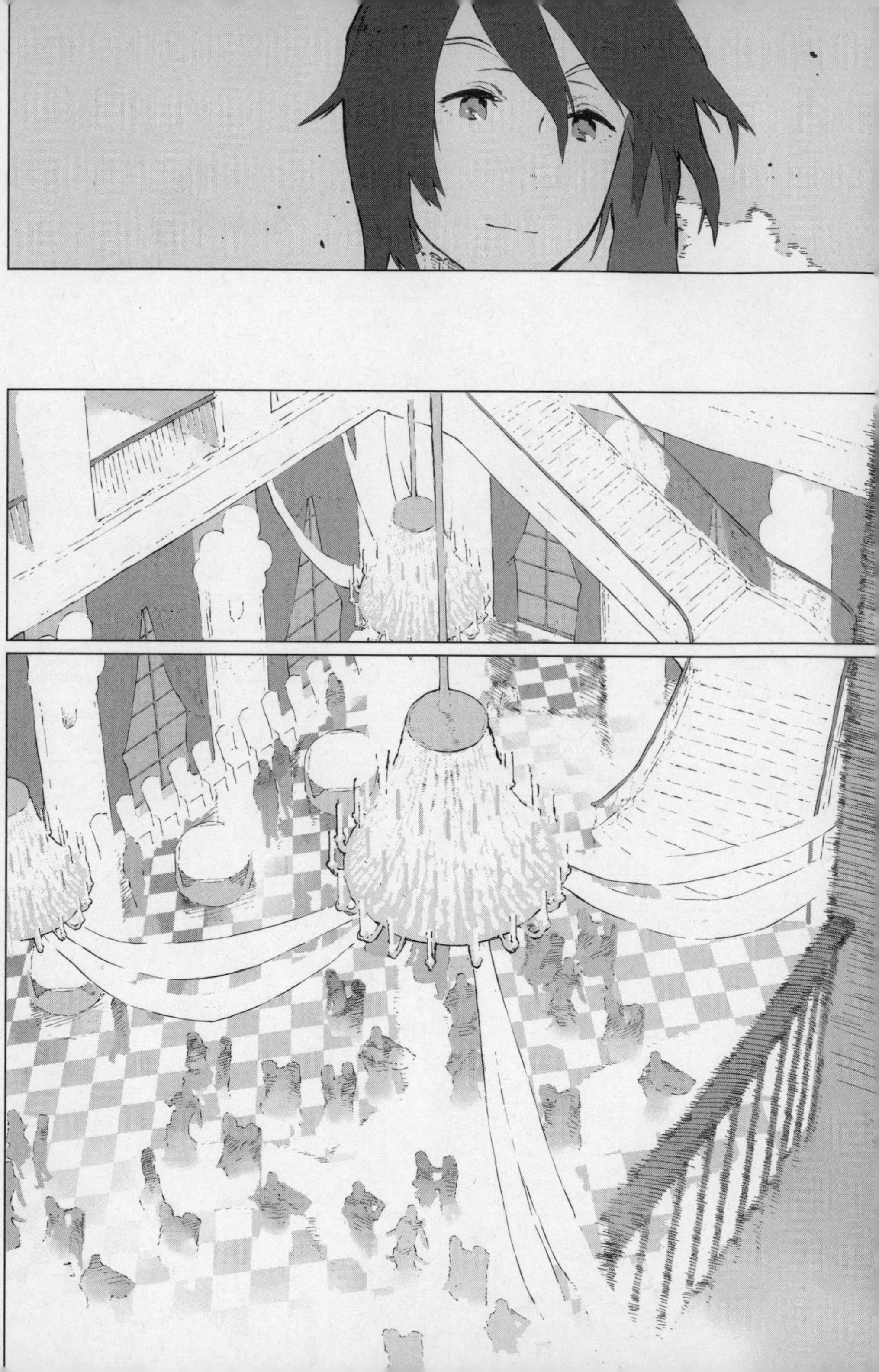

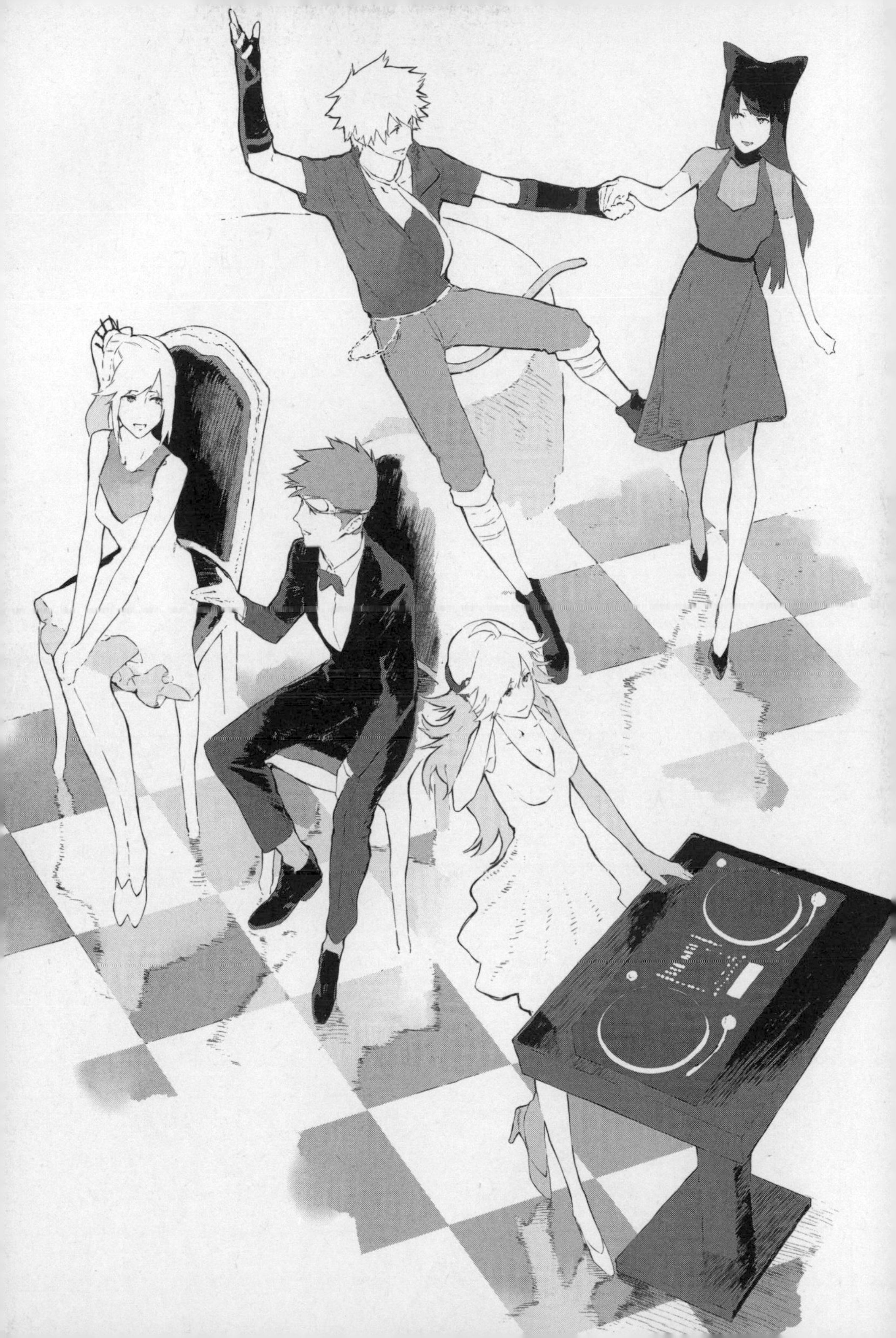

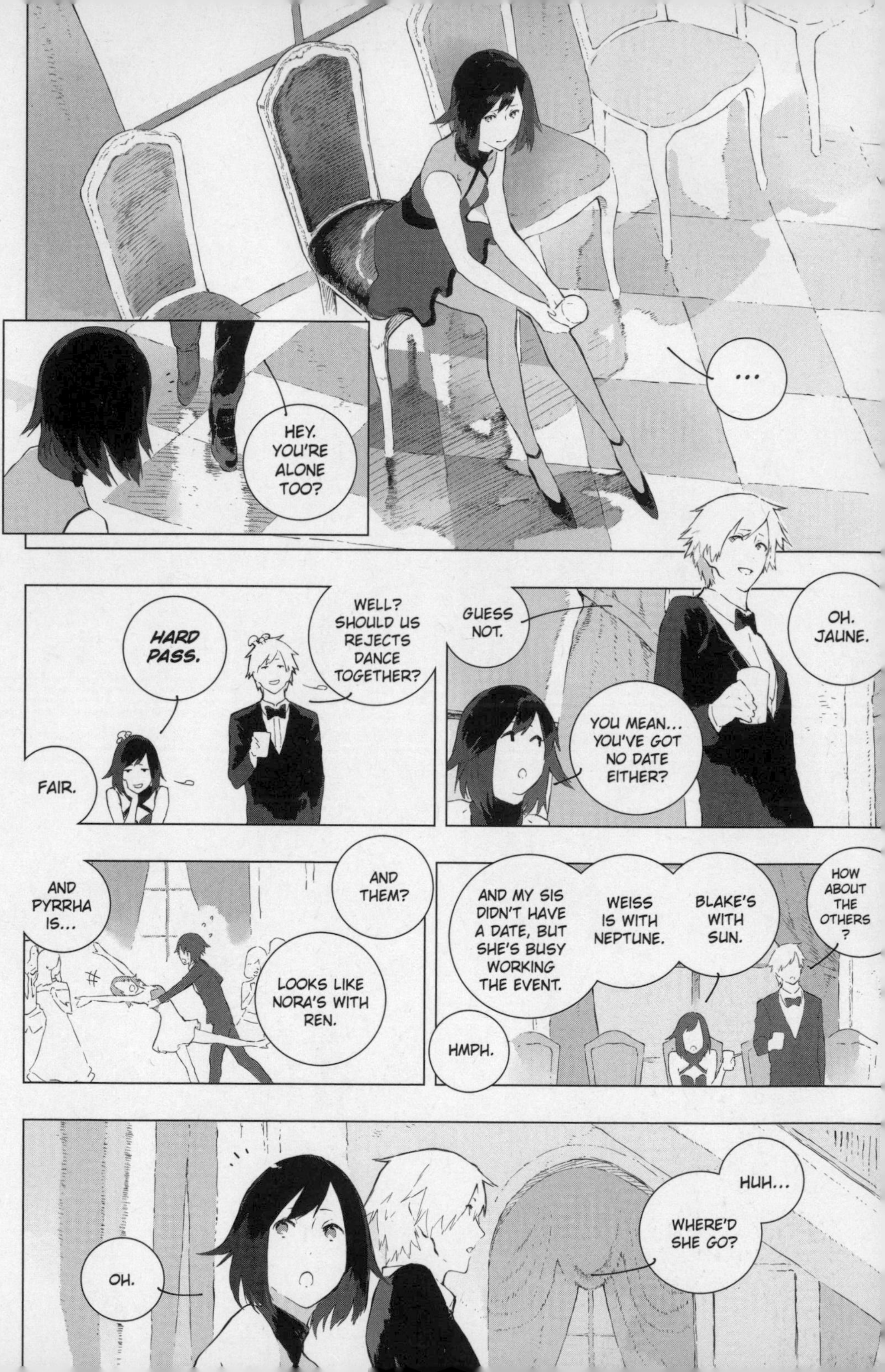
...
HEY. YOU'RE ALONE TOO?
OH. JAUNE.
YOU MEAN... YOU'VE GOT NO DATE EITHER?
GUESS NOT.
WELL? SHOULD US REJECTS DANCE TOGETHER?
HARD PASS.
FAIR.
HOW ABOUT THE OTHERS?
BLAKE'S WITH SUN.
WEISS IS WITH NEPTUNE.
AND MY SIS DIDN'T HAVE A DATE, BUT SHE'S BUSY WORKING THE EVENT.
HMPH.
AND THEM?
LOOKS LIKE NORA'S WITH REN.
AND PYRRHA IS...
HUH...
WHERE'D SHE GO?
OH.

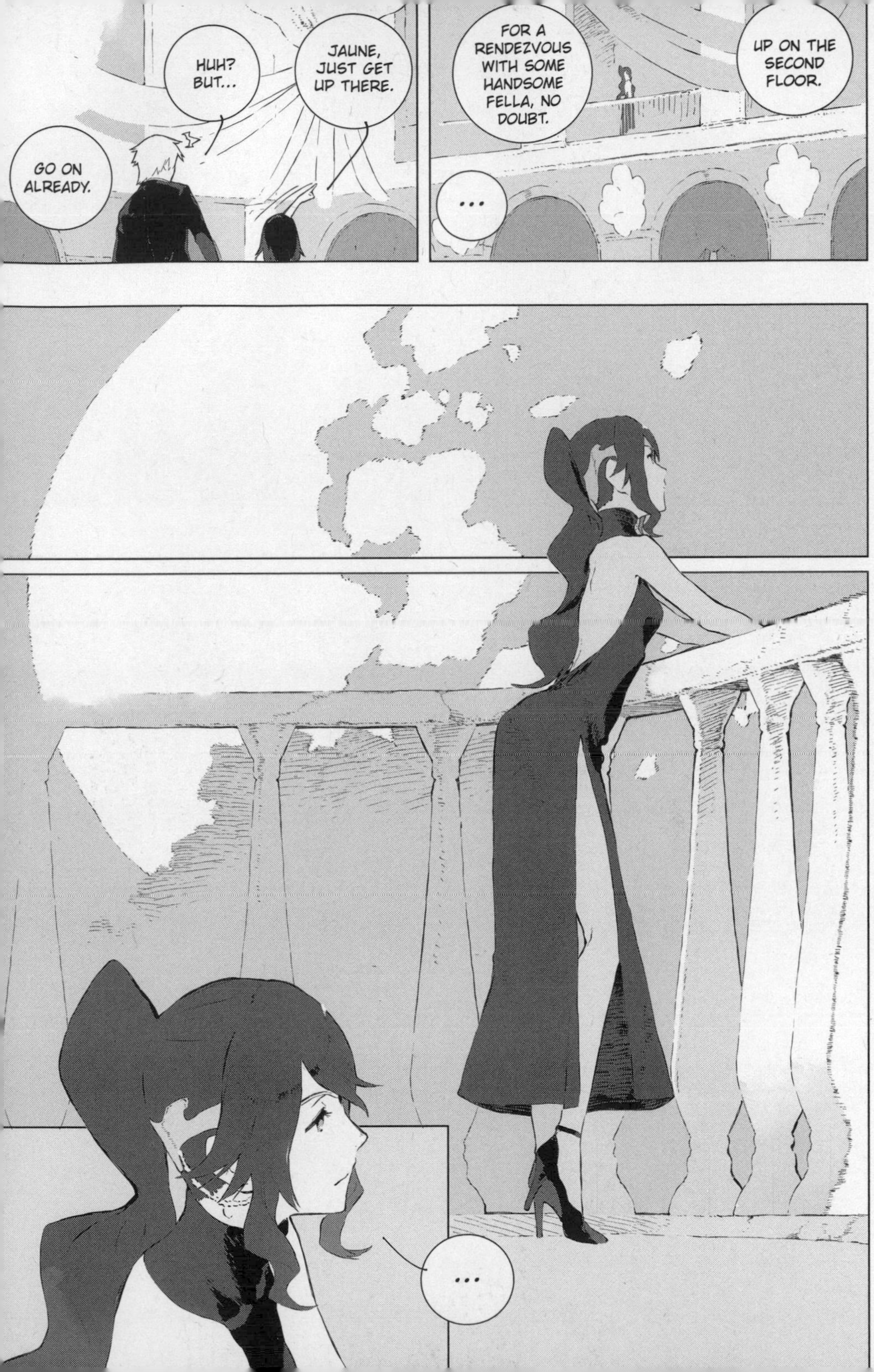
UP ON THE SECOND FLOOR.
FOR A RENDEZVOUS WITH SOME HANDSOME FELLA, NO DOUBT.
...
JAUNE, JUST GET UP THERE.
HUH? BUT...
GO ON ALREADY.
...

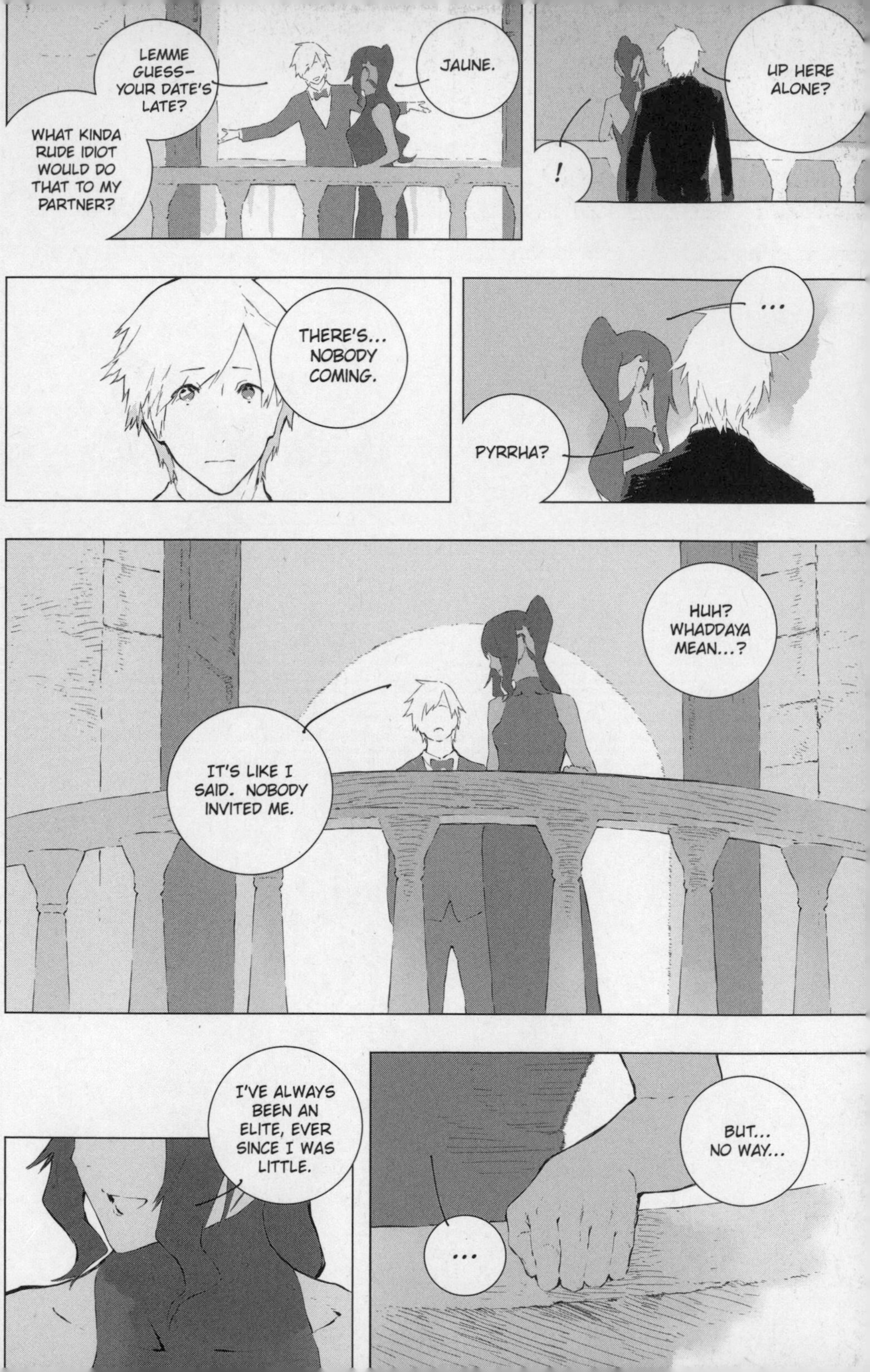
UP HERE ALONE?
!
JAUNE.
LEMME GUESS— YOUR DATE'S LATE?
WHAT KINDA RUDE IDIOT WOULD DO THAT TO MY PARTNER?
...
PYRRHA?
THERE'S... NOBODY COMING.
HUH? WHADDAYA MEAN...?
IT'S LIKE I SAID. NOBODY INVITED ME.
BUT... NO WAY...
...
I'VE ALWAYS BEEN AN ELITE, EVER SINCE I WAS LITTLE.

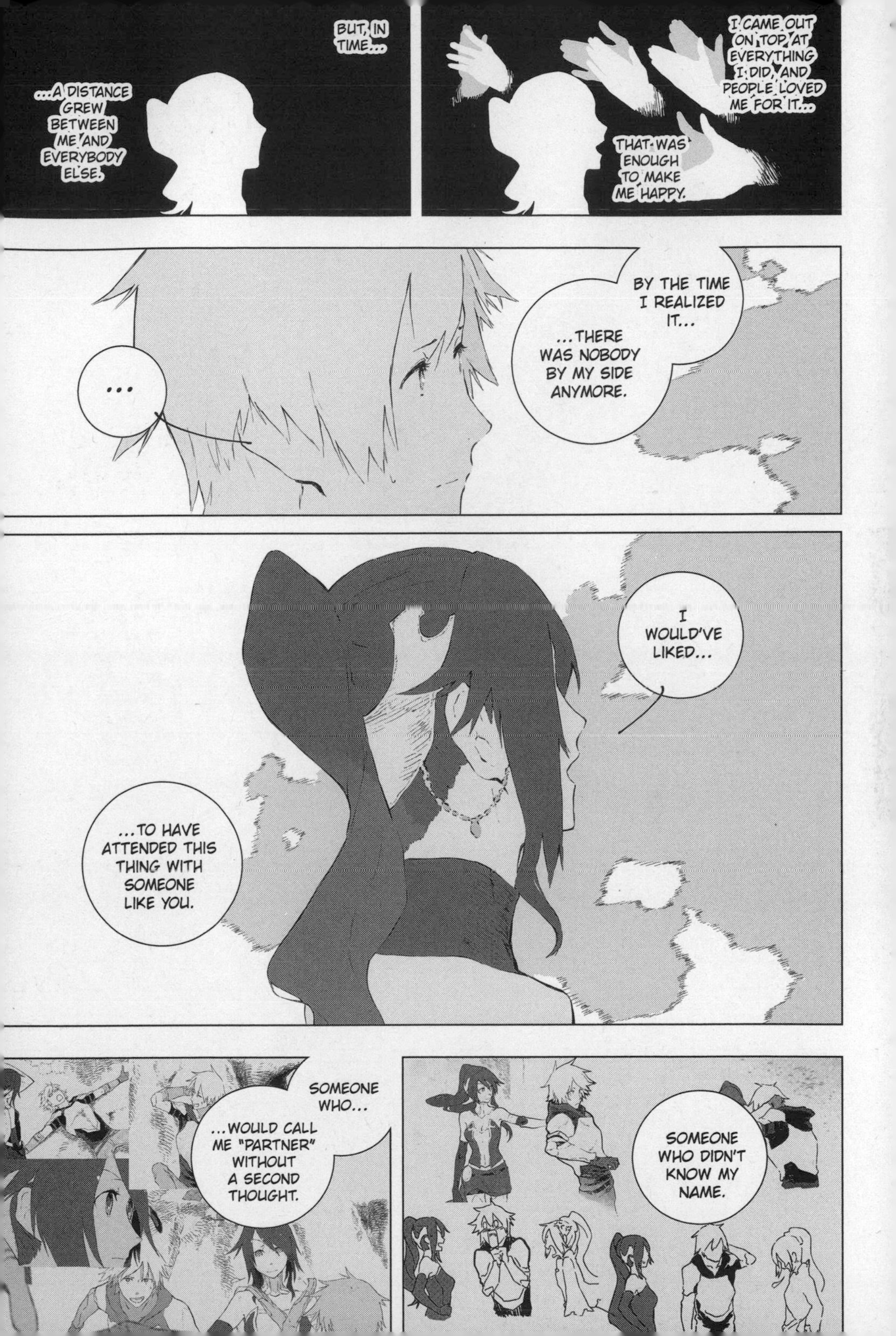
I CAME OUT ON TOP AT EVERYTHING I DID, AND PEOPLE LOVED ME FOR IT...
THAT WAS ENOUGH TO MAKE ME HAPPY.
BUT, IN TIME...
...A DISTANCE GREW BETWEEN ME AND EVERYBODY ELSE.
BY THE TIME I REALIZED IT...
...THERE WAS NOBODY BY MY SIDE ANYMORE.
...
I WOULD'VE LIKED...
...TO HAVE ATTENDED THIS THING WITH SOMEONE LIKE YOU.
SOMEONE WHO DIDN'T KNOW MY NAME.
SOMEONE WHO...
...WOULD CALL ME "PARTNER" WITHOUT A SECOND THOUGHT.

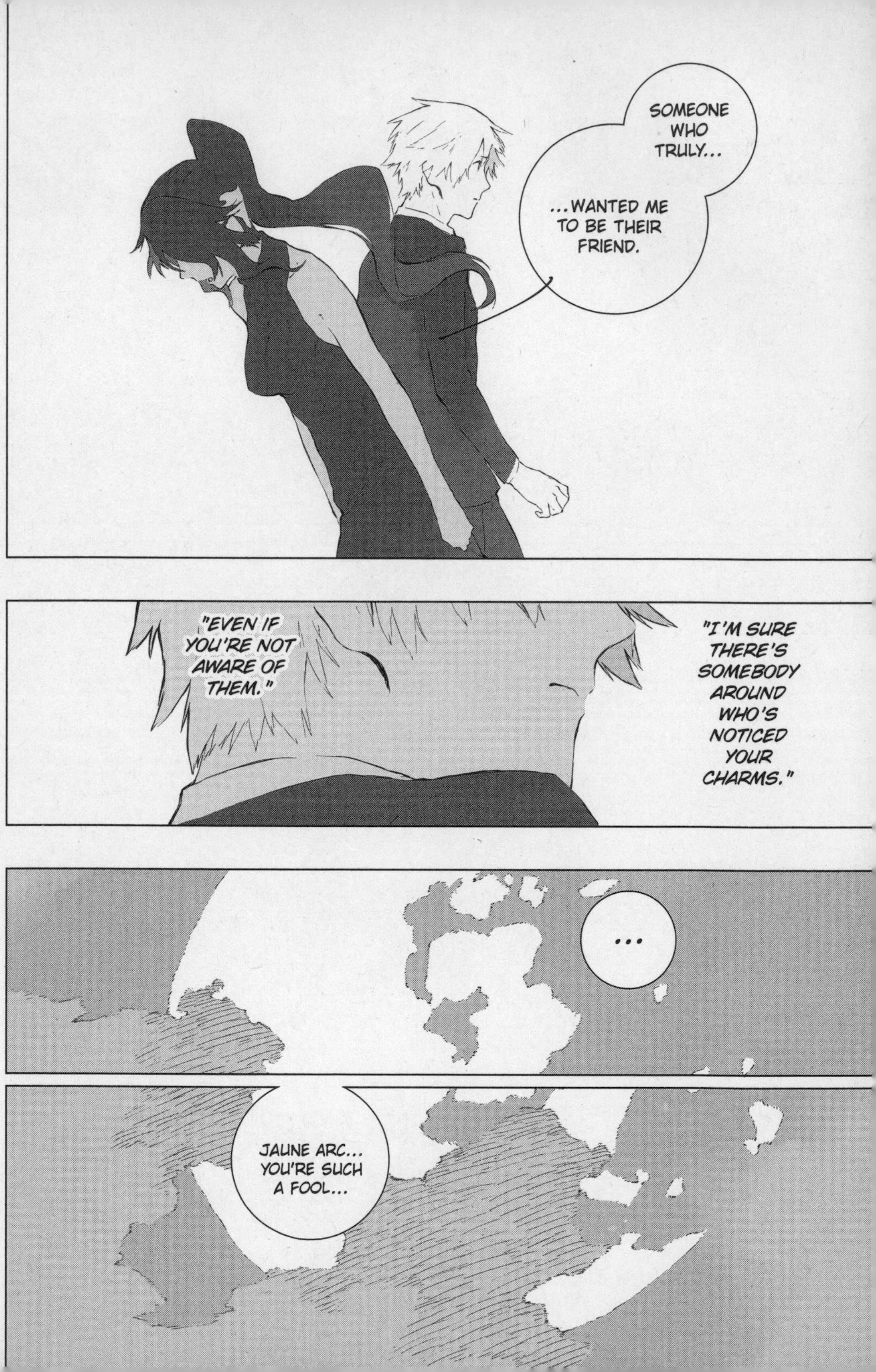
SOMEONE WHO TRULY...
...WANTED ME TO BE THEIR FRIEND.
"I'M SURE THERE'S SOMEBODY AROUND WHO'S NOTICED YOUR CHARMS."
"EVEN IF YOU'RE NOT AWARE OF THEM."
...
JAUNE ARC... YOU'RE SUCH A FOOL...

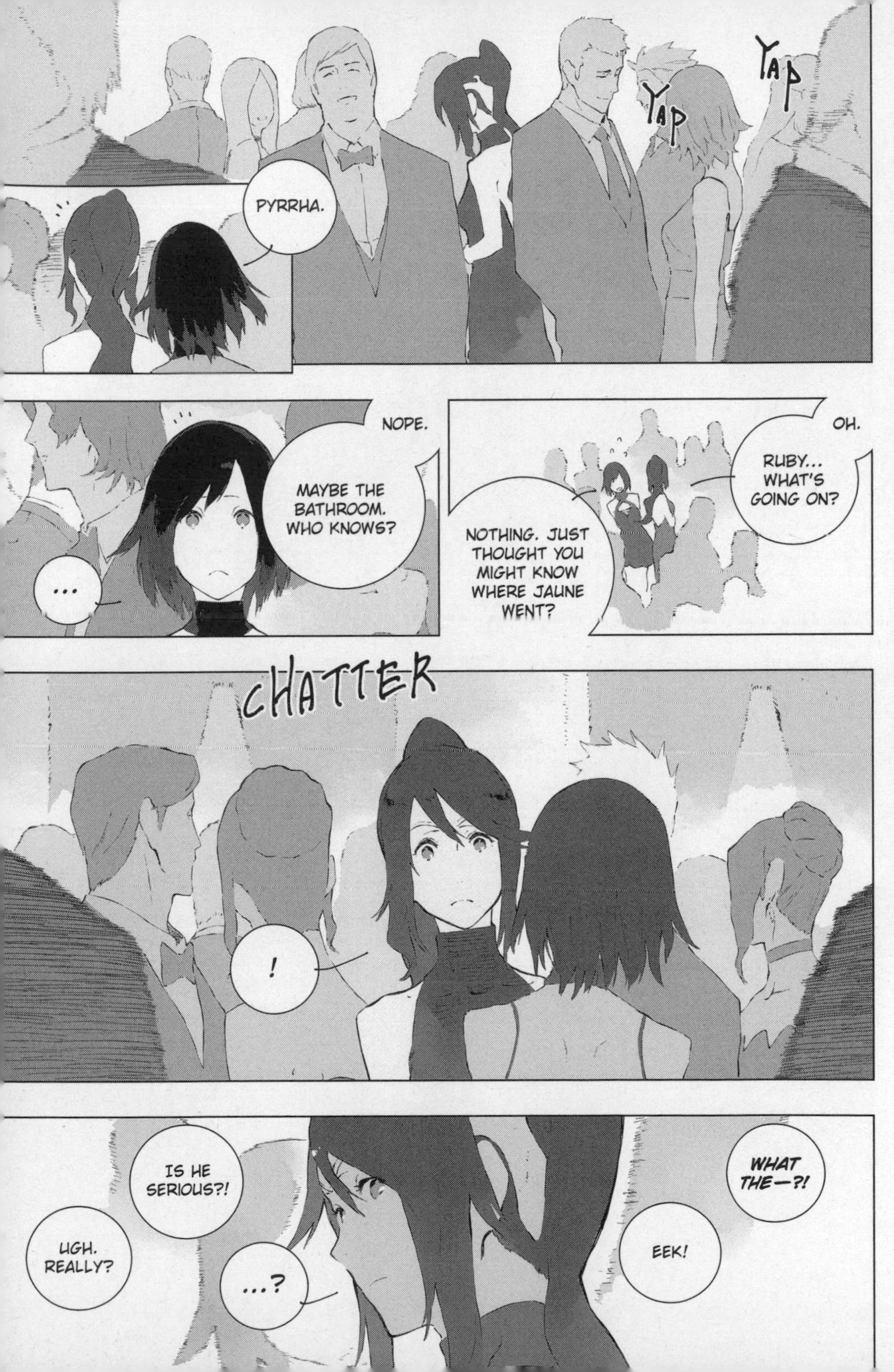
YAP
YAP
PYRRHA.
OH.
RUBY... WHAT'S GOING ON?
NOTHING. JUST THOUGHT YOU MIGHT KNOW WHERE JAUNE WENT?
NOPE.
MAYBE THE BATHROOM. WHO KNOWS?
...
CHATTER
!
WHAT THE—?!
IS HE SERIOUS?!
EEK!
UGH. REALLY?
...?

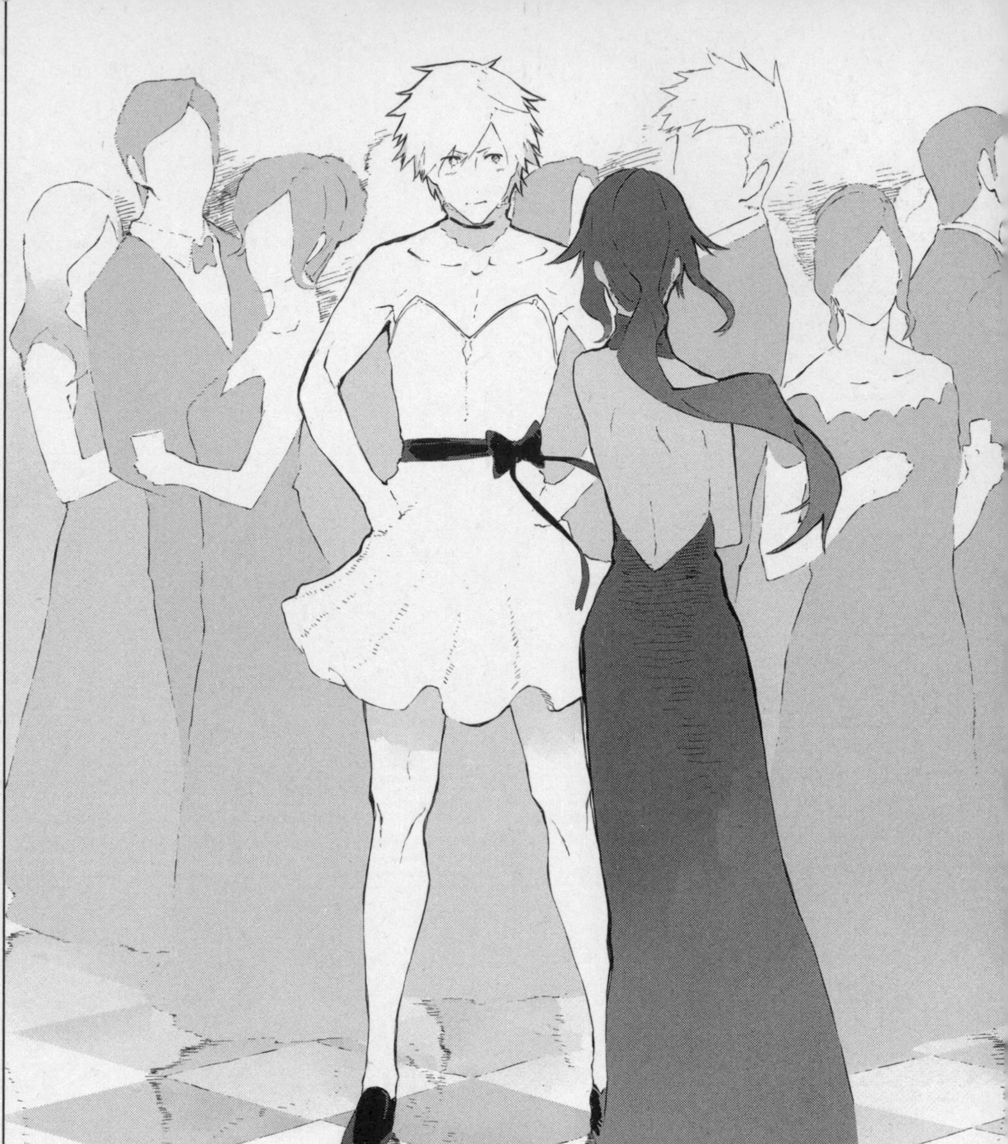

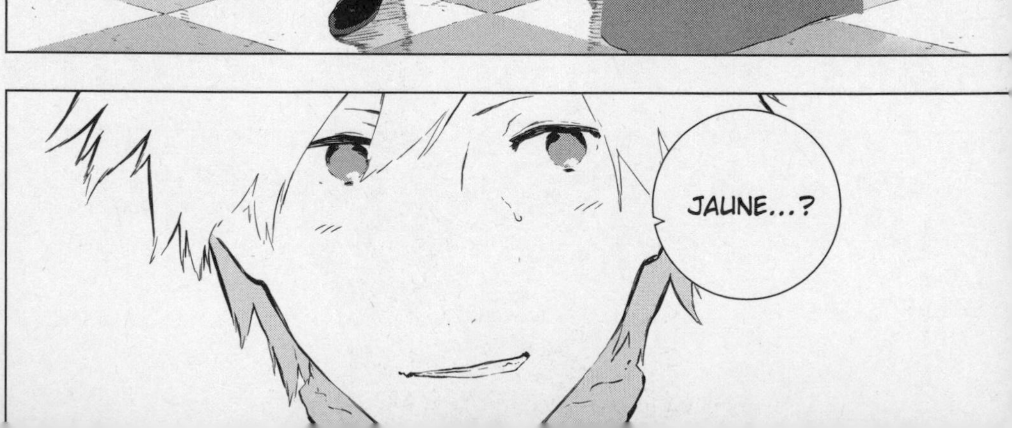
JAUNE...?

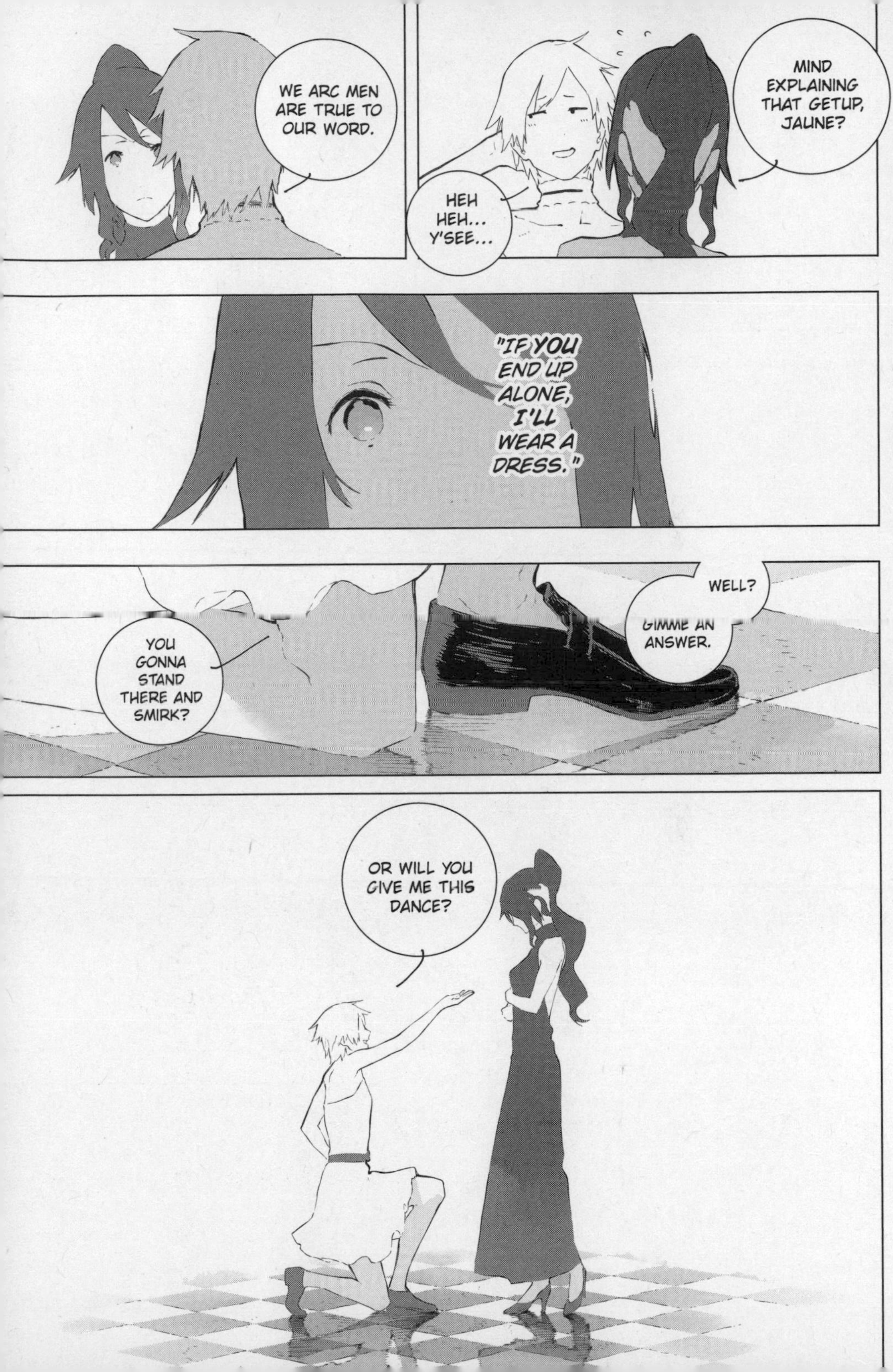
MIND EXPLAINING THAT GETUP, JAUNE?
HEH HEH... Y'SEE...
WE ARC MEN ARE TRUE TO OUR WORD.
"IF YOU END UP ALONE, I'LL WEAR A DRESS."
WELL? GIMME AN ANSWER.
YOU GONNA STAND THERE AND SMIRK?
OR WILL YOU GIVE ME THIS DANCE?

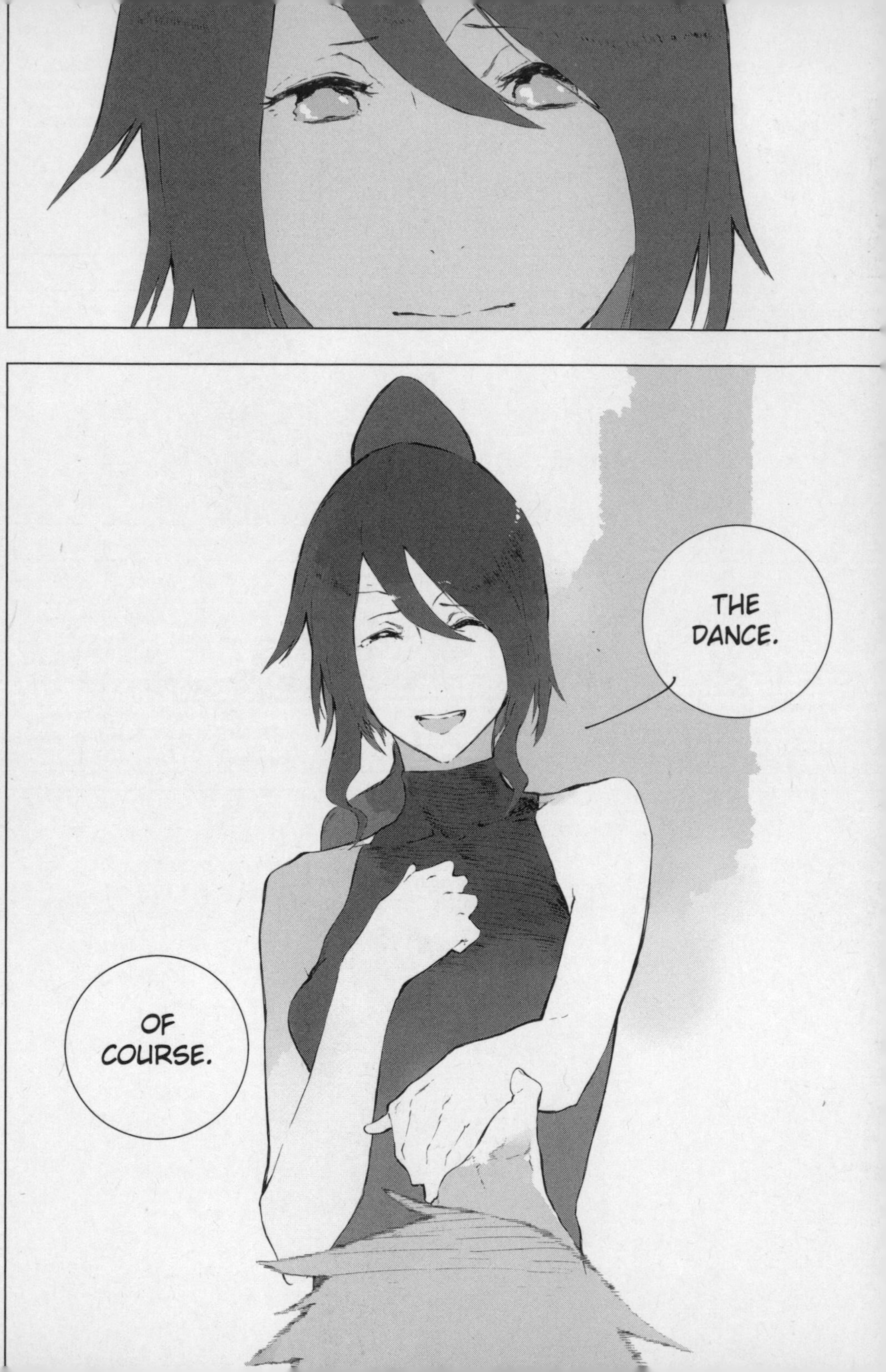
THE DANCE.
OF COURSE.

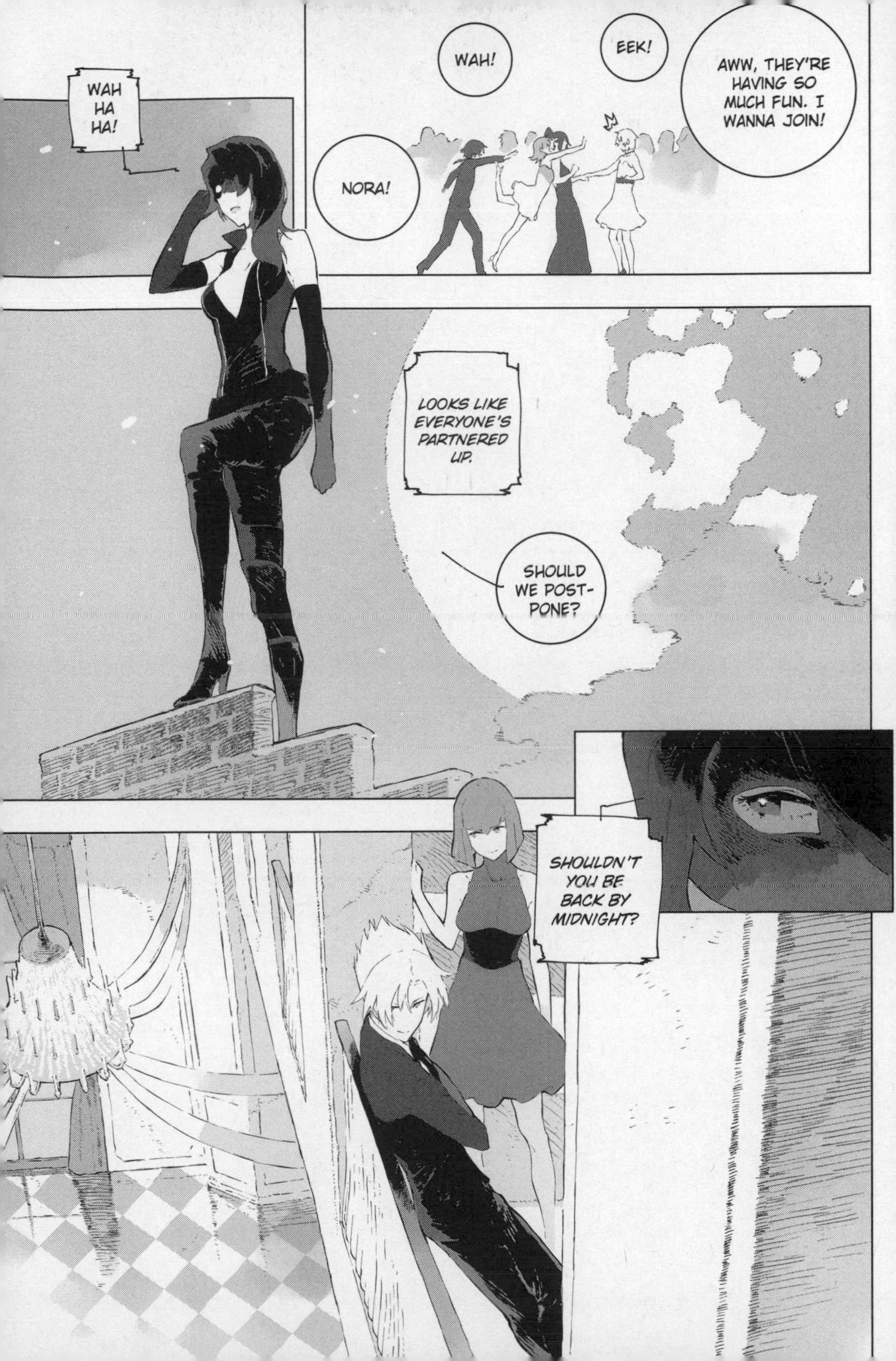
AWW, THEY'RE HAVING SO MUCH FUN. I WANNA JOIN!
EEK!
WAH!
NORA!
WAH HA HA!
LOOKS LIKE EVERYONE'S PARTNERED UP.
SHOULD WE POST-PONE?
SHOULDN'T YOU BE BACK BY MIDNIGHT?

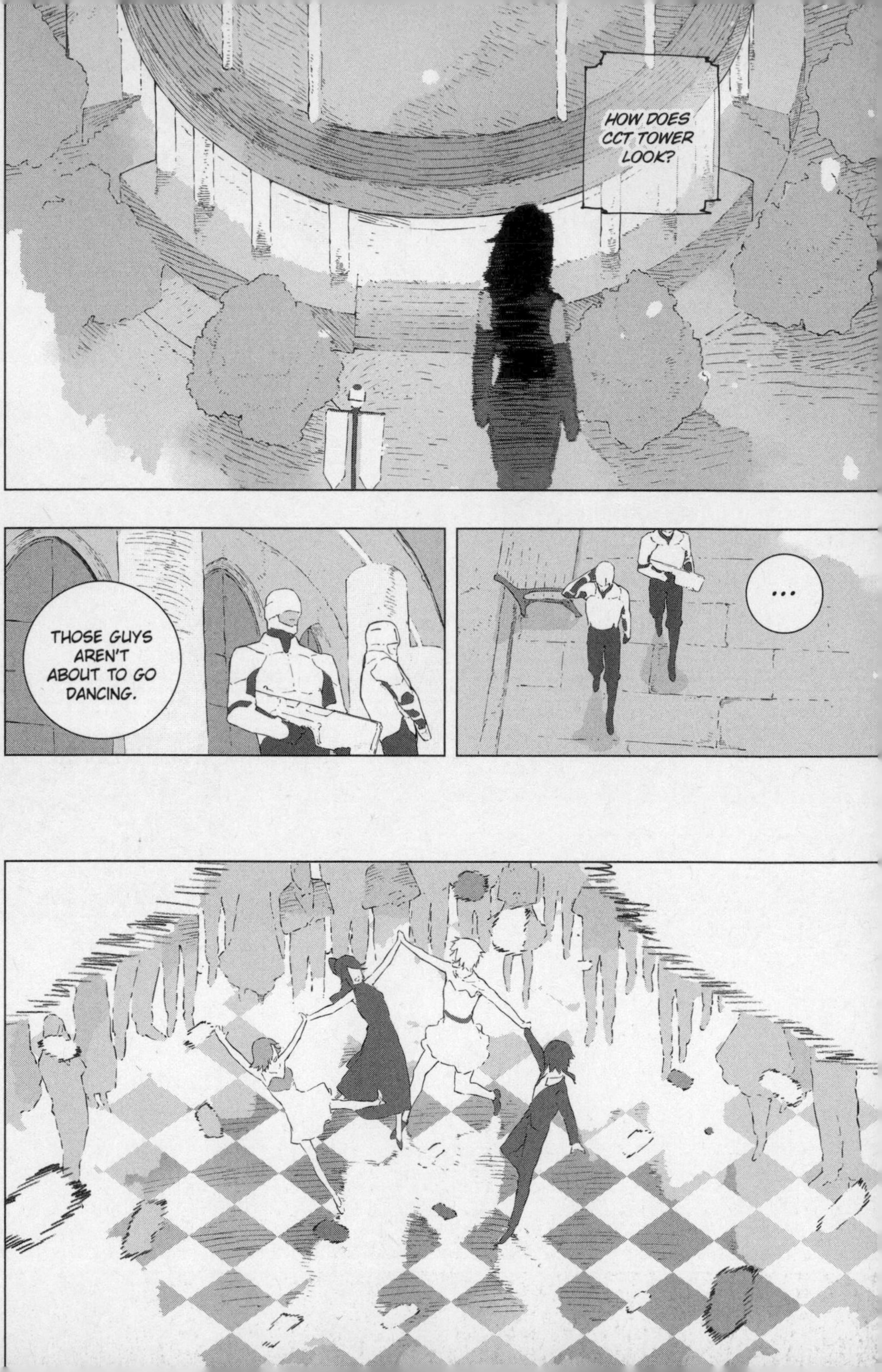
HOW DOES CCT TOWER LOOK?
...
THOSE GUYS AREN'T ABOUT TO GO DANCING.

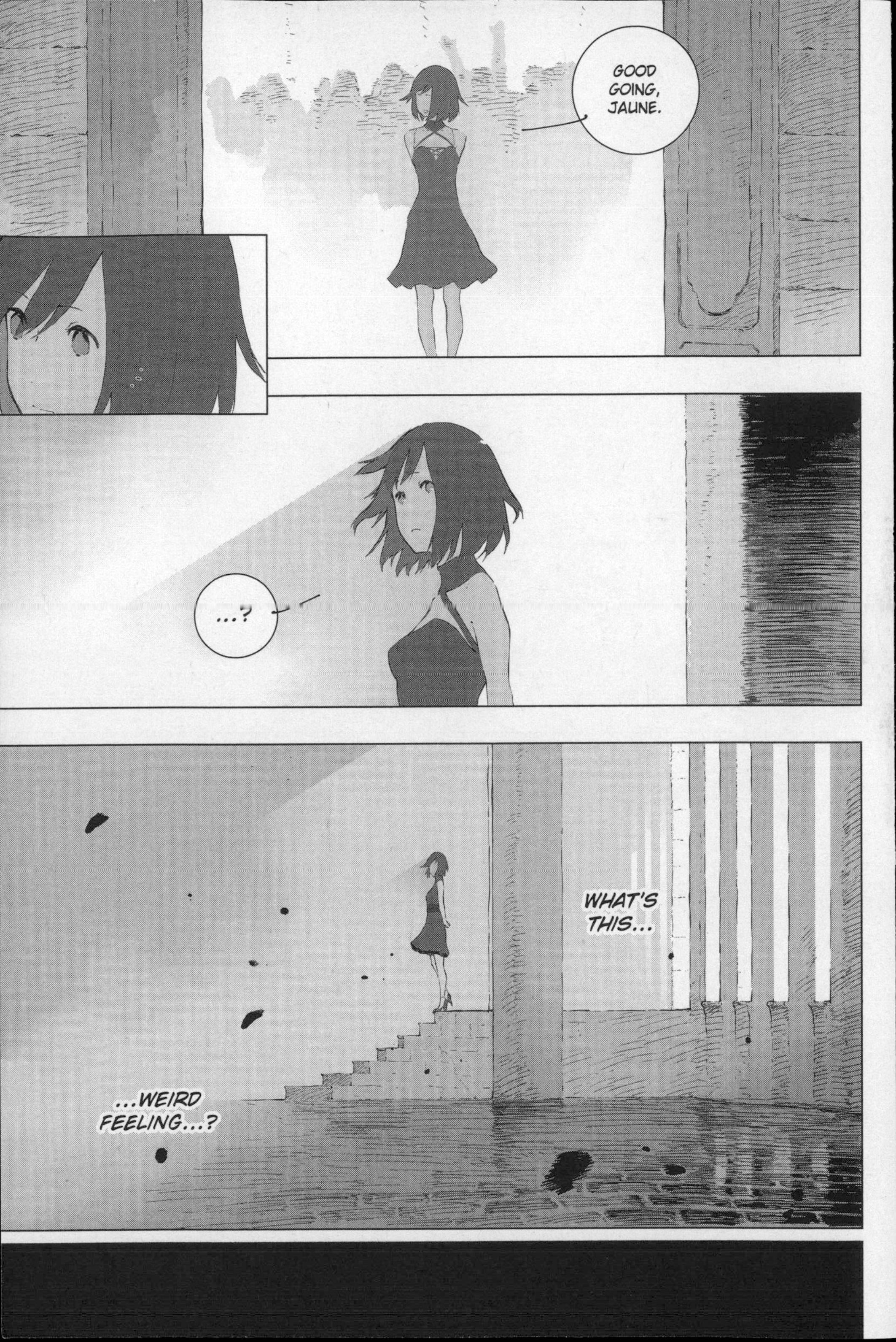
GOOD GOING, JAUNE.
...?
WHAT'S THIS...
...WEIRD FEELING...?

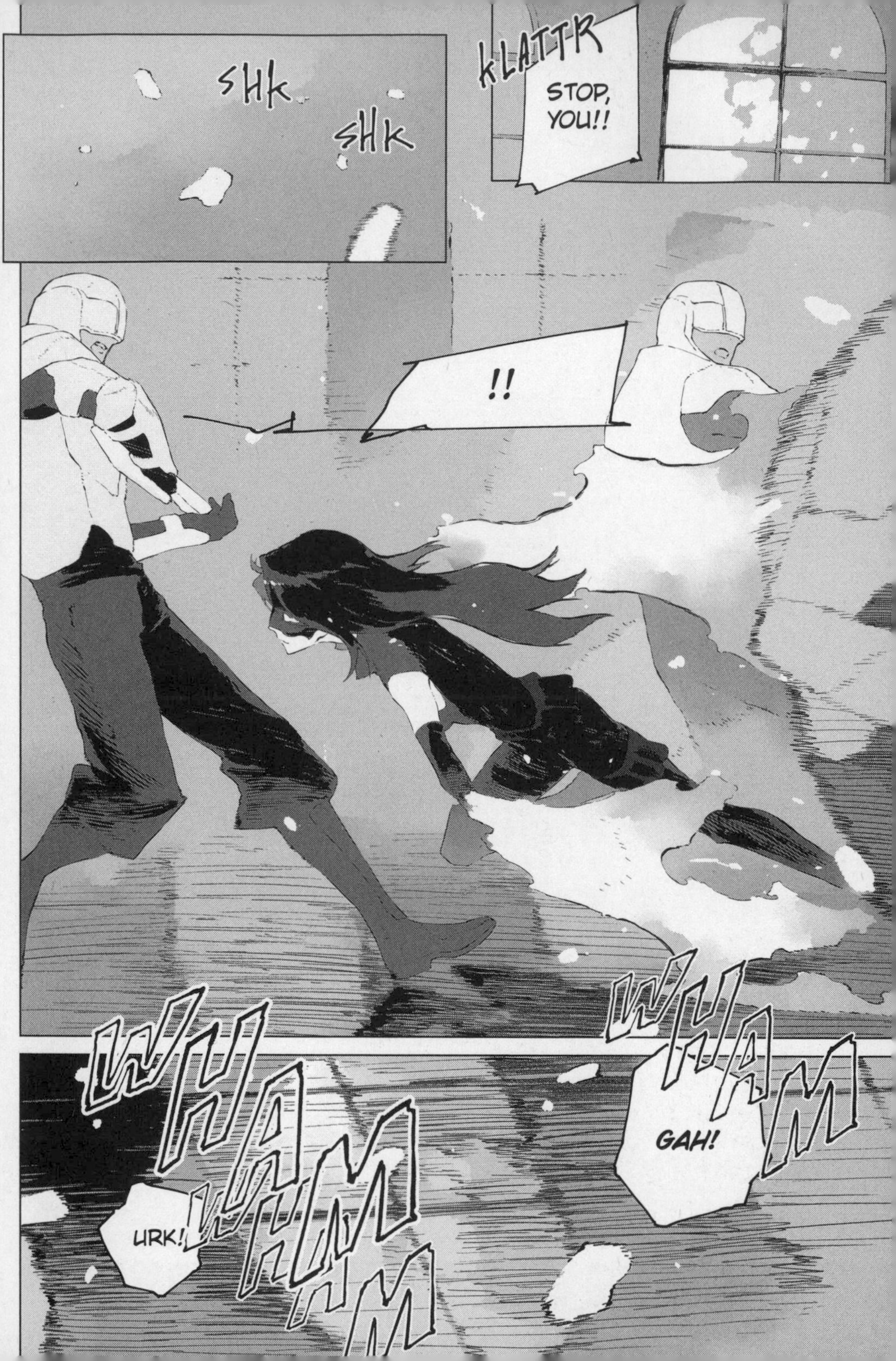
KLATTR
STOP, YOU!!
SHK
SHK
!!
WHAM
GAH!
WHAM
WHAM
URK!

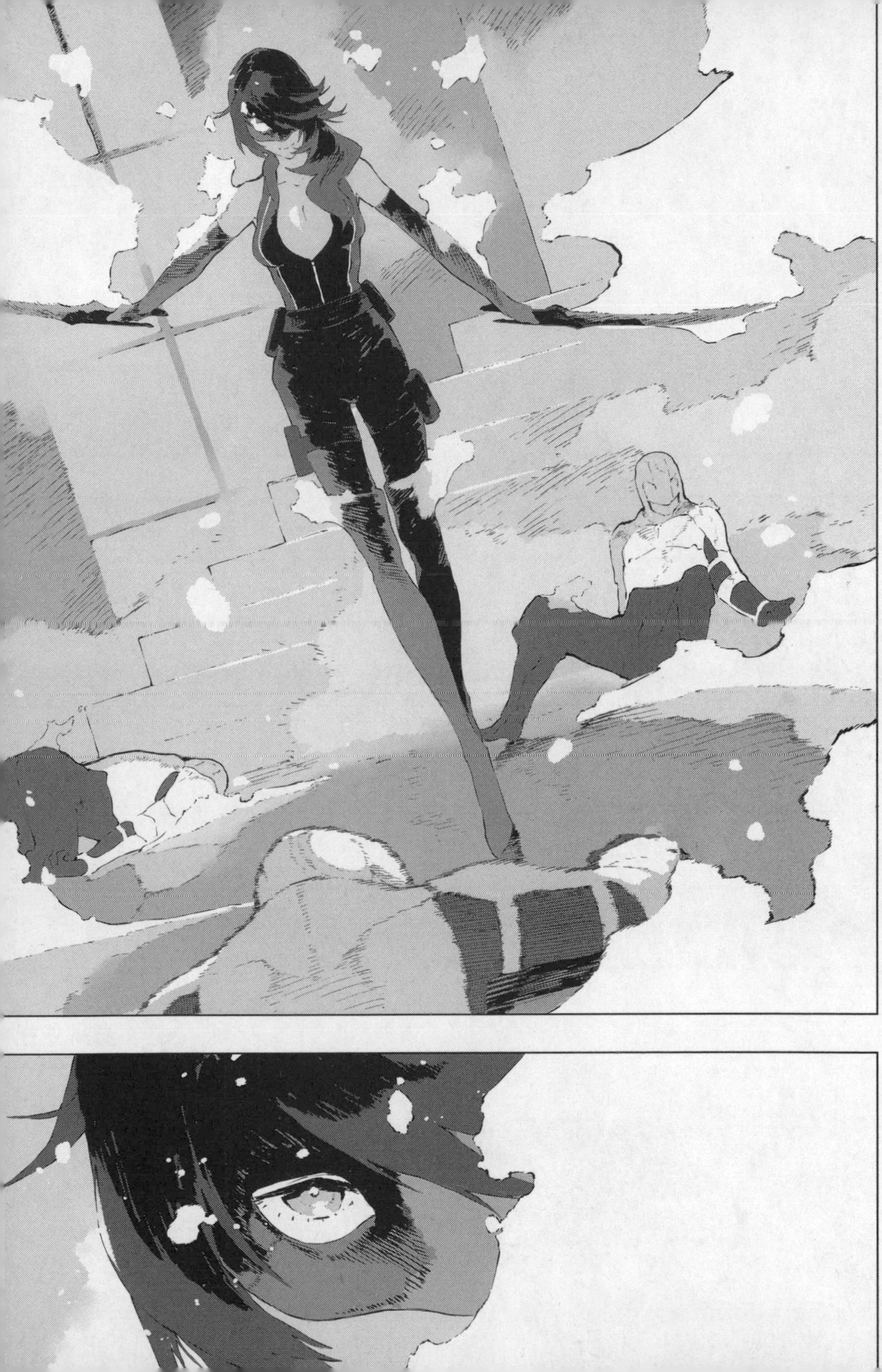

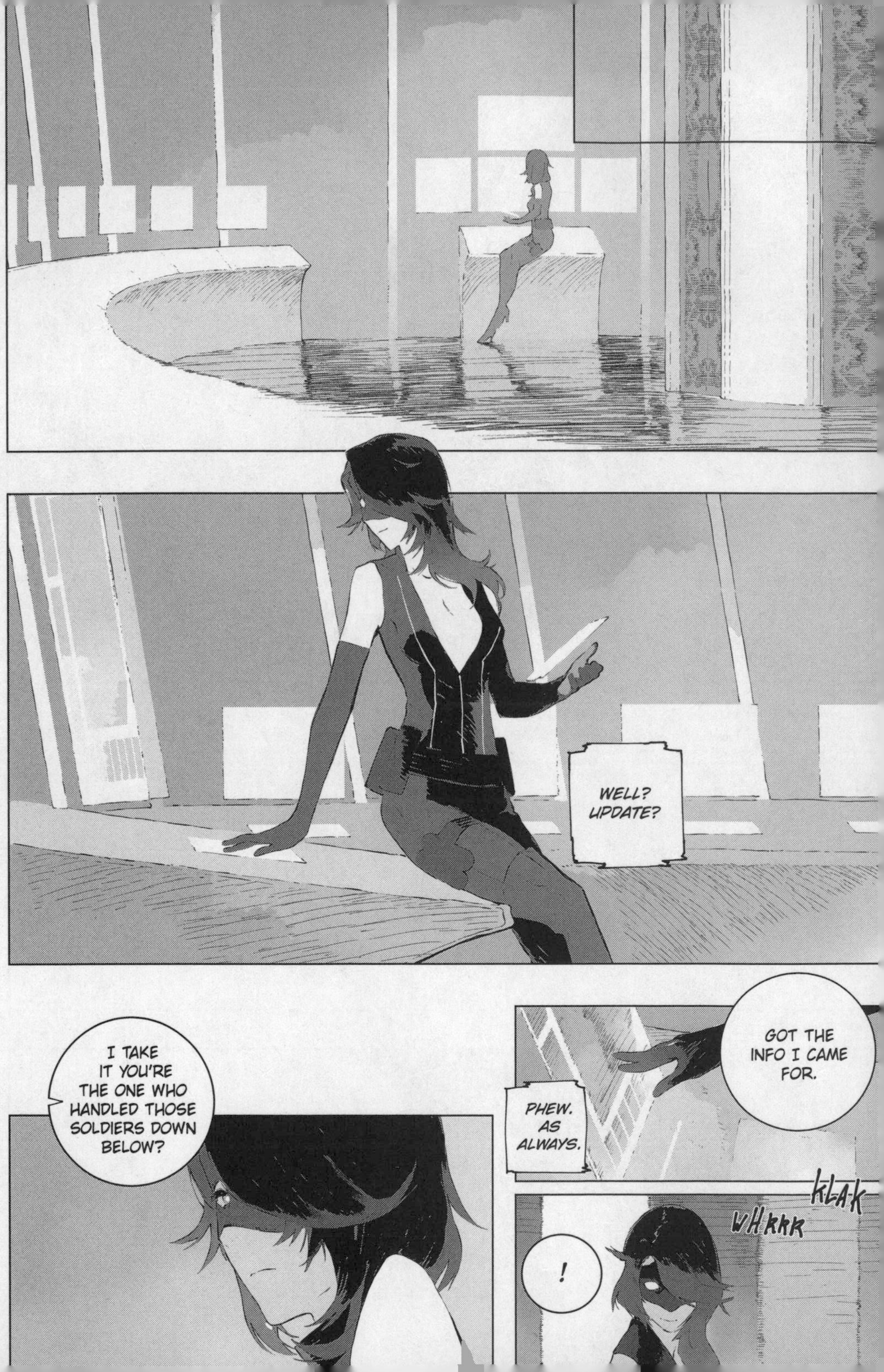
WELL? UPDATE?
GOT THE INFO I CAME FOR.
PHEW. AS ALWAYS.
KLAK
WHRRR
!
I TAKE IT YOU'RE THE ONE WHO HANDLED THOSE SOLDIERS DOWN BELOW?

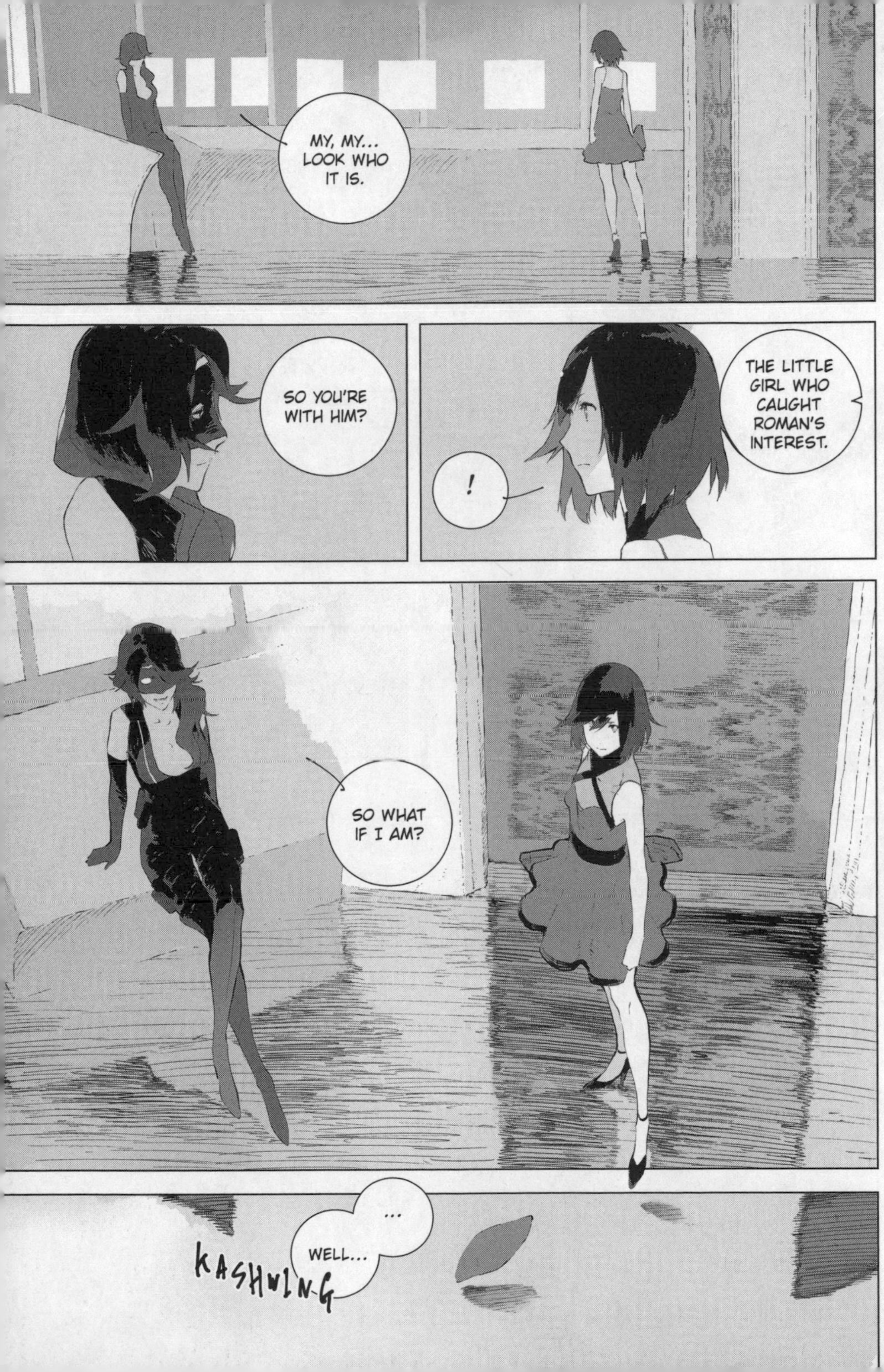
MY, MY... LOOK WHO IT IS.
THE LITTLE GIRL WHO CAUGHT ROMAN'S INTEREST.
!
SO YOU'RE WITH HIM?
SO WHAT IF I AM?
...
WELL...
KASHWING

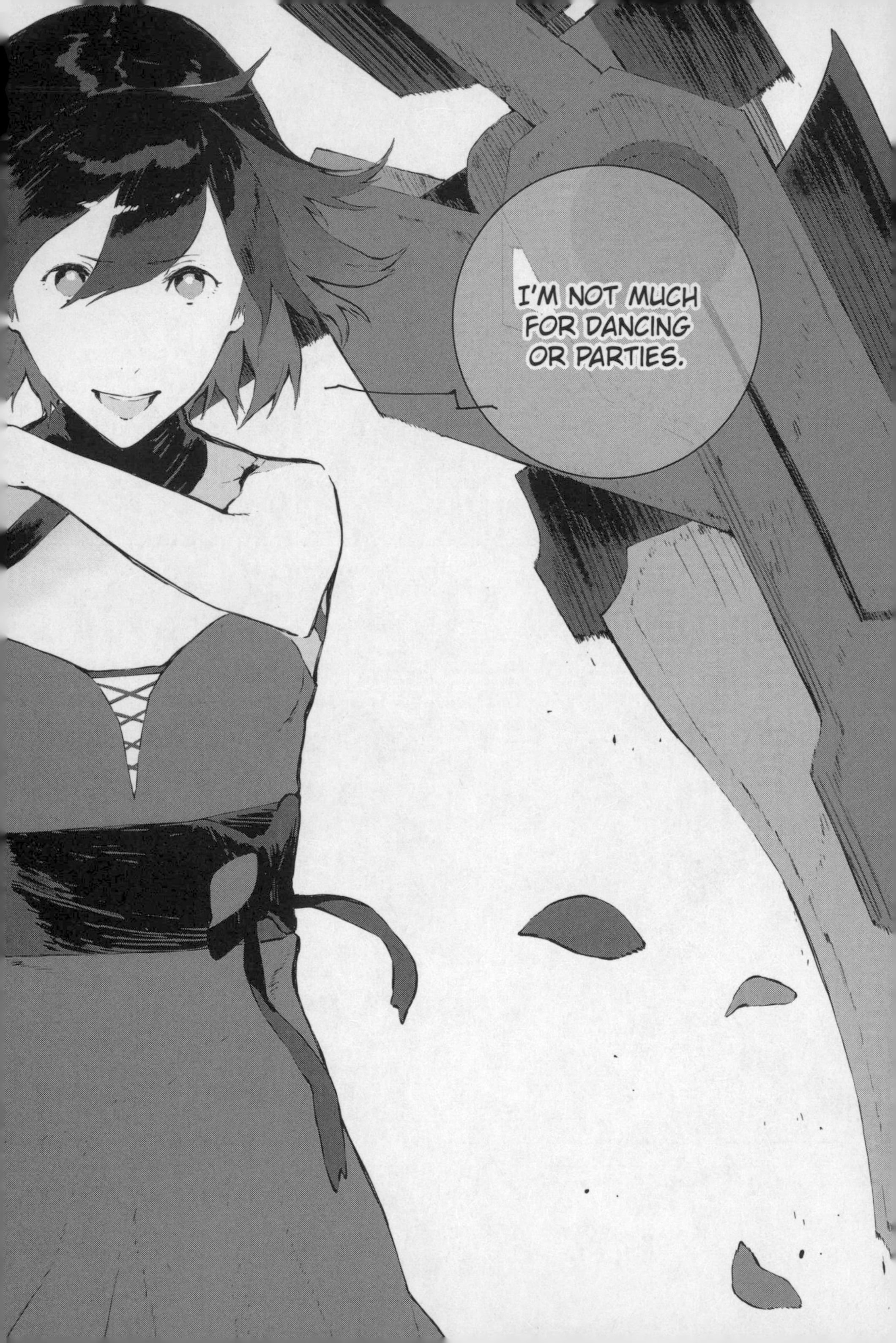
I'M NOT MUCH FOR DANCING OR PARTIES.

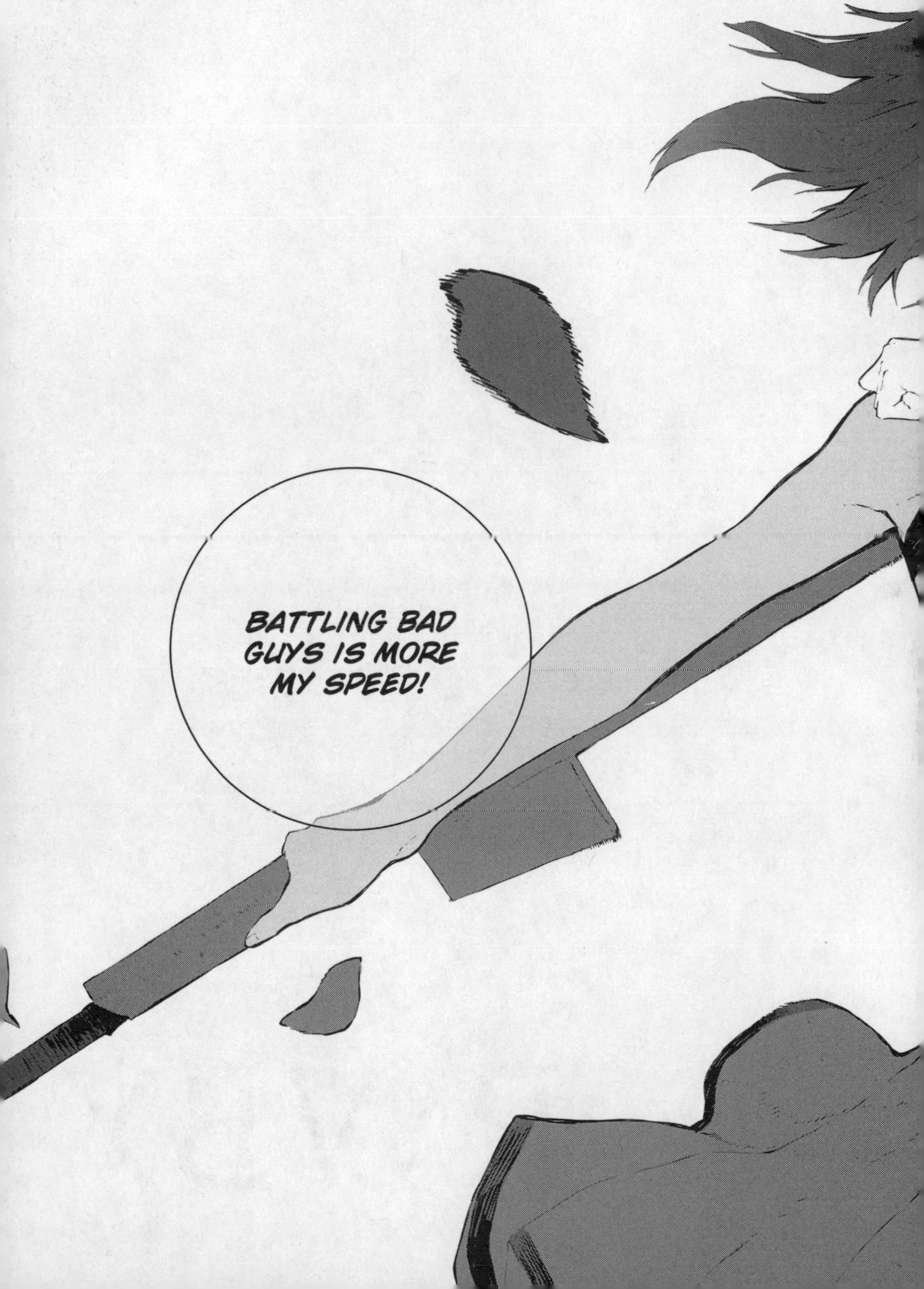
BATTLING BAD GUYS IS MORE MY SPEED!

RWBY

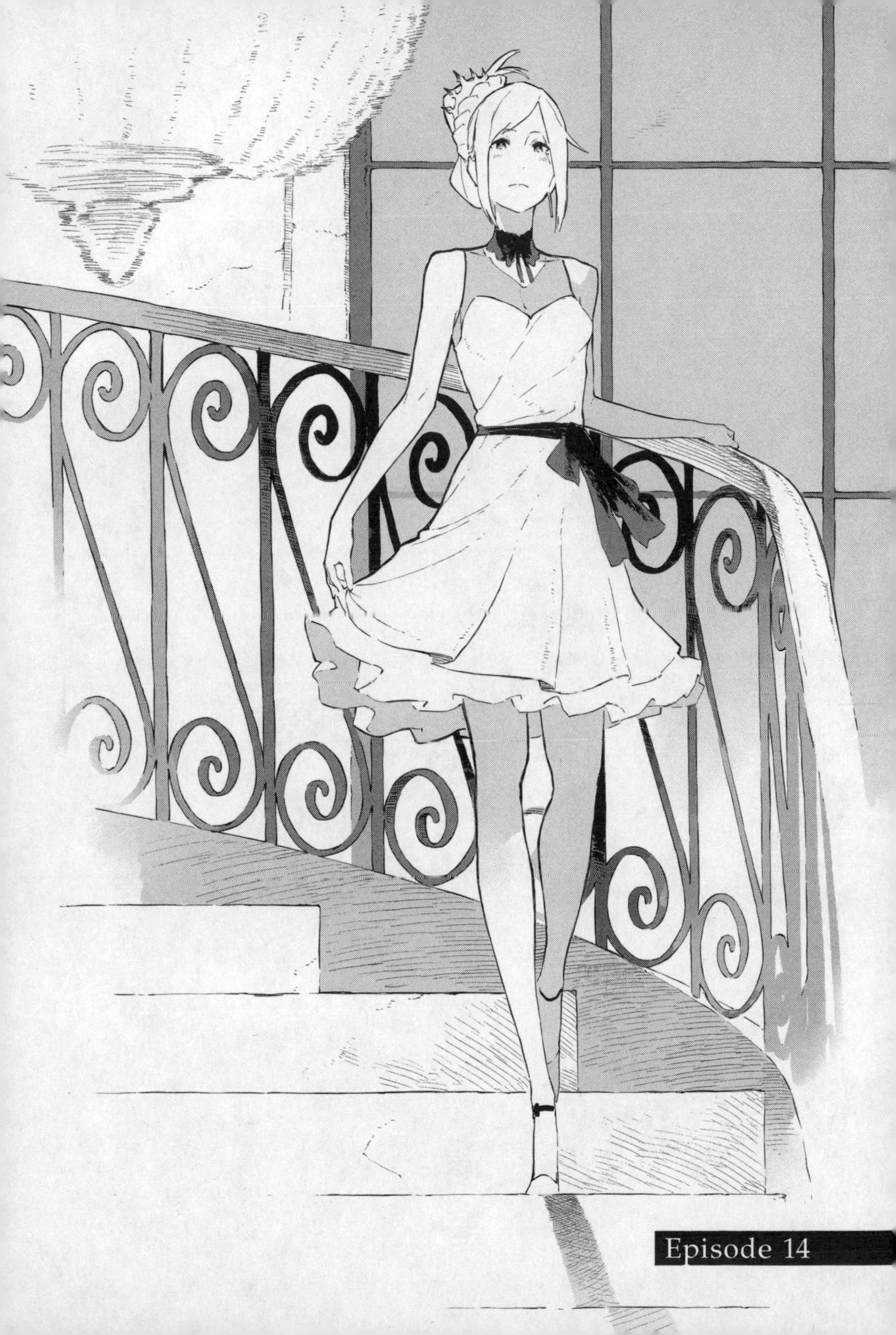

Episode 14

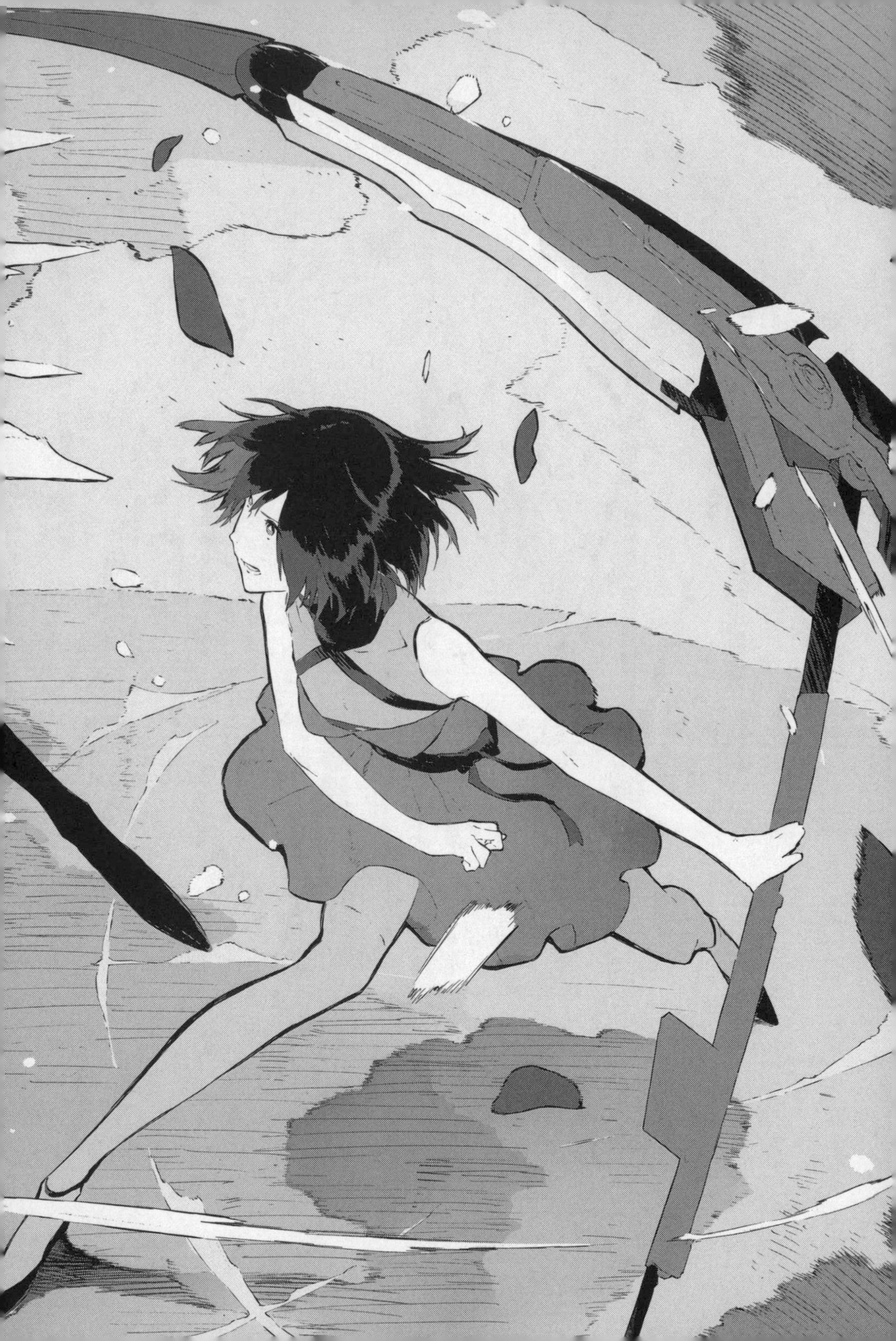

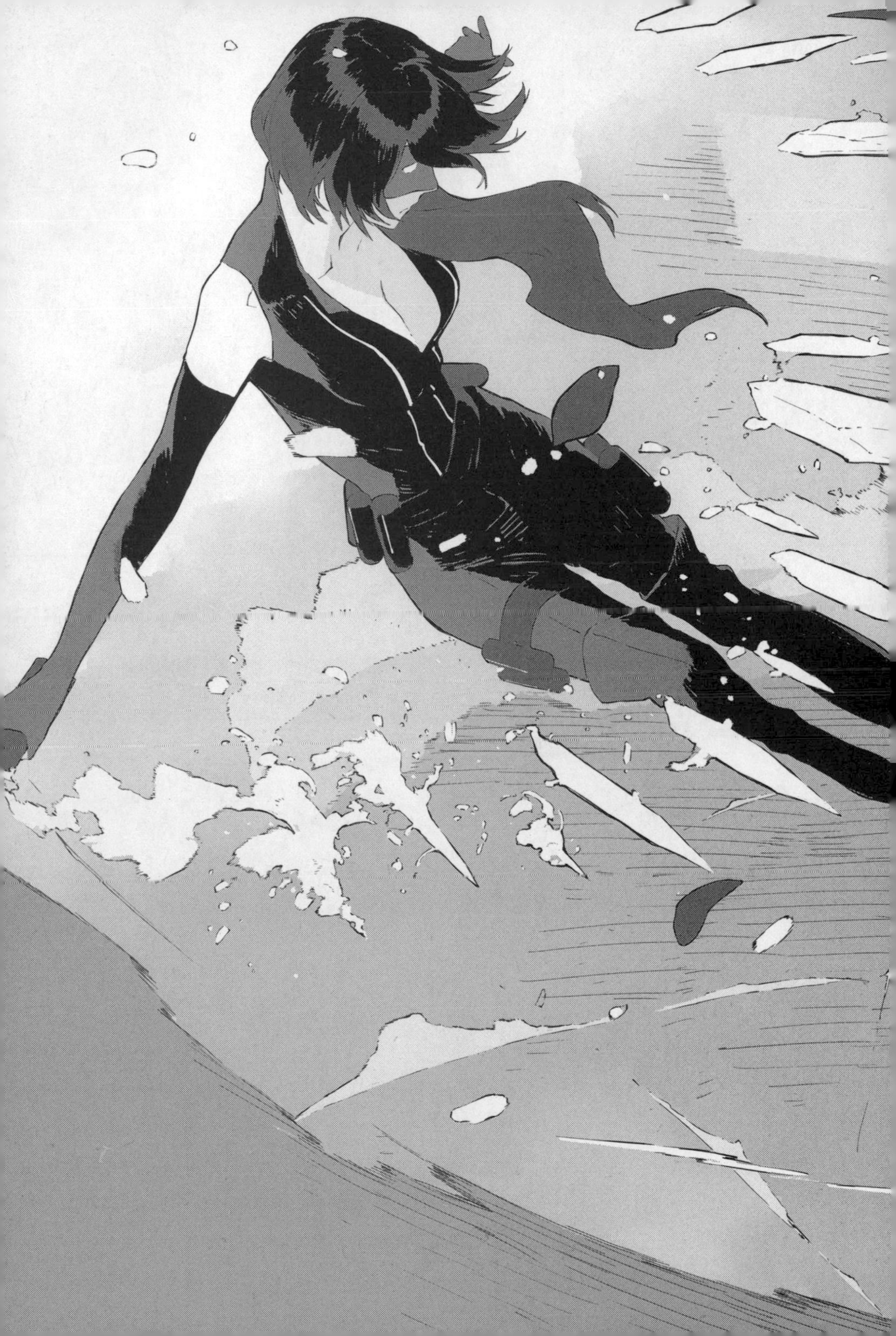

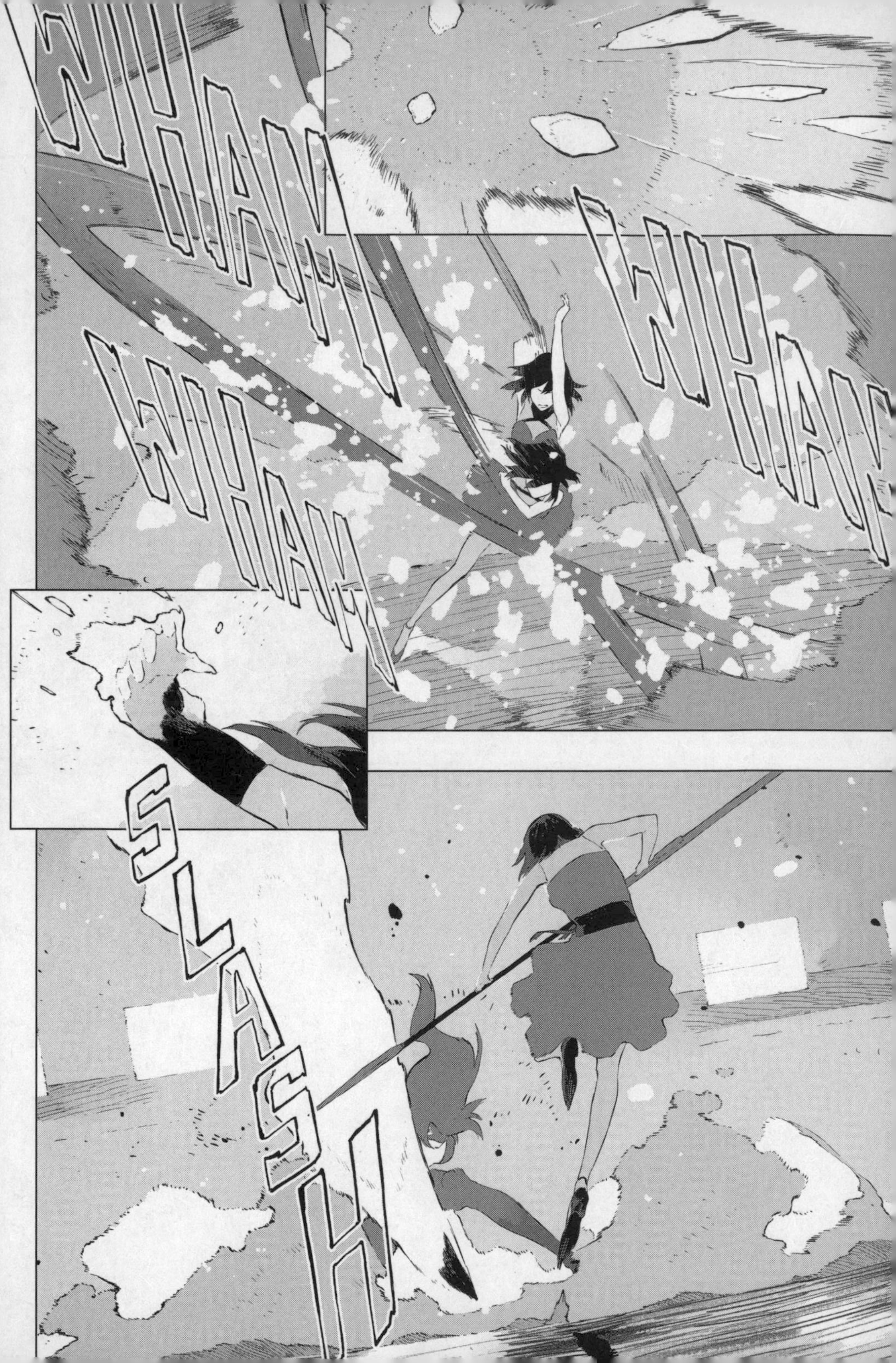
WHAM
WHAM
WHAM
SLASH

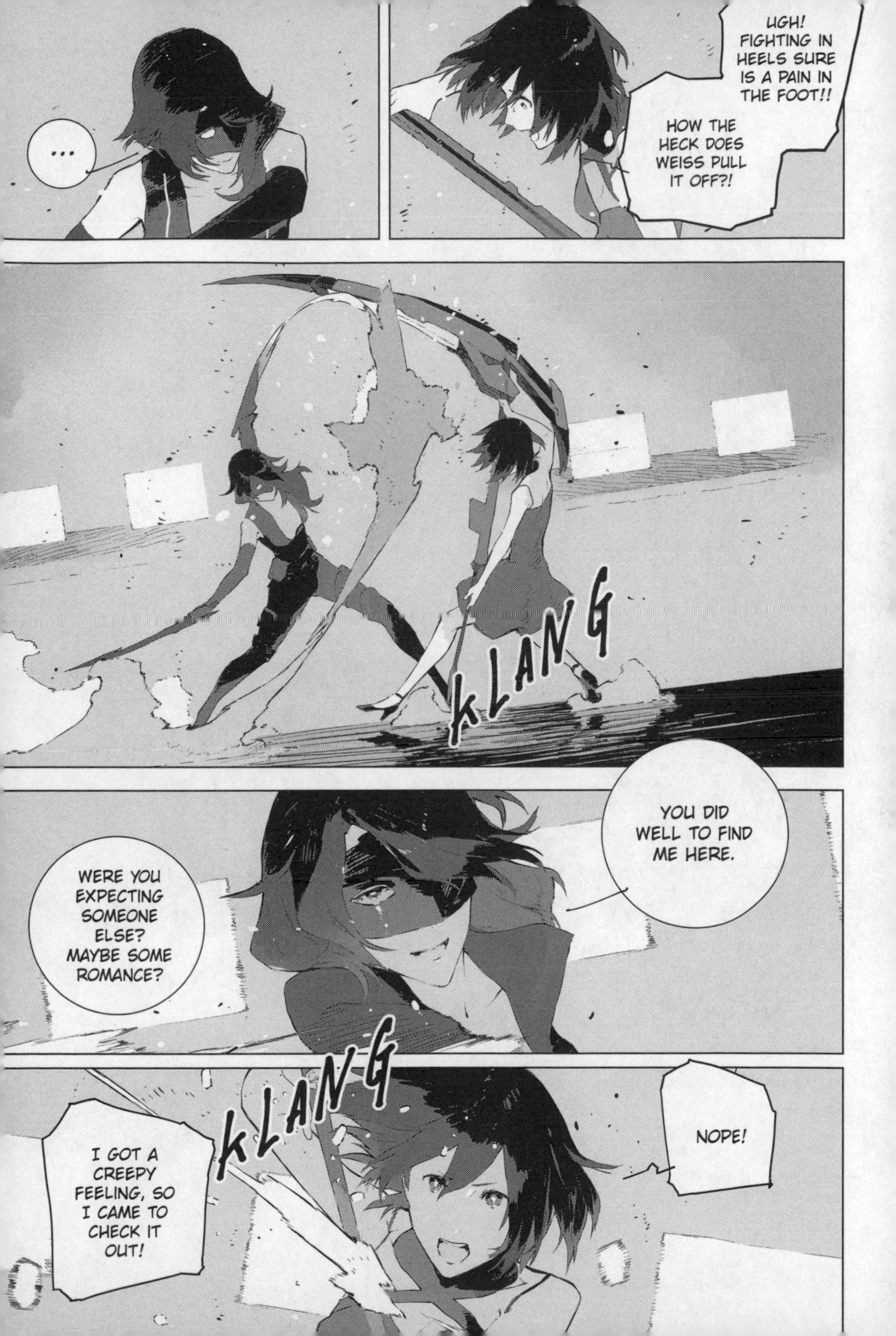
UGH! FIGHTING IN HEELS SURE IS A PAIN IN THE FOOT!!
HOW THE HECK DOES WEISS PULL IT OFF?!
...
KLANG
YOU DID WELL TO FIND ME HERE.
WERE YOU EXPECTING SOMEONE ELSE? MAYBE SOME ROMANCE?
KLANG
NOPE!
I GOT A CREEPY FEELING, SO I CAME TO CHECK IT OUT!

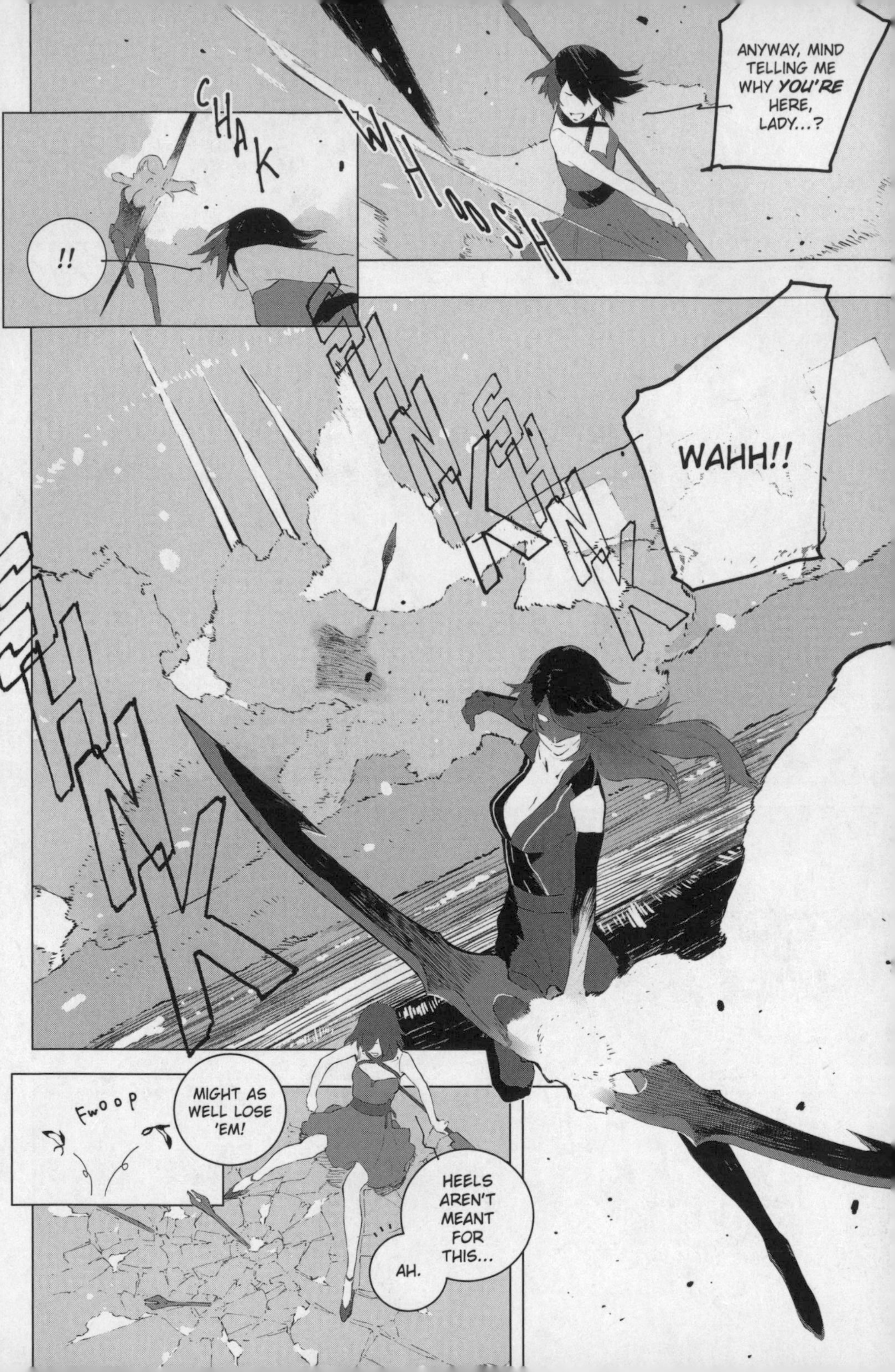

ANYWAY, MIND TELLING ME WHY *YOU'RE* HERE, LADY...?
WHOOSH
CHAK
!!
SHINK
SHINK
WAHH!!
SHINK
HEELS AREN'T MEANT FOR THIS...
...AH.
MIGHT AS WELL LOSE 'EM!
Fwoop

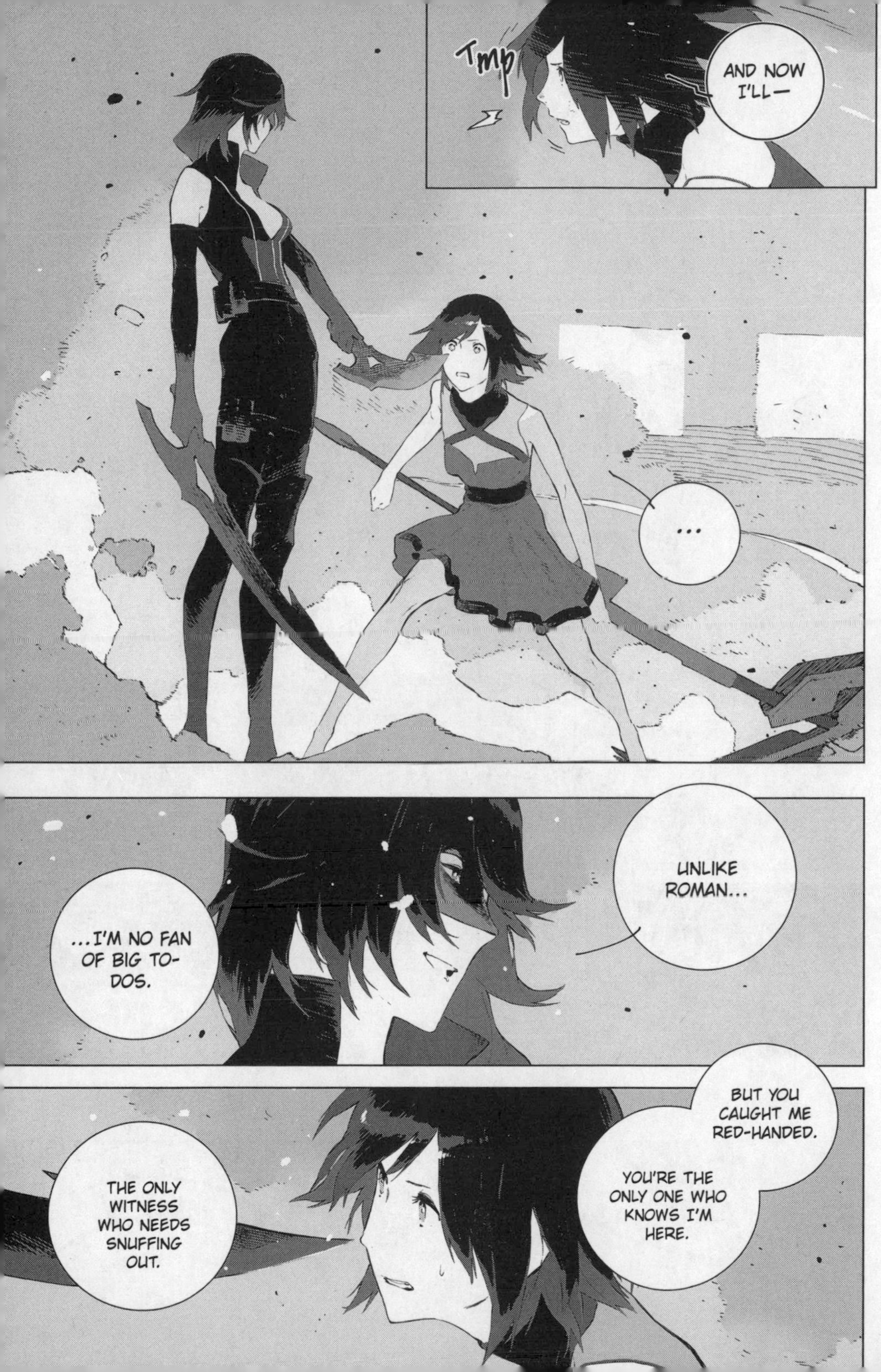
Tmp
AND NOW I'LL—
...
UNLIKE ROMAN...
...I'M NO FAN OF BIG TO-DOS.
BUT YOU CAUGHT ME RED-HANDED.
YOU'RE THE ONLY ONE WHO KNOWS I'M HERE.
THE ONLY WITNESS WHO NEEDS SNUFFING OUT.

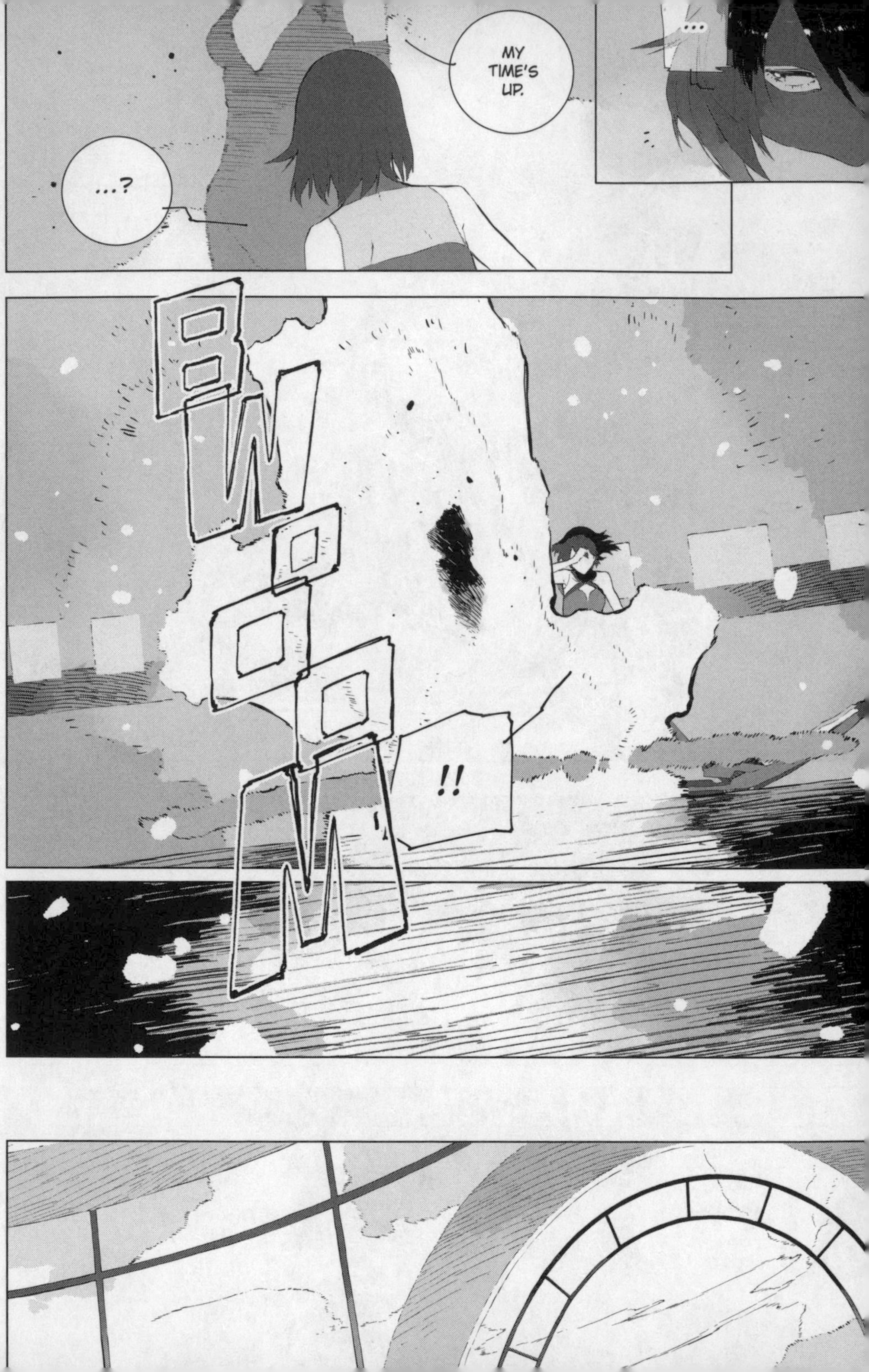
...
MY TIME'S UP.
...?
BWOOOM
!!

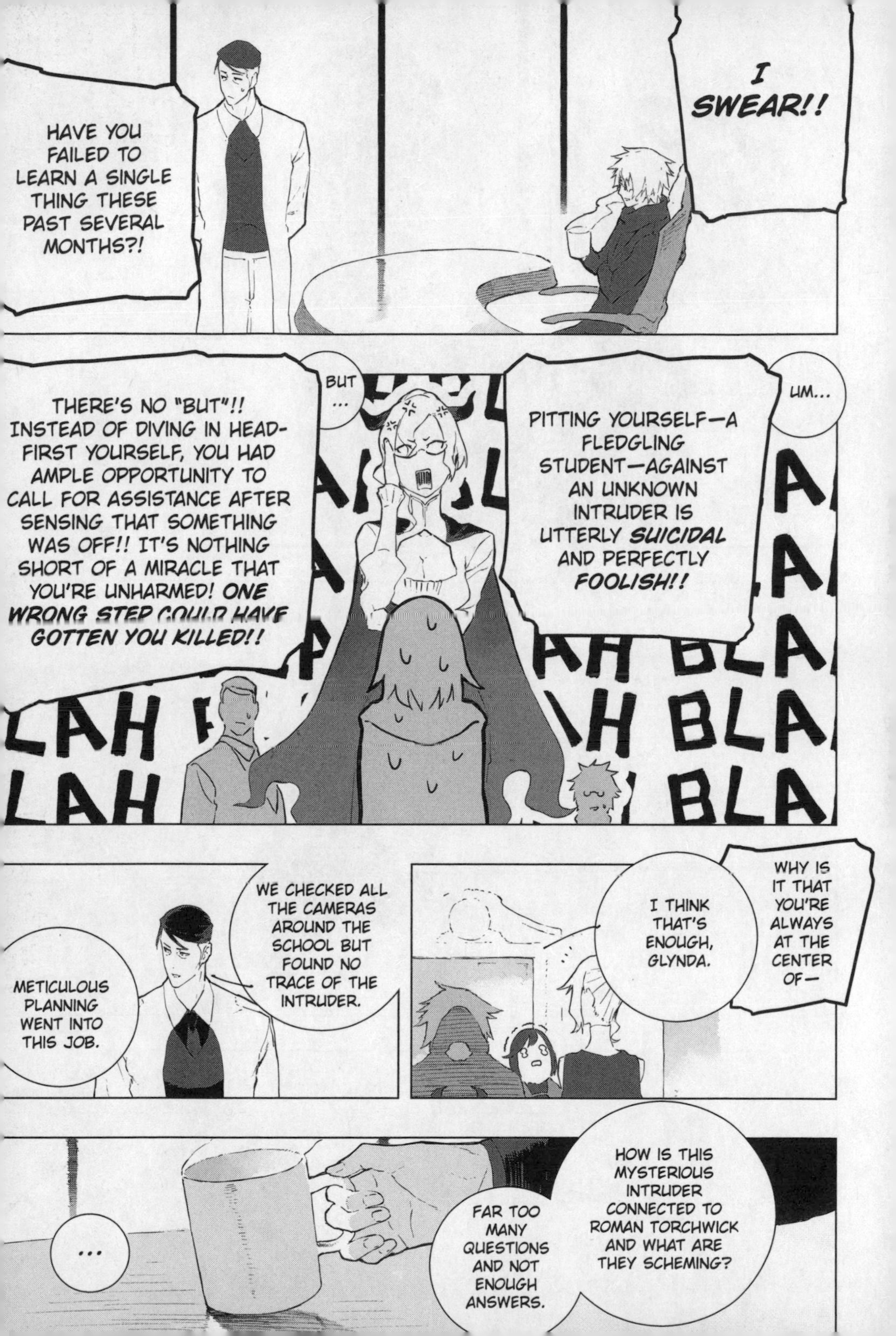
I SWEAR!!
HAVE YOU FAILED TO LEARN A SINGLE THING THESE PAST SEVERAL MONTHS?!
UM...
PITTING YOURSELF—A FLEDGLING STUDENT—AGAINST AN UNKNOWN INTRUDER IS UTTERLY SUICIDAL AND PERFECTLY FOOLISH!!
BUT ...
THERE'S NO "BUT"!! INSTEAD OF DIVING IN HEAD-FIRST YOURSELF, YOU HAD AMPLE OPPORTUNITY TO CALL FOR ASSISTANCE AFTER SENSING THAT SOMETHING WAS OFF!! IT'S NOTHING SHORT OF A MIRACLE THAT YOU'RE UNHARMED! ONE WRONG STEP COULD HAVE GOTTEN YOU KILLED!!
WHY IS IT THAT YOU'RE ALWAYS AT THE CENTER OF—
I THINK THAT'S ENOUGH, GLYNDA.
WE CHECKED ALL THE CAMERAS AROUND THE SCHOOL BUT FOUND NO TRACE OF THE INTRUDER.
METICULOUS PLANNING WENT INTO THIS JOB.
HOW IS THIS MYSTERIOUS INTRUDER CONNECTED TO ROMAN TORCHWICK AND WHAT ARE THEY SCHEMING?
FAR TOO MANY QUESTIONS AND NOT ENOUGH ANSWERS.
...

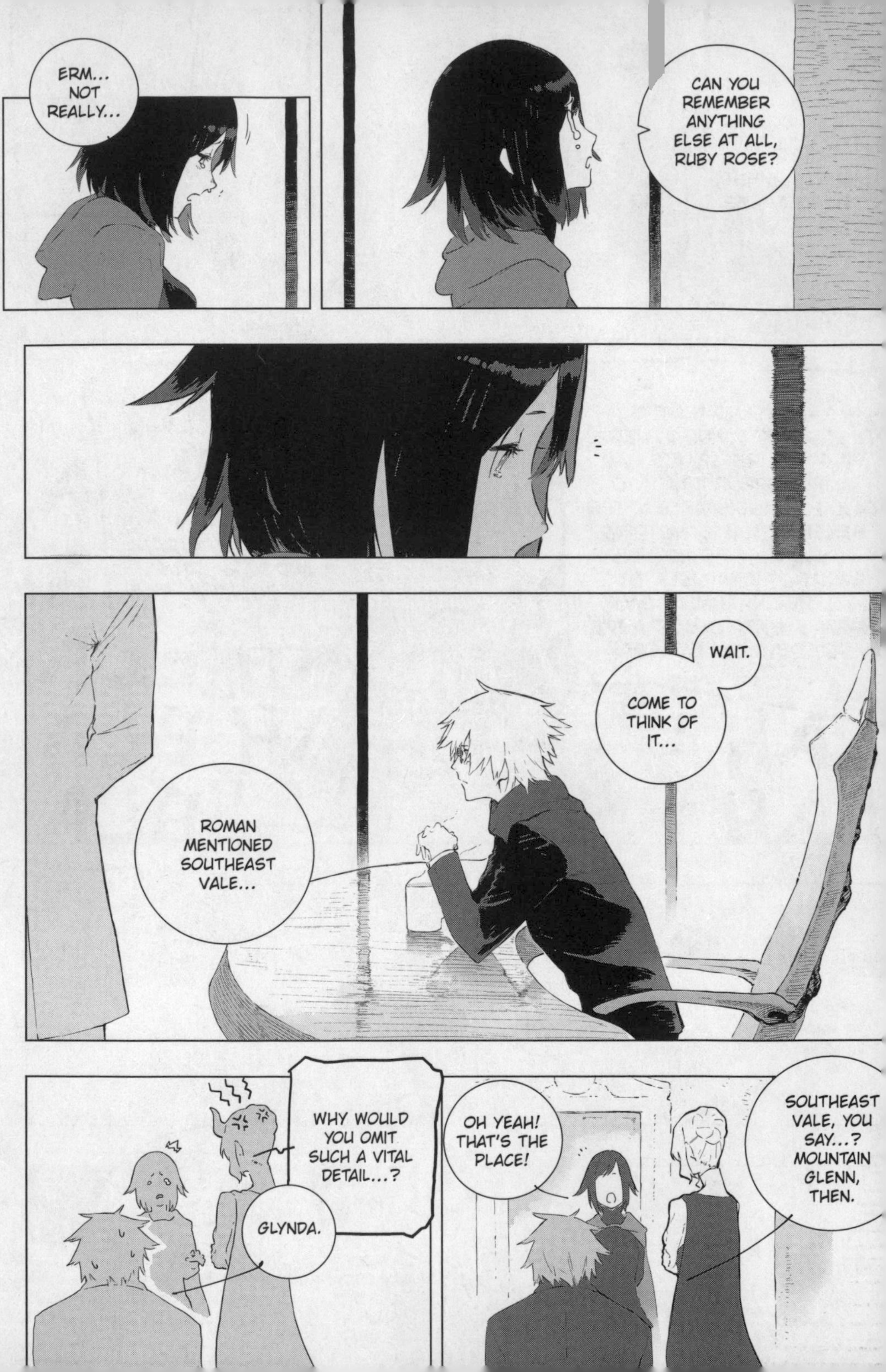
CAN YOU REMEMBER ANYTHING ELSE AT ALL, RUBY ROSE?
ERM... NOT REALLY...
WAIT.
COME TO THINK OF IT...
ROMAN MENTIONED SOUTHEAST VALE...
SOUTHEAST VALE, YOU SAY...? MOUNTAIN GLENN, THEN.
OH YEAH! THAT'S THE PLACE!
WHY WOULD YOU OMIT SUCH A VITAL DETAIL...?
GLYNDA.

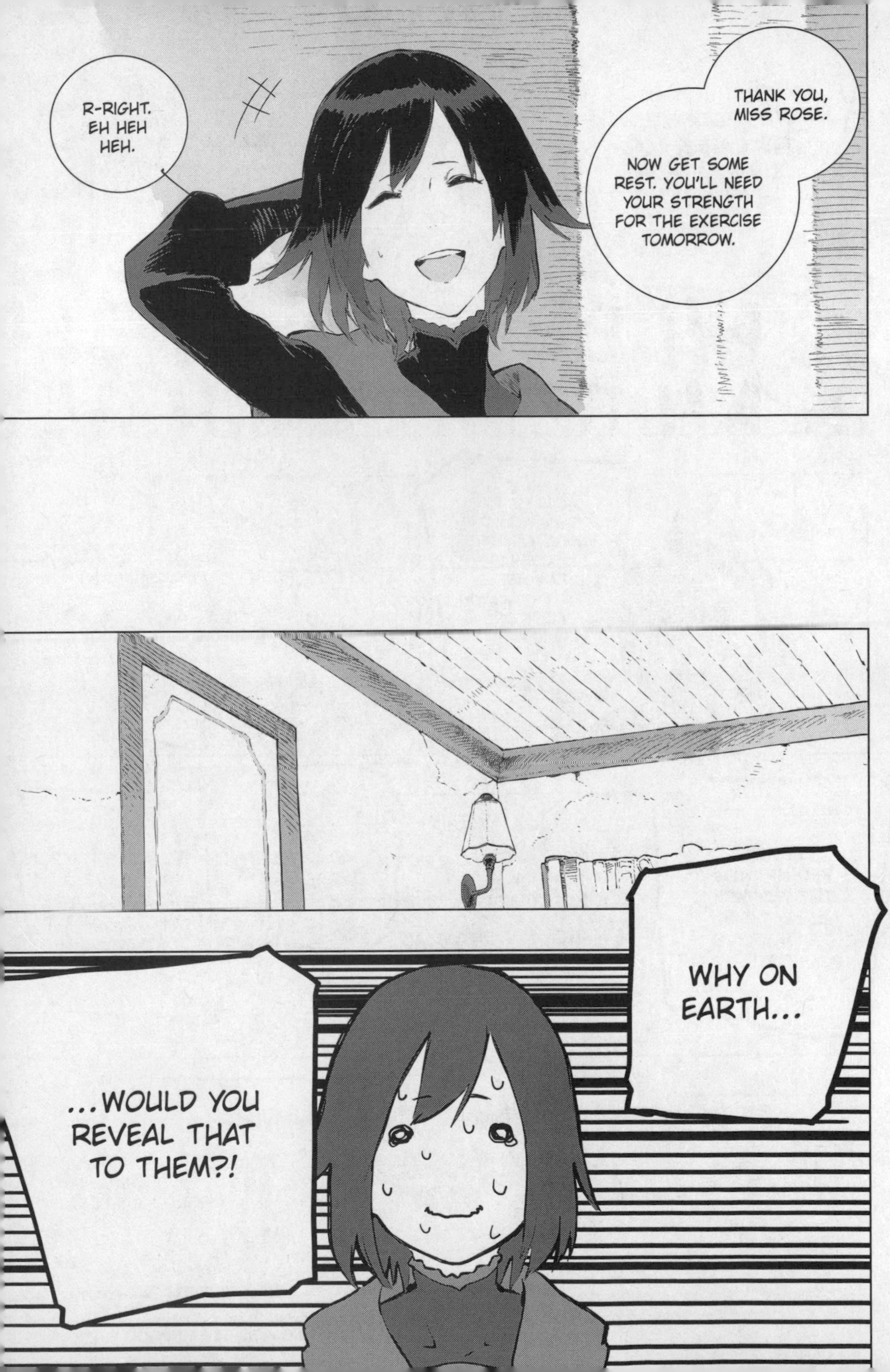
THANK YOU, MISS ROSE.
NOW GET SOME REST. YOU'LL NEED YOUR STRENGTH FOR THE EXERCISE TOMORROW.
R-RIGHT. EH HEH HEH.
WHY ON EARTH...
...WOULD YOU REVEAL THAT TO THEM?!

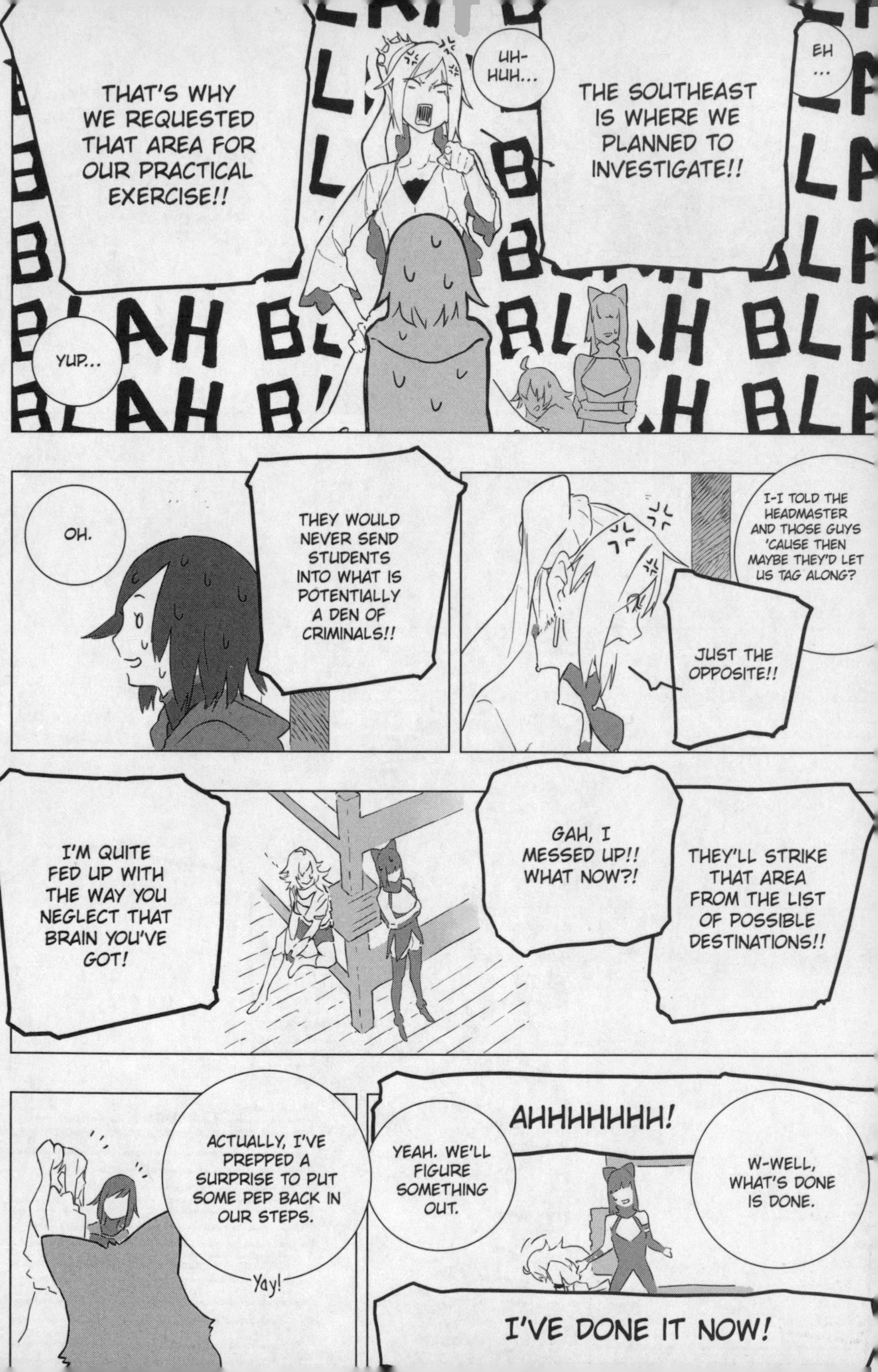
EH ...
THE SOUTHEAST IS WHERE WE PLANNED TO INVESTIGATE!!
UH-HUH...
THAT'S WHY WE REQUESTED THAT AREA FOR OUR PRACTICAL EXERCISE!!
BLAH BLAH
YUP...
I-I TOLD THE HEADMASTER AND THOSE GUYS 'CAUSE THEN MAYBE THEY'D LET US TAG ALONG?
JUST THE OPPOSITE!!
THEY WOULD NEVER SEND STUDENTS INTO WHAT IS POTENTIALLY A DEN OF CRIMINALS!!
OH.
THEY'LL STRIKE THAT AREA FROM THE LIST OF POSSIBLE DESTINATIONS!!
GAH, I MESSED UP!! WHAT NOW?!
I'M QUITE FED UP WITH THE WAY YOU NEGLECT THAT BRAIN YOU'VE GOT!
AHHHHHHH!
W-WELL, WHAT'S DONE IS DONE.
YEAH. WE'LL FIGURE SOMETHING OUT.
I'VE DONE IT NOW!
ACTUALLY, I'VE PREPPED A SURPRISE TO PUT SOME PEP BACK IN OUR STEPS.
Yay!

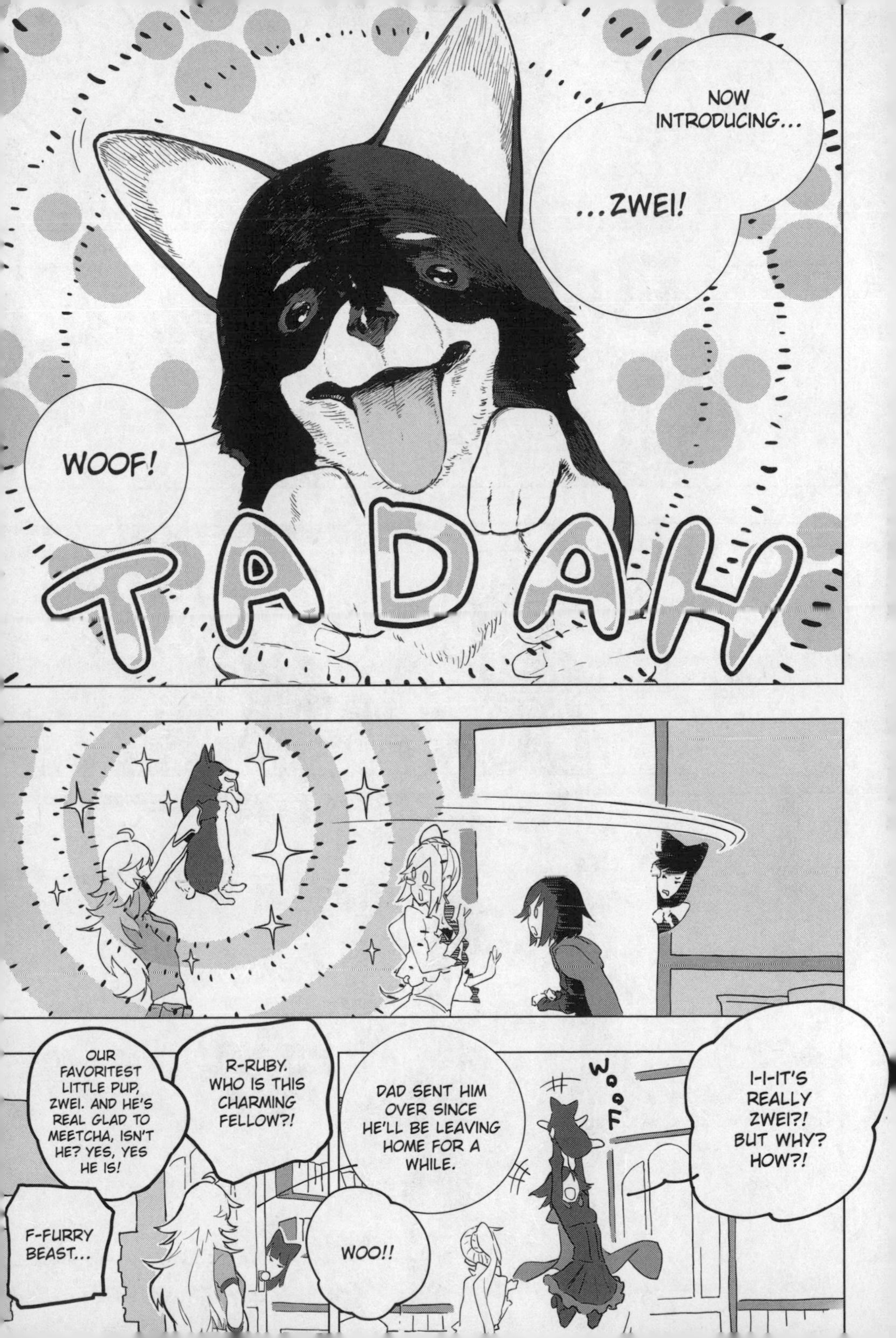
NOW INTRODUCING...
...ZWEI!
WOOF!
TADAH
I-I-IT'S REALLY ZWEI?! BUT WHY? HOW?!
WOOF
DAD SENT HIM OVER SINCE HE'LL BE LEAVING HOME FOR A WHILE.
WOO!!
R-RUBY. WHO IS THIS CHARMING FELLOW?!
OUR FAVORITEST LITTLE PUP, ZWEI. AND HE'S REAL GLAD TO MEETCHA, ISN'T HE? YES, YES HE IS!
F-FURRY BEAST...

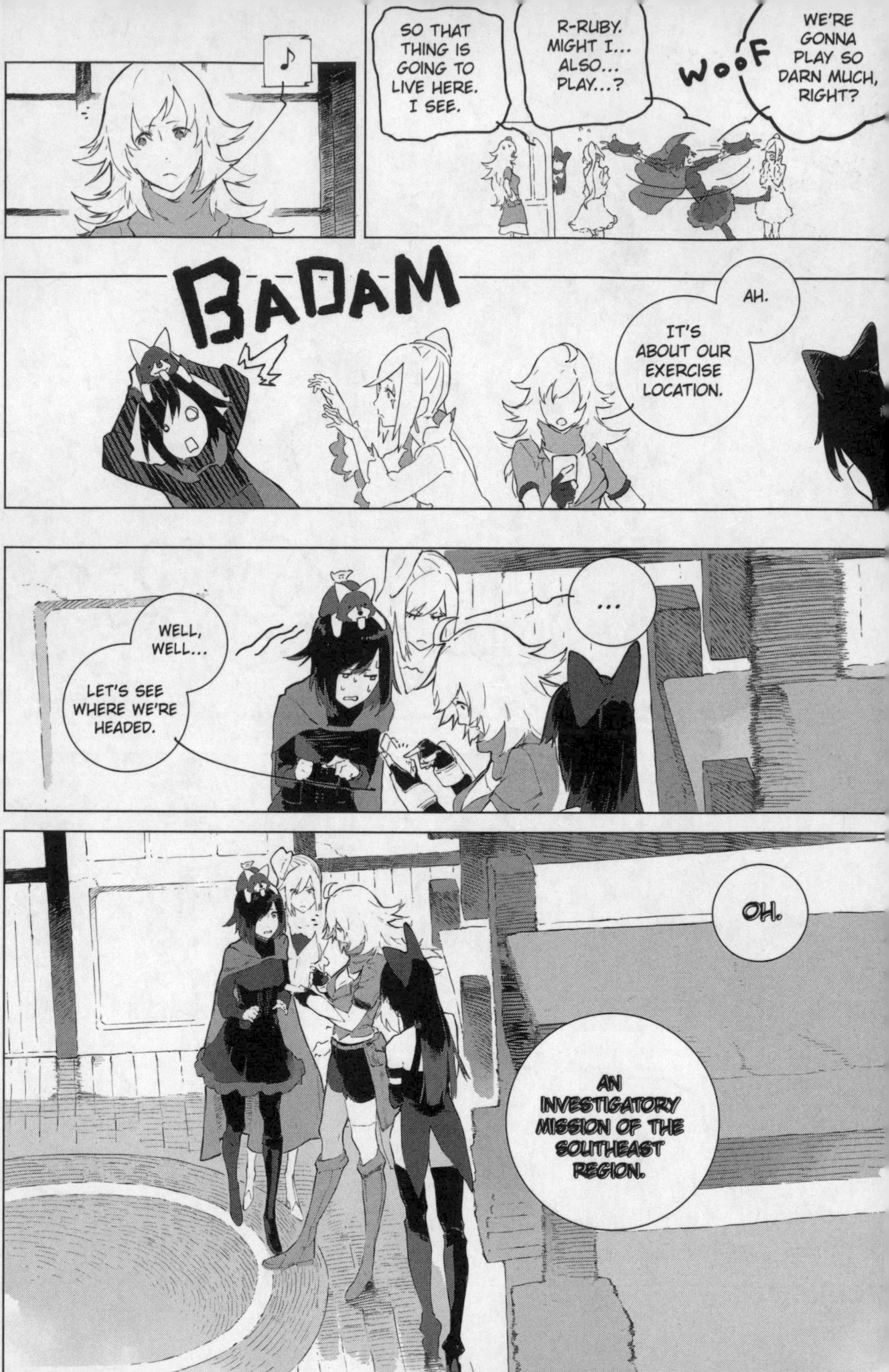
WE'RE GONNA PLAY SO DARN MUCH, RIGHT?
WOOF
R-RUBY. MIGHT I... ALSO... PLAY...?
SO THAT THING IS GOING TO LIVE HERE. I SEE.
♪
AH.
IT'S ABOUT OUR EXERCISE LOCATION.
BADAM
...
WELL, WELL...
LET'S SEE WHERE WE'RE HEADED.
OH.
AN INVESTIGATORY MISSION OF THE SOUTHEAST REGION.

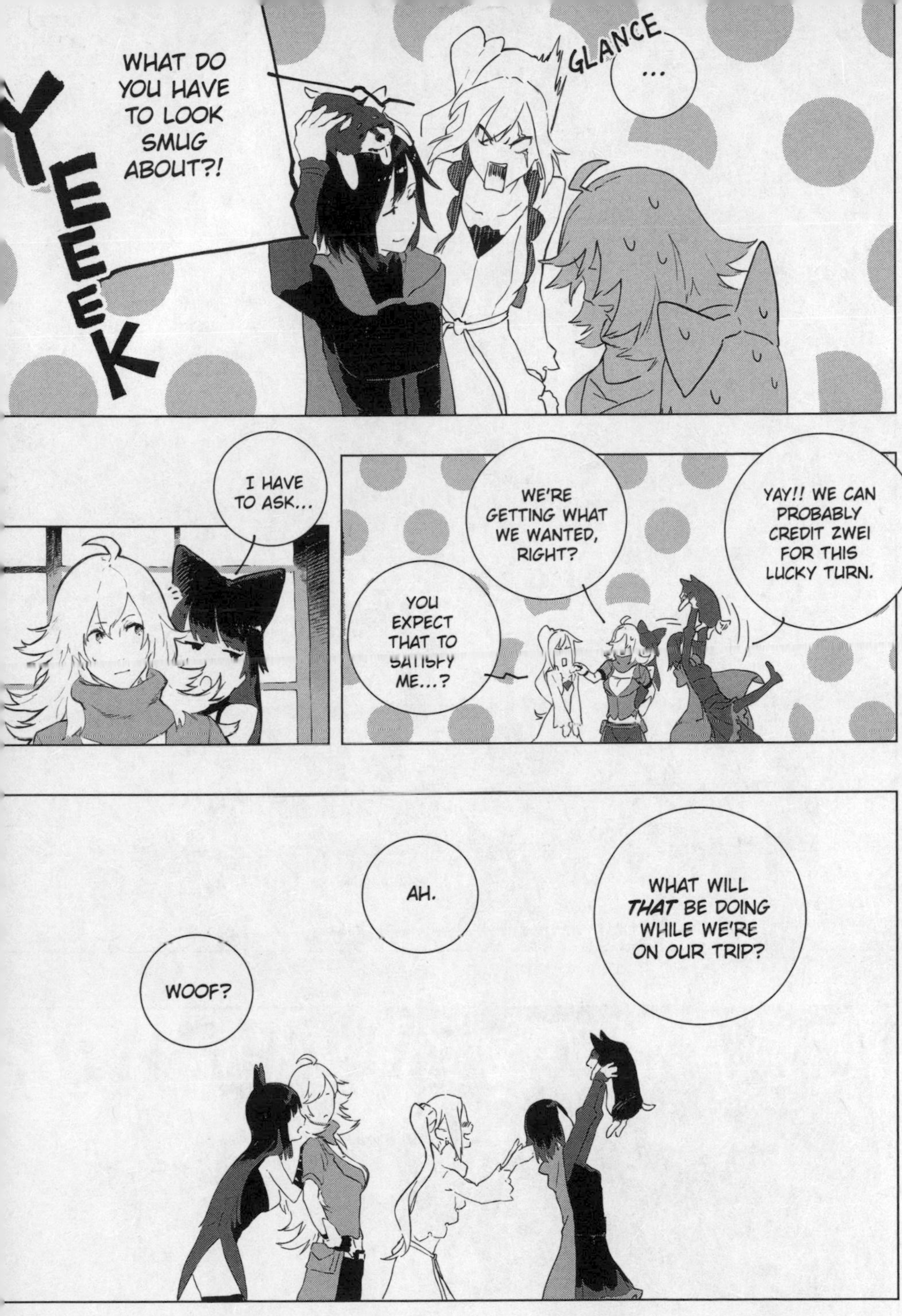
GLANCE
...
YEEEK
WHAT DO YOU HAVE TO LOOK SMUG ABOUT?!
YAY!! WE CAN PROBABLY CREDIT ZWEI FOR THIS LUCKY TURN.
WE'RE GETTING WHAT WE WANTED, RIGHT?
YOU EXPECT THAT TO SATISFY ME...?
I HAVE TO ASK...
WHAT WILL *THAT* BE DOING WHILE WE'RE ON OUR TRIP?
AH.
WOOF?

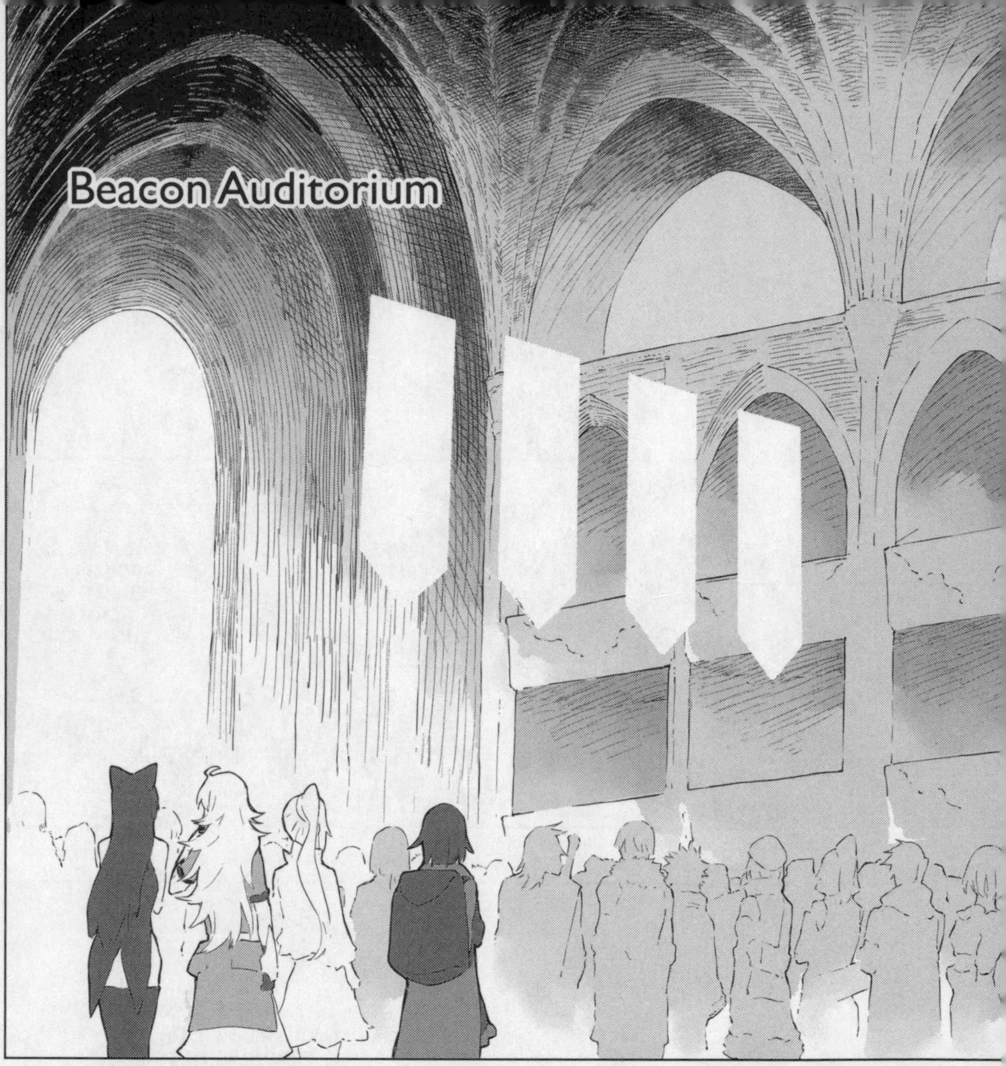
Beacon Auditorium
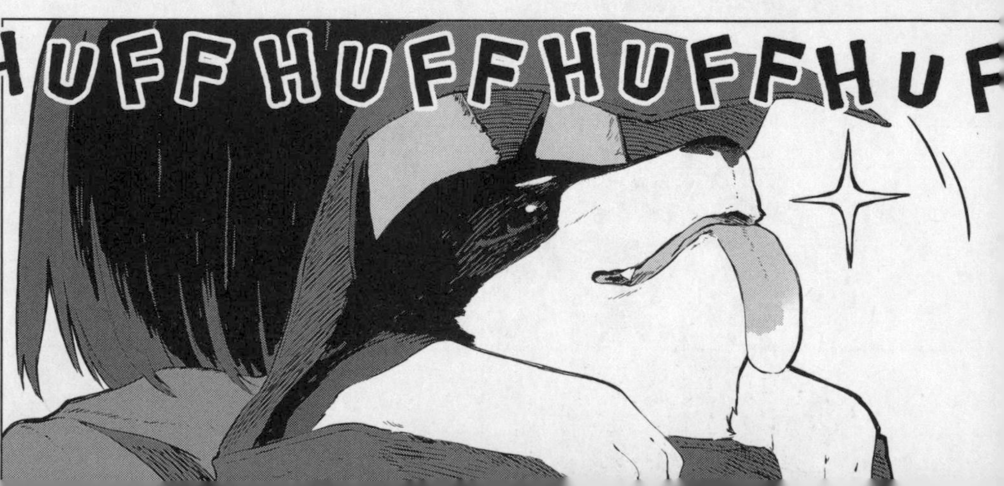
HUFF HUFF HUFF HUF

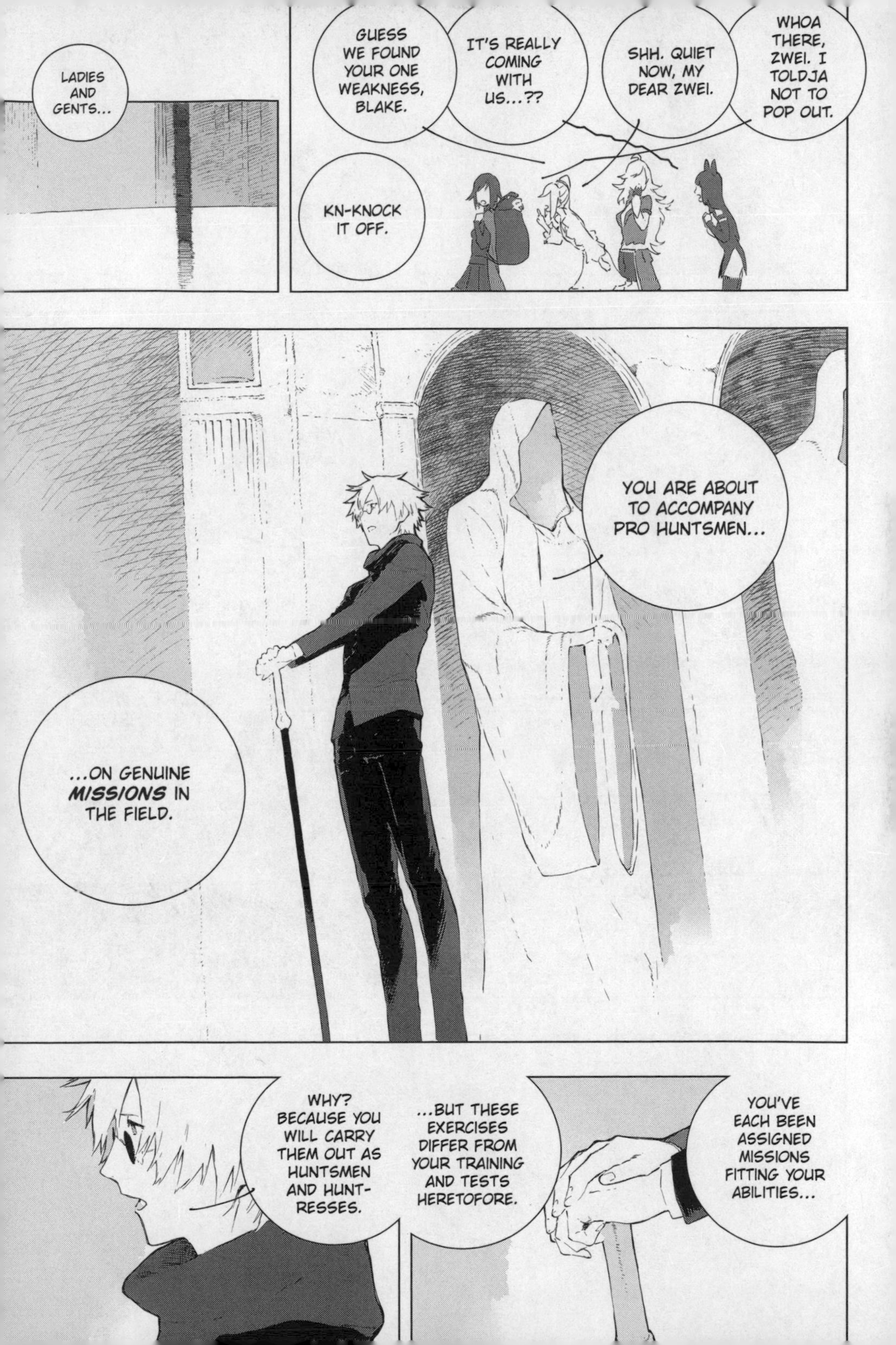
WHOA THERE, ZWEI. I TOLDJA NOT TO POP OUT.
SHH. QUIET NOW, MY DEAR ZWEI.
IT'S REALLY COMING WITH US...??
GUESS WE FOUND YOUR ONE WEAKNESS, BLAKE.
KN-KNOCK IT OFF.
LADIES AND GENTS...
YOU ARE ABOUT TO ACCOMPANY PRO HUNTSMEN...
...ON GENUINE **MISSIONS** IN THE FIELD.
YOU'VE EACH BEEN ASSIGNED MISSIONS FITTING YOUR ABILITIES...
...BUT THESE EXERCISES DIFFER FROM YOUR TRAINING AND TESTS HERETOFORE.
WHY? BECAUSE YOU WILL CARRY THEM OUT AS HUNTSMEN AND HUNT-RESSES.

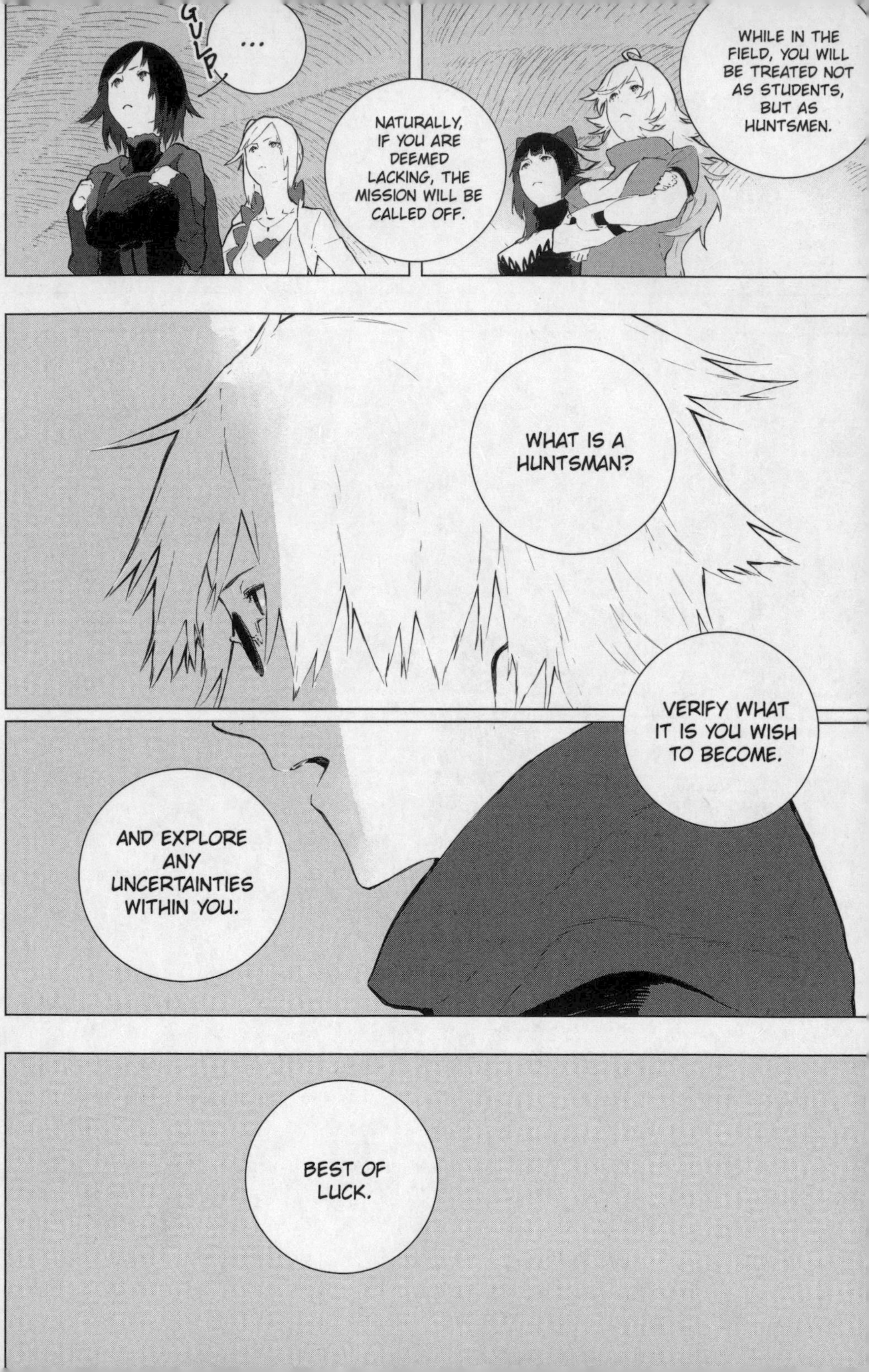
WHILE IN THE FIELD, YOU WILL BE TREATED NOT AS STUDENTS, BUT AS HUNTSMEN.
NATURALLY, IF YOU ARE DEEMED LACKING, THE MISSION WILL BE CALLED OFF.
...
GULP
WHAT IS A HUNTSMAN?
VERIFY WHAT IT IS YOU WISH TO BECOME.
AND EXPLORE ANY UNCERTAINTIES WITHIN YOU.
BEST OF LUCK.

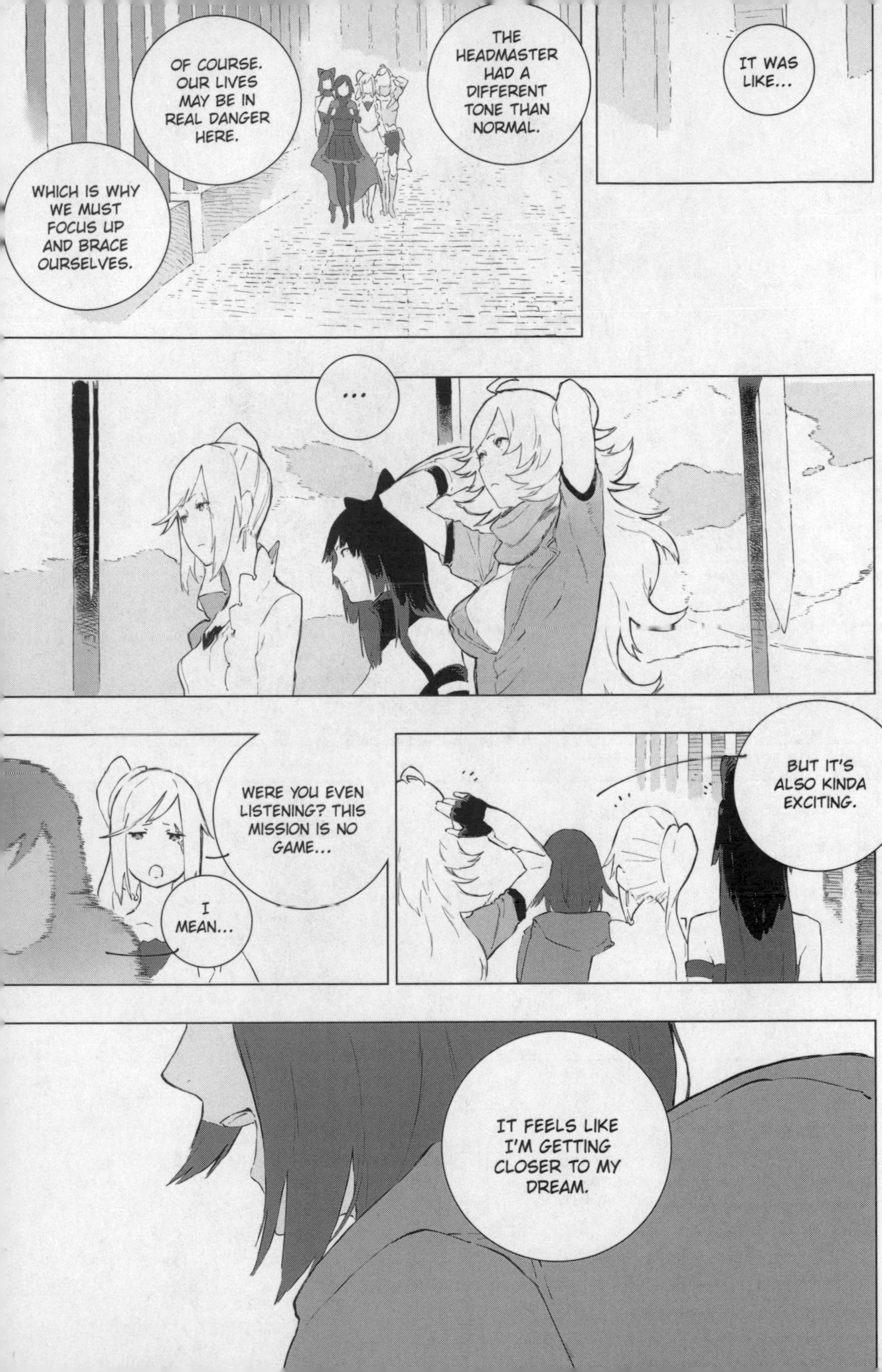
IT WAS LIKE...
THE HEADMASTER HAD A DIFFERENT TONE THAN NORMAL.
OF COURSE. OUR LIVES MAY BE IN REAL DANGER HERE.
WHICH IS WHY WE MUST FOCUS UP AND BRACE OURSELVES.
...
BUT IT'S ALSO KINDA EXCITING.
WERE YOU EVEN LISTENING? THIS MISSION IS NO GAME...
I MEAN...
IT FEELS LIKE I'M GETTING CLOSER TO MY DREAM.

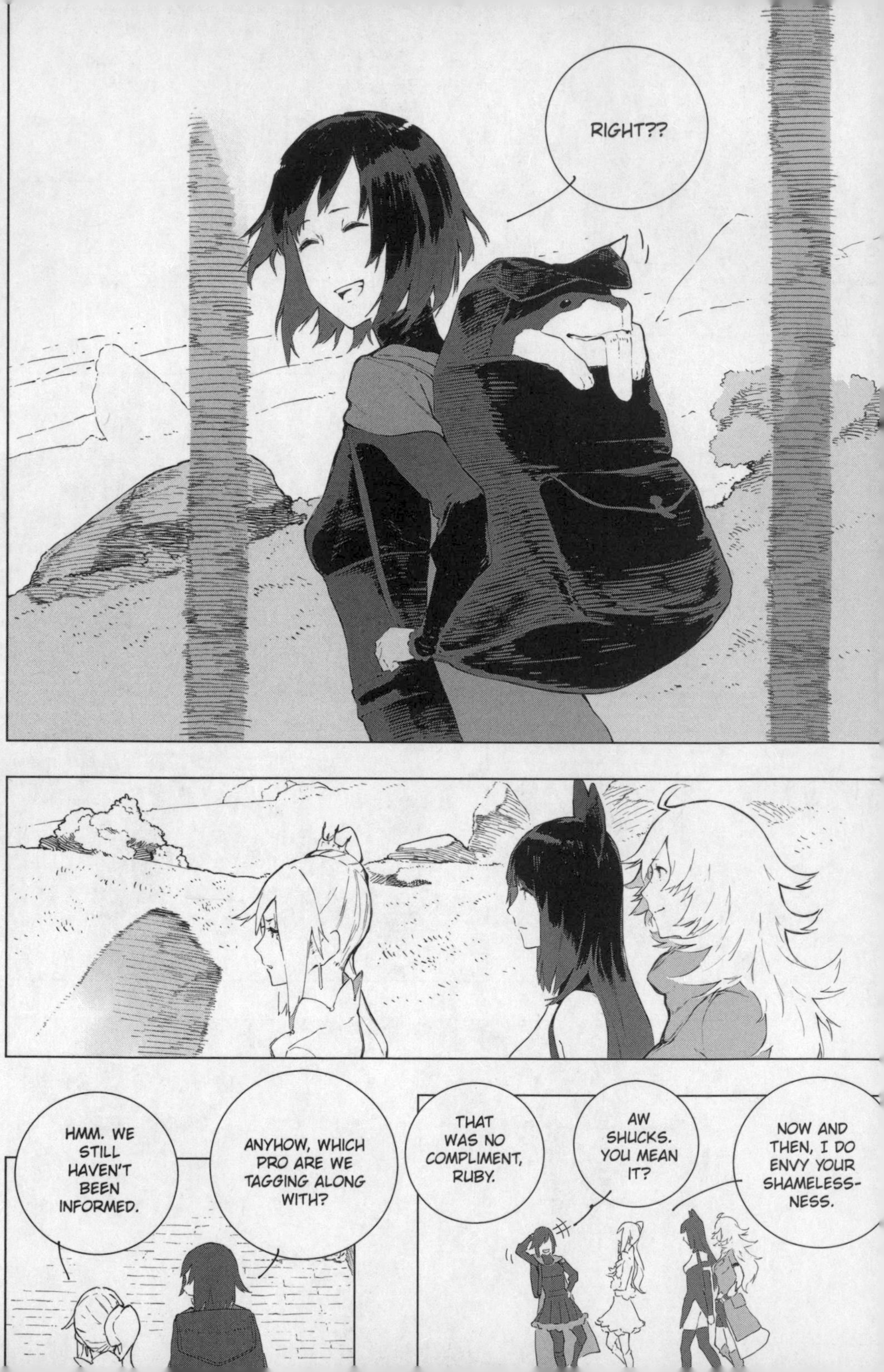
RIGHT??
NOW AND THEN, I DO ENVY YOUR SHAMELESS-NESS.
AW SHUCKS. YOU MEAN IT?
THAT WAS NO COMPLIMENT, RUBY.
ANYHOW, WHICH PRO ARE WE TAGGING ALONG WITH?
HMM. WE STILL HAVEN'T BEEN INFORMED.

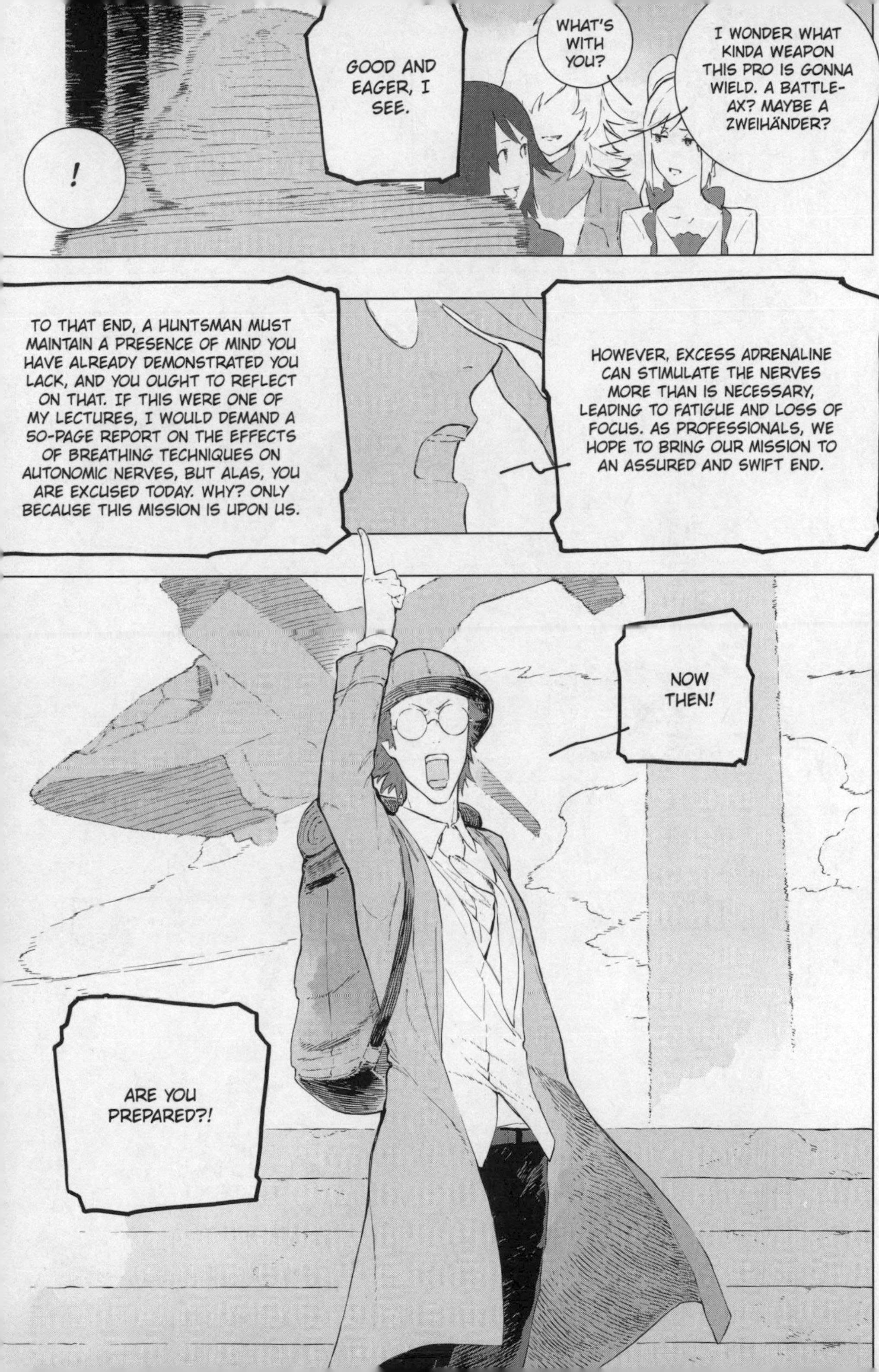
I WONDER WHAT KINDA WEAPON THIS PRO IS GONNA WIELD. A BATTLE-AX? MAYBE A ZWEIHÄNDER?
WHAT'S WITH YOU?
GOOD AND EAGER, I SEE.
!
HOWEVER, EXCESS ADRENALINE CAN STIMULATE THE NERVES MORE THAN IS NECESSARY, LEADING TO FATIGUE AND LOSS OF FOCUS. AS PROFESSIONALS, WE HOPE TO BRING OUR MISSION TO AN ASSURED AND SWIFT END.
TO THAT END, A HUNTSMAN MUST MAINTAIN A PRESENCE OF MIND YOU HAVE ALREADY DEMONSTRATED YOU LACK, AND YOU OUGHT TO REFLECT ON THAT. IF THIS WERE ONE OF MY LECTURES, I WOULD DEMAND A 50-PAGE REPORT ON THE EFFECTS OF BREATHING TECHNIQUES ON AUTONOMIC NERVES, BUT ALAS, YOU ARE EXCUSED TODAY. WHY? ONLY BECAUSE THIS MISSION IS UPON US.
NOW THEN!
ARE YOU PREPARED?!

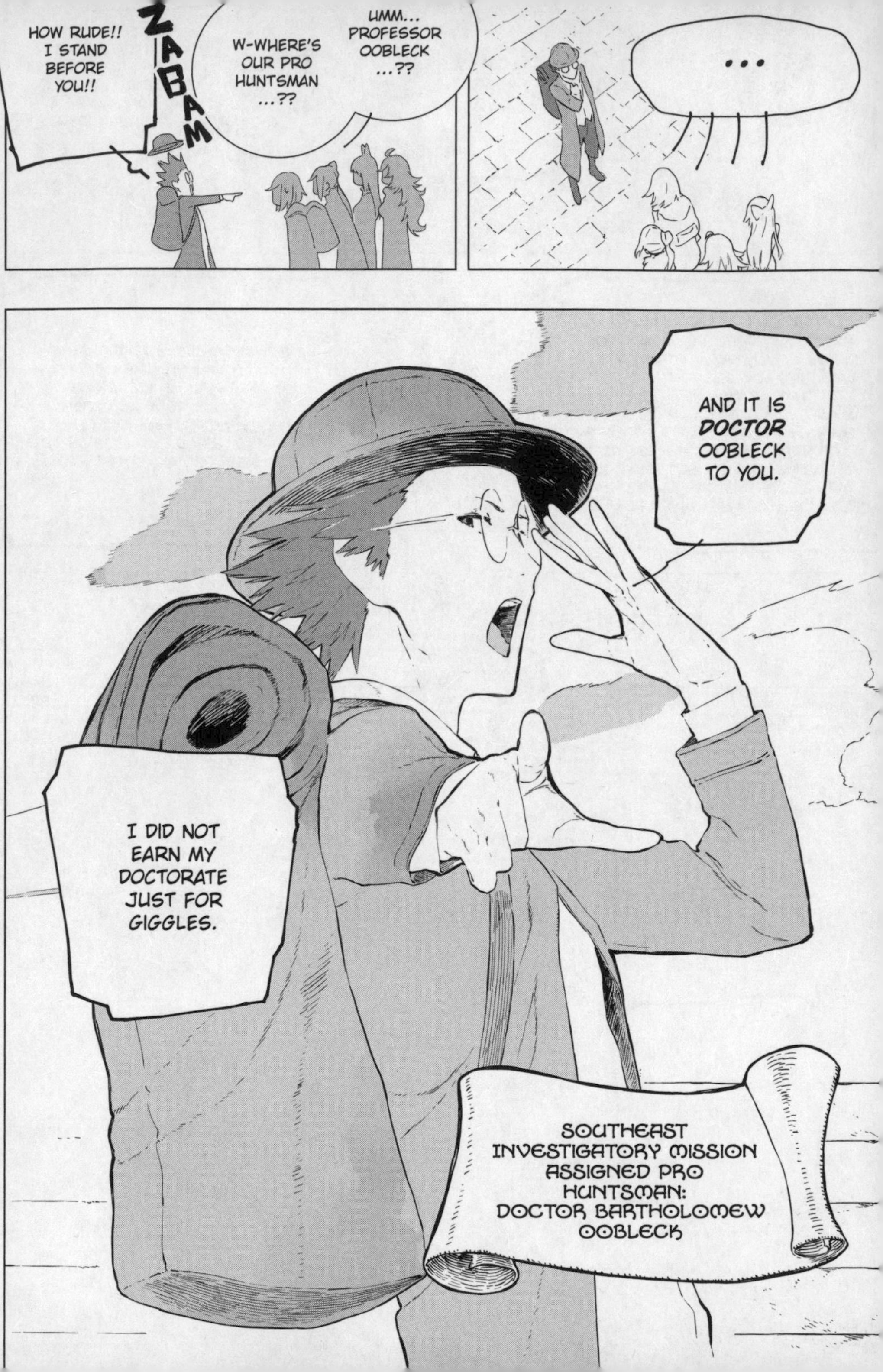
...
UMM... PROFESSOR OOBLECK ...??
W-WHERE'S OUR PRO HUNTSMAN ...??
HOW RUDE!! I STAND BEFORE YOU!!
ZABAM
AND IT IS *DOCTOR* OOBLECK TO YOU.
I DID NOT EARN MY DOCTORATE JUST FOR GIGGLES.
SOUTHEAST INVESTIGATORY MISSION ASSIGNED PRO HUNTSMAN: DOCTOR BARTHOLOMEW OOBLECK

TALLYHO!

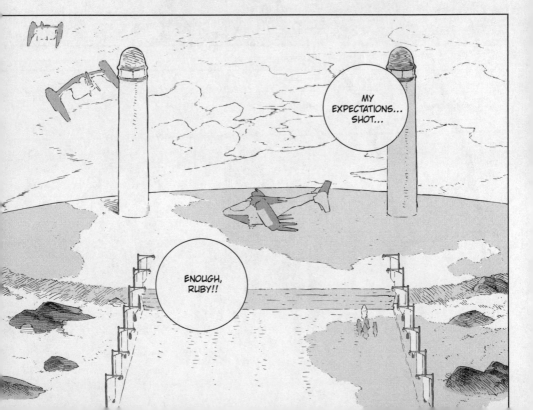

MY EXPECTATIONS... SHOT...

ENOUGH, RUBY!!

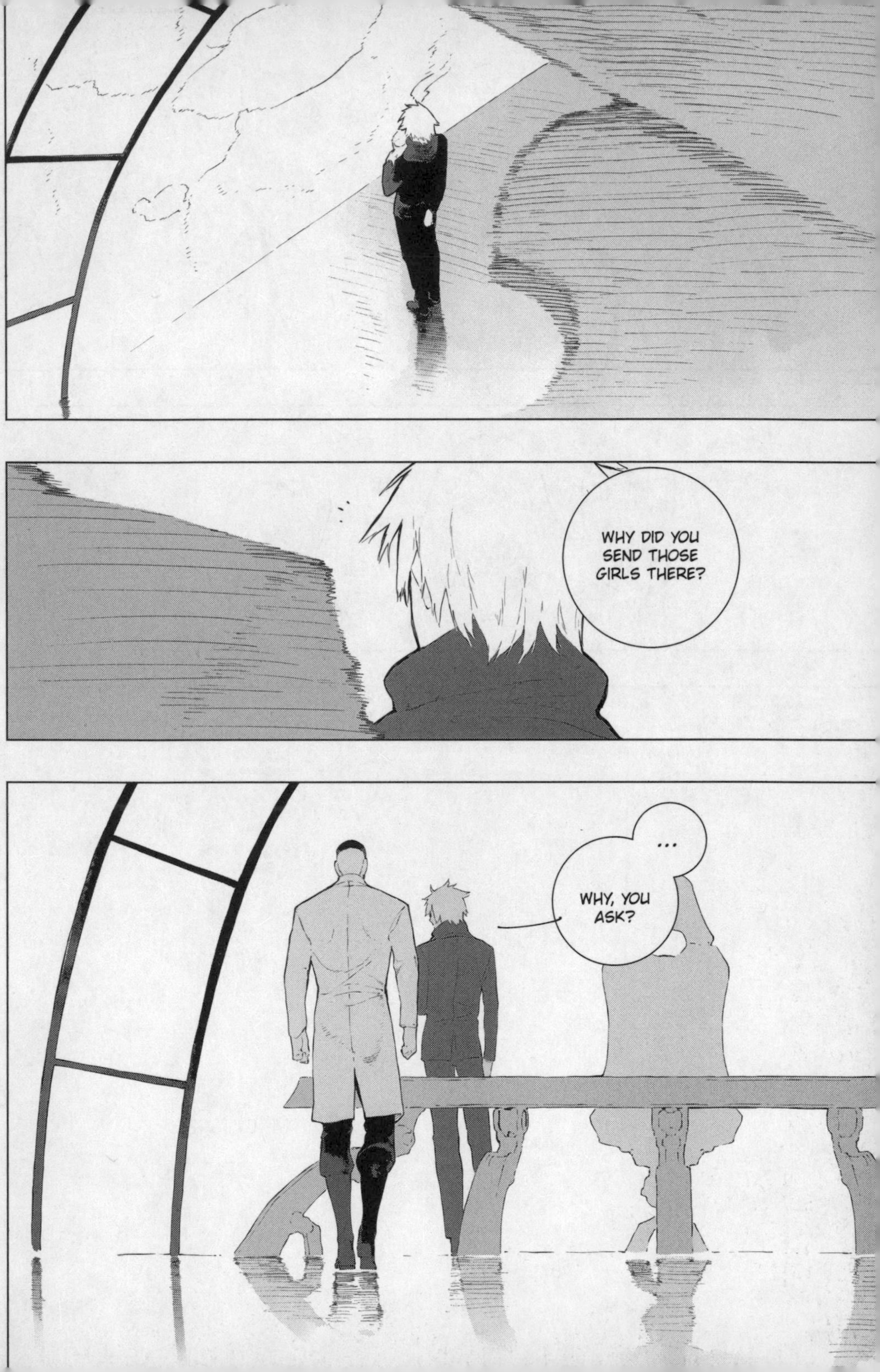
WHY DID YOU SEND THOSE GIRLS THERE?
...
WHY, YOU ASK?

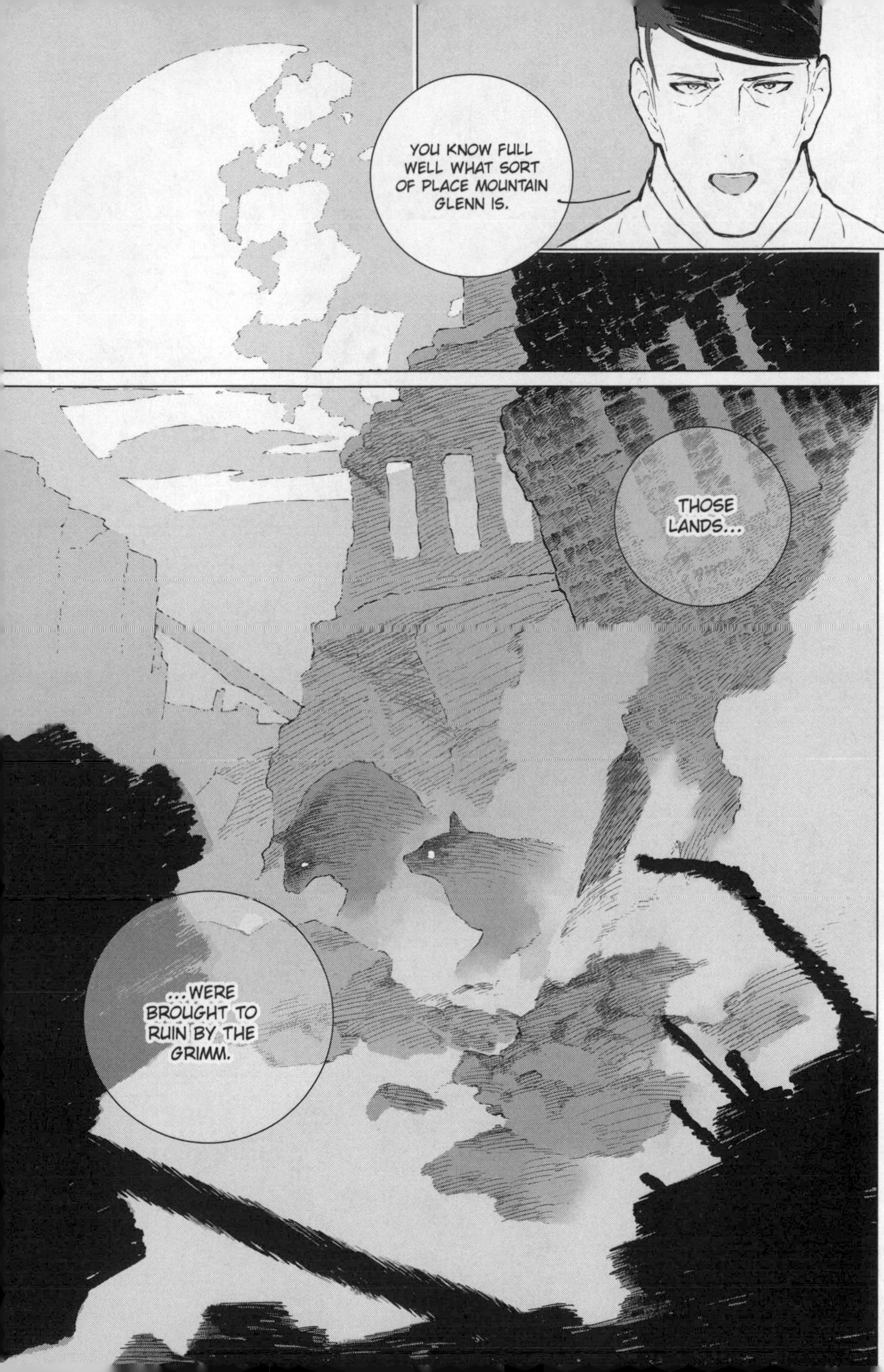
YOU KNOW FULL WELL WHAT SORT OF PLACE MOUNTAIN GLENN IS.
THOSE LANDS...
...WERE BROUGHT TO RUIN BY THE GRIMM.

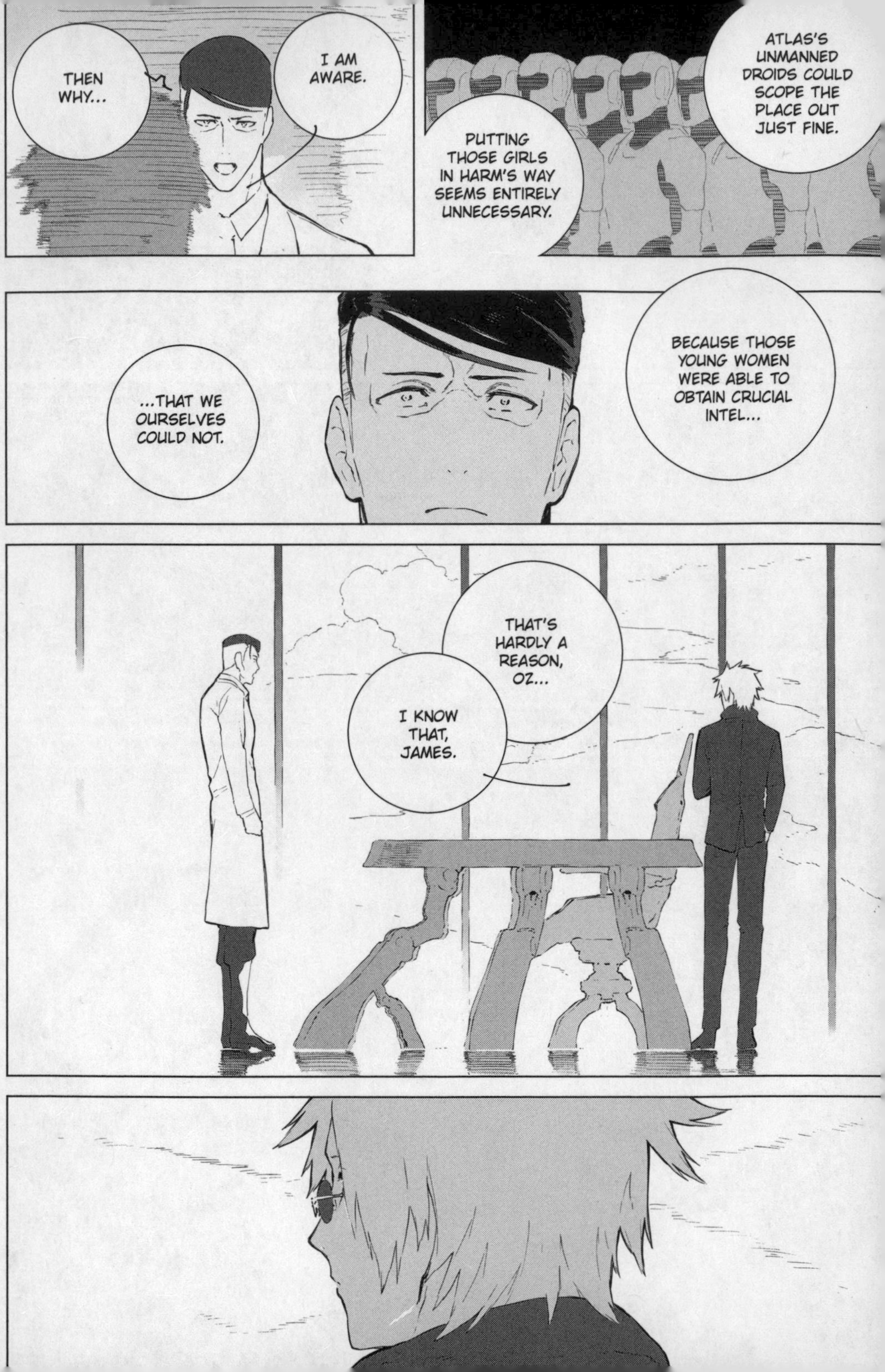
ATLAS'S UNMANNED DROIDS COULD SCOPE THE PLACE OUT JUST FINE.
PUTTING THOSE GIRLS IN HARM'S WAY SEEMS ENTIRELY UNNECESSARY.
I AM AWARE.
THEN WHY...
BECAUSE THOSE YOUNG WOMEN WERE ABLE TO OBTAIN CRUCIAL INTEL...
...THAT WE OURSELVES COULD NOT.
THAT'S HARDLY A REASON, OZ...
I KNOW THAT, JAMES.

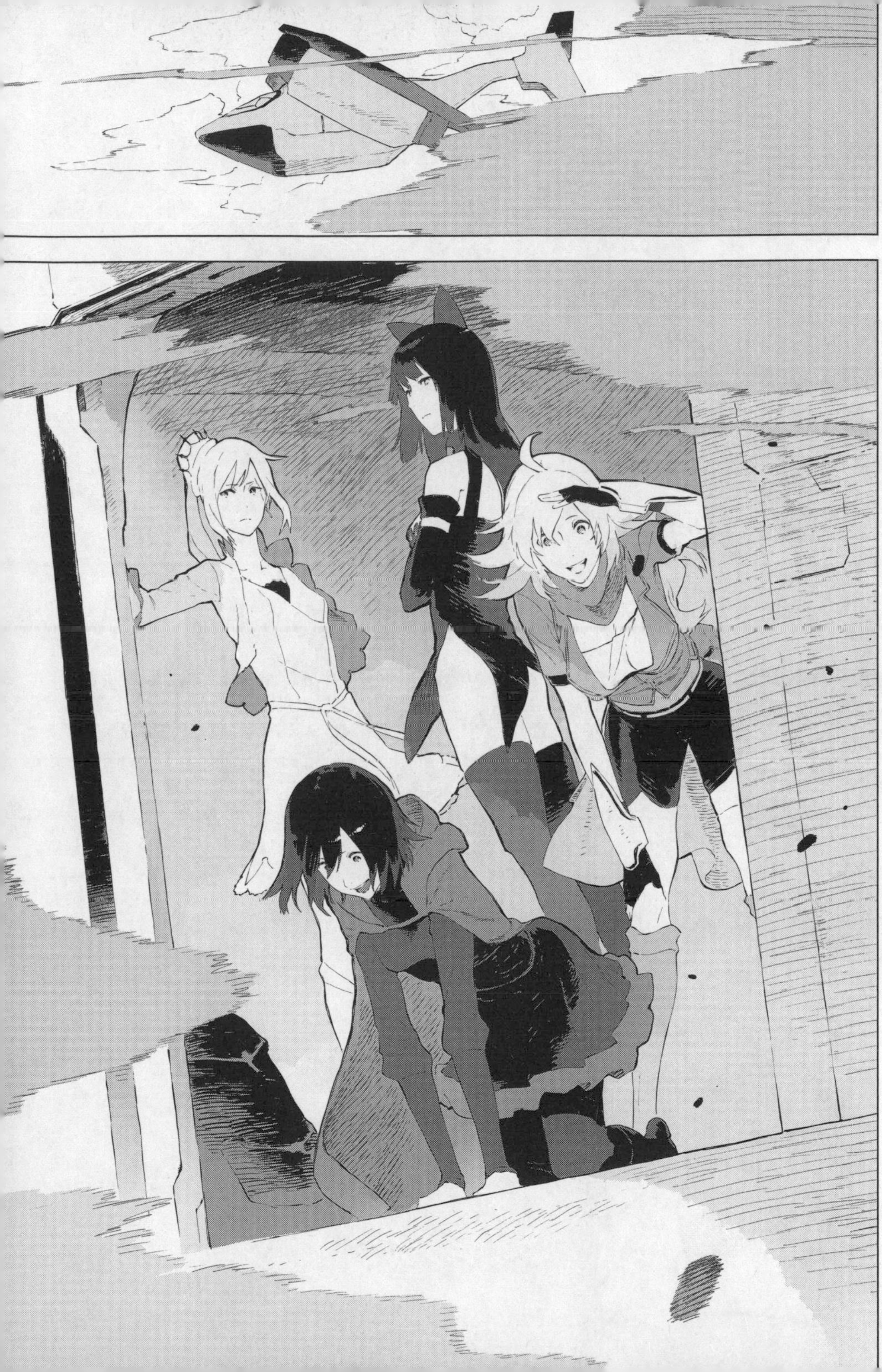

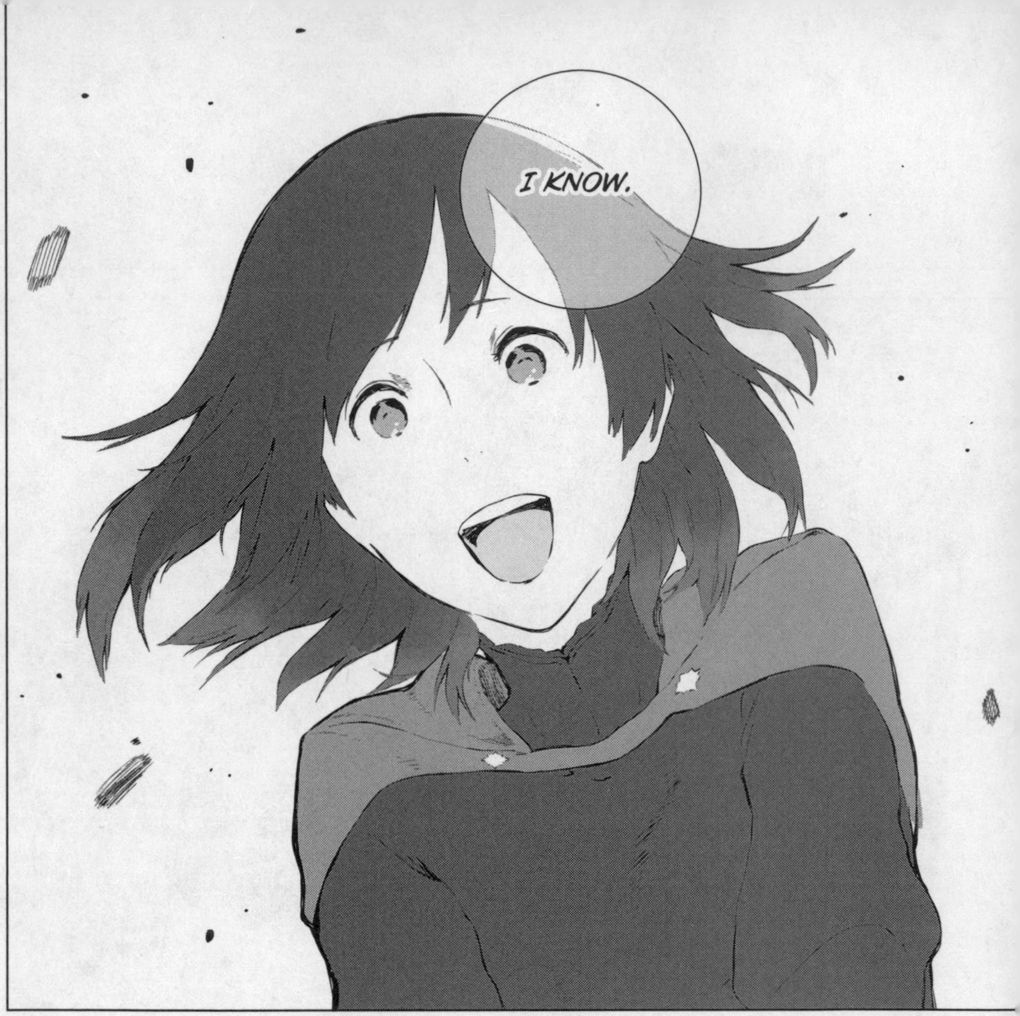
I KNOW.

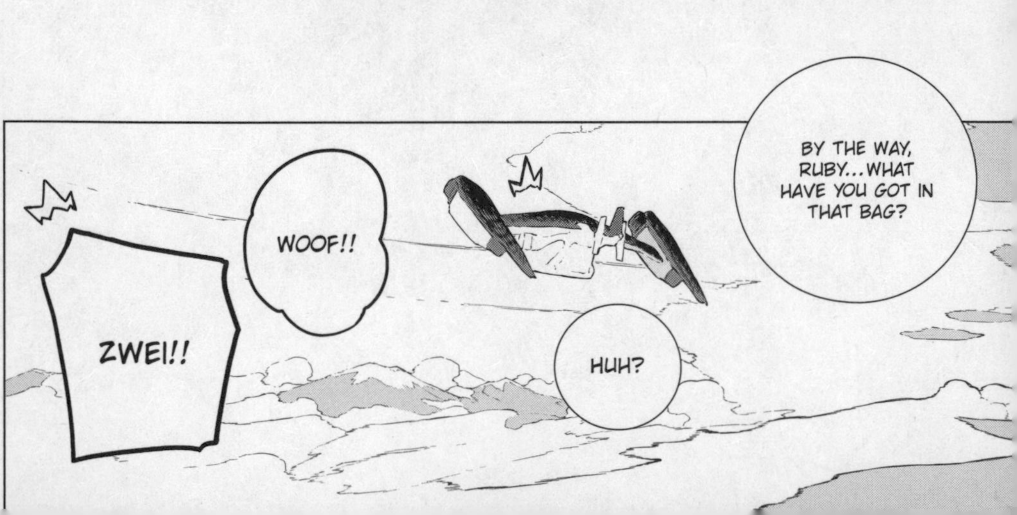
BY THE WAY, RUBY...WHAT HAVE YOU GOT IN THAT BAG?
HUH?
WOOF!!
ZWEI!!

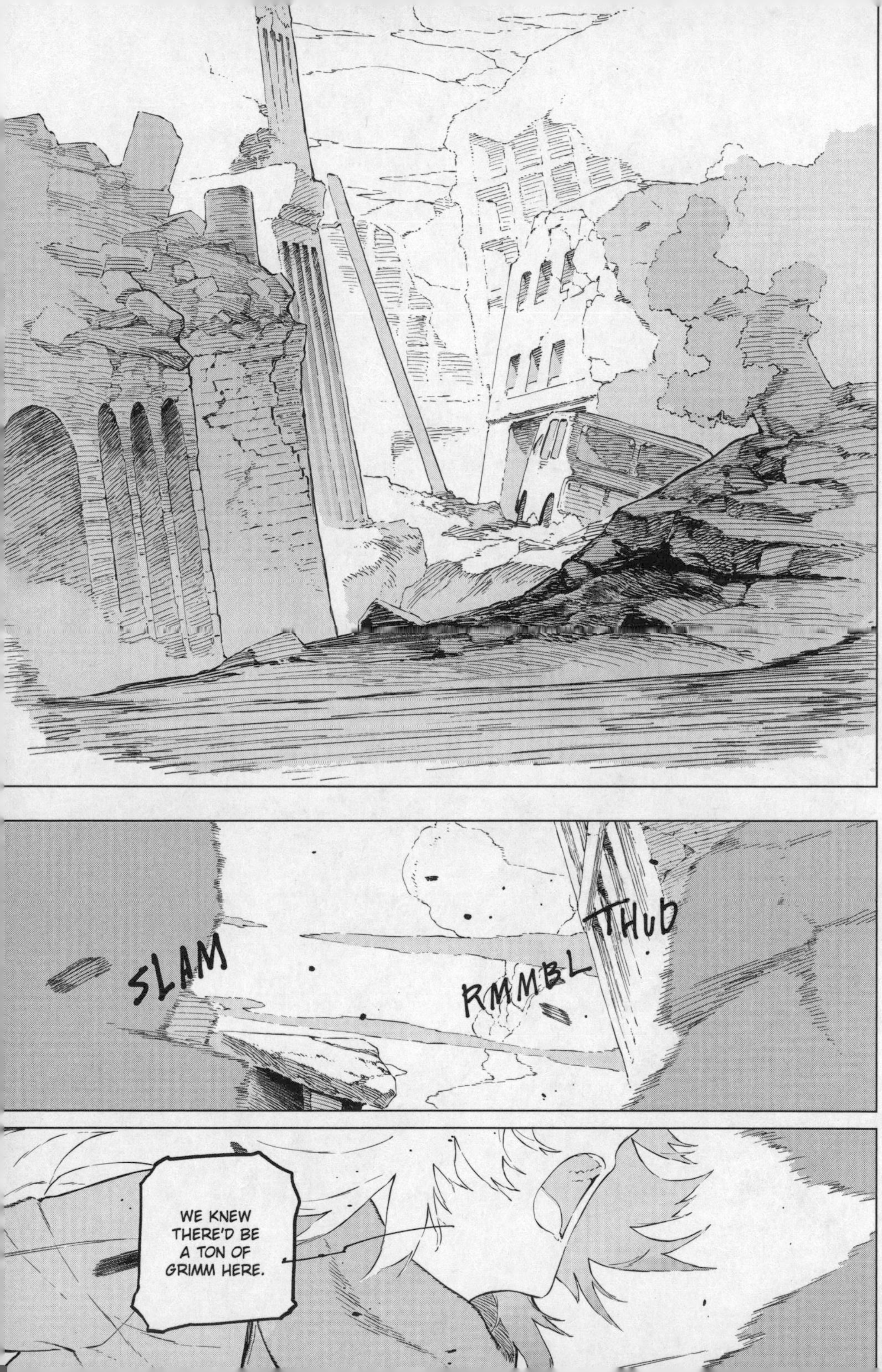
THUD
RMMBL
SLAM
WE KNEW THERE'D BE A TON OF GRIMM HERE.

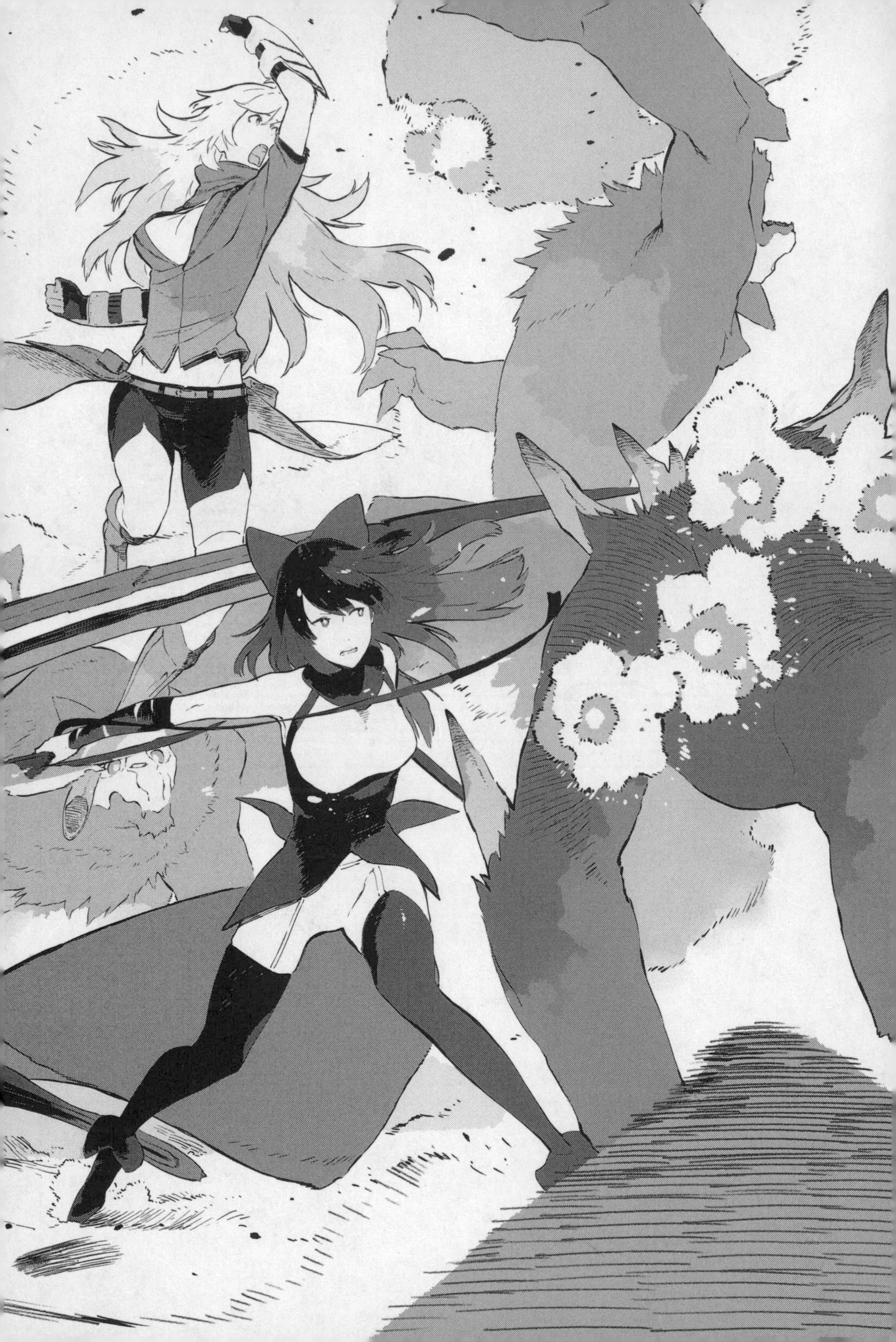

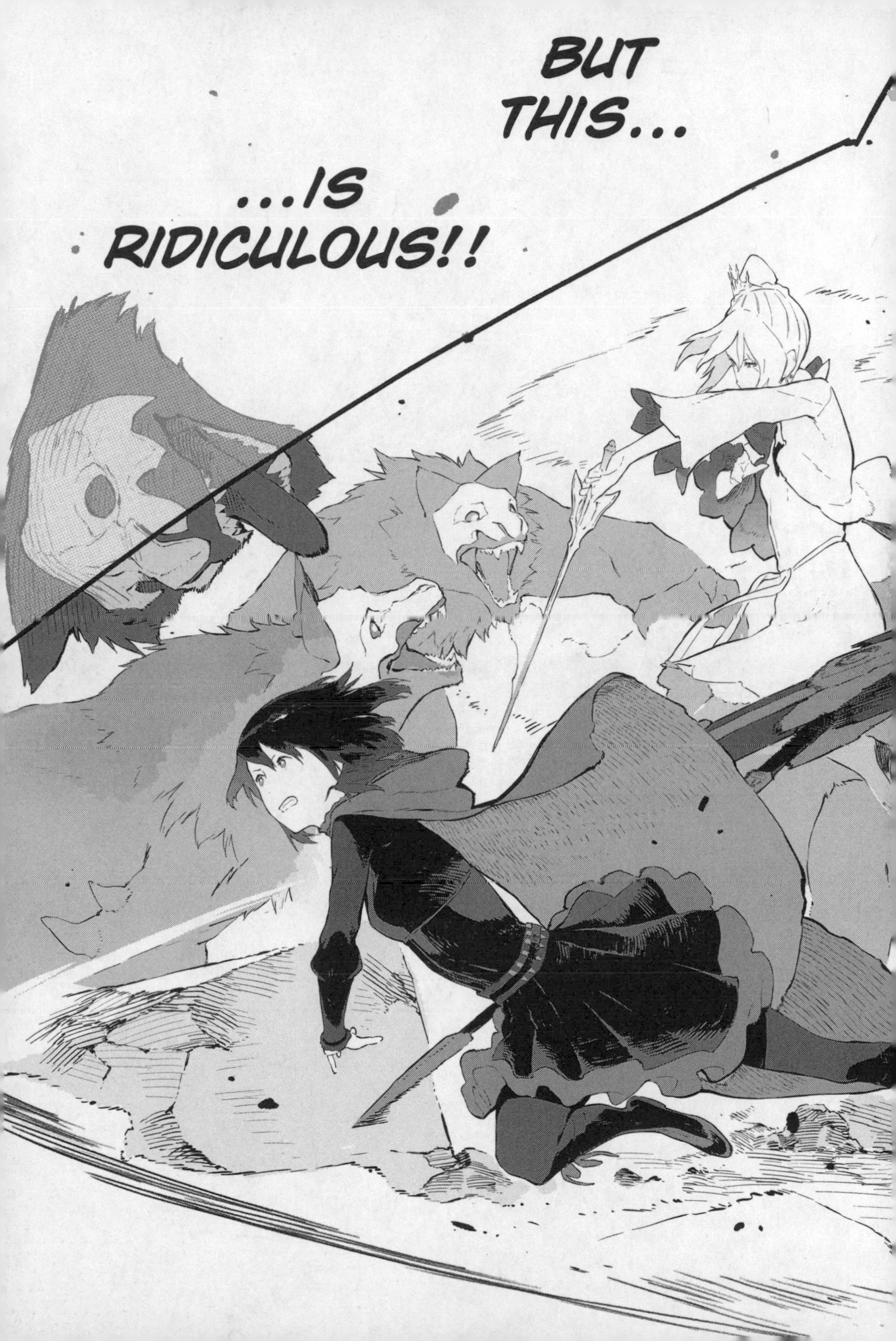
BUT THIS...
...IS RIDICULOUS!!

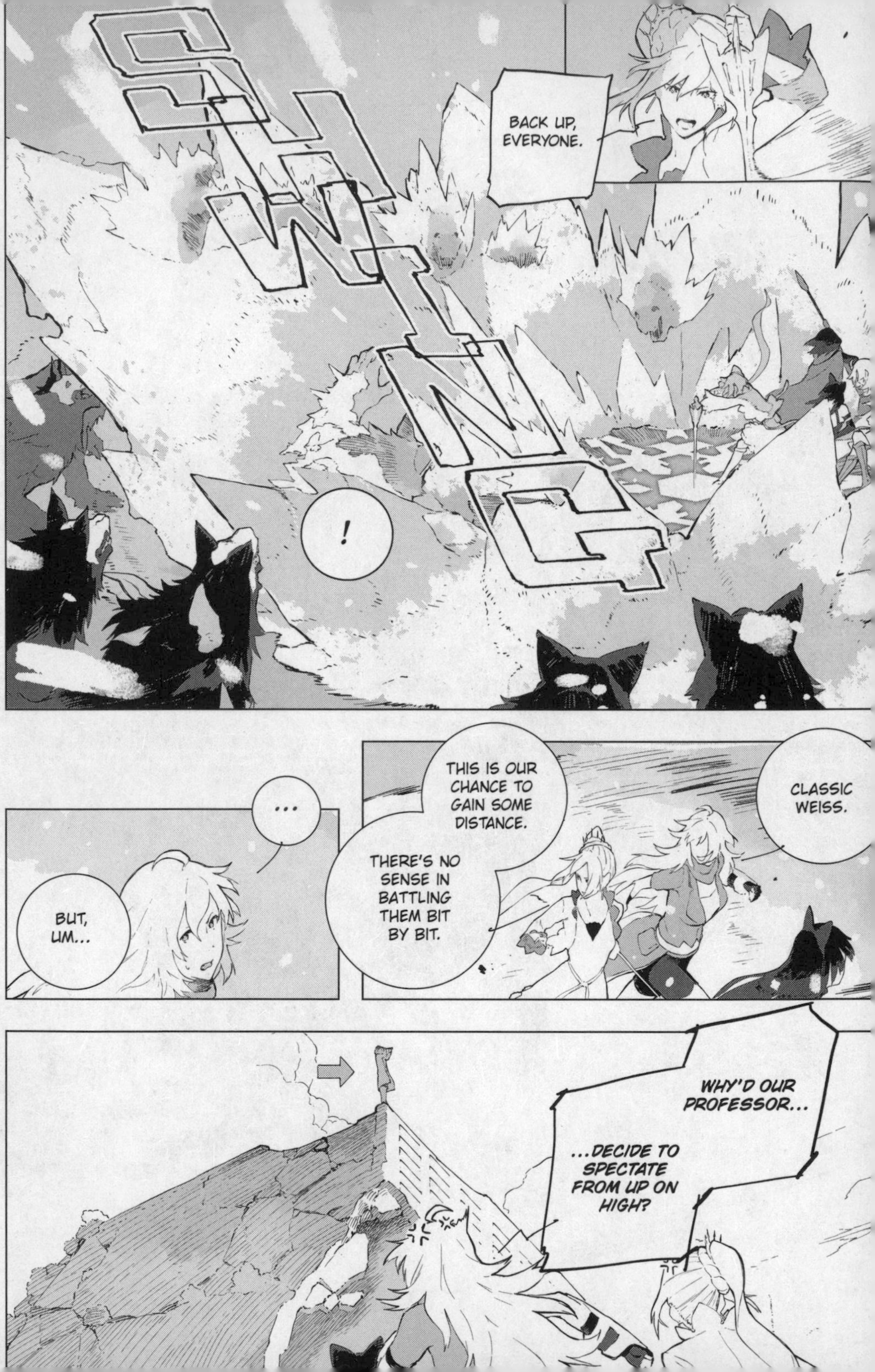
BACK UP, EVERYONE.
SHWING
!
CLASSIC WEISS.
THIS IS OUR CHANCE TO GAIN SOME DISTANCE.
THERE'S NO SENSE IN BATTLING THEM BIT BY BIT.
...
BUT, UM...
WHY'D OUR PROFESSOR...
...DECIDE TO SPECTATE FROM UP ON HIGH?

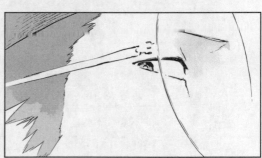

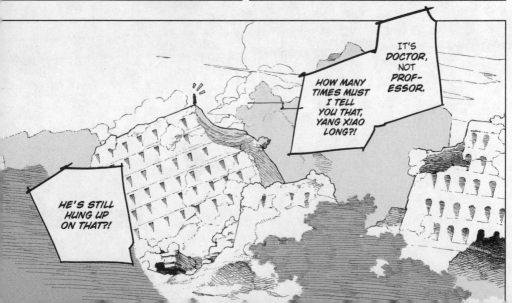

IT'S DOCTOR, NOT PROFESSOR.

HOW MANY TIMES MUST I TELL YOU THAT, YANG XIAO LONG?!

HE'S STILL HUNG UP ON THAT?!

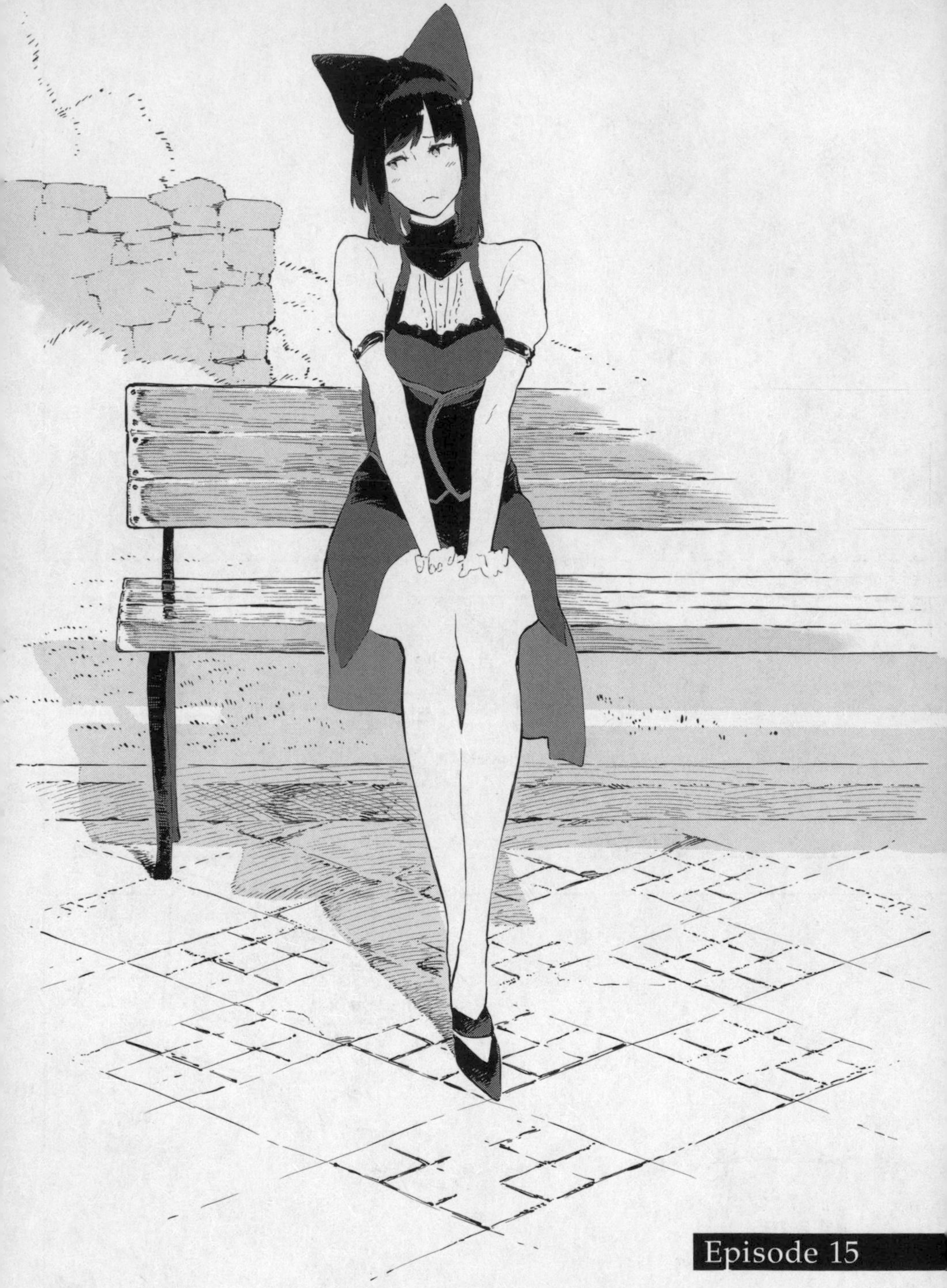

Episode 15

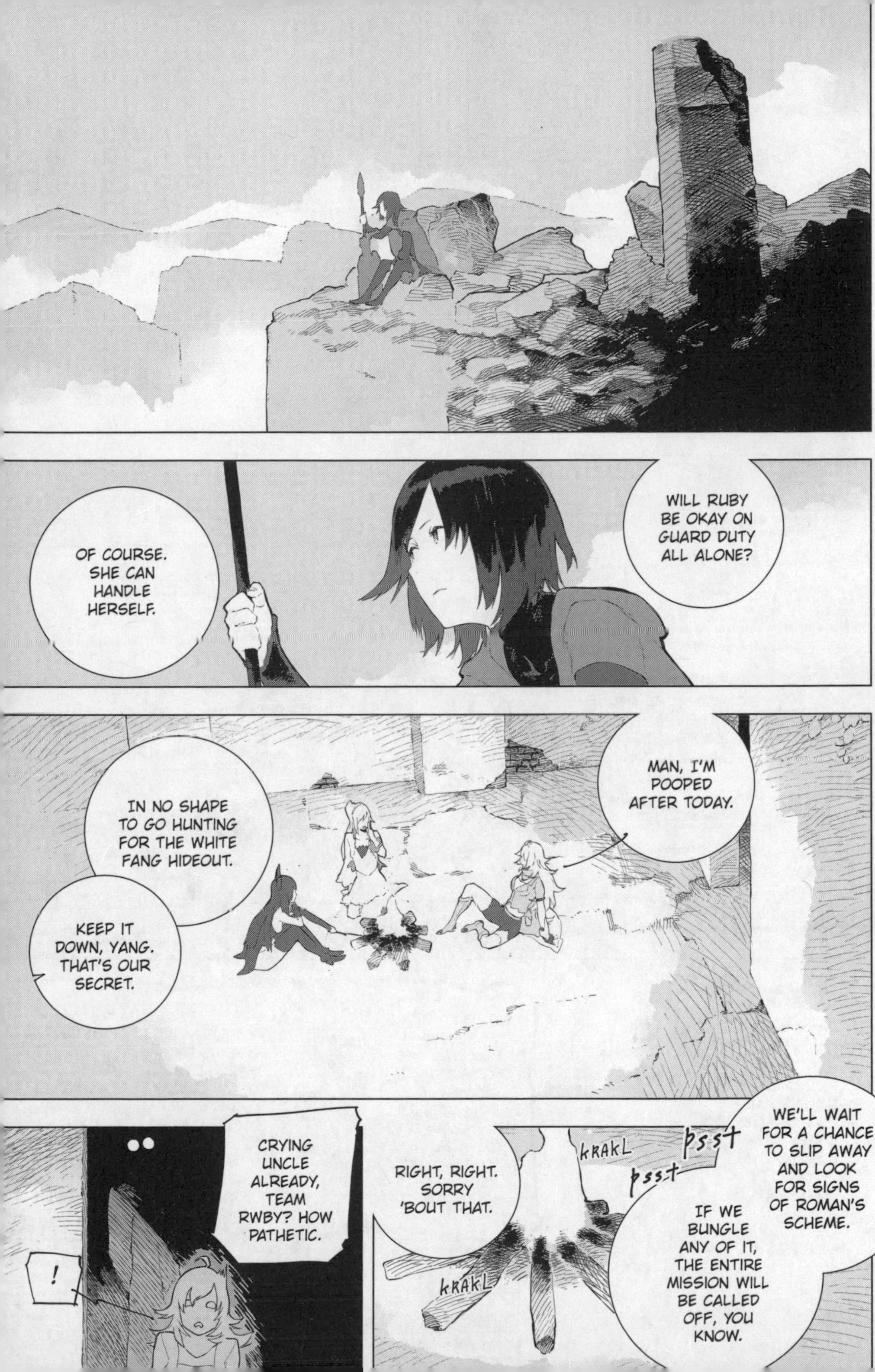
WILL RUBY BE OKAY ON GUARD DUTY ALL ALONE?
OF COURSE. SHE CAN HANDLE HERSELF.
MAN, I'M POOPED AFTER TODAY.
IN NO SHAPE TO GO HUNTING FOR THE WHITE FANG HIDEOUT.
KEEP IT DOWN, YANG. THAT'S OUR SECRET.
WE'LL WAIT FOR A CHANCE TO SLIP AWAY AND LOOK FOR SIGNS OF ROMAN'S SCHEME.
psst
psst
krakl
IF WE BUNGLE ANY OF IT, THE ENTIRE MISSION WILL BE CALLED OFF, YOU KNOW.
RIGHT, RIGHT. SORRY 'BOUT THAT.
krakl
CRYING UNCLE ALREADY, TEAM RWBY? HOW PATHETIC.
!

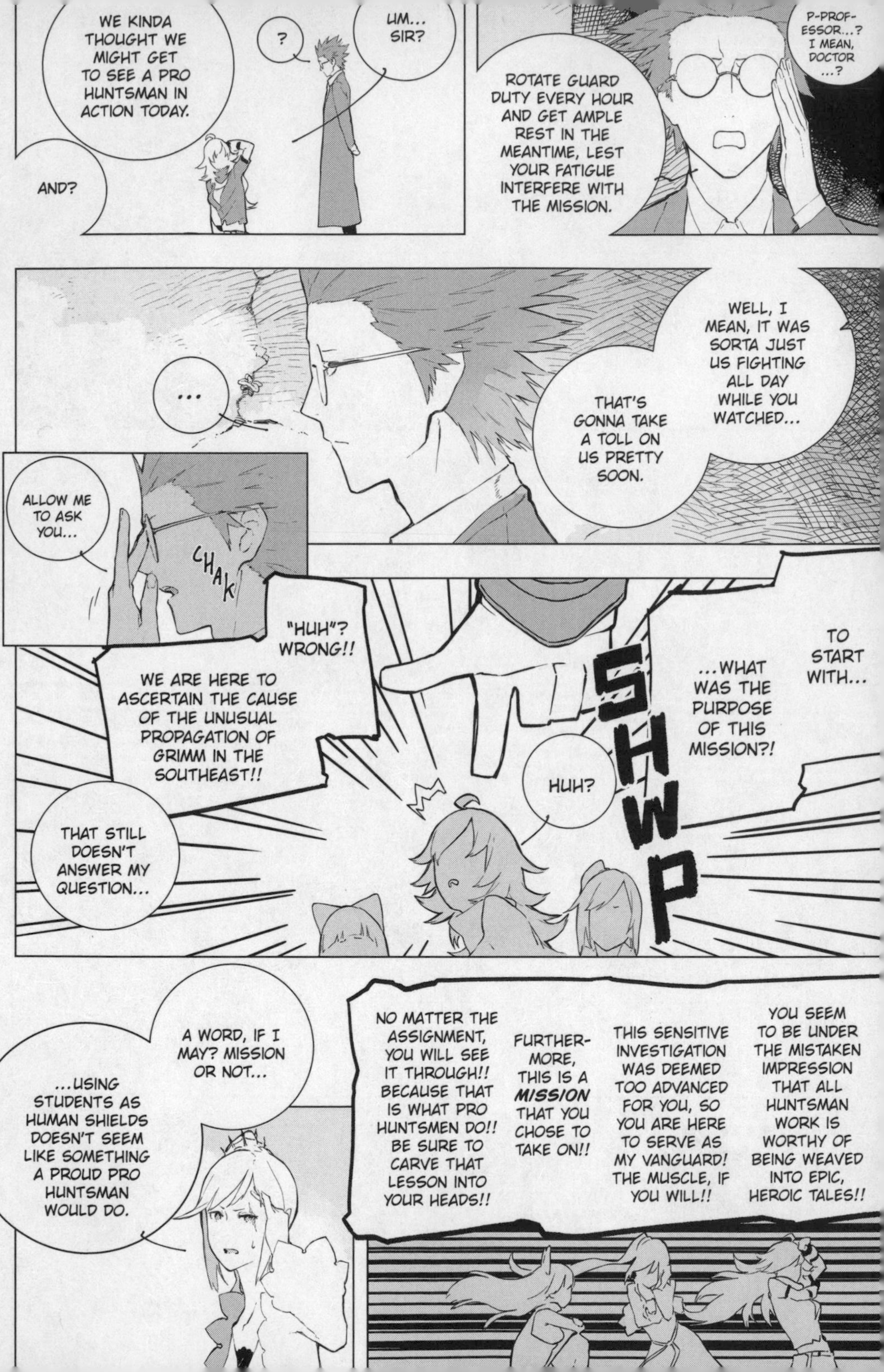
P-PROFESSOR...? I MEAN, DOCTOR ...?
ROTATE GUARD DUTY EVERY HOUR AND GET AMPLE REST IN THE MEANTIME, LEST YOUR FATIGUE INTERFERE WITH THE MISSION.
UM... SIR?
?
WE KINDA THOUGHT WE MIGHT GET TO SEE A PRO HUNTSMAN IN ACTION TODAY.
AND?
WELL, I MEAN, IT WAS SORTA JUST US FIGHTING ALL DAY WHILE YOU WATCHED...
THAT'S GONNA TAKE A TOLL ON US PRETTY SOON.
...
ALLOW ME TO ASK YOU...
CHAK
TO START WITH...
...WHAT WAS THE PURPOSE OF THIS MISSION?!
SHWP
HUH?
"HUH"? WRONG!!
WE ARE HERE TO ASCERTAIN THE CAUSE OF THE UNUSUAL PROPAGATION OF GRIMM IN THE SOUTHEAST!!
THAT STILL DOESN'T ANSWER MY QUESTION...
YOU SEEM TO BE UNDER THE MISTAKEN IMPRESSION THAT ALL HUNTSMAN WORK IS WORTHY OF BEING WEAVED INTO EPIC, HEROIC TALES!!
THIS SENSITIVE INVESTIGATION WAS DEEMED TOO ADVANCED FOR YOU, SO YOU ARE HERE TO SERVE AS MY VANGUARD! THE MUSCLE, IF YOU WILL!!
FURTHERMORE, THIS IS A *MISSION* THAT YOU CHOSE TO TAKE ON!!
NO MATTER THE ASSIGNMENT, YOU WILL SEE IT THROUGH!! BECAUSE THAT IS WHAT PRO HUNTSMEN DO!! BE SURE TO CARVE THAT LESSON INTO YOUR HEADS!!
A WORD, IF I MAY? MISSION OR NOT...
...USING STUDENTS AS HUMAN SHIELDS DOESN'T SEEM LIKE SOMETHING A PROUD PRO HUNTSMAN WOULD DO.

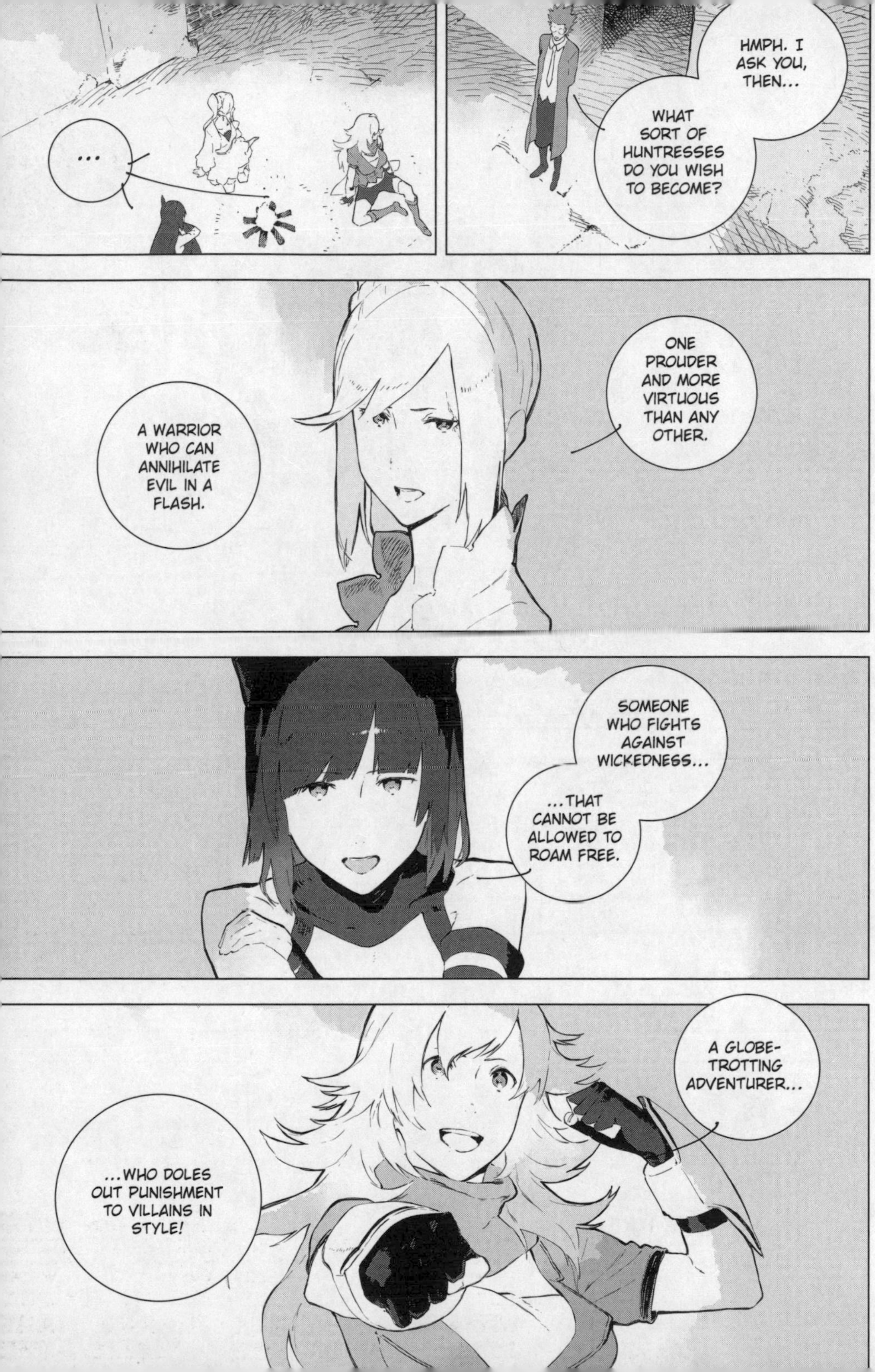
HMPH. I ASK YOU, THEN...
WHAT SORT OF HUNTRESSES DO YOU WISH TO BECOME?
...
ONE PROUDER AND MORE VIRTUOUS THAN ANY OTHER.
A WARRIOR WHO CAN ANNIHILATE EVIL IN A FLASH.
SOMEONE WHO FIGHTS AGAINST WICKEDNESS...
...THAT CANNOT BE ALLOWED TO ROAM FREE.
A GLOBE-TROTTING ADVENTURER...
...WHO DOLES OUT PUNISHMENT TO VILLAINS IN STYLE!

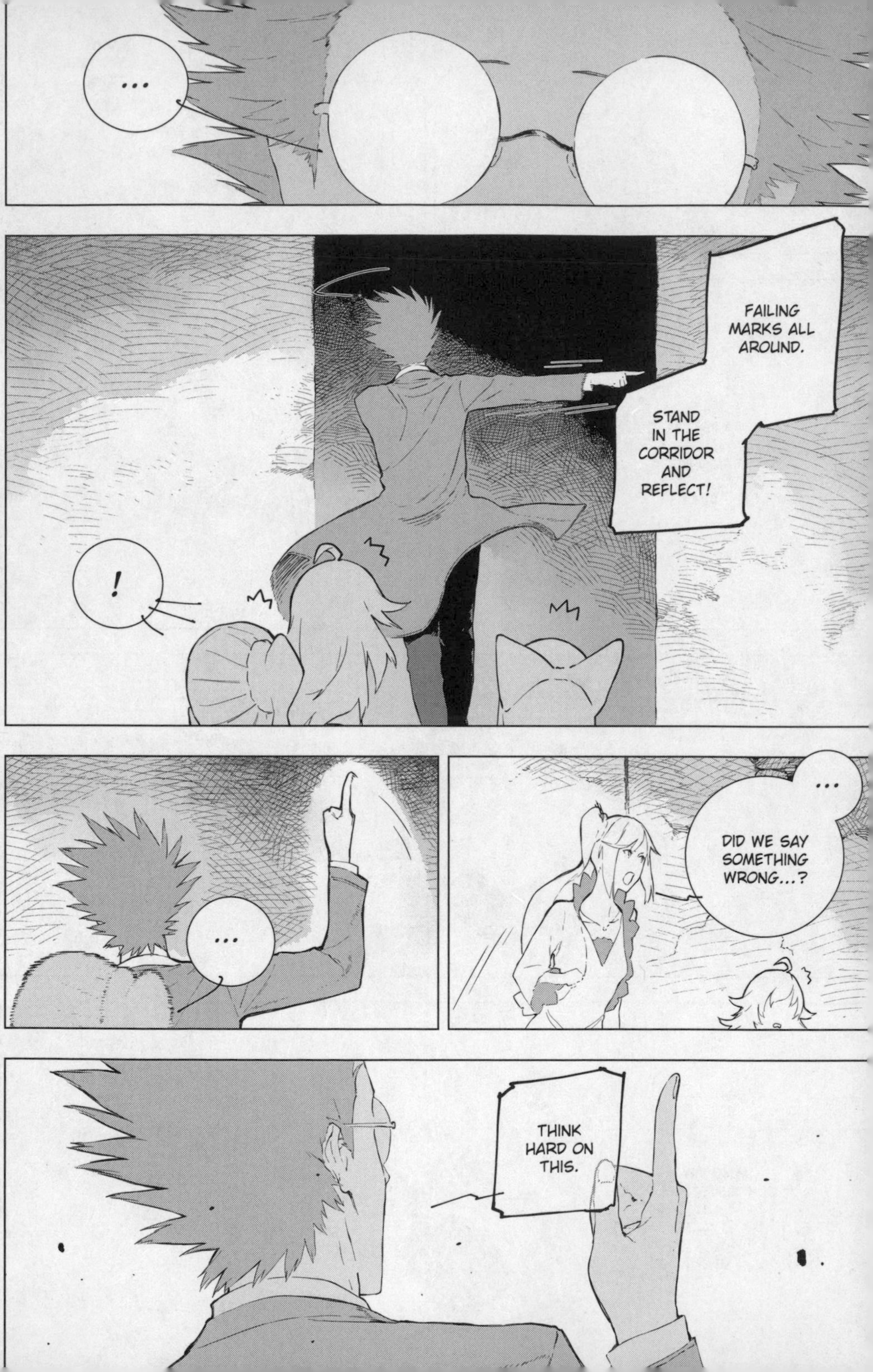
...
FAILING MARKS ALL AROUND.
STAND IN THE CORRIDOR AND REFLECT!
!
...
DID WE SAY SOMETHING WRONG...?
...
THINK HARD ON THIS.

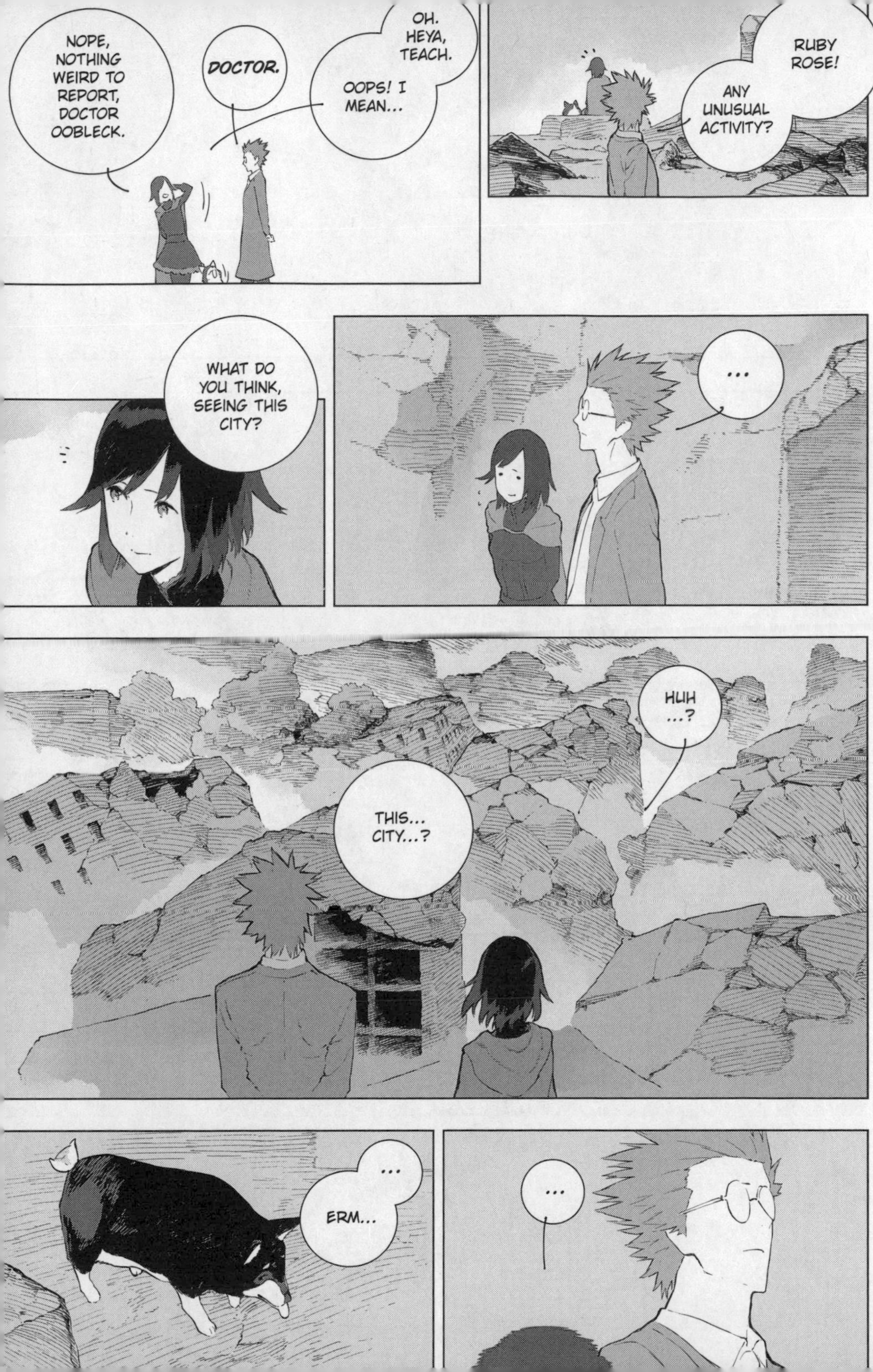
RUBY ROSE!
ANY UNUSUAL ACTIVITY?
OH. HEYA, TEACH.
OOPS! I MEAN...
DOCTOR.
NOPE, NOTHING WEIRD TO REPORT, DOCTOR OOBLECK.
...
WHAT DO YOU THINK, SEEING THIS CITY?
HUH ...?
THIS... CITY...?
...
...
ERM...

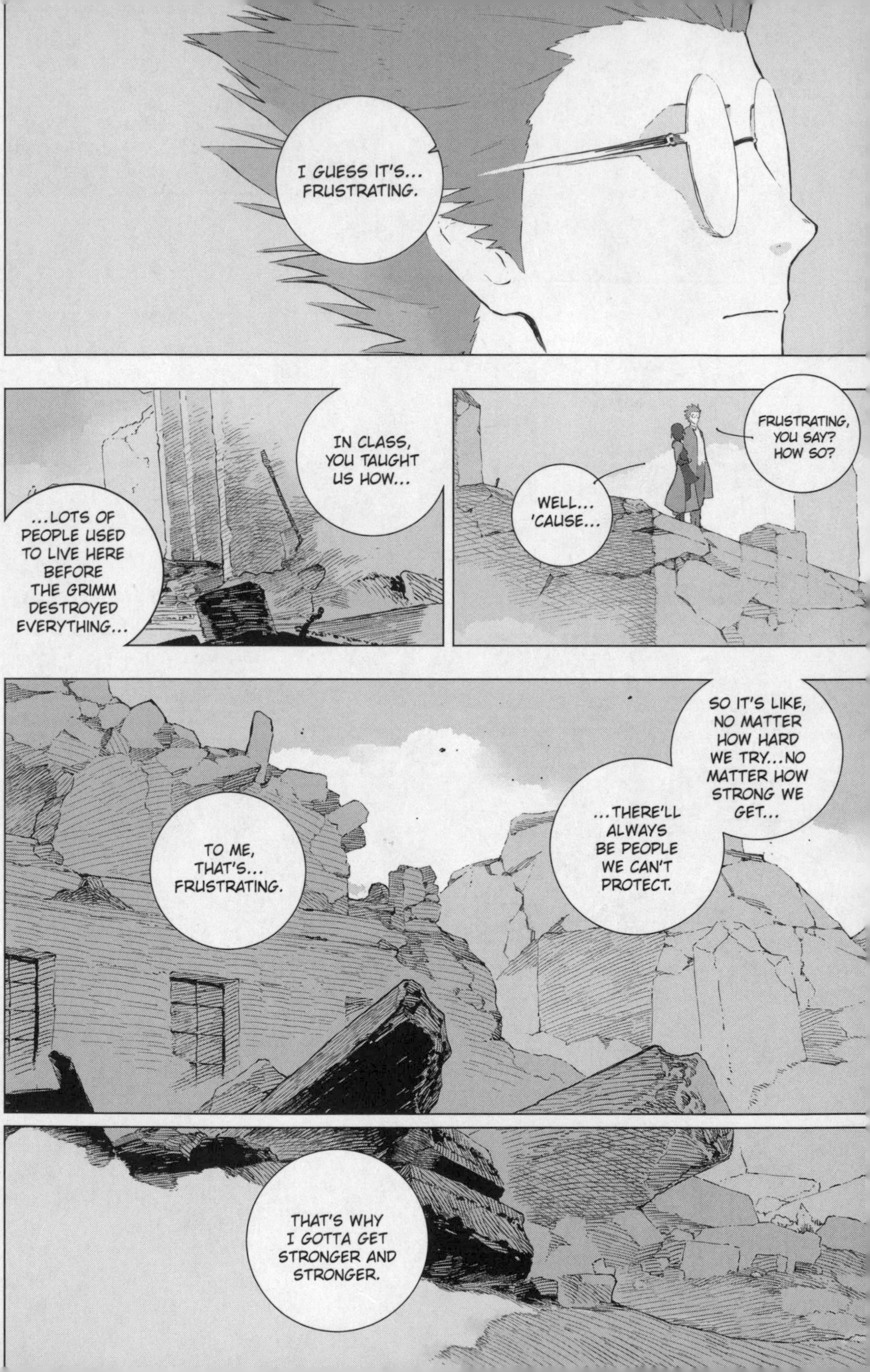
I GUESS IT'S... FRUSTRATING.
FRUSTRATING, YOU SAY? HOW SO?
WELL... 'CAUSE...
IN CLASS, YOU TAUGHT US HOW...
...LOTS OF PEOPLE USED TO LIVE HERE BEFORE THE GRIMM DESTROYED EVERYTHING...
SO IT'S LIKE, NO MATTER HOW HARD WE TRY...NO MATTER HOW STRONG WE GET...
...THERE'LL ALWAYS BE PEOPLE WE CAN'T PROTECT.
TO ME, THAT'S... FRUSTRATING.
THAT'S WHY I GOTTA GET STRONGER AND STRONGER.

SO THAT NEXT TIME...

...I CAN PROTECT THEM.

I SEE.

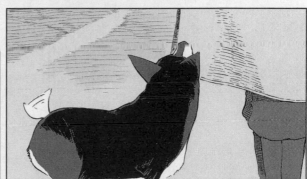

BE WARY OF OUR SURROUNDINGS.

AH, R-ROGER THAT.

WOOF! WOOF!

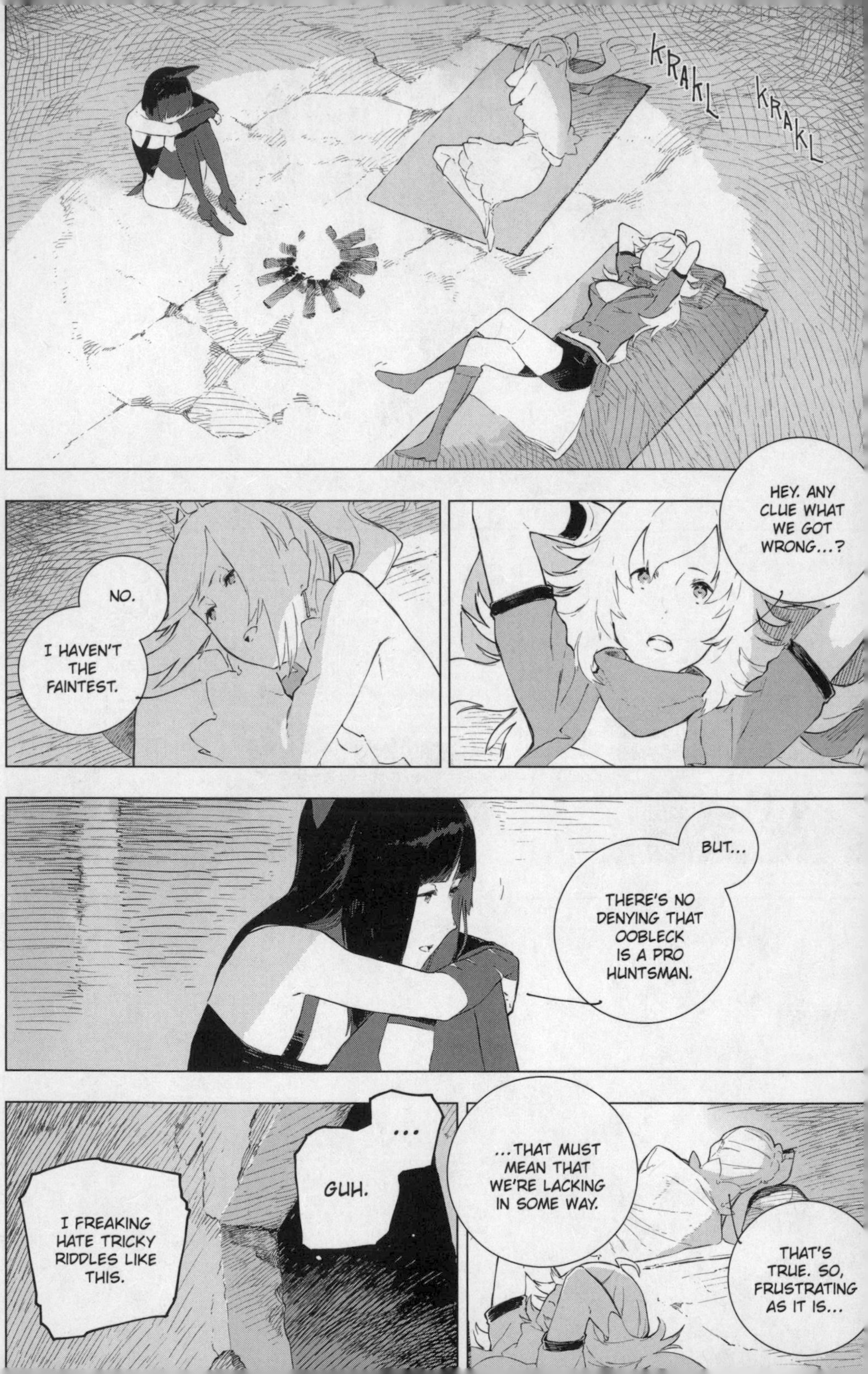
KRAKL KRAKL
HEY. ANY CLUE WHAT WE GOT WRONG...?
NO.
I HAVEN'T THE FAINTEST.
BUT...
THERE'S NO DENYING THAT OOBLECK IS A PRO HUNTSMAN.
THAT'S TRUE. SO, FRUSTRATING AS IT IS...
...THAT MUST MEAN THAT WE'RE LACKING IN SOME WAY.
...
GUH.
I FREAKING HATE TRICKY RIDDLES LIKE THIS.

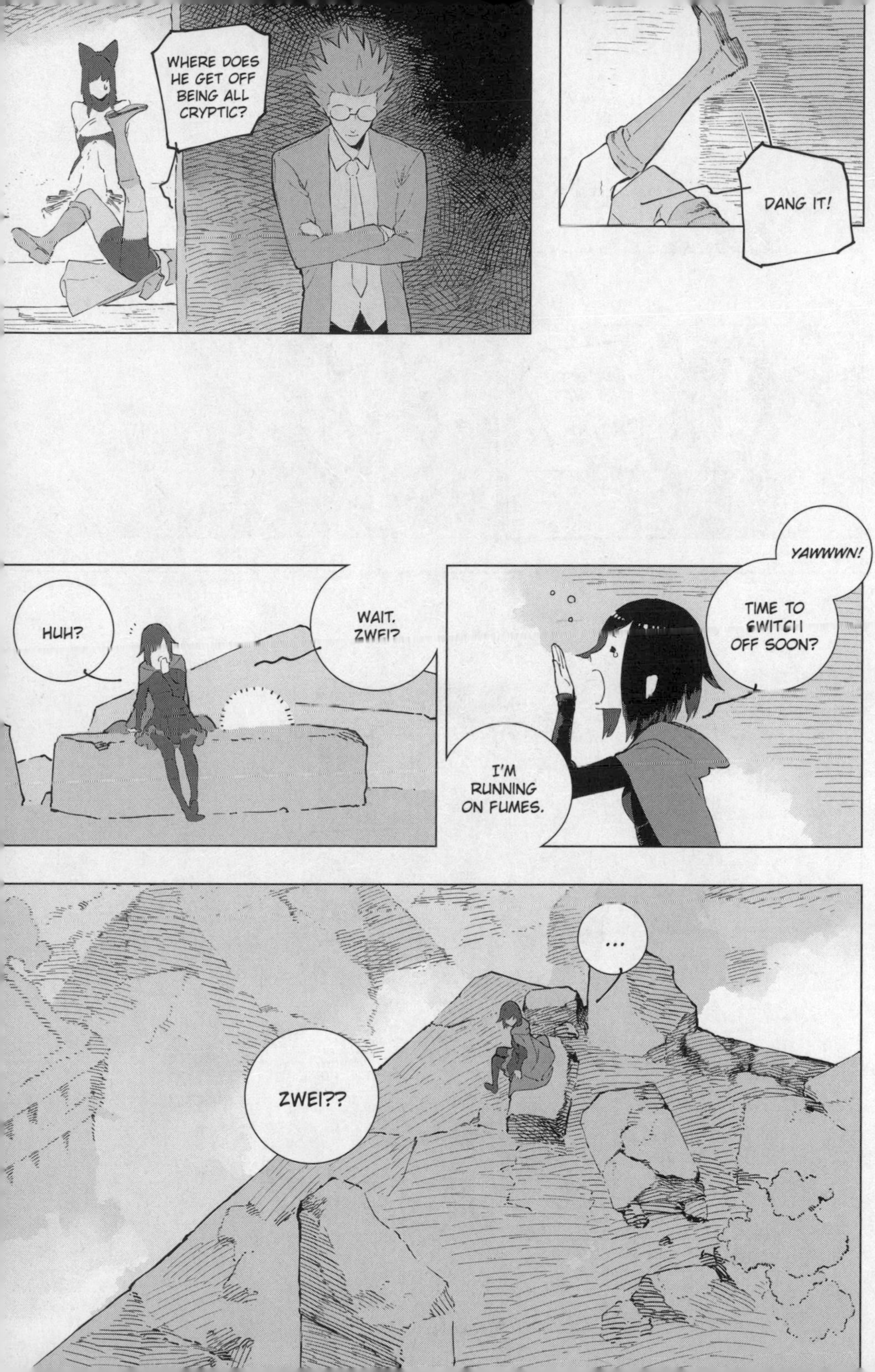
DANG IT!
WHERE DOES HE GET OFF BEING ALL CRYPTIC?
YAWWWN!
TIME TO SWITCH OFF SOON?
I'M RUNNING ON FUMES.
WAIT. ZWEI?
HUH?
...
ZWEI??

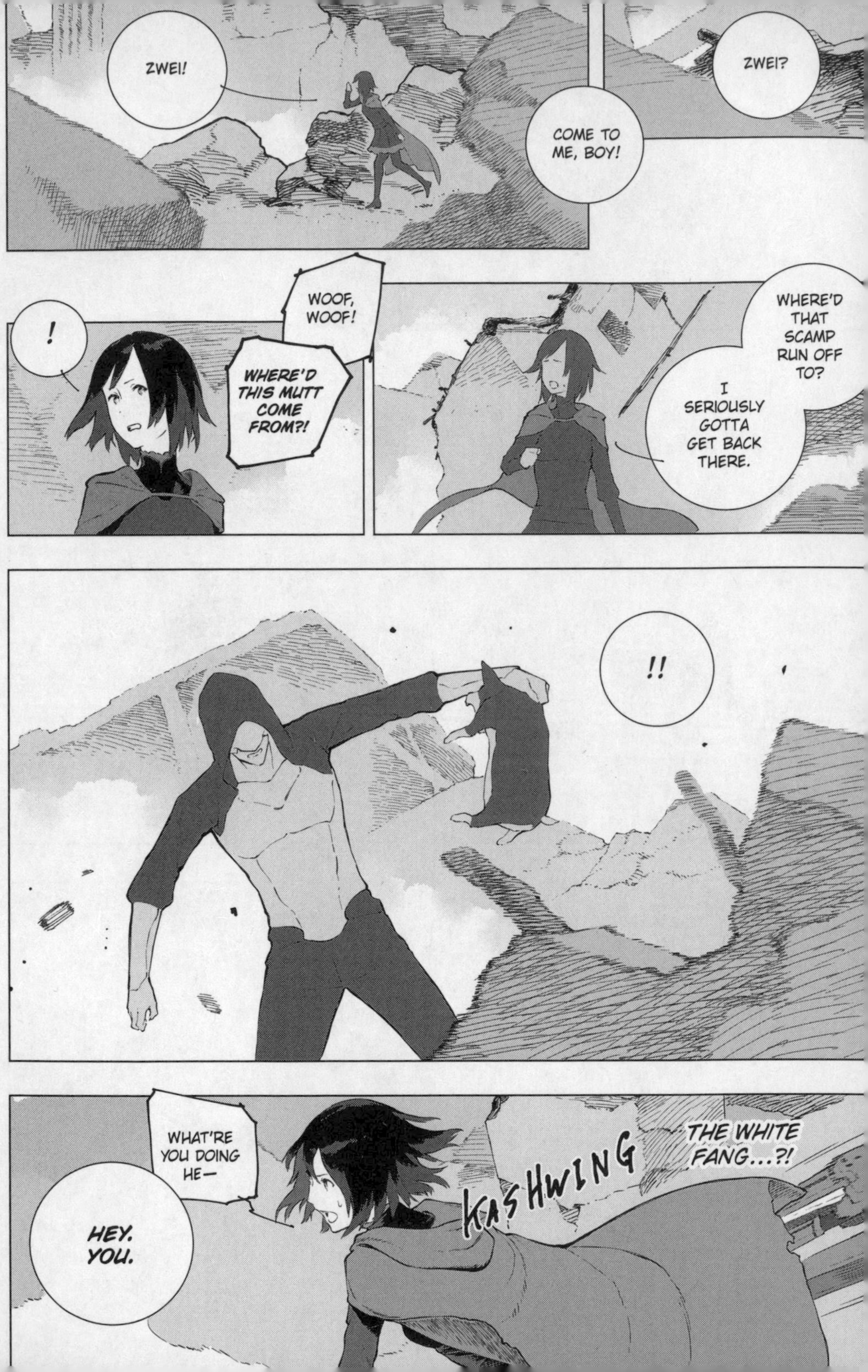
ZWEI?
COME TO ME, BOY!
ZWEI!
WHERE'D THAT SCAMP RUN OFF TO?
I SERIOUSLY GOTTA GET BACK THERE.
WOOF, WOOF!
!
WHERE'D THIS MUTT COME FROM?!
!!
THE WHITE FANG...?!
WHAT'RE YOU DOING HE—
KASHWING
HEY. YOU.

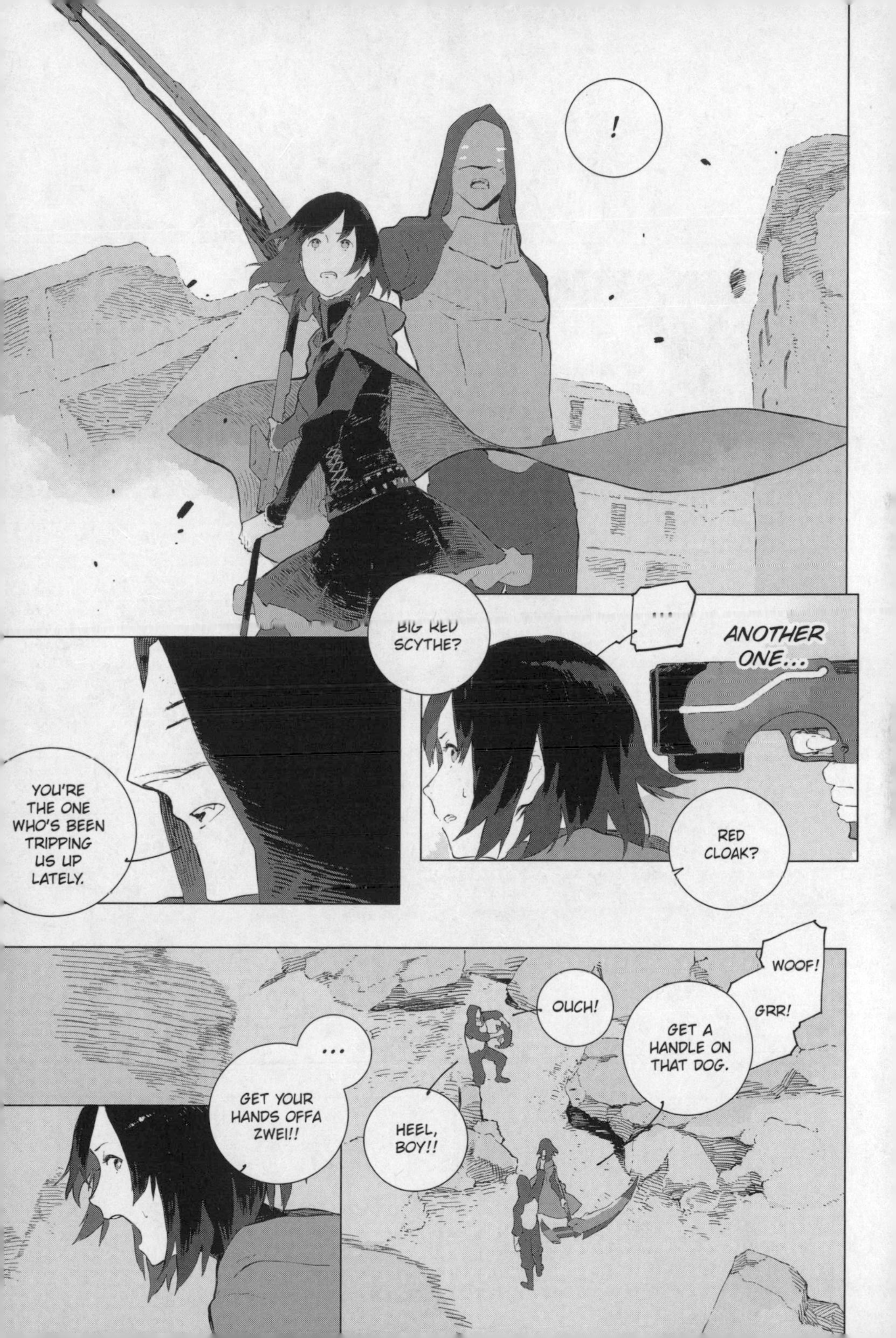
!
ANOTHER ONE...
...
RED CLOAK?
BIG RED SCYTHE?
YOU'RE THE ONE WHO'S BEEN TRIPPING US UP LATELY.
WOOF!
GRR!
GET A HANDLE ON THAT DOG.
OUCH!
HEEL, BOY!!
...
GET YOUR HANDS OFFA ZWEI!!

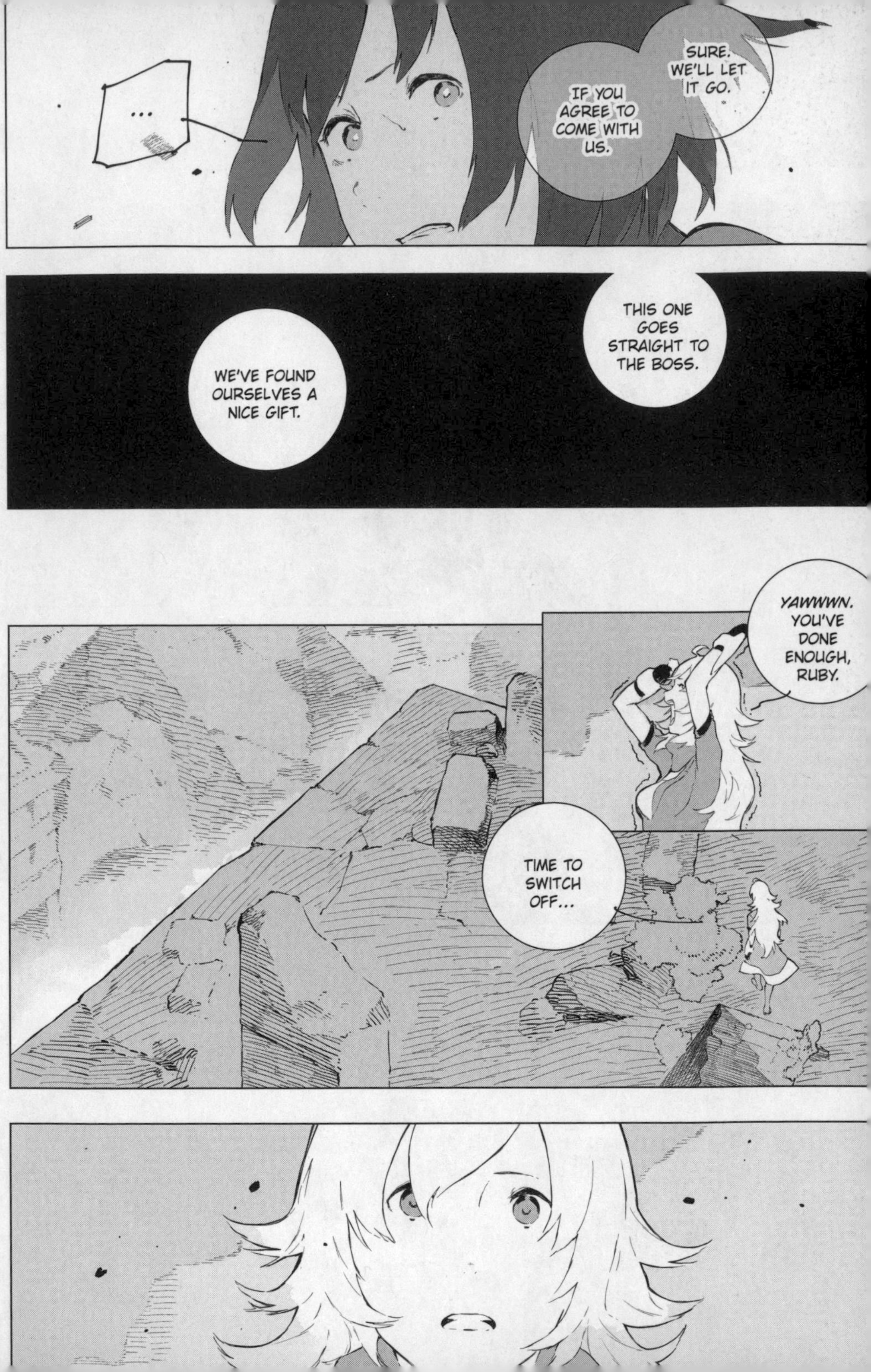
SURE. WE'LL LET IT GO.
IF YOU AGREE TO COME WITH US.
...
THIS ONE GOES STRAIGHT TO THE BOSS.
WE'VE FOUND OURSELVES A NICE GIFT.
YAWWWN. YOU'VE DONE ENOUGH, RUBY.
TIME TO SWITCH OFF...

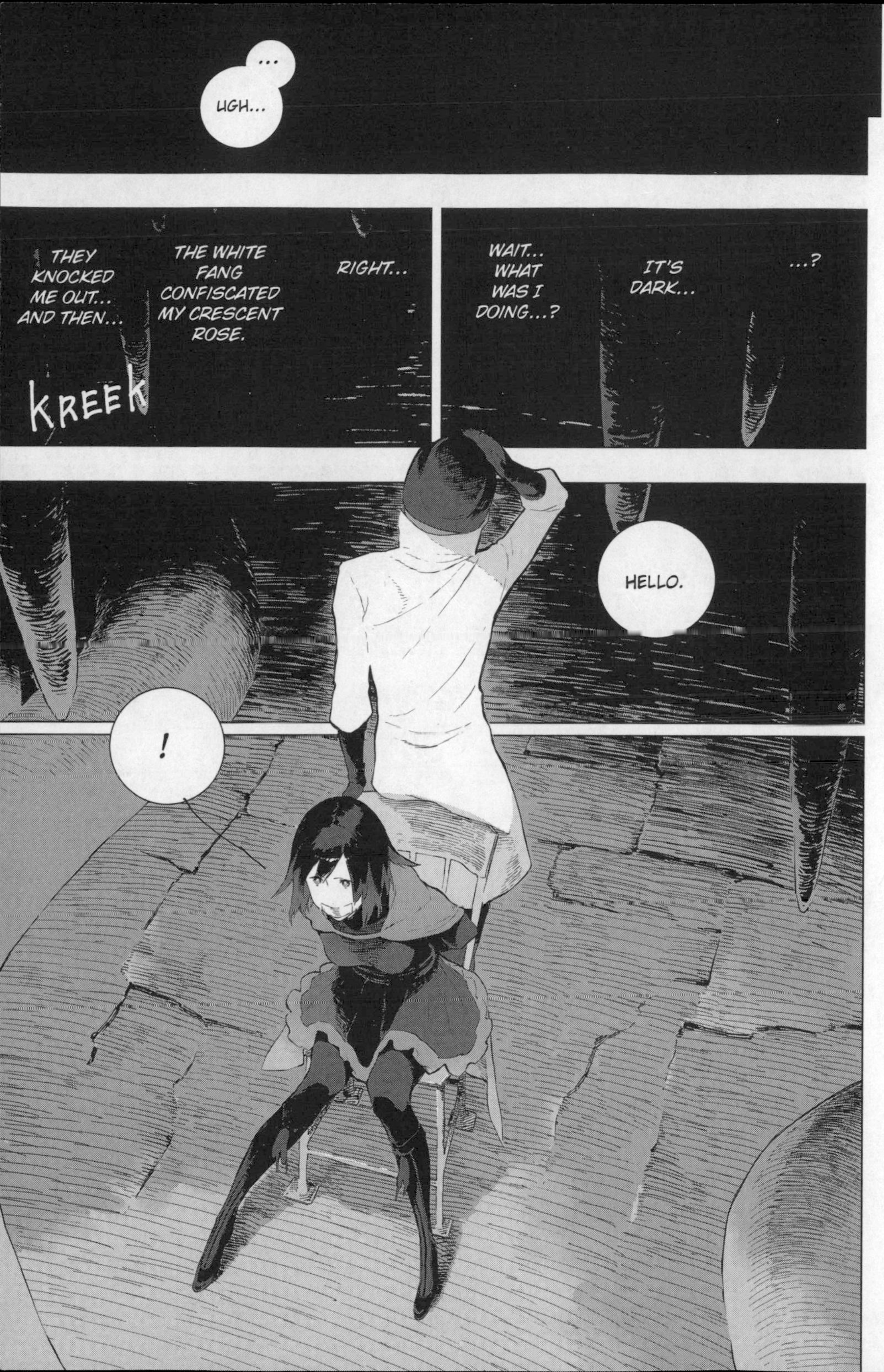
...
UGH...
...?
IT'S DARK...
WAIT... WHAT WAS I DOING...?
RIGHT...
THE WHITE FANG CONFISCATED MY CRESCENT ROSE.
THEY KNOCKED ME OUT... AND THEN...
KREEK
HELLO.
!

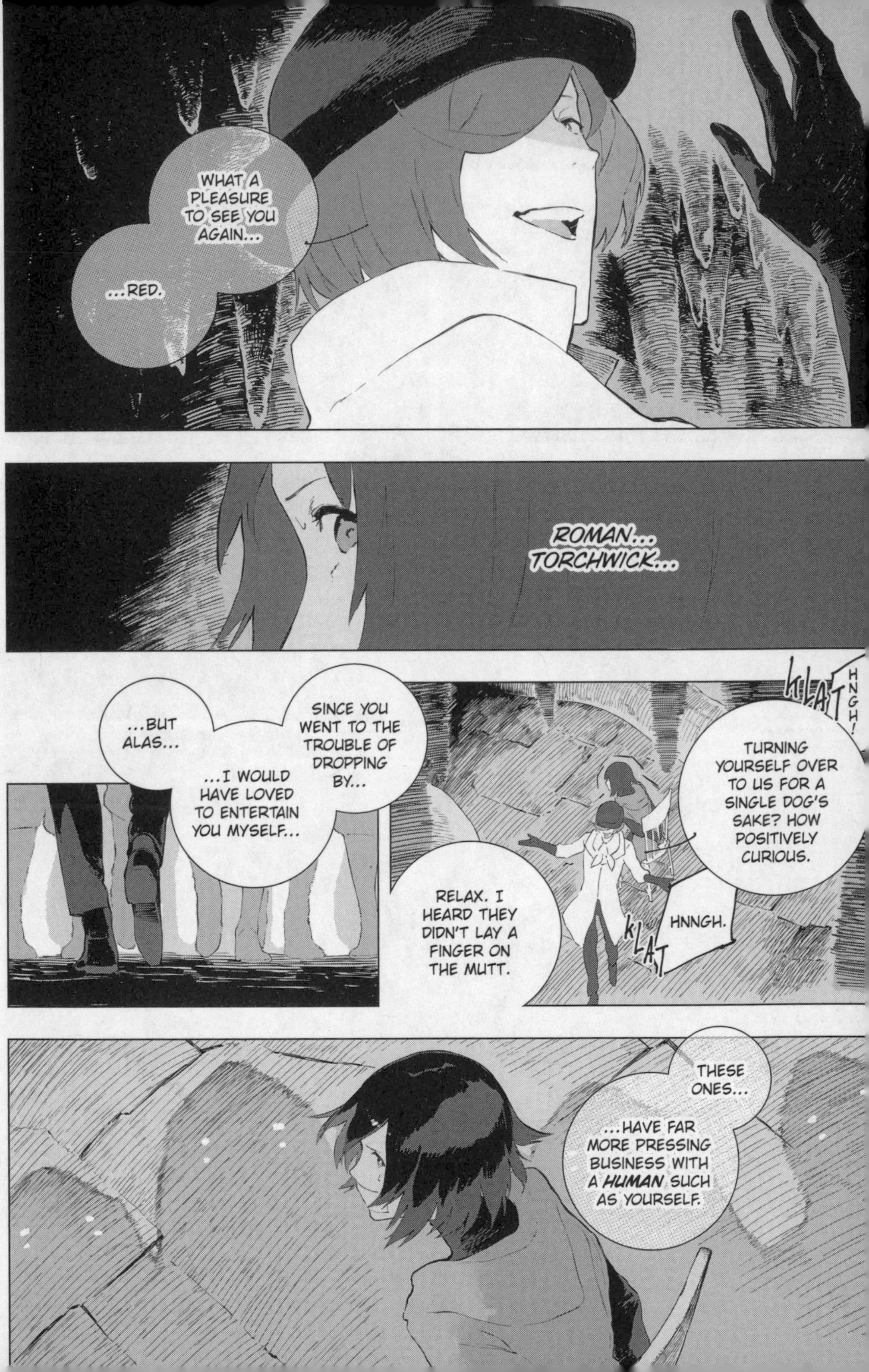
WHAT A PLEASURE TO SEE YOU AGAIN...
...RED.
ROMAN... TORCHWICK...
KLAT
HNGH!
TURNING YOURSELF OVER TO US FOR A SINGLE DOG'S SAKE? HOW POSITIVELY CURIOUS.
RELAX. I HEARD THEY DIDN'T LAY A FINGER ON THE MUTT.
HNNGH.
KLAT
SINCE YOU WENT TO THE TROUBLE OF DROPPING BY...
...I WOULD HAVE LOVED TO ENTERTAIN YOU MYSELF...
...BUT ALAS...
THESE ONES...
...HAVE FAR MORE PRESSING BUSINESS WITH A *HUMAN* SUCH AS YOURSELF.

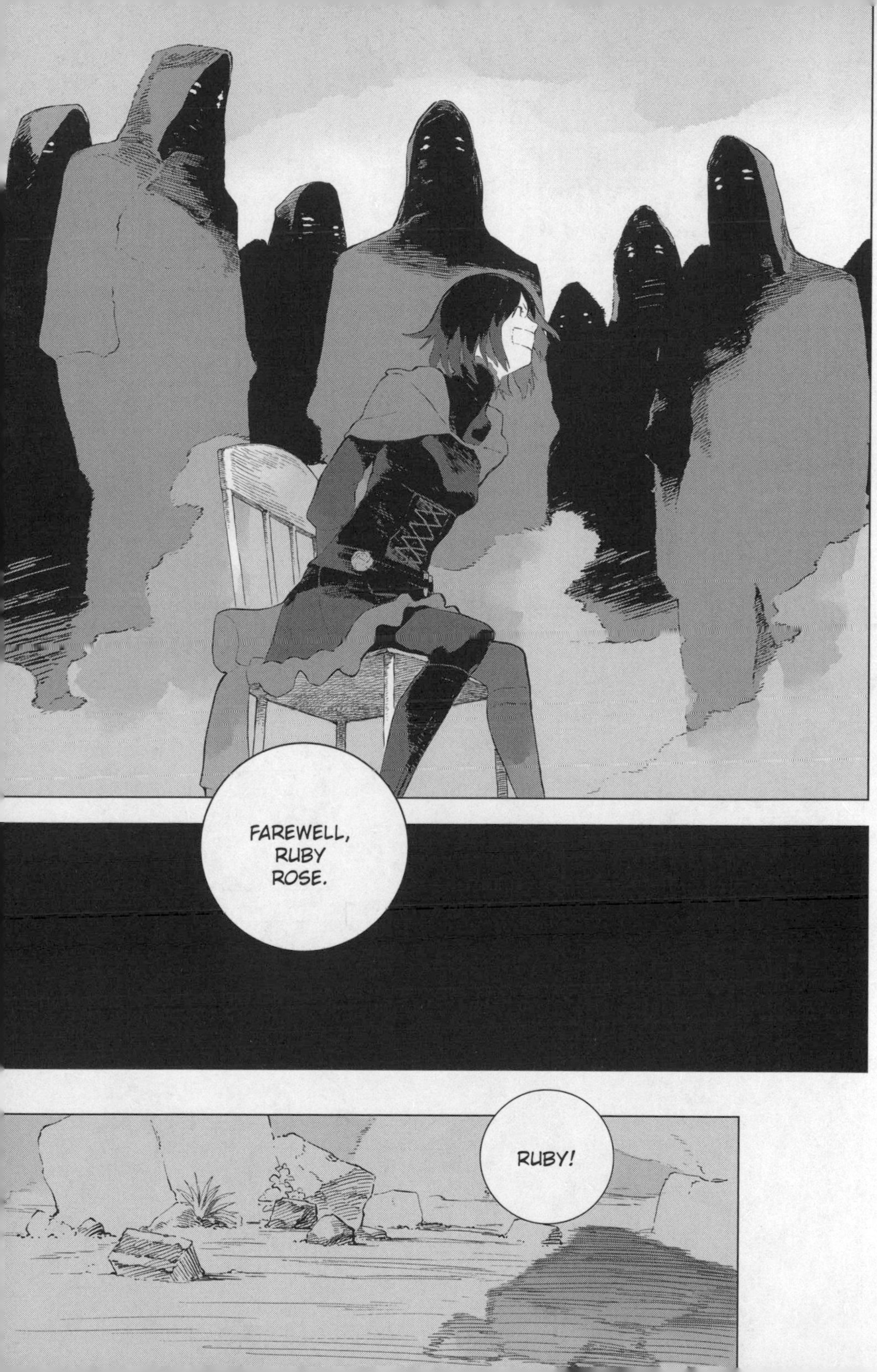
FAREWELL, RUBY ROSE.
RUBY!

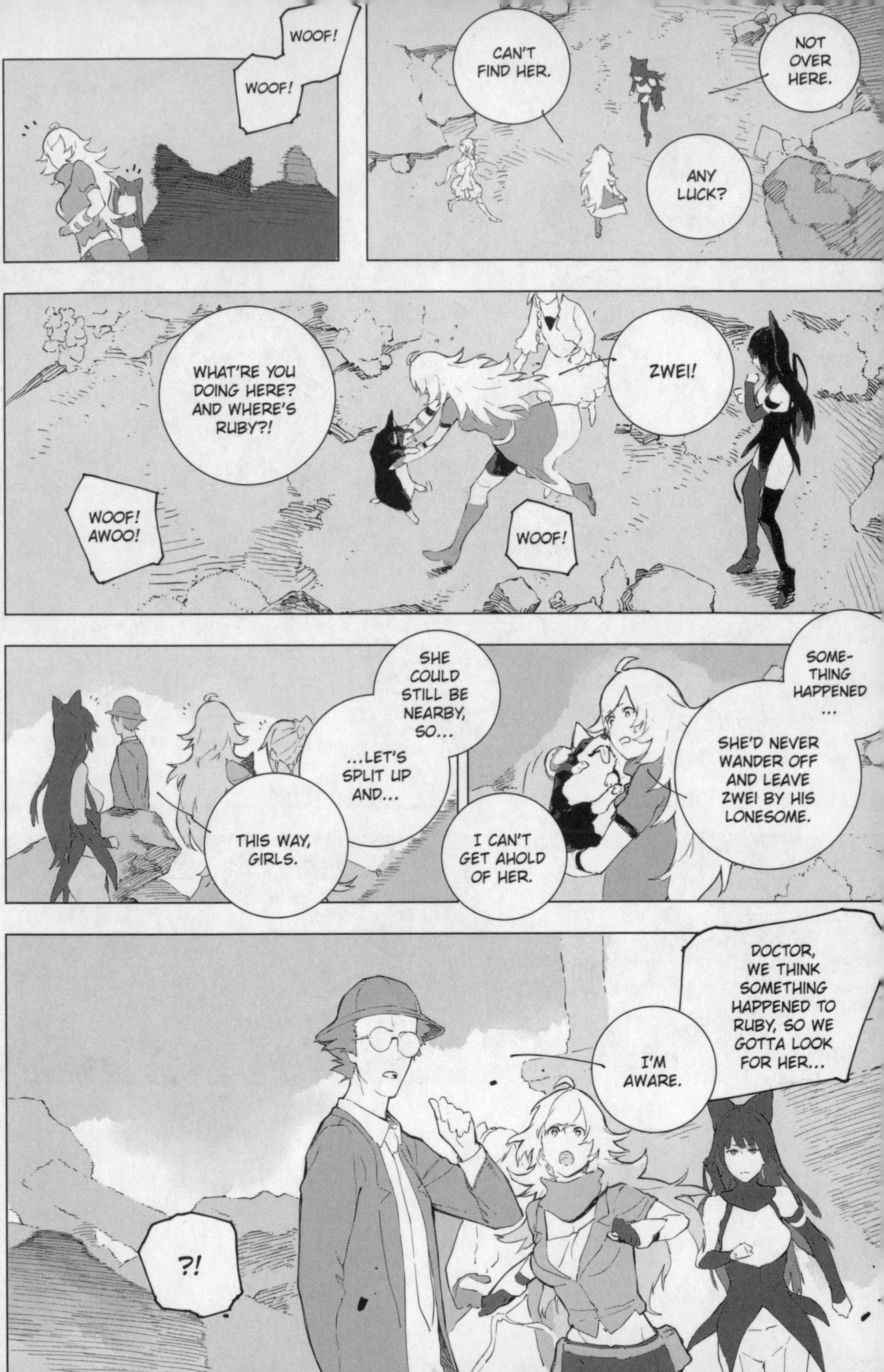
NOT OVER HERE.
CAN'T FIND HER.
ANY LUCK?
WOOF!
WOOF!
ZWEI!
WHAT'RE YOU DOING HERE? AND WHERE'S RUBY?!
WOOF!
WOOF! AWOO!
SOME-THING HAPPENED...
SHE'D NEVER WANDER OFF AND LEAVE ZWEI BY HIS LONESOME.
I CAN'T GET AHOLD OF HER.
SHE COULD STILL BE NEARBY, SO...
...LET'S SPLIT UP AND...
THIS WAY, GIRLS.
DOCTOR, WE THINK SOMETHING HAPPENED TO RUBY, SO WE GOTTA LOOK FOR HER...
I'M AWARE.
?!

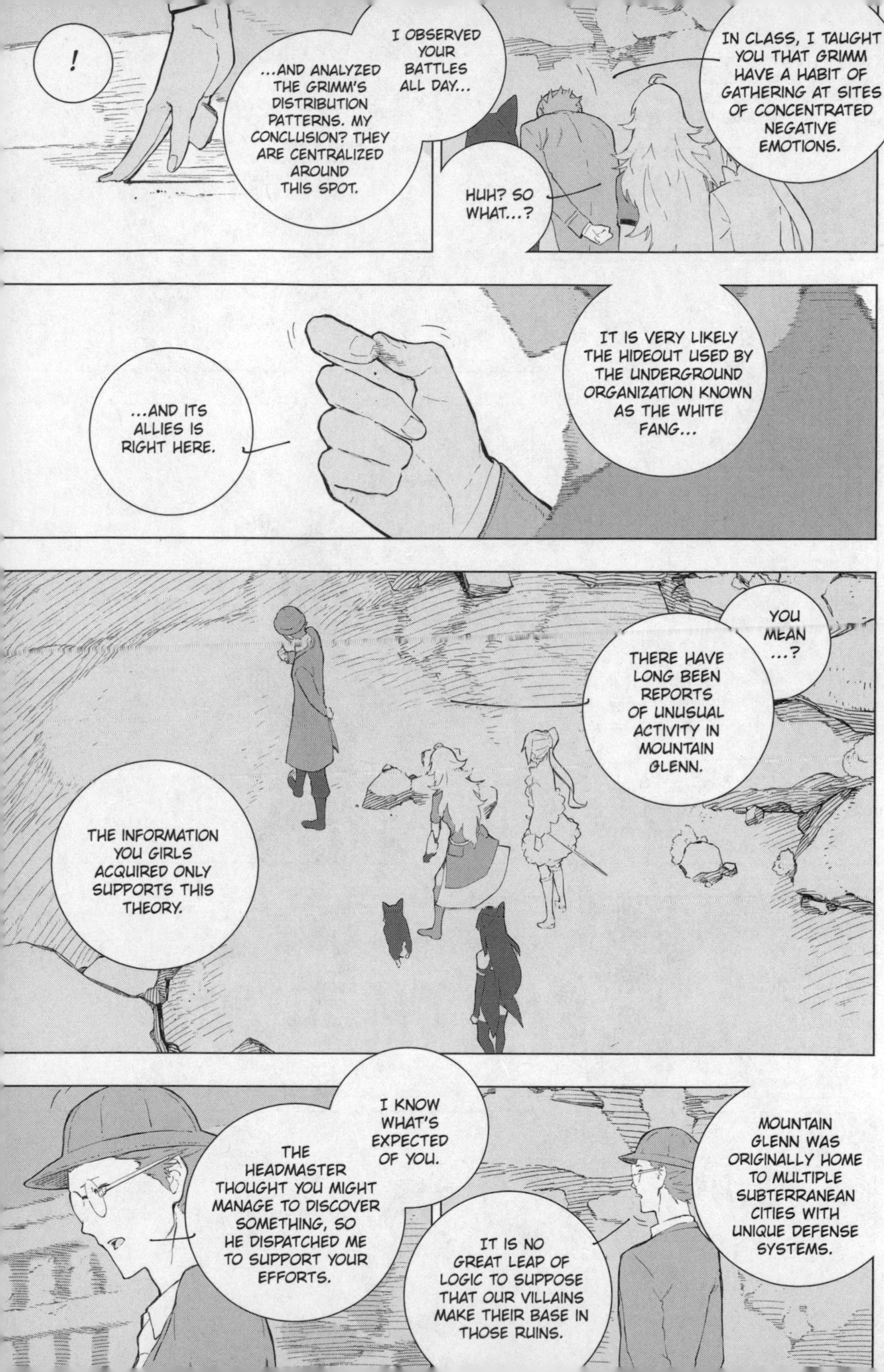
IN CLASS, I TAUGHT YOU THAT GRIMM HAVE A HABIT OF GATHERING AT SITES OF CONCENTRATED NEGATIVE EMOTIONS.
HUH? SO WHAT...?
I OBSERVED YOUR BATTLES ALL DAY...
...AND ANALYZED THE GRIMM'S DISTRIBUTION PATTERNS. MY CONCLUSION? THEY ARE CENTRALIZED AROUND THIS SPOT.
!
IT IS VERY LIKELY THE HIDEOUT USED BY THE UNDERGROUND ORGANIZATION KNOWN AS THE WHITE FANG...
...AND ITS ALLIES IS RIGHT HERE.
YOU MEAN ...?
THERE HAVE LONG BEEN REPORTS OF UNUSUAL ACTIVITY IN MOUNTAIN GLENN.
THE INFORMATION YOU GIRLS ACQUIRED ONLY SUPPORTS THIS THEORY.
MOUNTAIN GLENN WAS ORIGINALLY HOME TO MULTIPLE SUBTERRANEAN CITIES WITH UNIQUE DEFENSE SYSTEMS.
IT IS NO GREAT LEAP OF LOGIC TO SUPPOSE THAT OUR VILLAINS MAKE THEIR BASE IN THOSE RUINS.
I KNOW WHAT'S EXPECTED OF YOU.
THE HEADMASTER THOUGHT YOU MIGHT MANAGE TO DISCOVER SOMETHING, SO HE DISPATCHED ME TO SUPPORT YOUR EFFORTS.

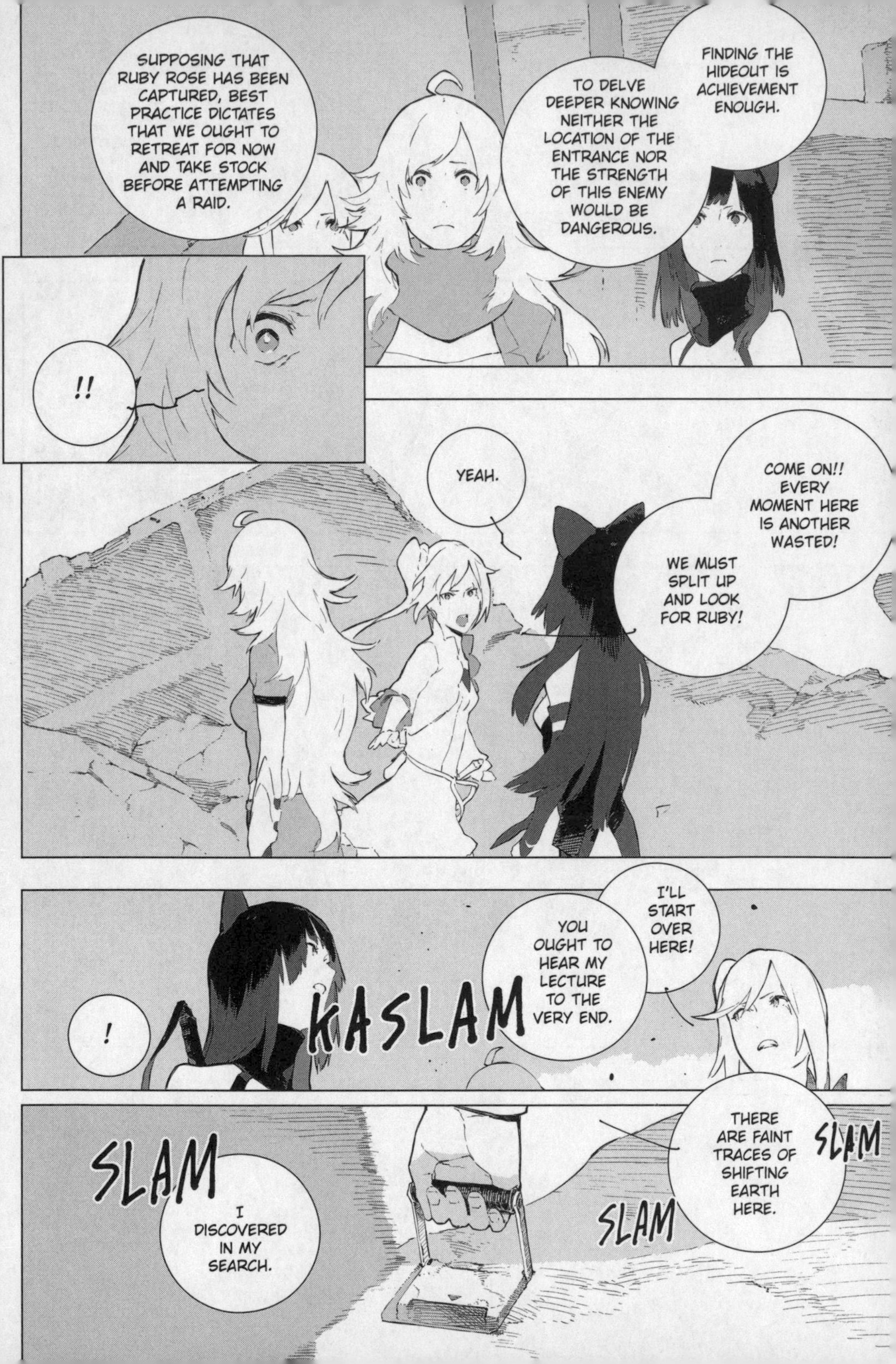
FINDING THE HIDEOUT IS ACHIEVEMENT ENOUGH.
TO DELVE DEEPER KNOWING NEITHER THE LOCATION OF THE ENTRANCE NOR THE STRENGTH OF THIS ENEMY WOULD BE DANGEROUS.
SUPPOSING THAT RUBY ROSE HAS BEEN CAPTURED, BEST PRACTICE DICTATES THAT WE OUGHT TO RETREAT FOR NOW AND TAKE STOCK BEFORE ATTEMPTING A RAID.
!!
COME ON!! EVERY MOMENT HERE IS ANOTHER WASTED!
WE MUST SPLIT UP AND LOOK FOR RUBY!
YEAH.
I'LL START OVER HERE!
YOU OUGHT TO HEAR MY LECTURE TO THE VERY END.
KASLAM
!
SLAM
THERE ARE FAINT TRACES OF SHIFTING EARTH HERE.
SLAM
SLAM
I DISCOVERED IN MY SEARCH.

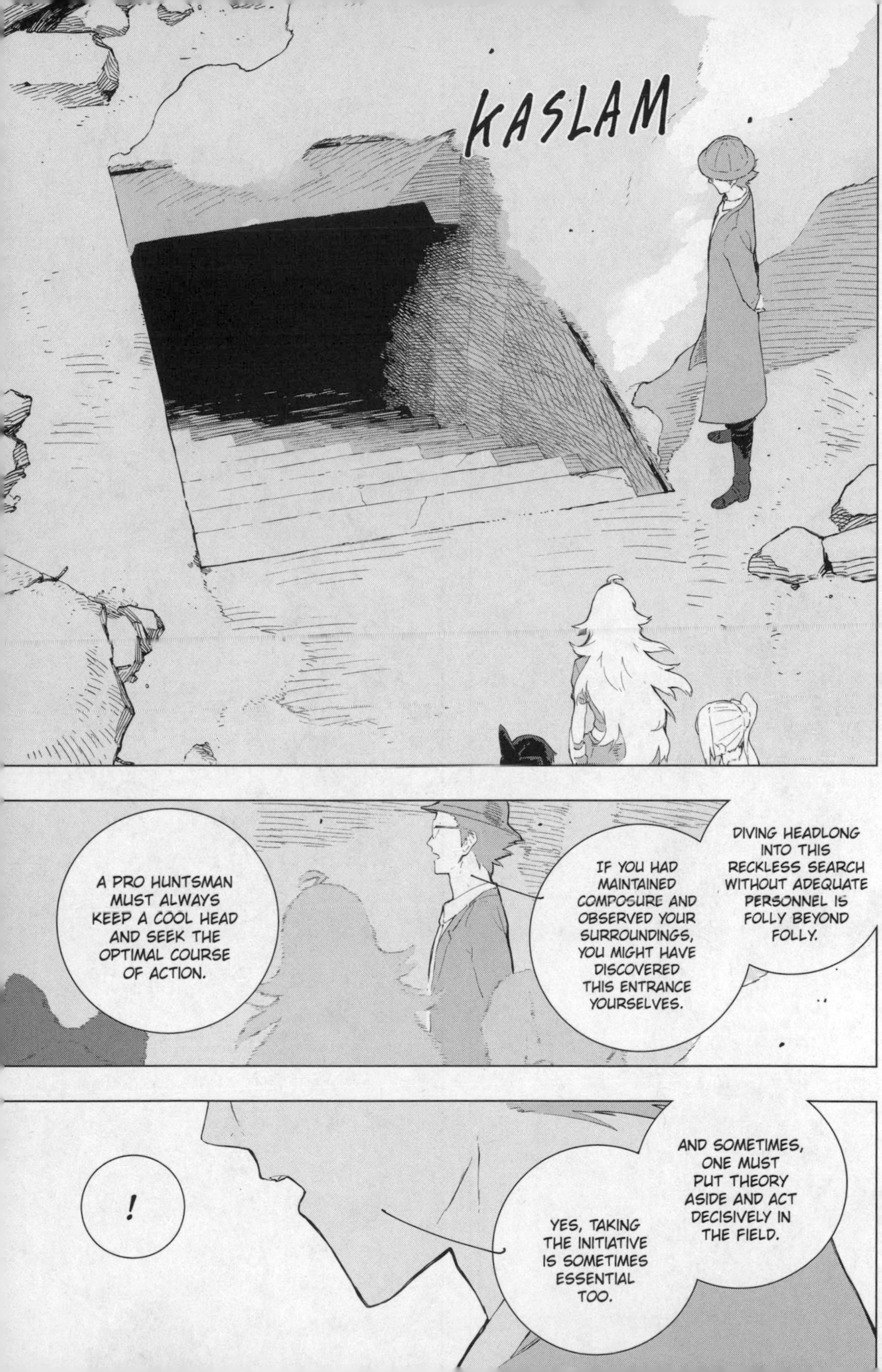
KASLAM
DIVING HEADLONG INTO THIS RECKLESS SEARCH WITHOUT ADEQUATE PERSONNEL IS FOLLY BEYOND FOLLY.
IF YOU HAD MAINTAINED COMPOSURE AND OBSERVED YOUR SURROUNDINGS, YOU MIGHT HAVE DISCOVERED THIS ENTRANCE YOURSELVES.
A PRO HUNTSMAN MUST ALWAYS KEEP A COOL HEAD AND SEEK THE OPTIMAL COURSE OF ACTION.
AND SOMETIMES, ONE MUST PUT THEORY ASIDE AND ACT DECISIVELY IN THE FIELD.
YES, TAKING THE INITIATIVE IS SOMETIMES ESSENTIAL TOO.
!

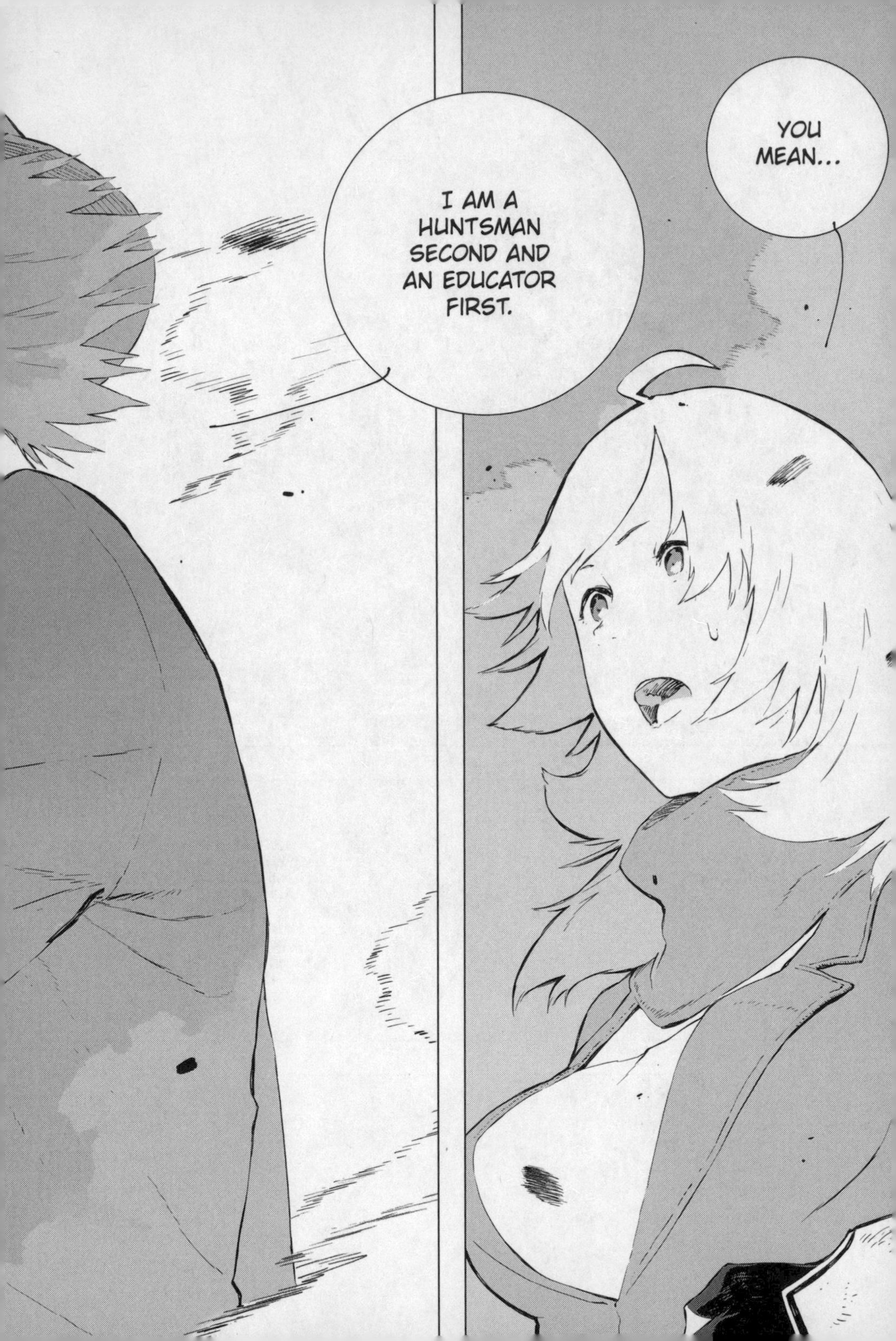
YOU MEAN...
I AM A HUNTSMAN SECOND AND AN EDUCATOR FIRST.

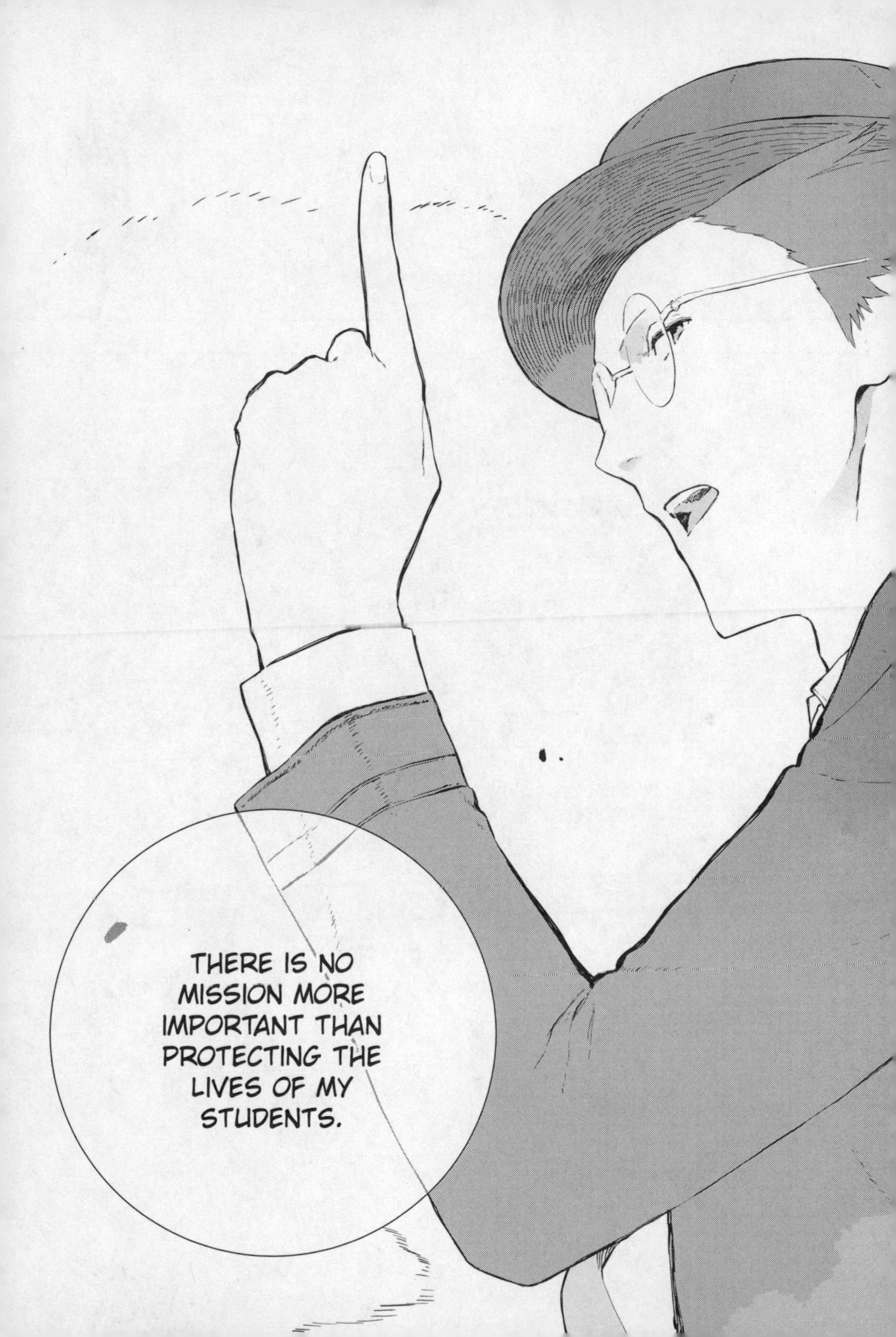
THERE IS NO MISSION MORE IMPORTANT THAN PROTECTING THE LIVES OF MY STUDENTS.

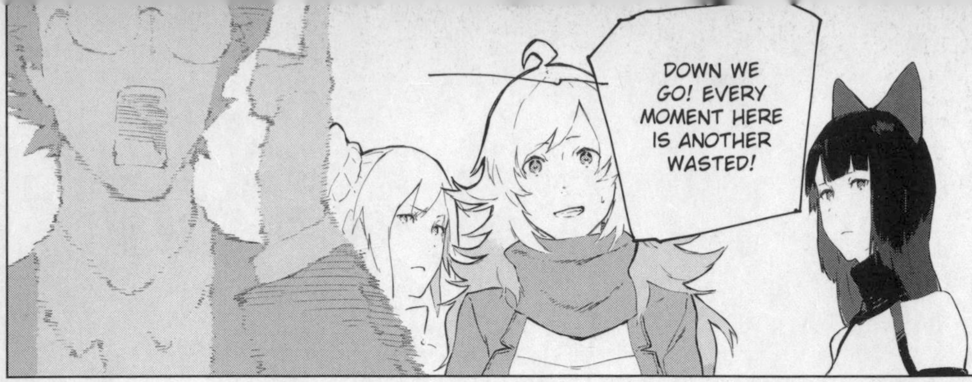
DOWN WE GO! EVERY MOMENT HERE IS ANOTHER WASTED!
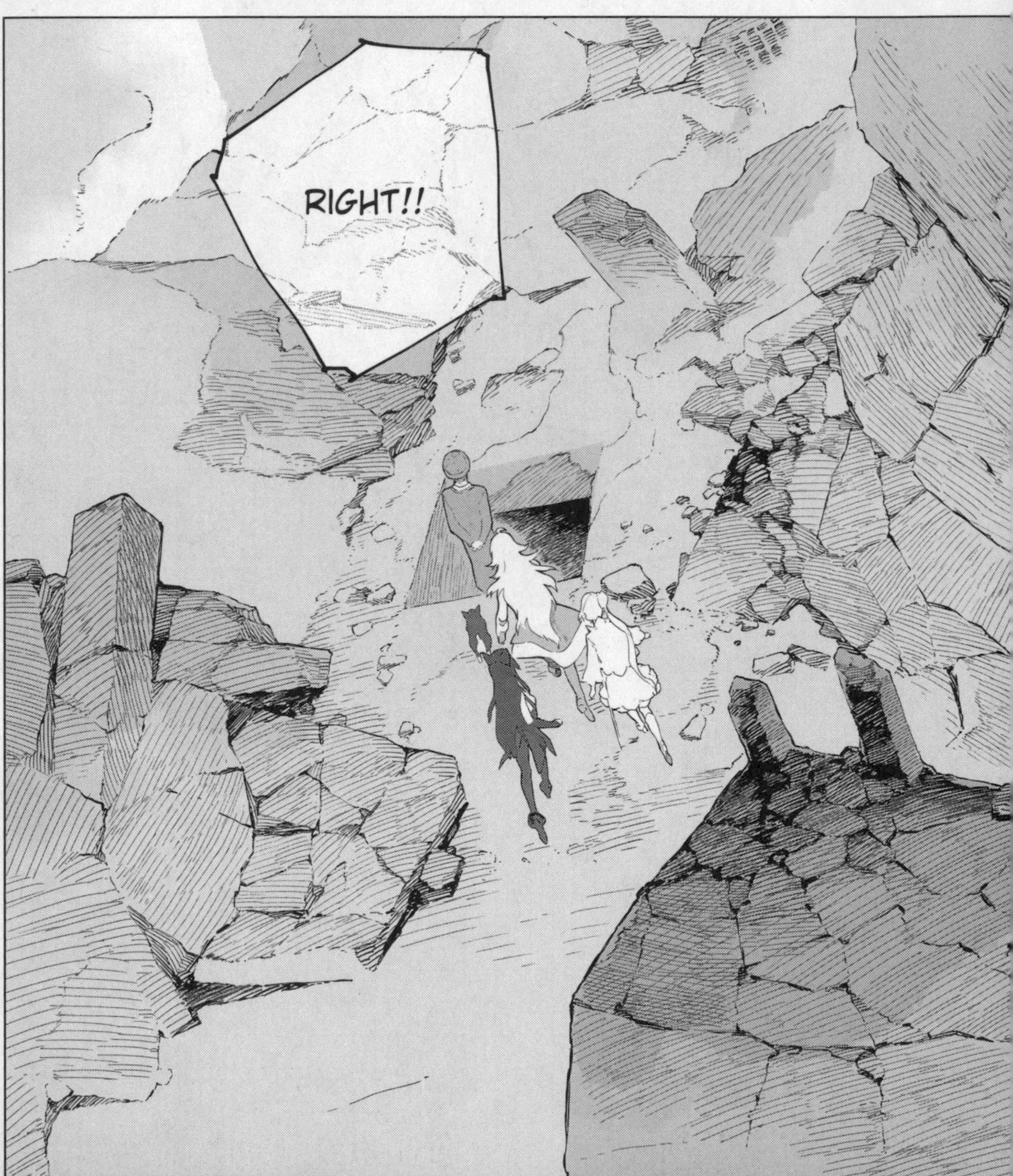
RIGHT!!

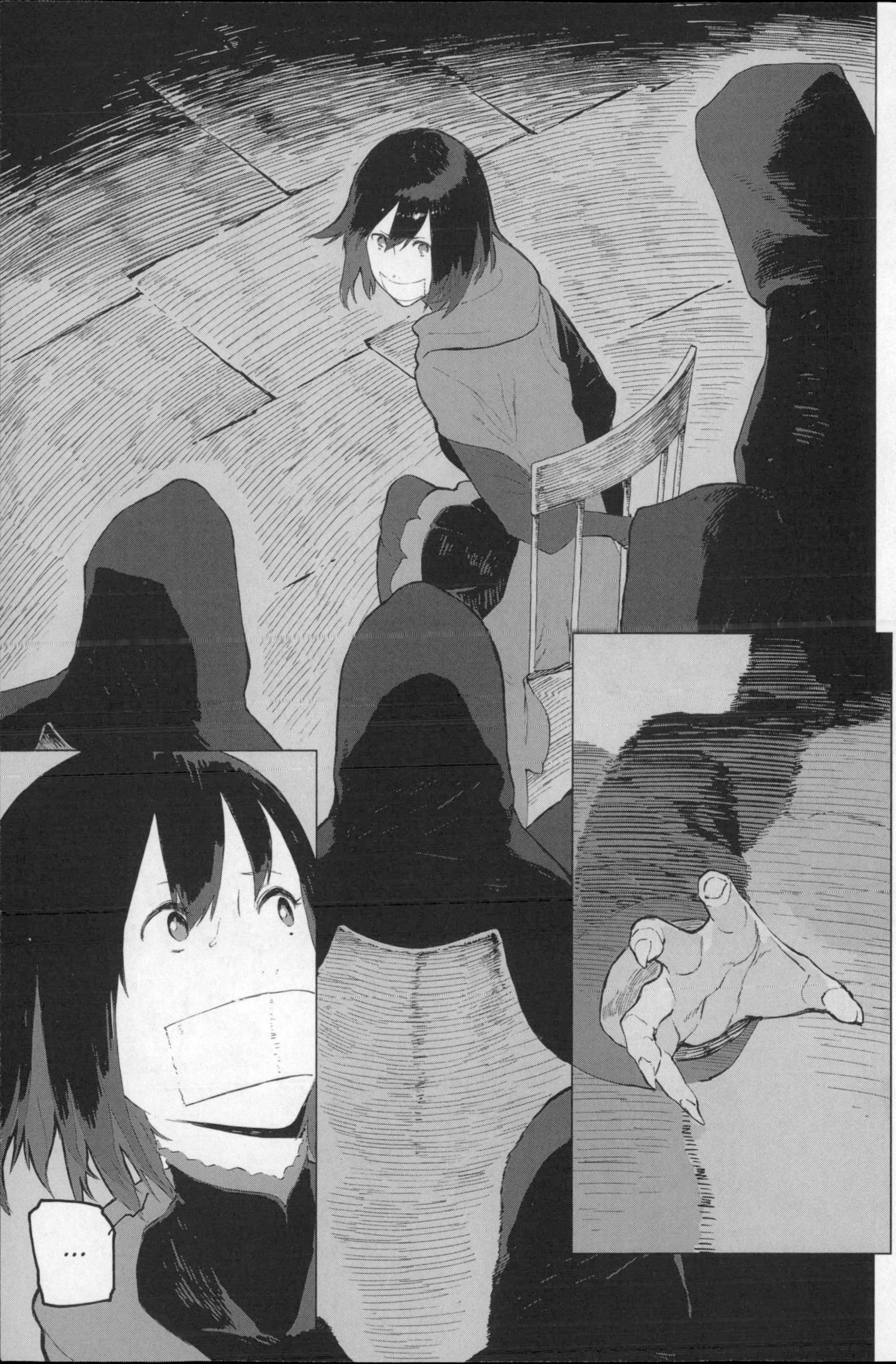
...

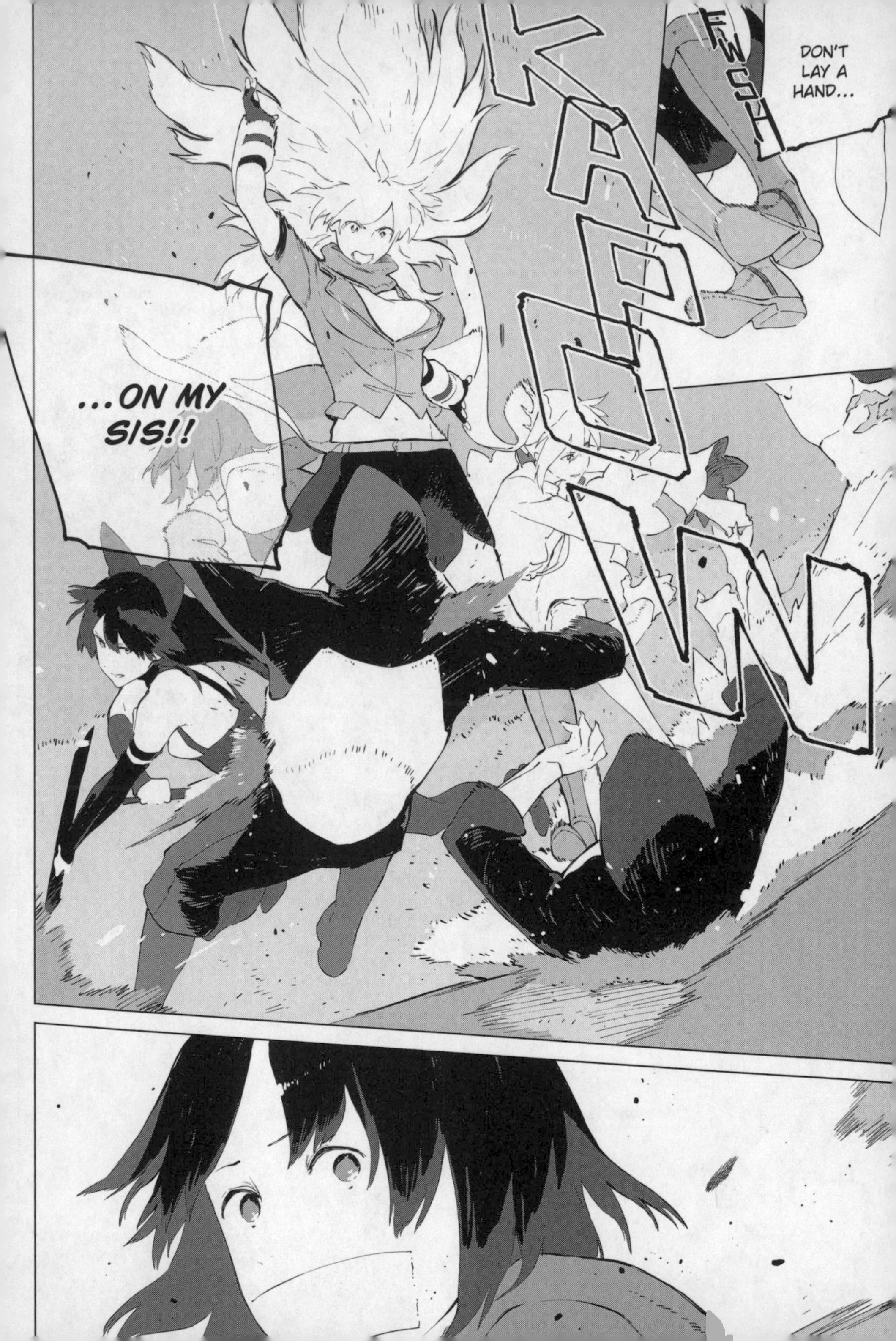
FWSH
DON'T LAY A HAND...
KAPOW
...ON MY SIS!!

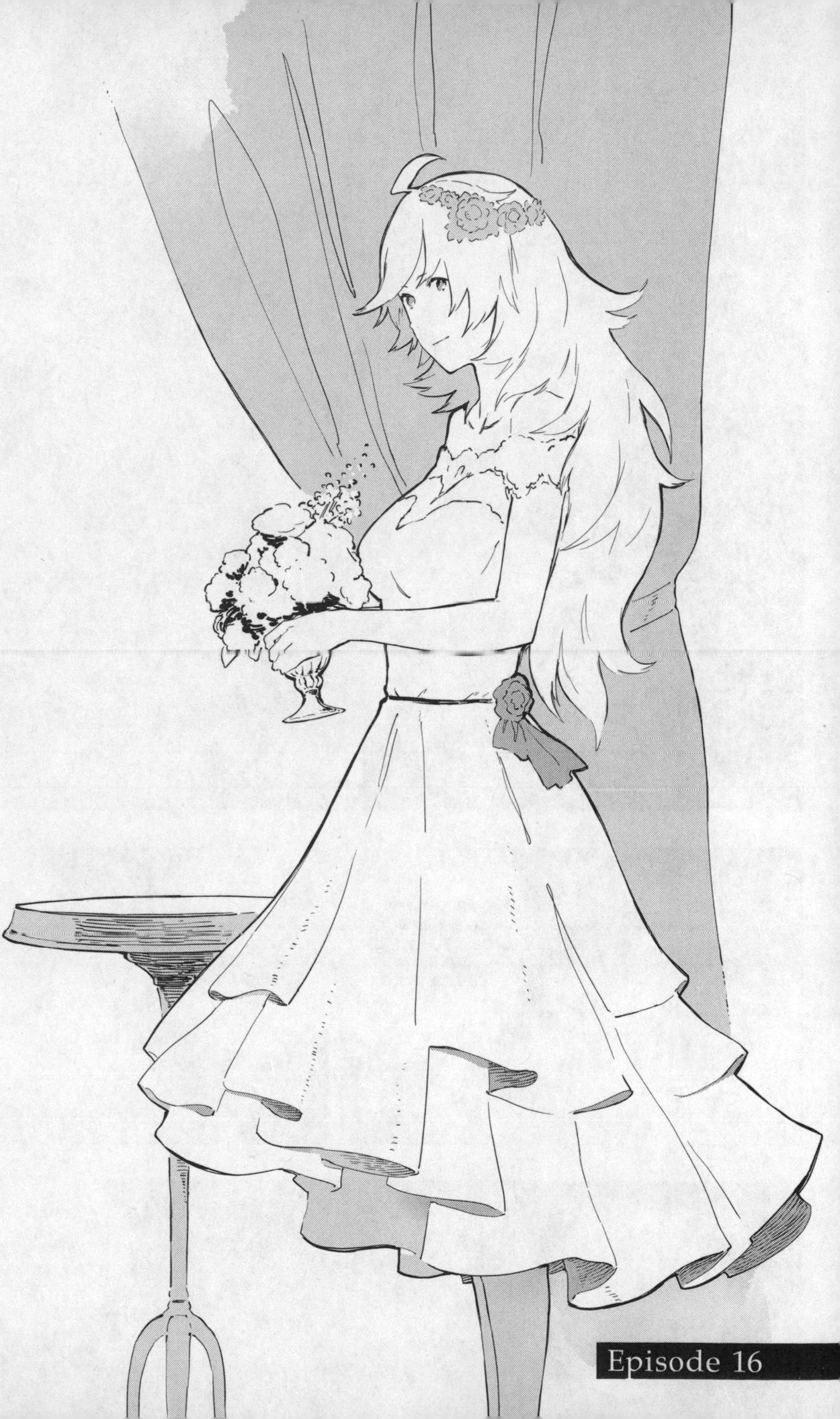
Episode 16

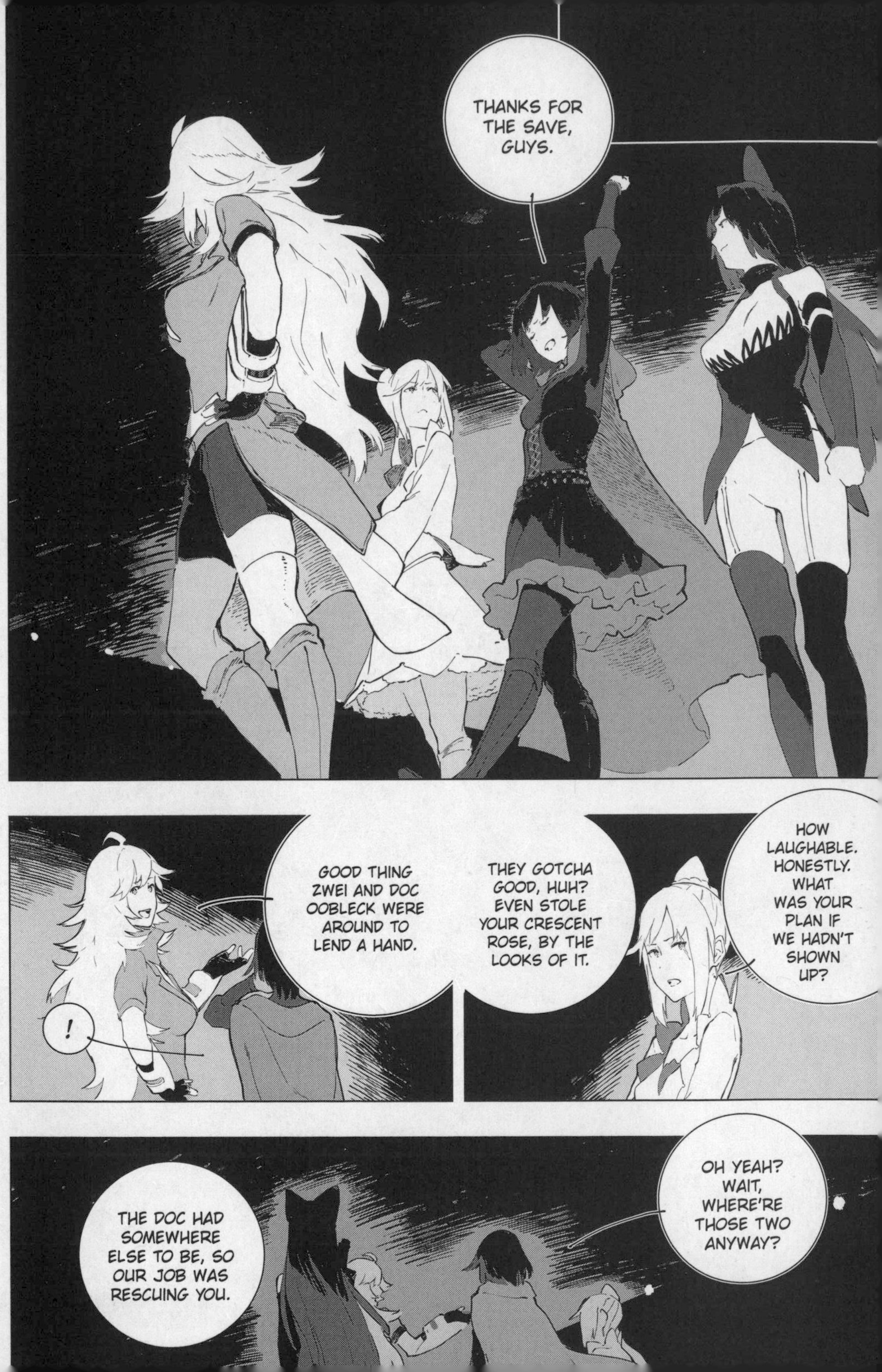
THANKS FOR THE SAVE, GUYS.
HOW LAUGHABLE. HONESTLY. WHAT WAS YOUR PLAN IF WE HADN'T SHOWN UP?
THEY GOTCHA GOOD, HUH? EVEN STOLE YOUR CRESCENT ROSE, BY THE LOOKS OF IT.
GOOD THING ZWEI AND DOC OOBLECK WERE AROUND TO LEND A HAND.
!
OH YEAH? WAIT, WHERE'RE THOSE TWO ANYWAY?
THE DOC HAD SOMEWHERE ELSE TO BE, SO OUR JOB WAS RESCUING YOU.

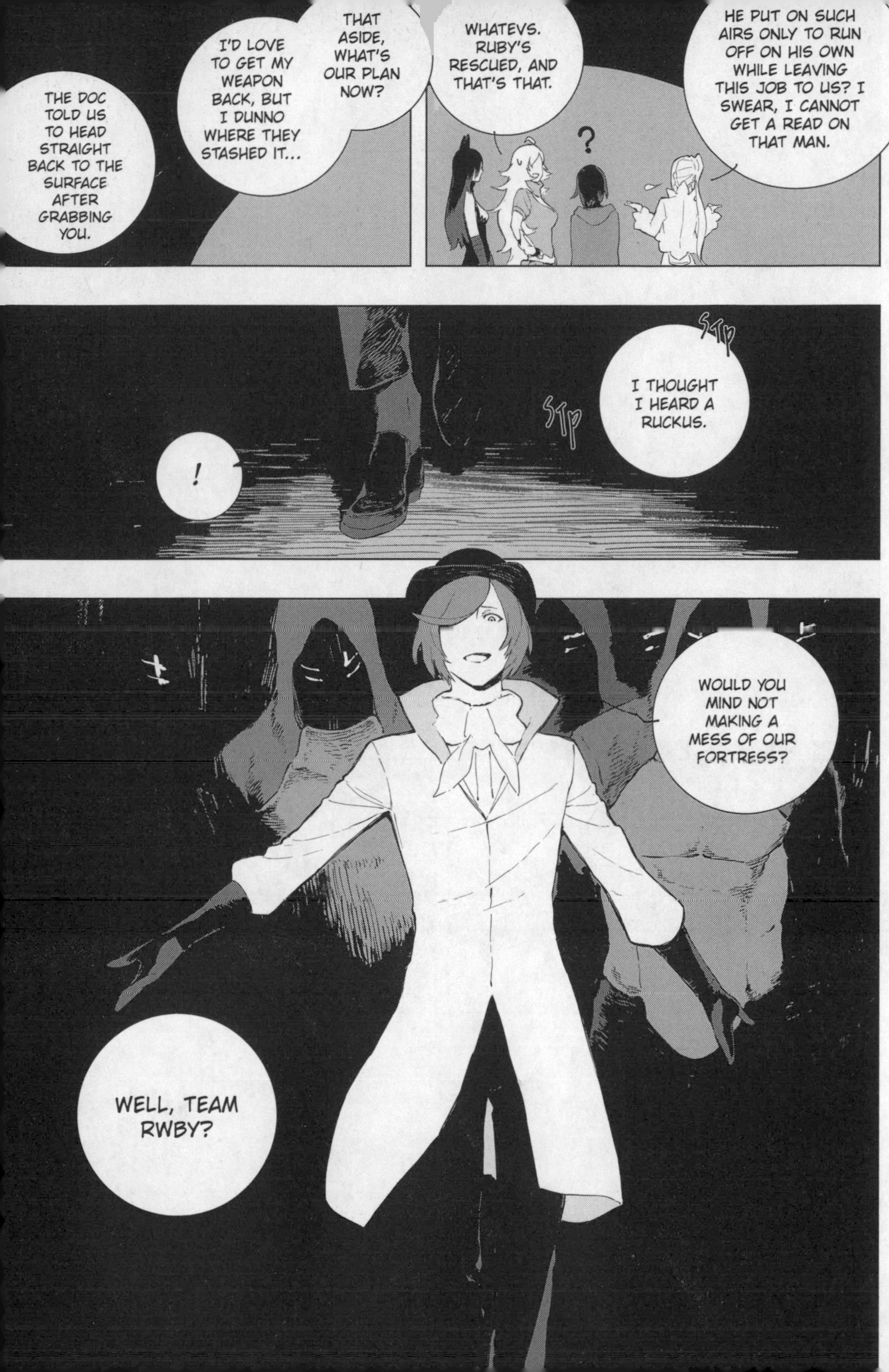
HE PUT ON SUCH AIRS ONLY TO RUN OFF ON HIS OWN WHILE LEAVING THIS JOB TO US? I SWEAR, I CANNOT GET A READ ON THAT MAN.
WHATEVS. RUBY'S RESCUED, AND THAT'S THAT.
?
THAT ASIDE, WHAT'S OUR PLAN NOW?
I'D LOVE TO GET MY WEAPON BACK, BUT I DUNNO WHERE THEY STASHED IT...
THE DOC TOLD US TO HEAD STRAIGHT BACK TO THE SURFACE AFTER GRABBING YOU.
STP
I THOUGHT I HEARD A RUCKUS.
STP
!
WOULD YOU MIND NOT MAKING A MESS OF OUR FORTRESS?
WELL, TEAM RWBY?

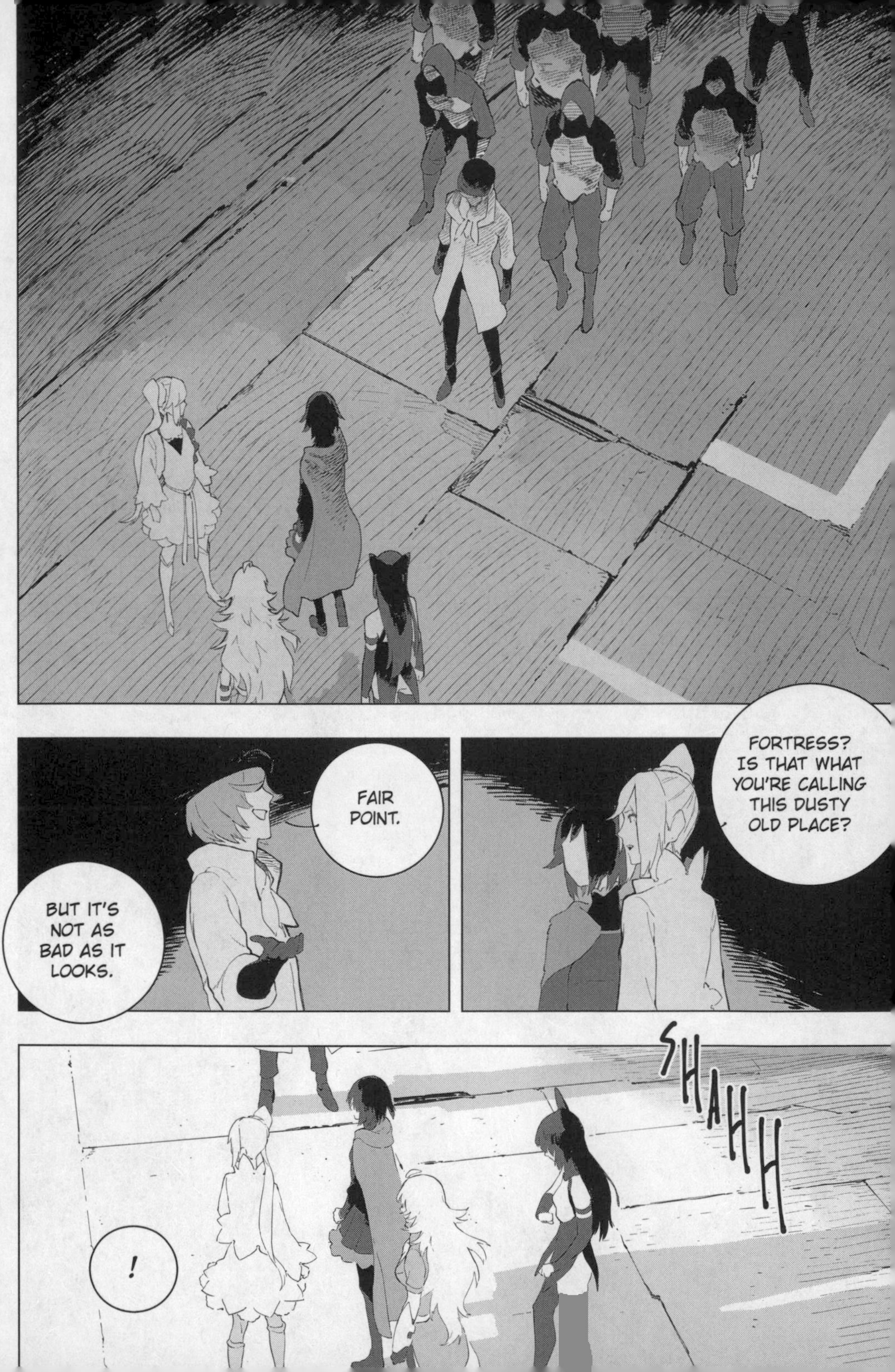
FORTRESS? IS THAT WHAT YOU'RE CALLING THIS DUSTY OLD PLACE?
FAIR POINT.
BUT IT'S NOT AS BAD AS IT LOOKS.
SHAHH
!

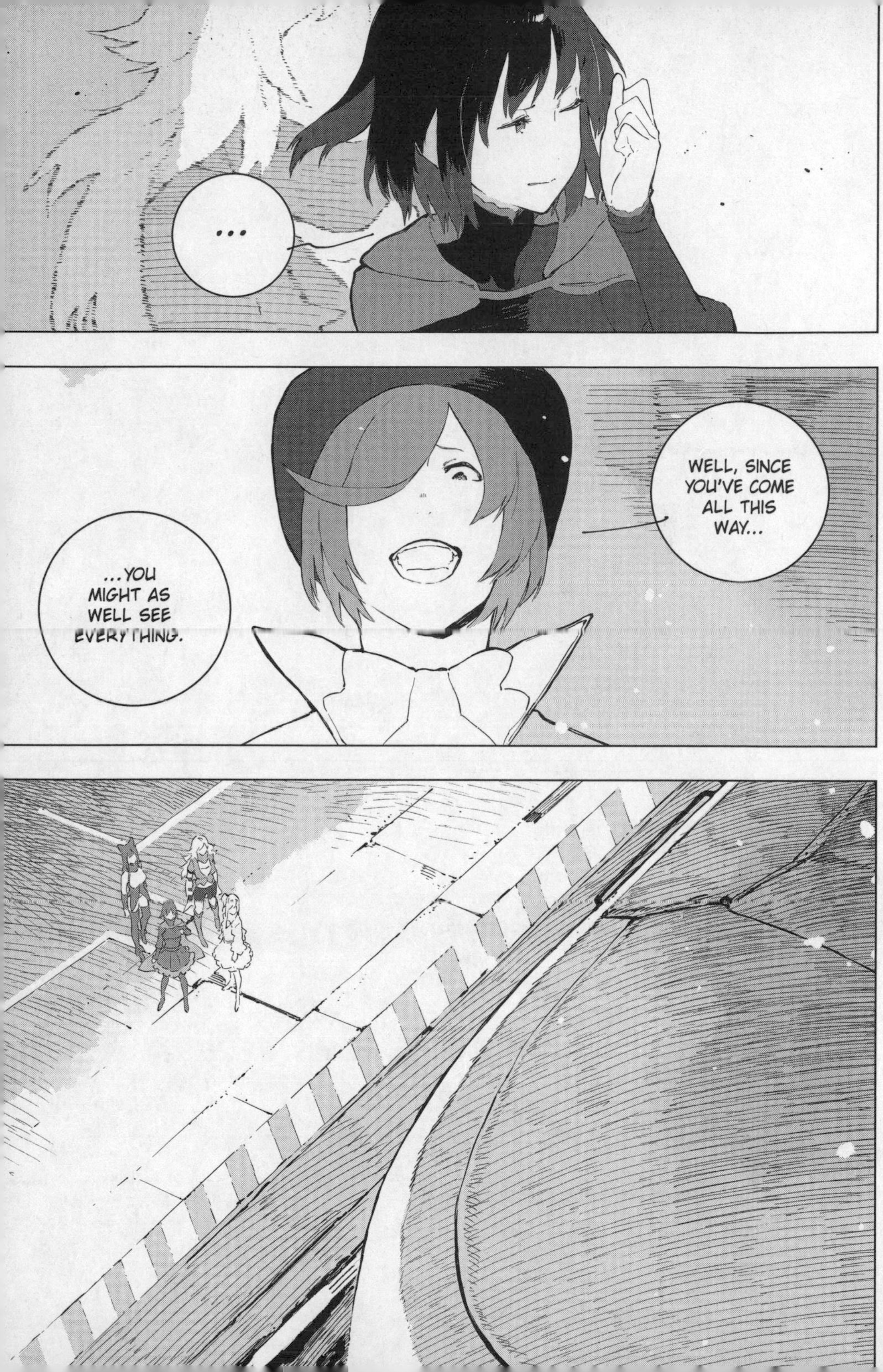
...
WELL, SINCE YOU'VE COME ALL THIS WAY...
...YOU MIGHT AS WELL SEE EVERYTHING.

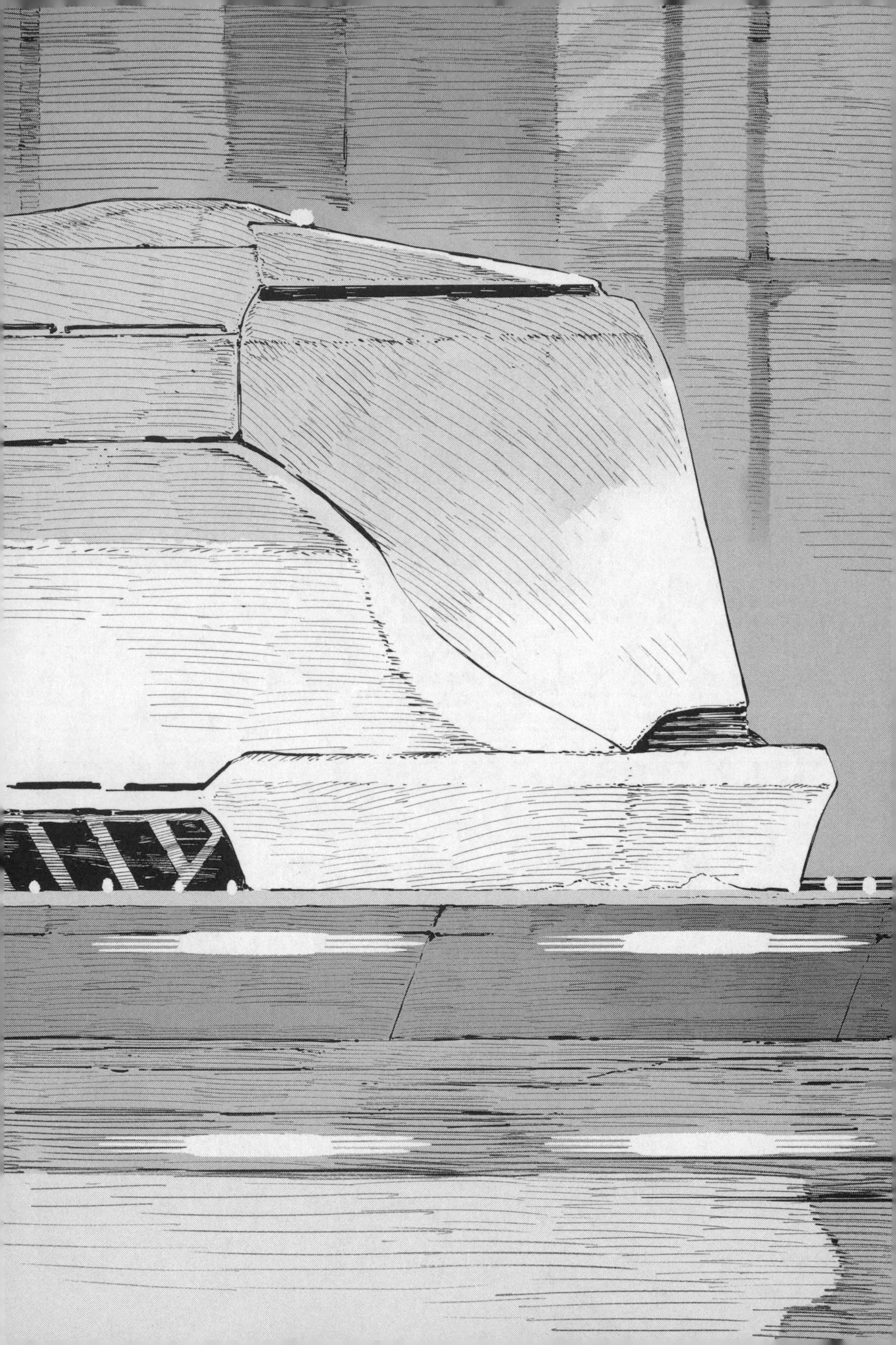

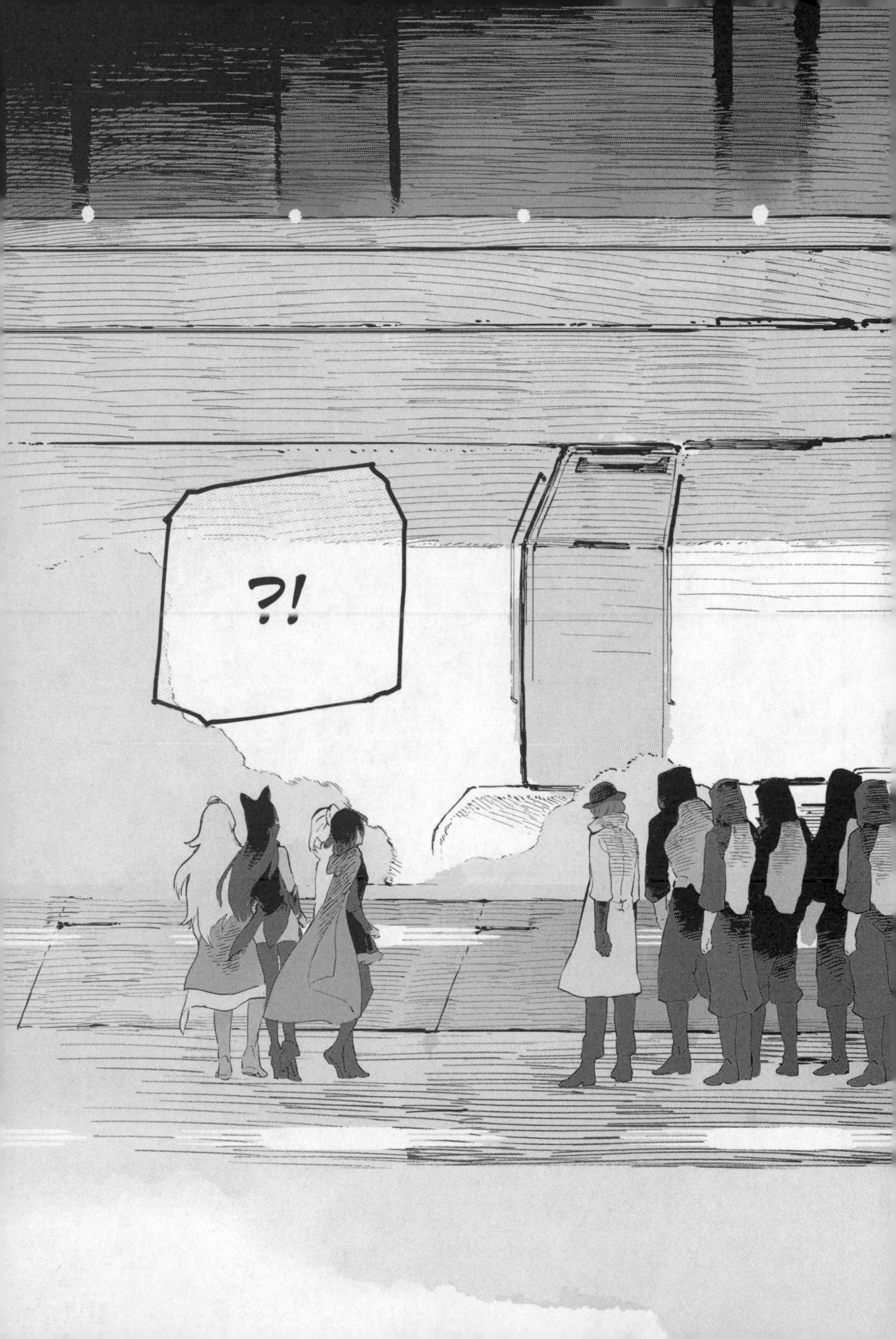
?!

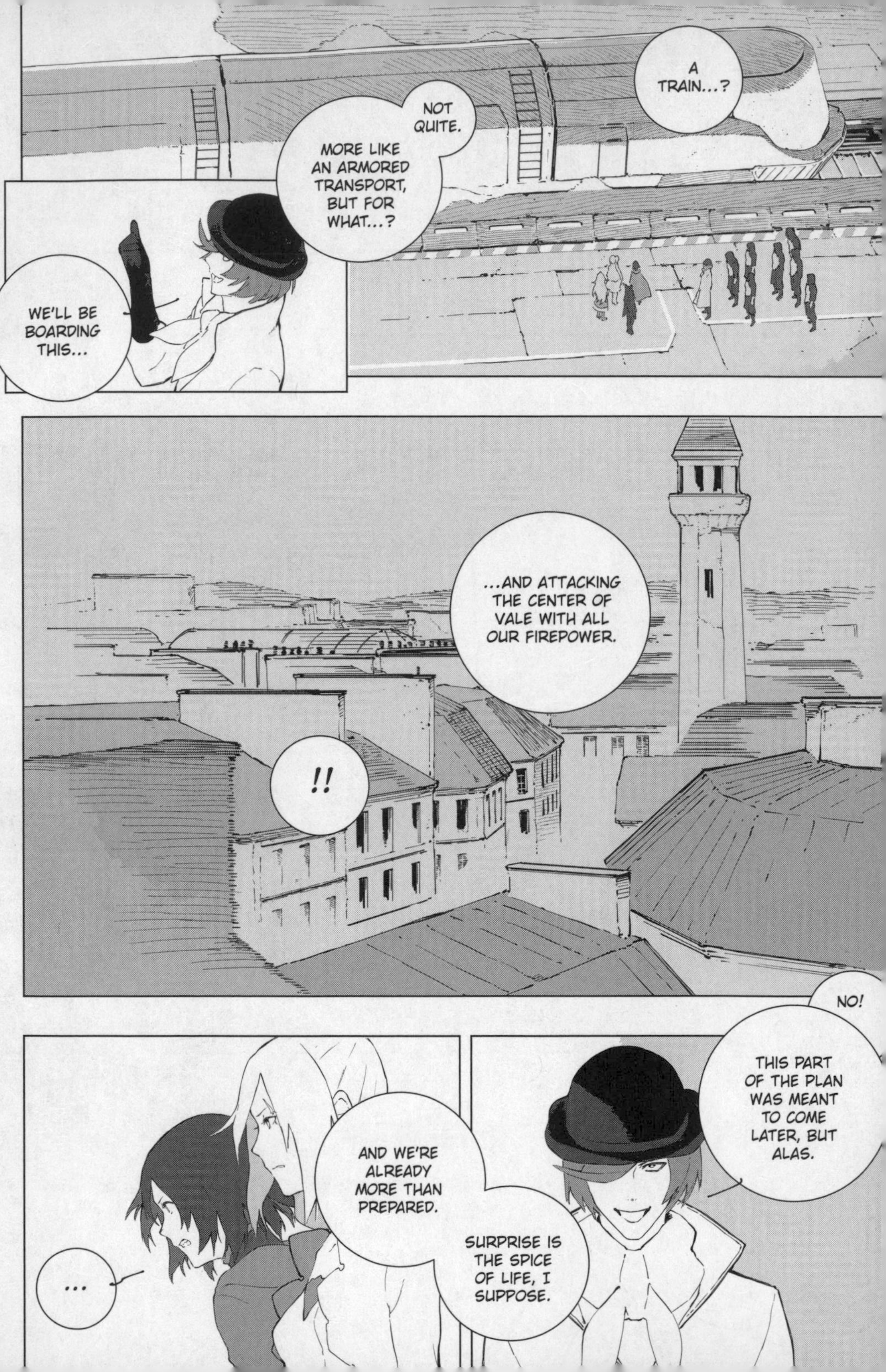
A TRAIN...?
NOT QUITE.
MORE LIKE AN ARMORED TRANSPORT, BUT FOR WHAT...?
WE'LL BE BOARDING THIS...
...AND ATTACKING THE CENTER OF VALE WITH ALL OUR FIREPOWER.
!!
NO!
THIS PART OF THE PLAN WAS MEANT TO COME LATER, BUT ALAS.
SURPRISE IS THE SPICE OF LIFE, I SUPPOSE.
AND WE'RE ALREADY MORE THAN PREPARED.
...

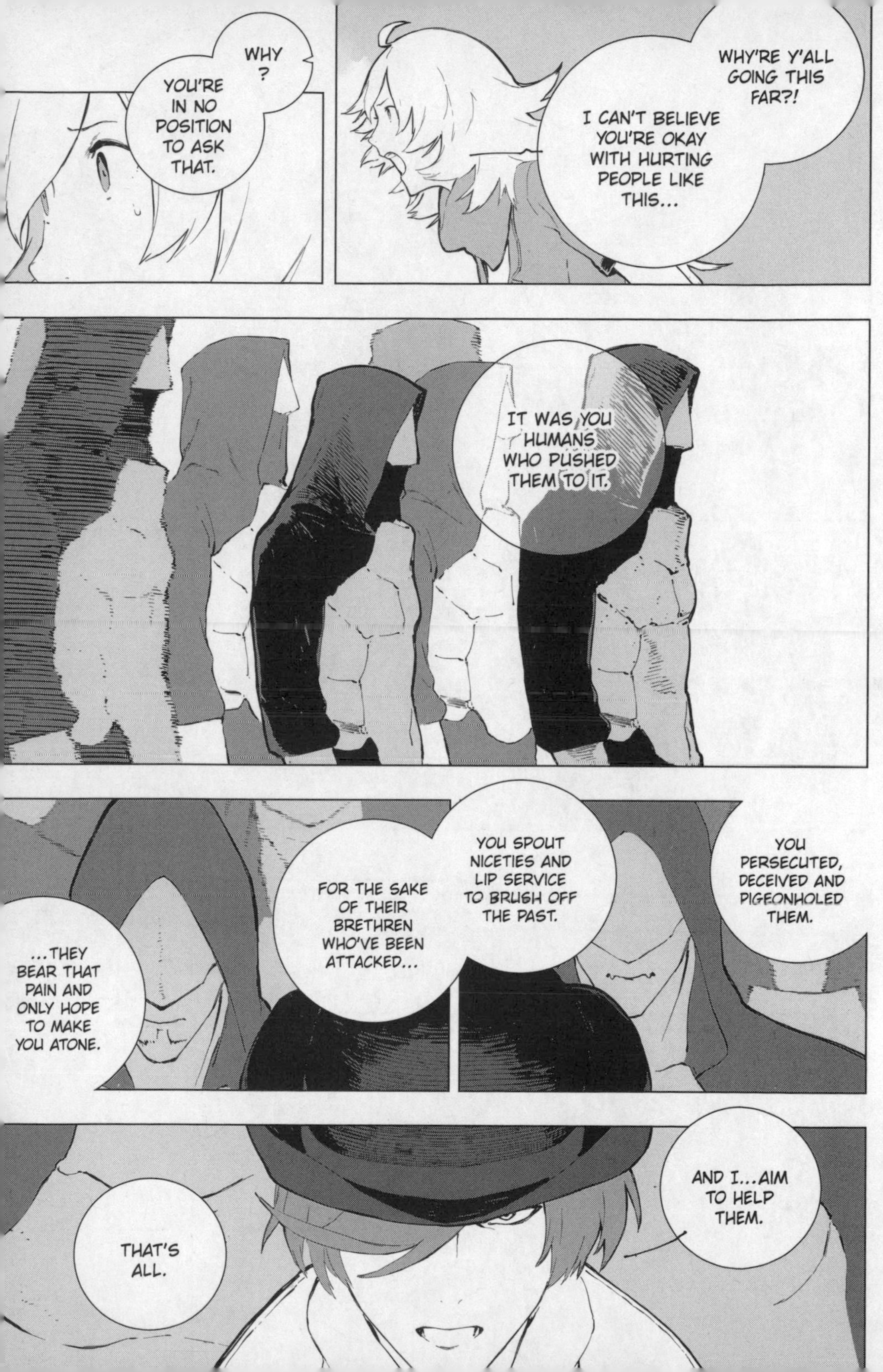
WHY'RE Y'ALL GOING THIS FAR?!
I CAN'T BELIEVE YOU'RE OKAY WITH HURTING PEOPLE LIKE THIS...
WHY? YOU'RE IN NO POSITION TO ASK THAT.
IT WAS YOU HUMANS WHO PUSHED THEM TO IT.
YOU PERSECUTED, DECEIVED AND PIGEONHOLED THEM.
YOU SPOUT NICETIES AND LIP SERVICE TO BRUSH OFF THE PAST.
FOR THE SAKE OF THEIR BRETHREN WHO'VE BEEN ATTACKED...
...THEY BEAR THAT PAIN AND ONLY HOPE TO MAKE YOU ATONE.
AND I...AIM TO HELP THEM.
THAT'S ALL.

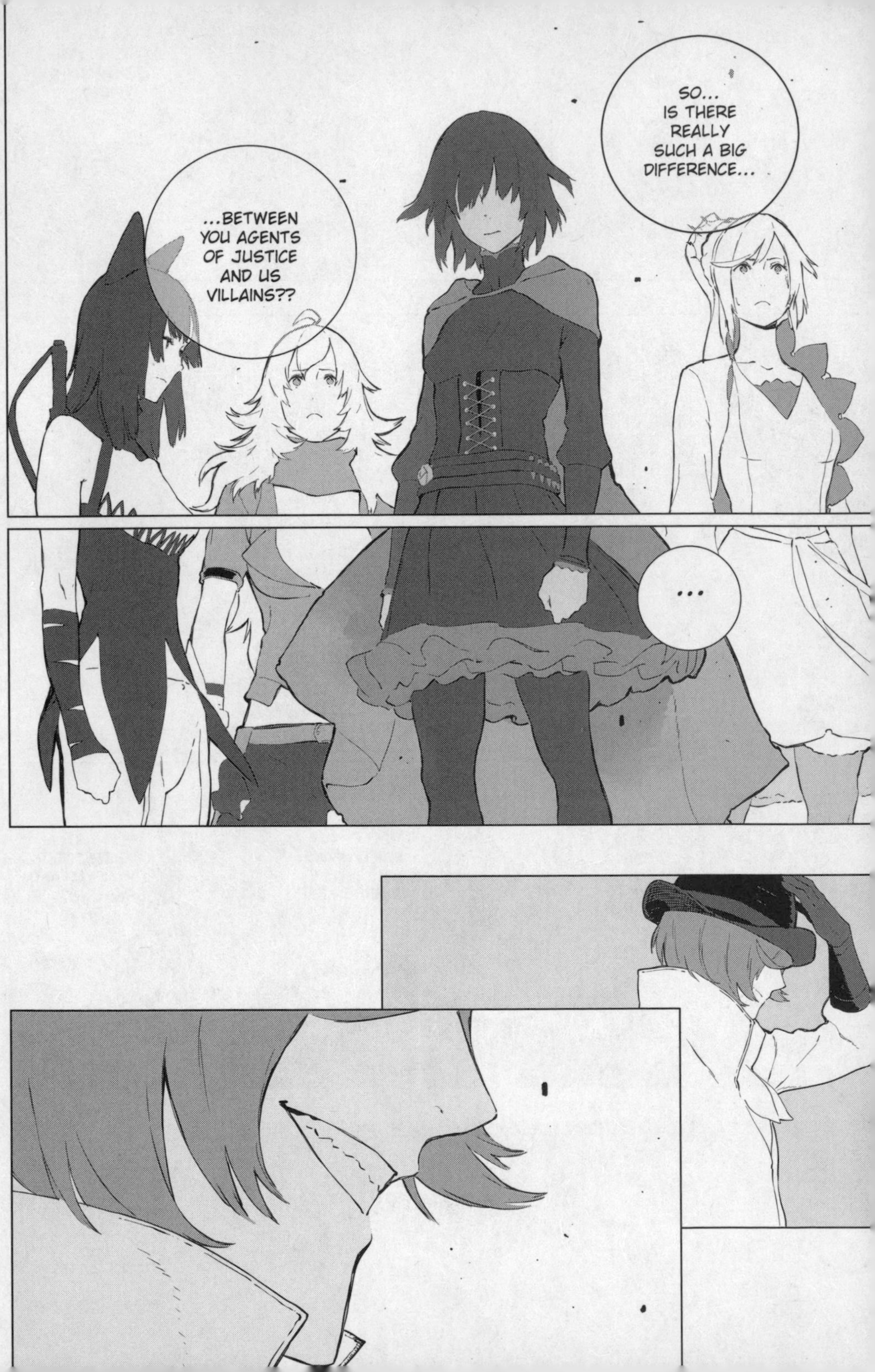
SO... IS THERE REALLY SUCH A BIG DIFFERENCE...
...BETWEEN YOU AGENTS OF JUSTICE AND US VILLAINS??
...

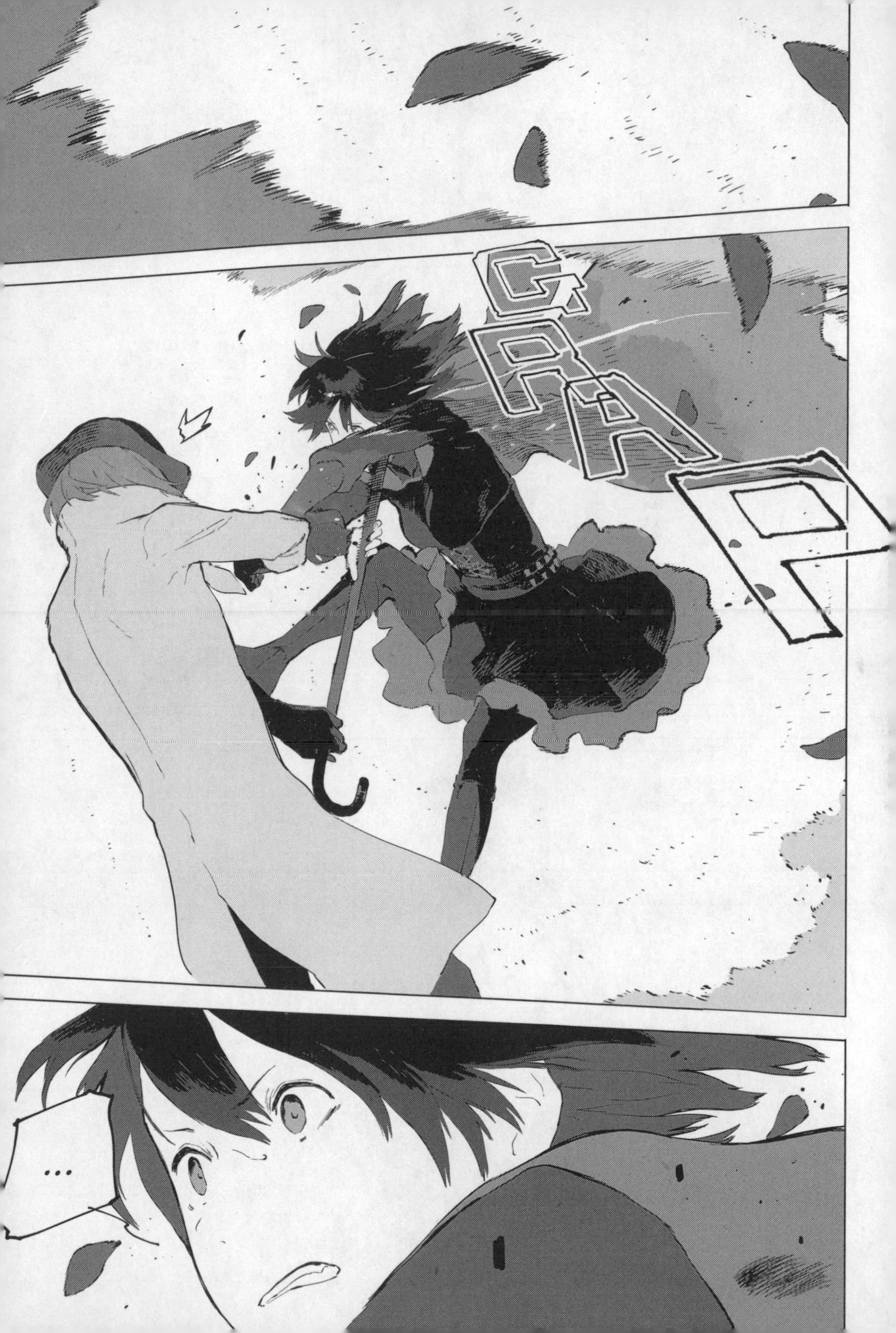
GRAB
...

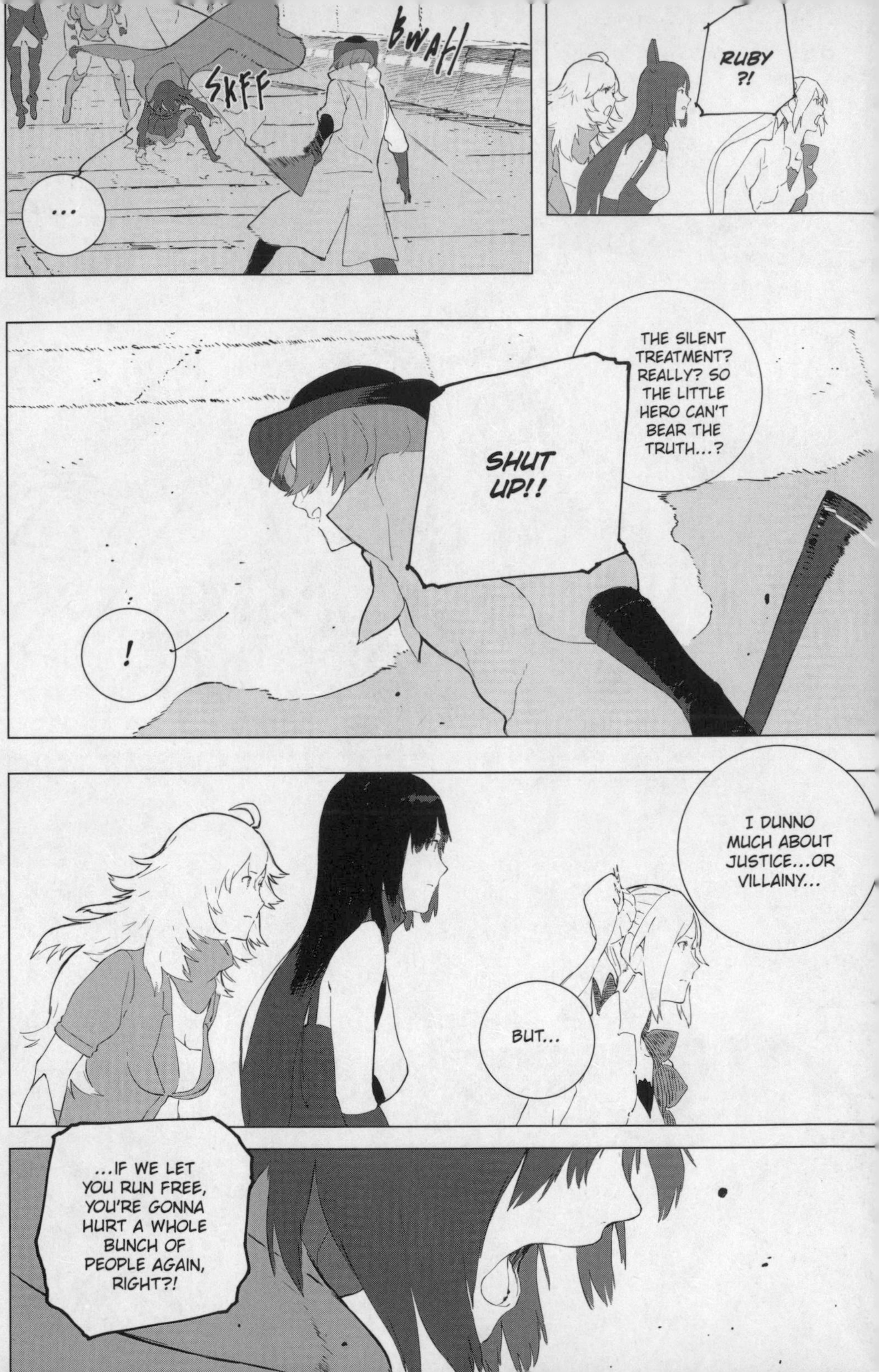
RUBY ?!
BWAH
SKFF
...
THE SILENT TREATMENT? REALLY? SO THE LITTLE HERO CAN'T BEAR THE TRUTH...?
SHUT UP!!
!
I DUNNO MUCH ABOUT JUSTICE...OR VILLAINY...
BUT...
...IF WE LET YOU RUN FREE, YOU'RE GONNA HURT A WHOLE BUNCH OF PEOPLE AGAIN, RIGHT?!

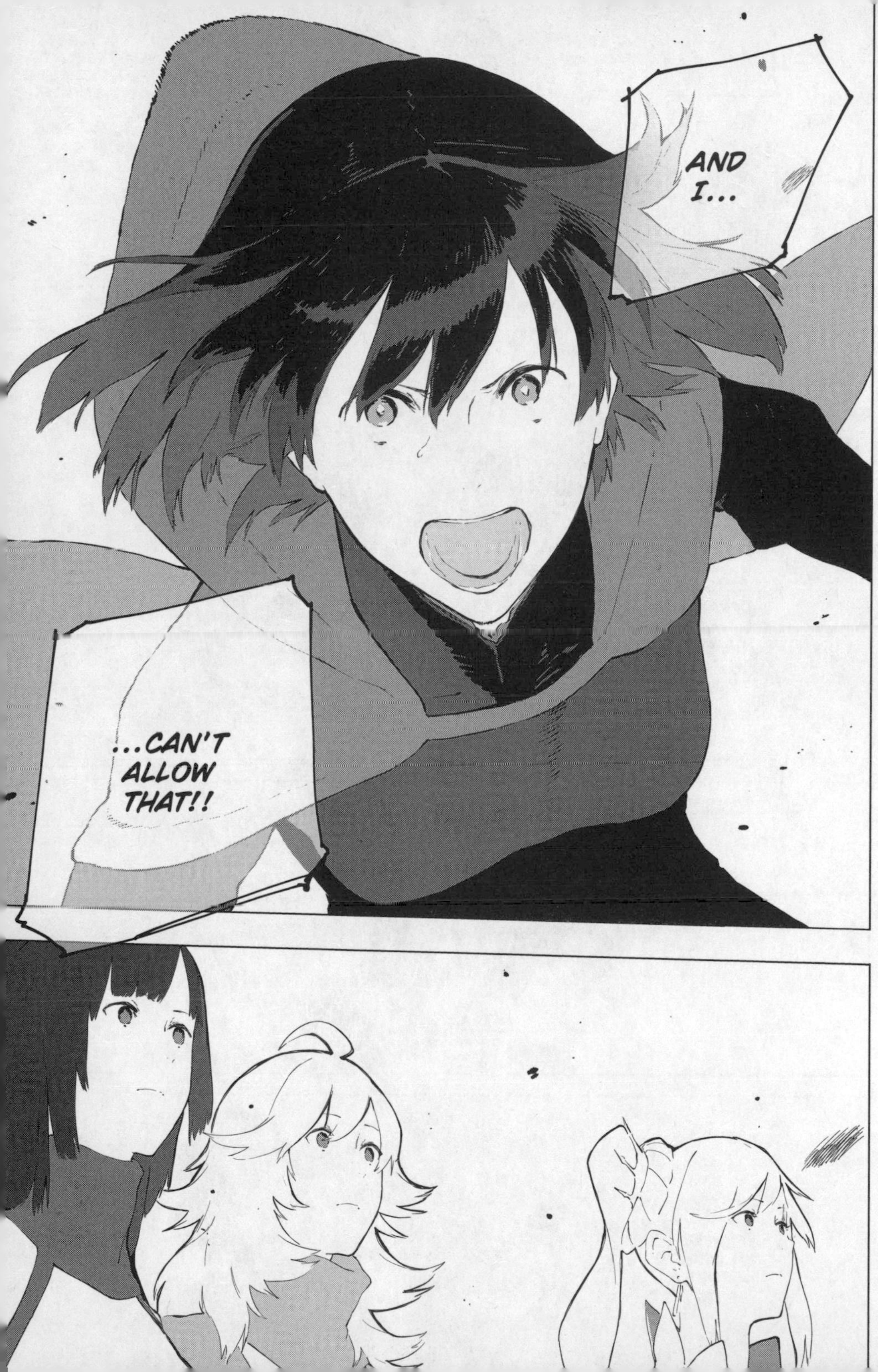
AND I...
...CAN'T ALLOW THAT!!

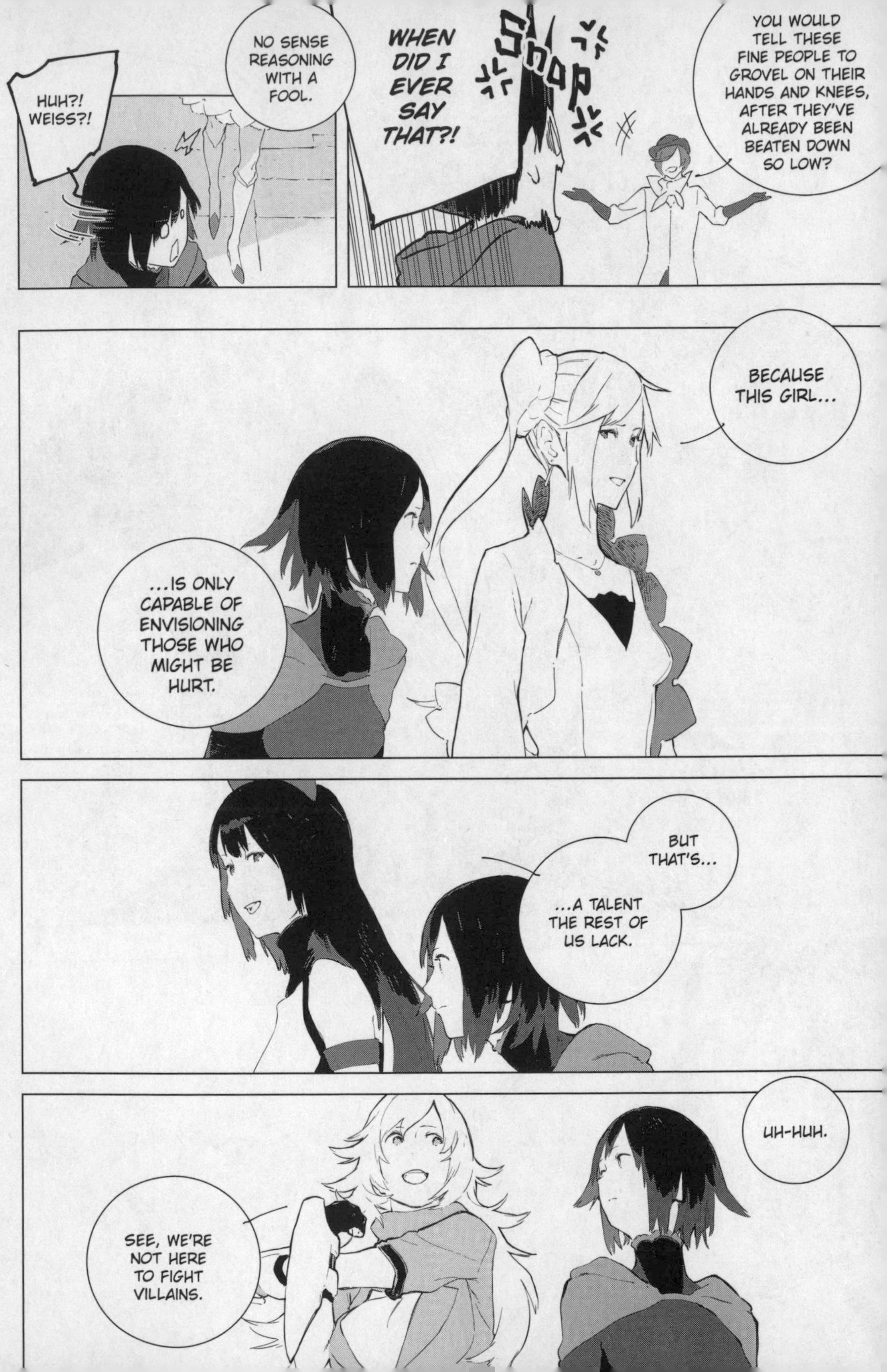
YOU WOULD TELL THESE FINE PEOPLE TO GROVEL ON THEIR HANDS AND KNEES, AFTER THEY'VE ALREADY BEEN BEATEN DOWN SO LOW?
SNAP
WHEN DID I EVER SAY THAT?!
NO SENSE REASONING WITH A FOOL.
HUH?! WEISS?!
BECAUSE THIS GIRL...
...IS ONLY CAPABLE OF ENVISIONING THOSE WHO MIGHT BE HURT.
BUT THAT'S...
...A TALENT THE REST OF US LACK.
UH-HUH.
SEE, WE'RE NOT HERE TO FIGHT VILLAINS.

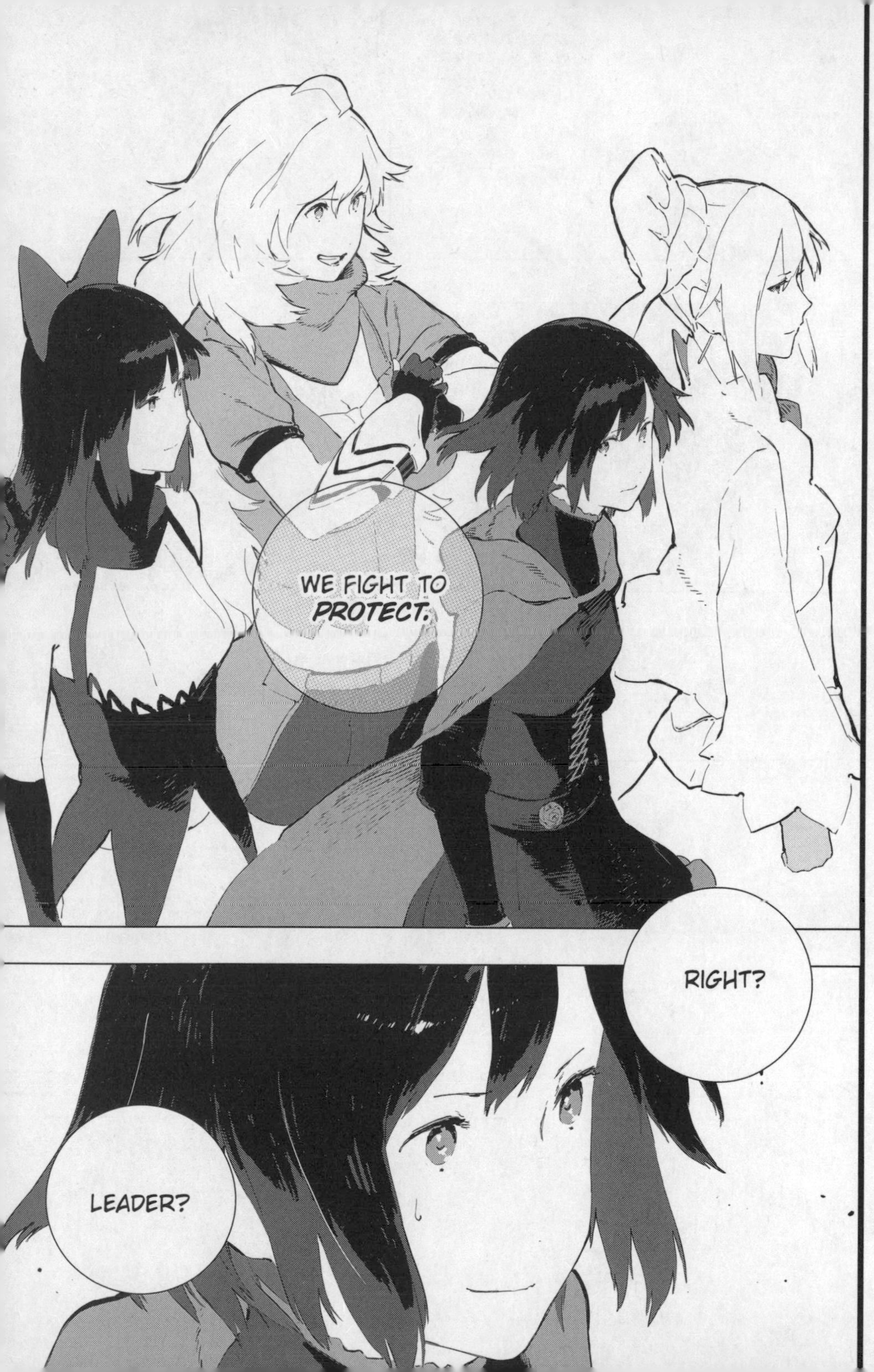
WE FIGHT TO PROTECT.
RIGHT?
LEADER?

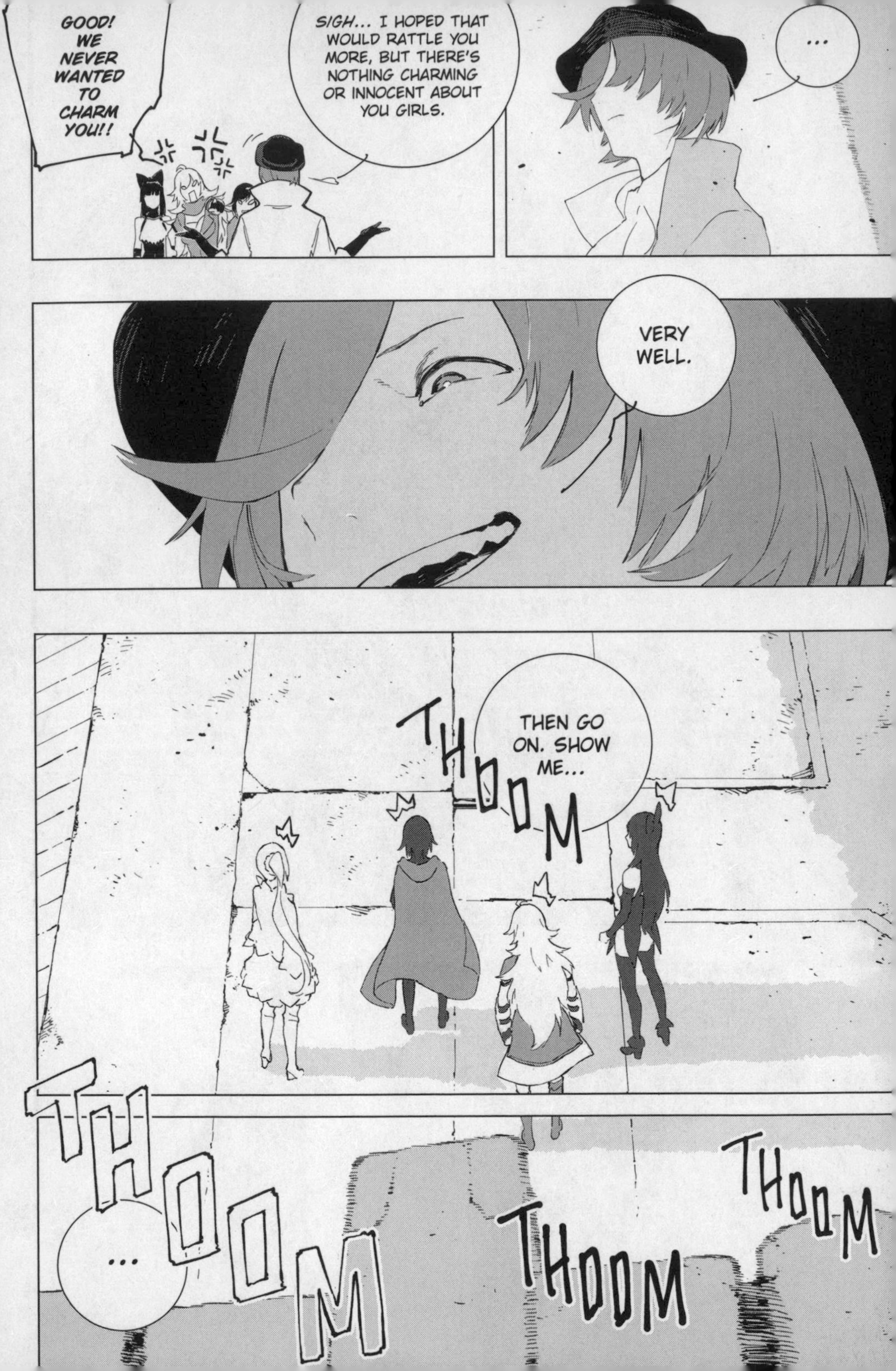
...
SIGH... I HOPED THAT WOULD RATTLE YOU MORE, BUT THERE'S NOTHING CHARMING OR INNOCENT ABOUT YOU GIRLS.
GOOD! WE NEVER WANTED TO CHARM YOU!!
VERY WELL.
THEN GO ON. SHOW ME...
THOOM
THOOM
THOOM
THOOM
...

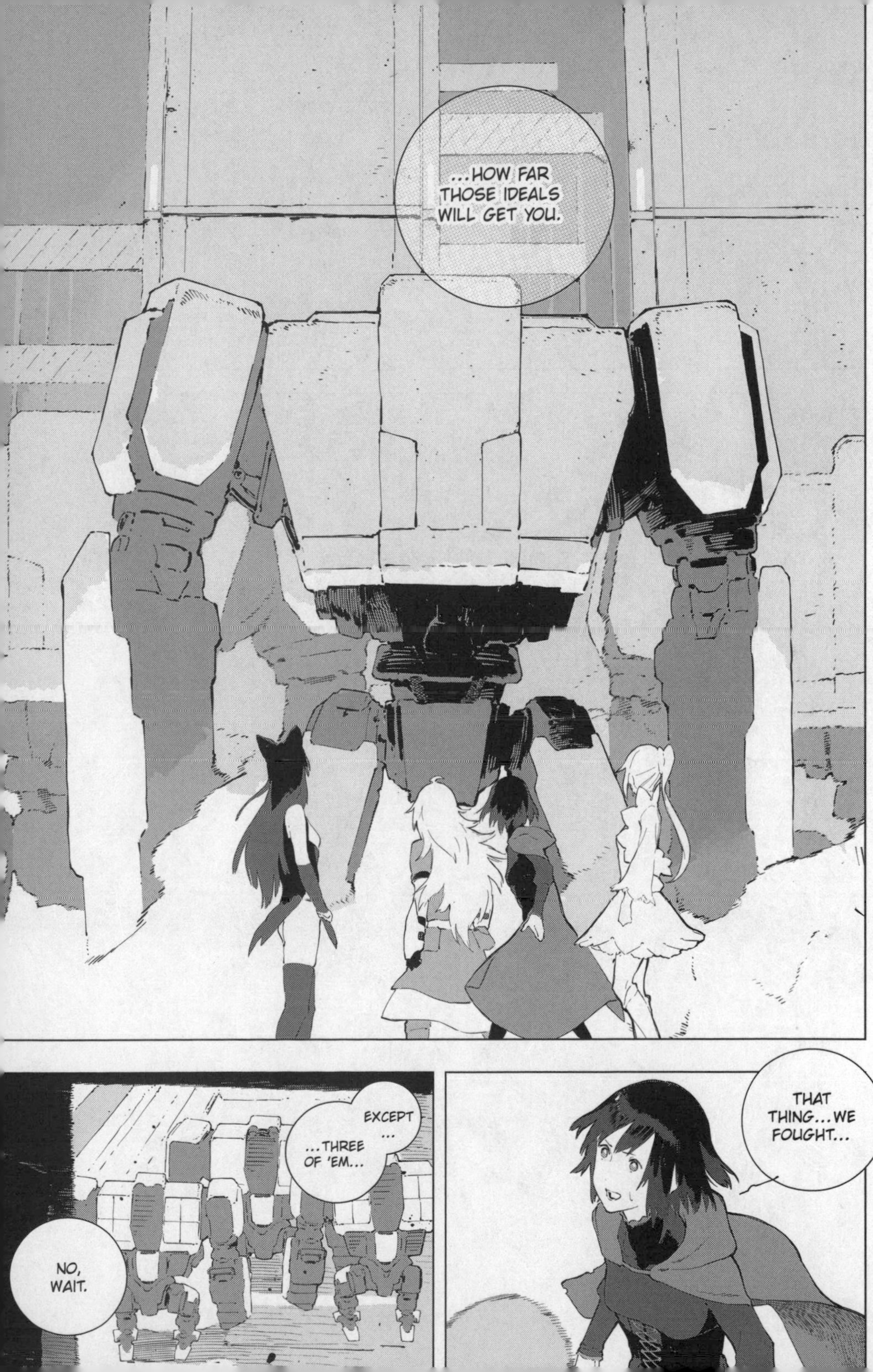
...HOW FAR THOSE IDEALS WILL GET YOU.
THAT THING...WE FOUGHT...
EXCEPT ...
...THREE OF 'EM...
NO, WAIT.

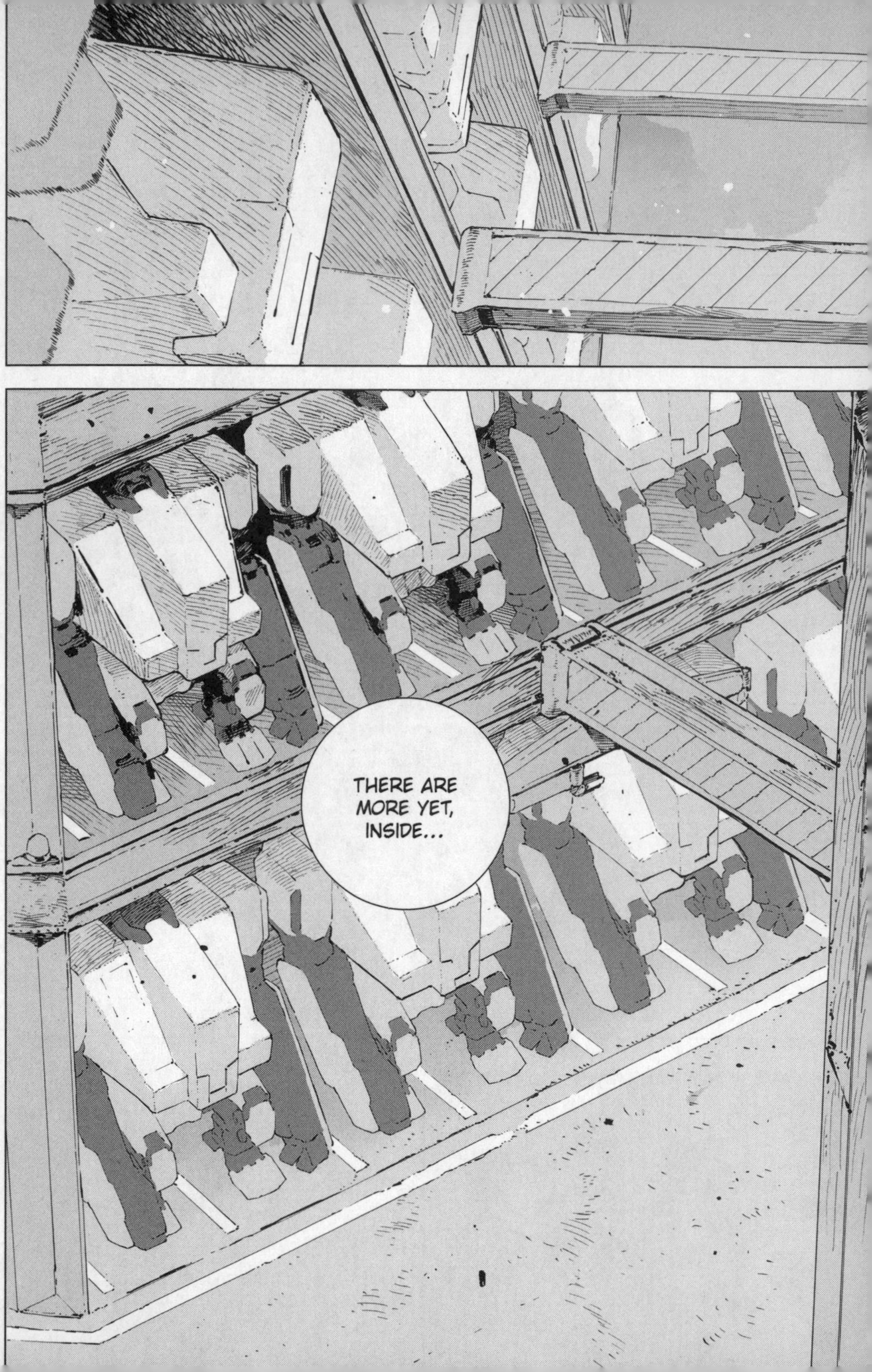
THERE ARE MORE YET, INSIDE...

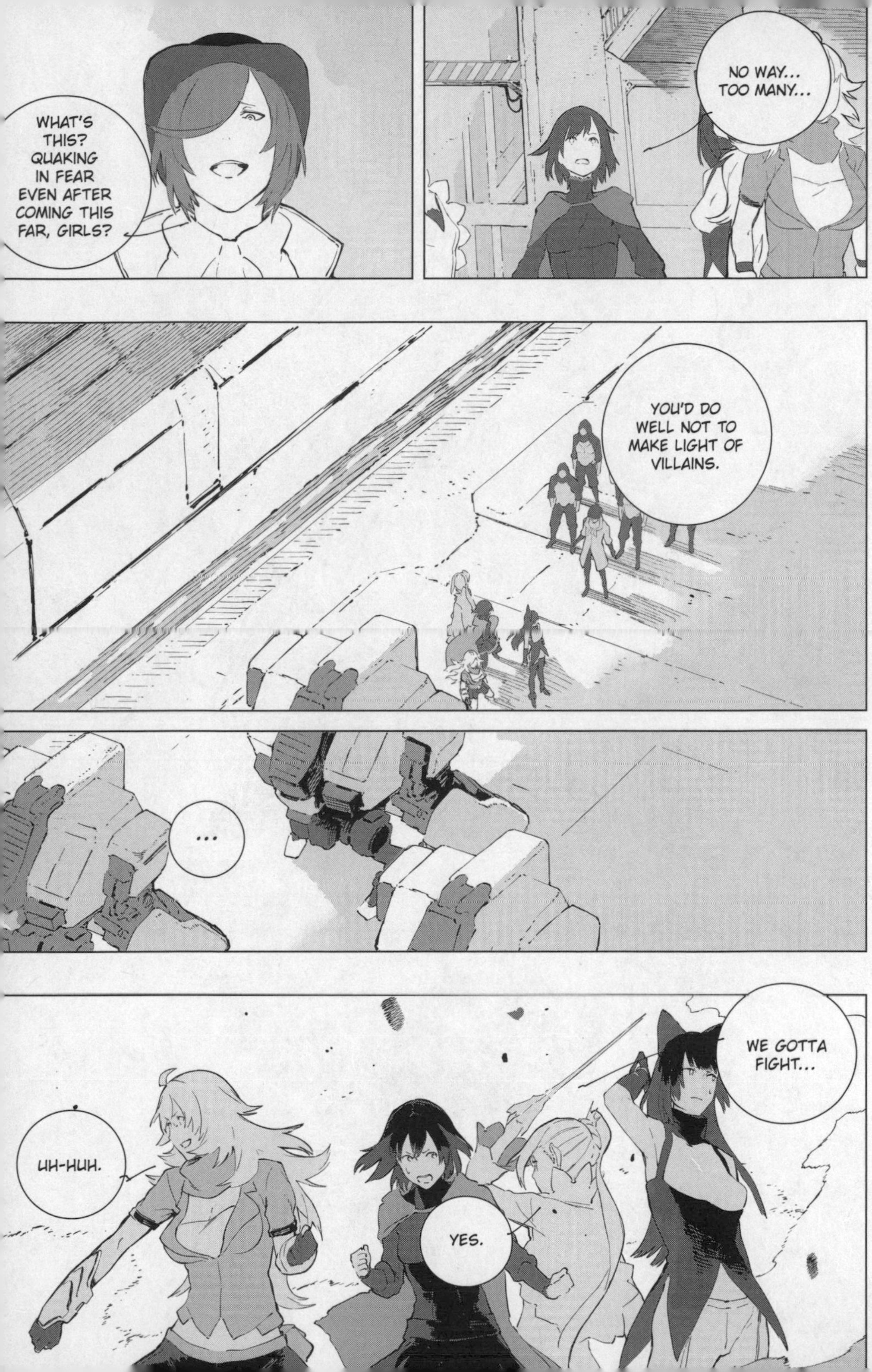
NO WAY... TOO MANY...
WHAT'S THIS? QUAKING IN FEAR EVEN AFTER COMING THIS FAR, GIRLS?
YOU'D DO WELL NOT TO MAKE LIGHT OF VILLAINS.
...
WE GOTTA FIGHT...
YES.
UH-HUH.

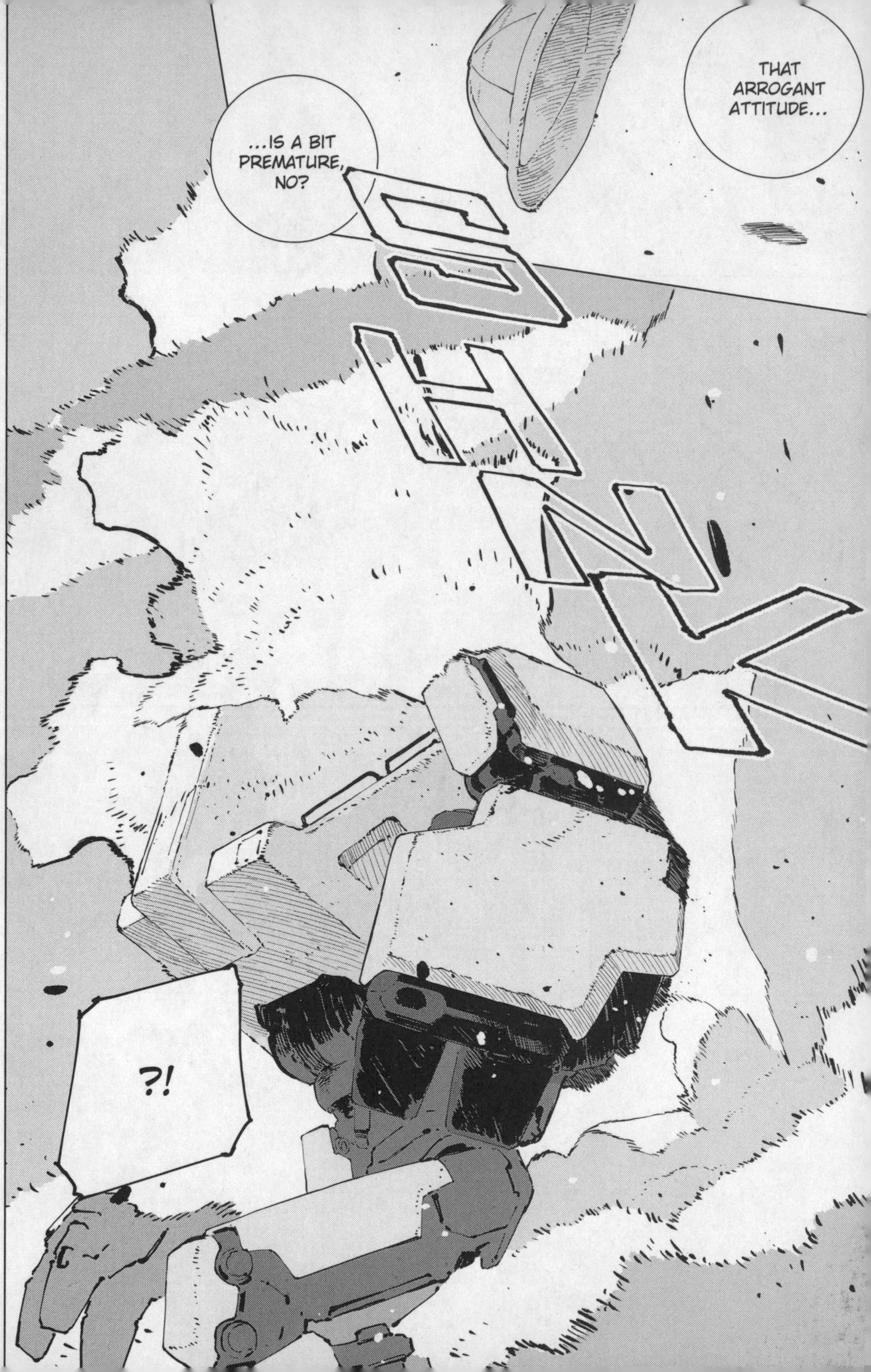
THAT ARROGANT ATTITUDE...
...IS A BIT PREMATURE, NO?
?!

KATHUD

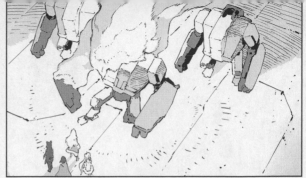

STP

!

I APOLOGIZE
FOR MY TARDY
ENTRANCE,
LADIES.

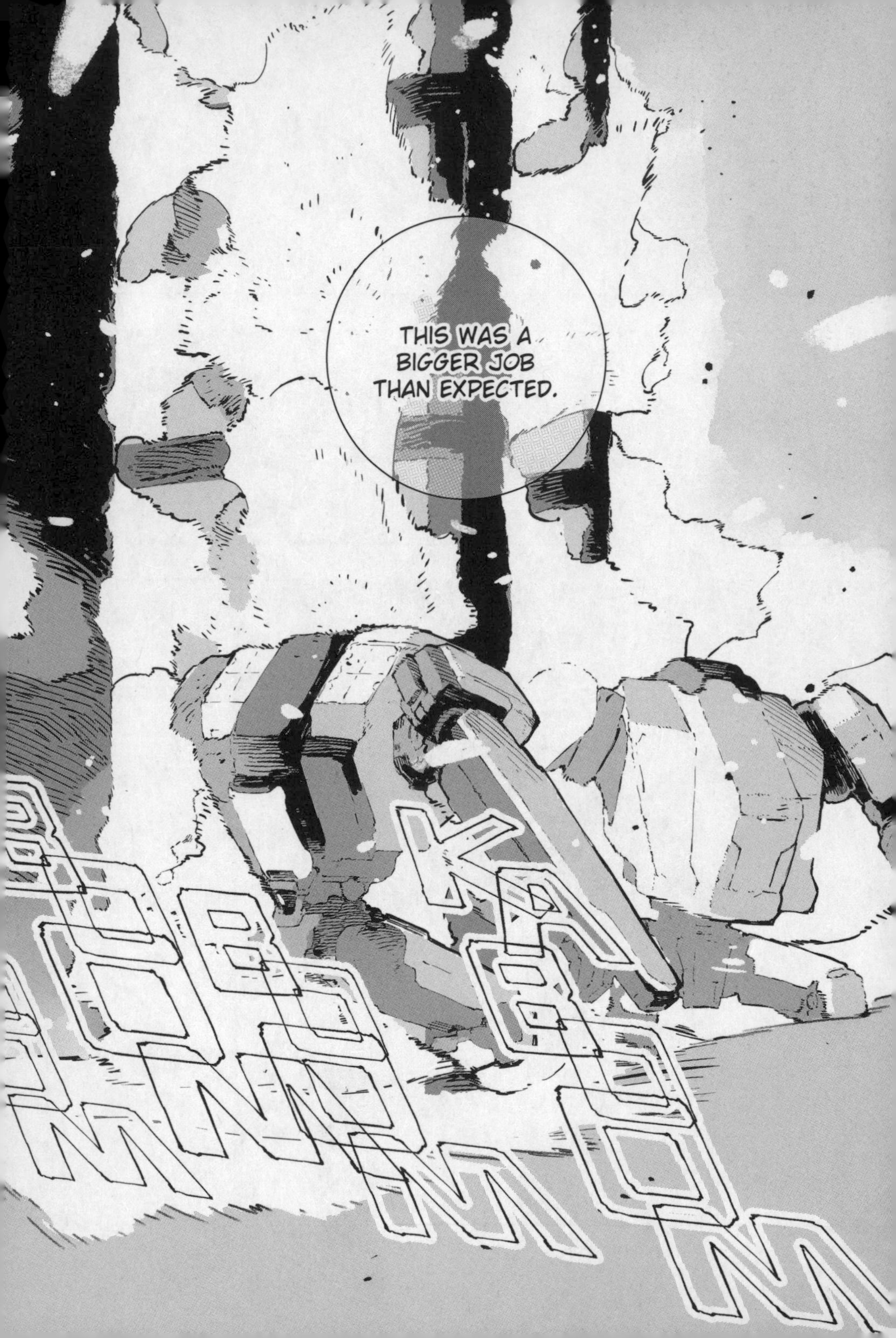
THIS WAS A BIGGER JOB THAN EXPECTED.

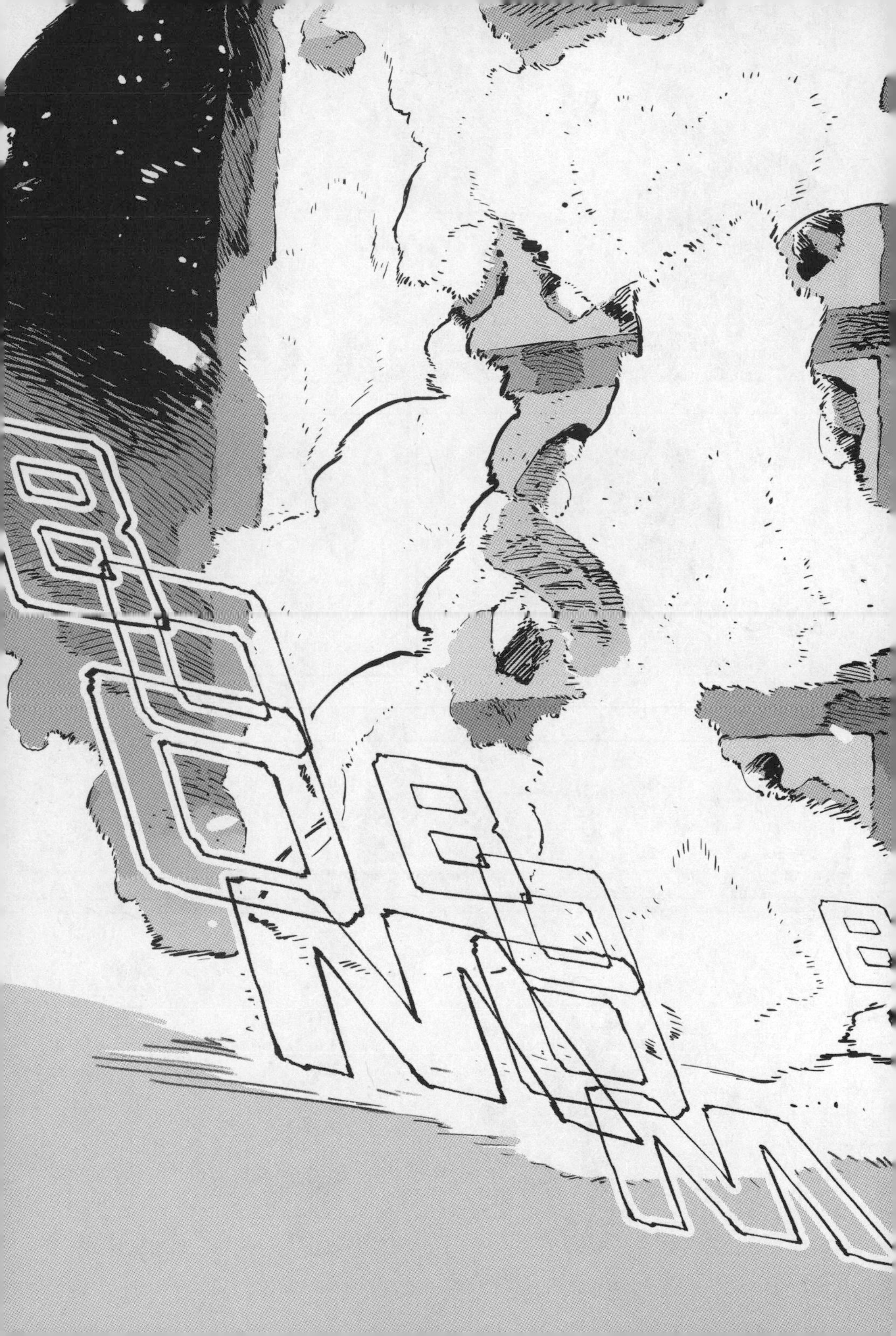

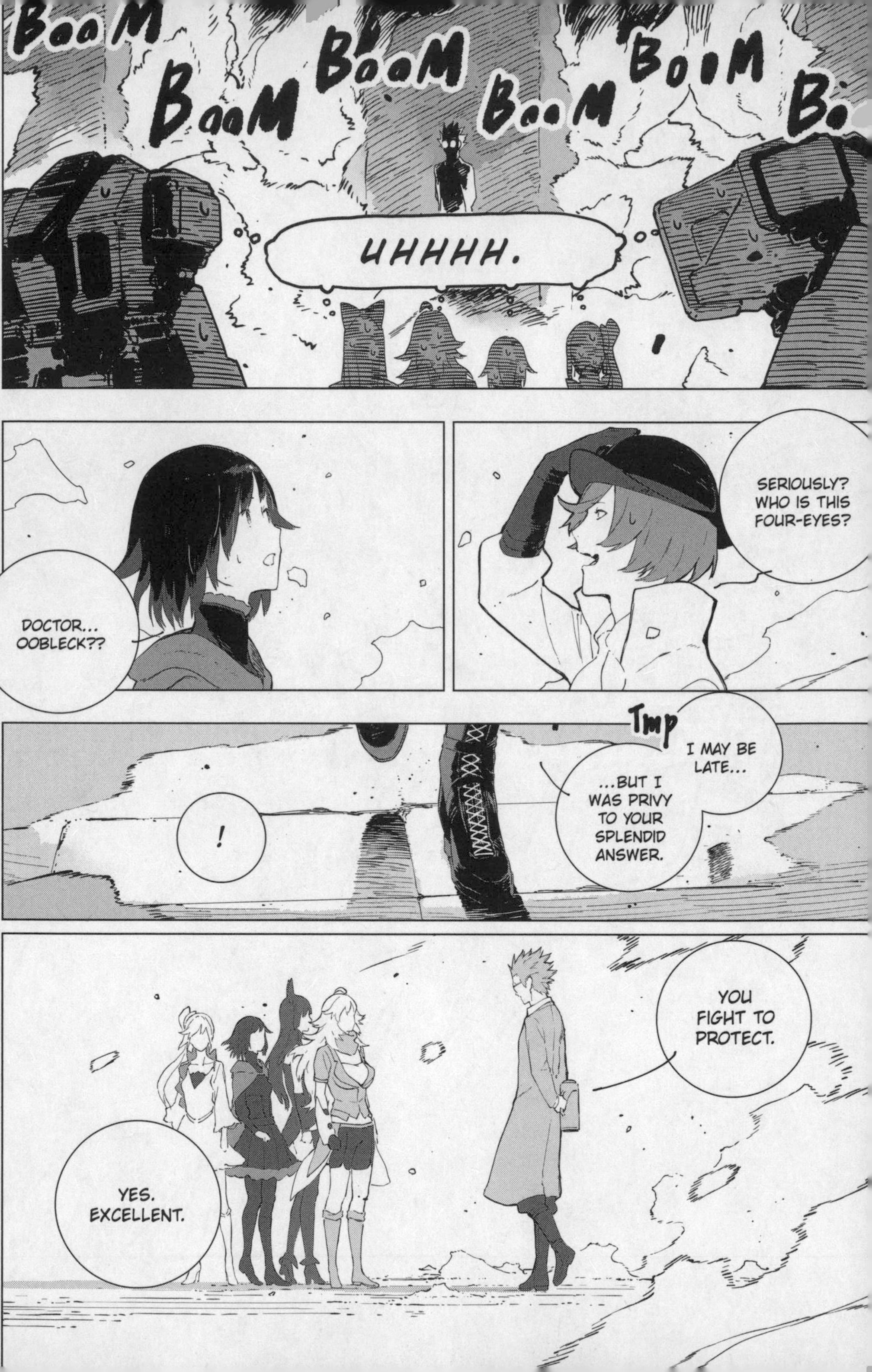
BooM
BooM
BooM
BooM
BooM
BooM
UHHHH.
!
SERIOUSLY? WHO IS THIS FOUR-EYES?
DOCTOR... OOBLECK??
Tmp
I MAY BE LATE...
...BUT I WAS PRIVY TO YOUR SPLENDID ANSWER.
!
YOU FIGHT TO PROTECT.
YES. EXCELLENT.

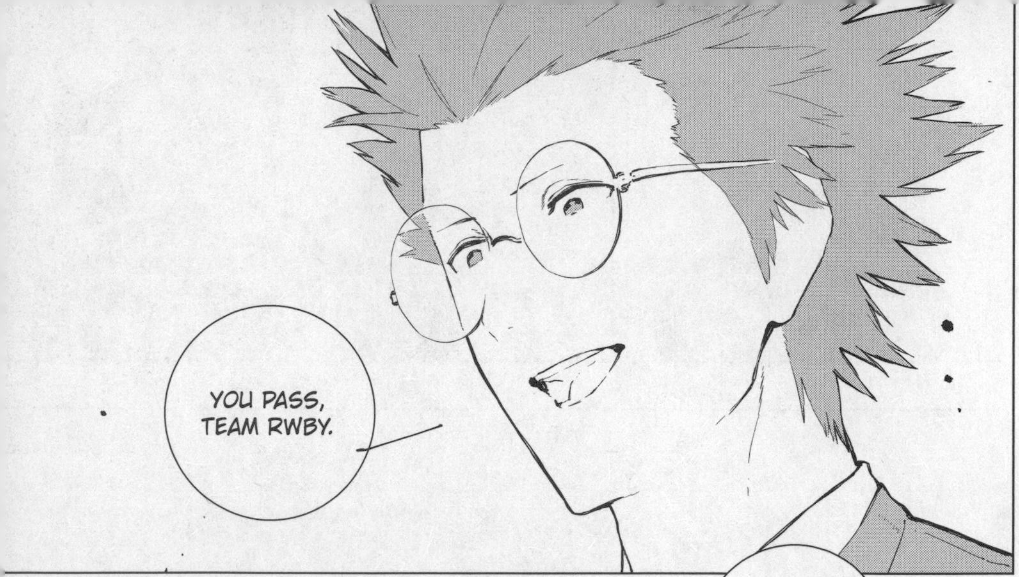
YOU PASS, TEAM RWBY.

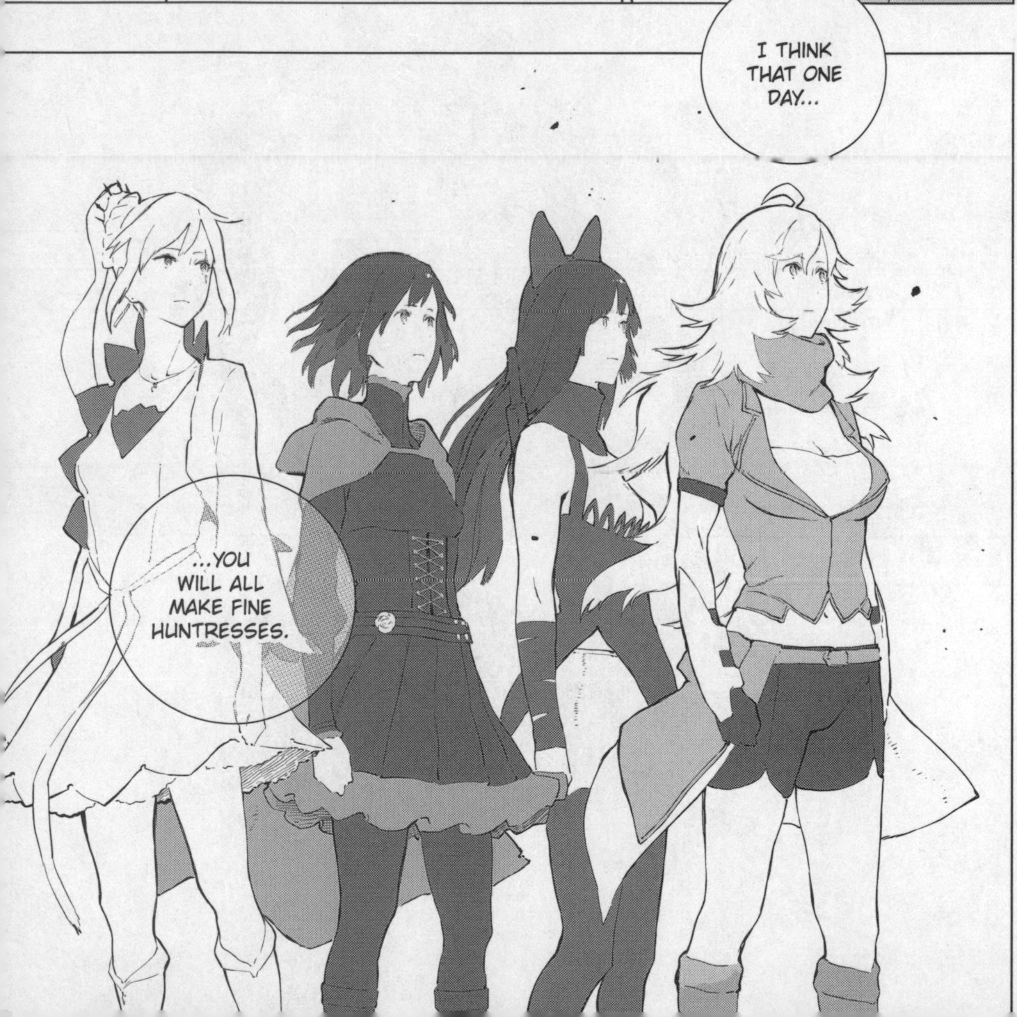
I THINK THAT ONE DAY...
...YOU WILL ALL MAKE FINE HUNTRESSES.

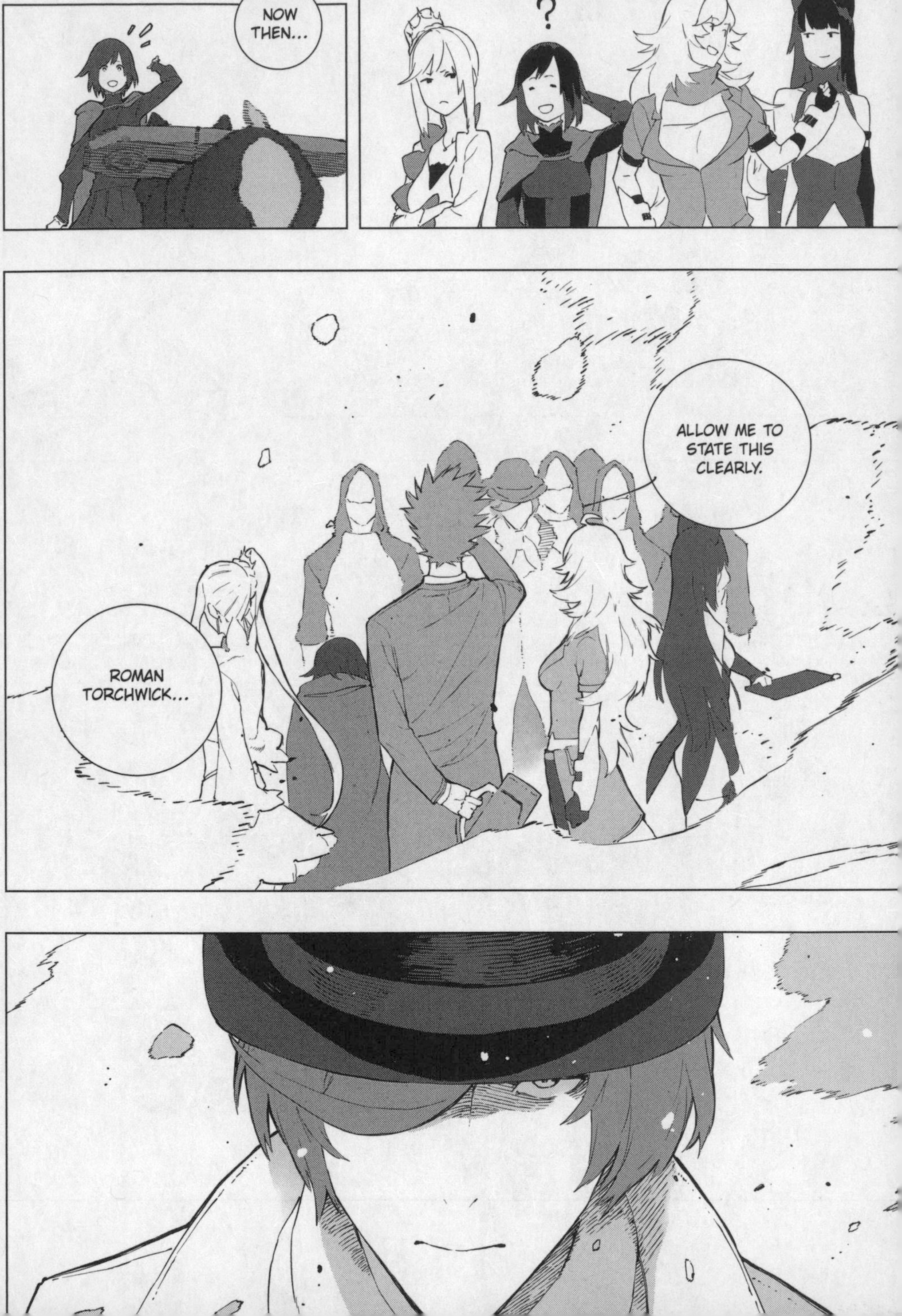
?
NOW THEN...
ALLOW ME TO STATE THIS CLEARLY.
ROMAN TORCHWICK...

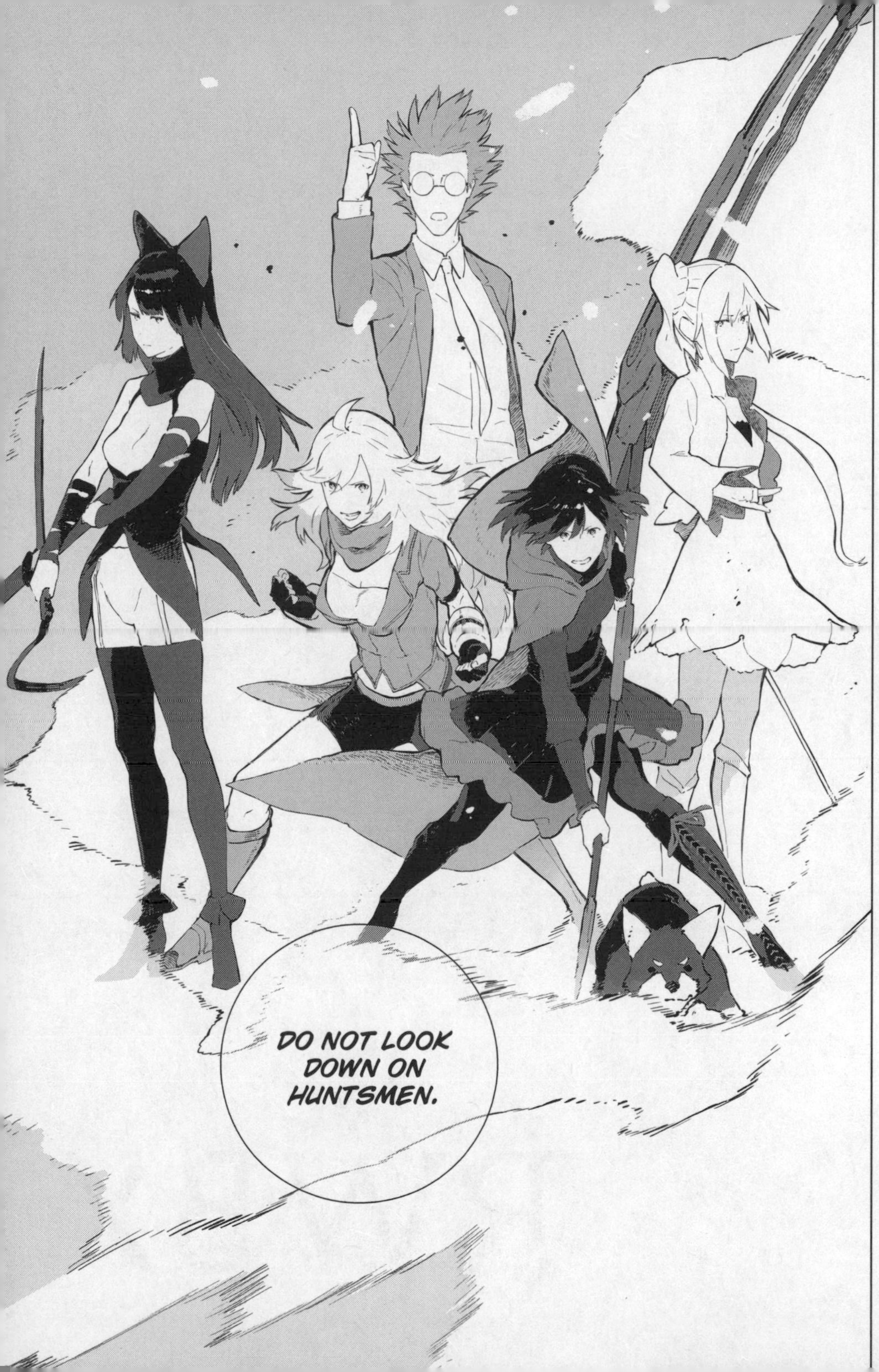
DO NOT LOOK DOWN ON HUNTSMEN.

RWBY

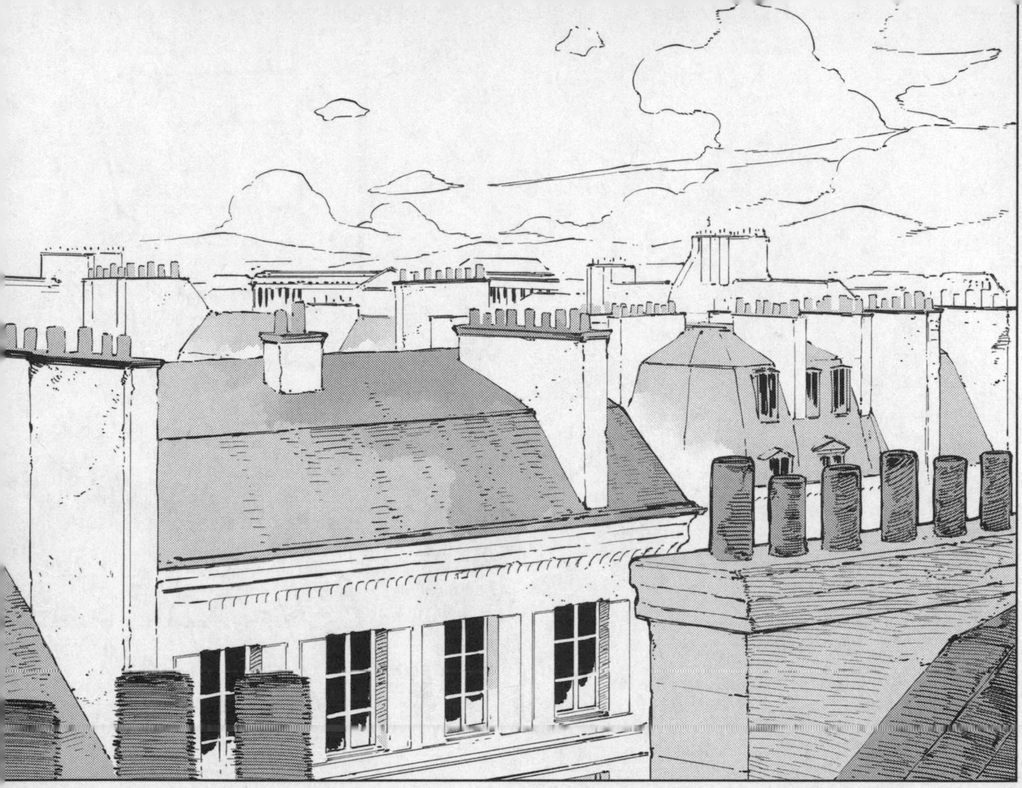

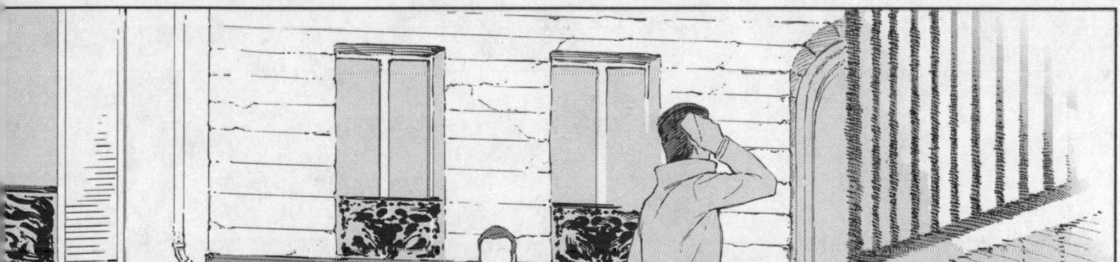

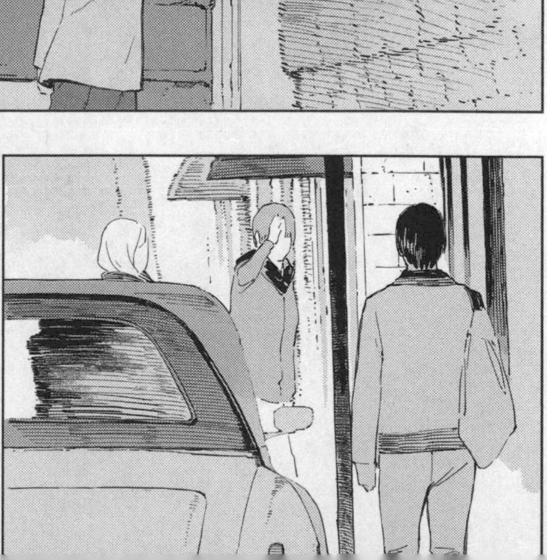

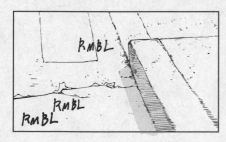

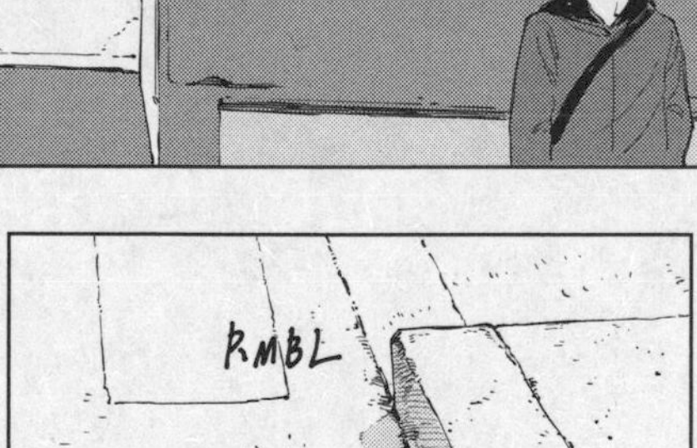
RMBL
RMBL
RMBL

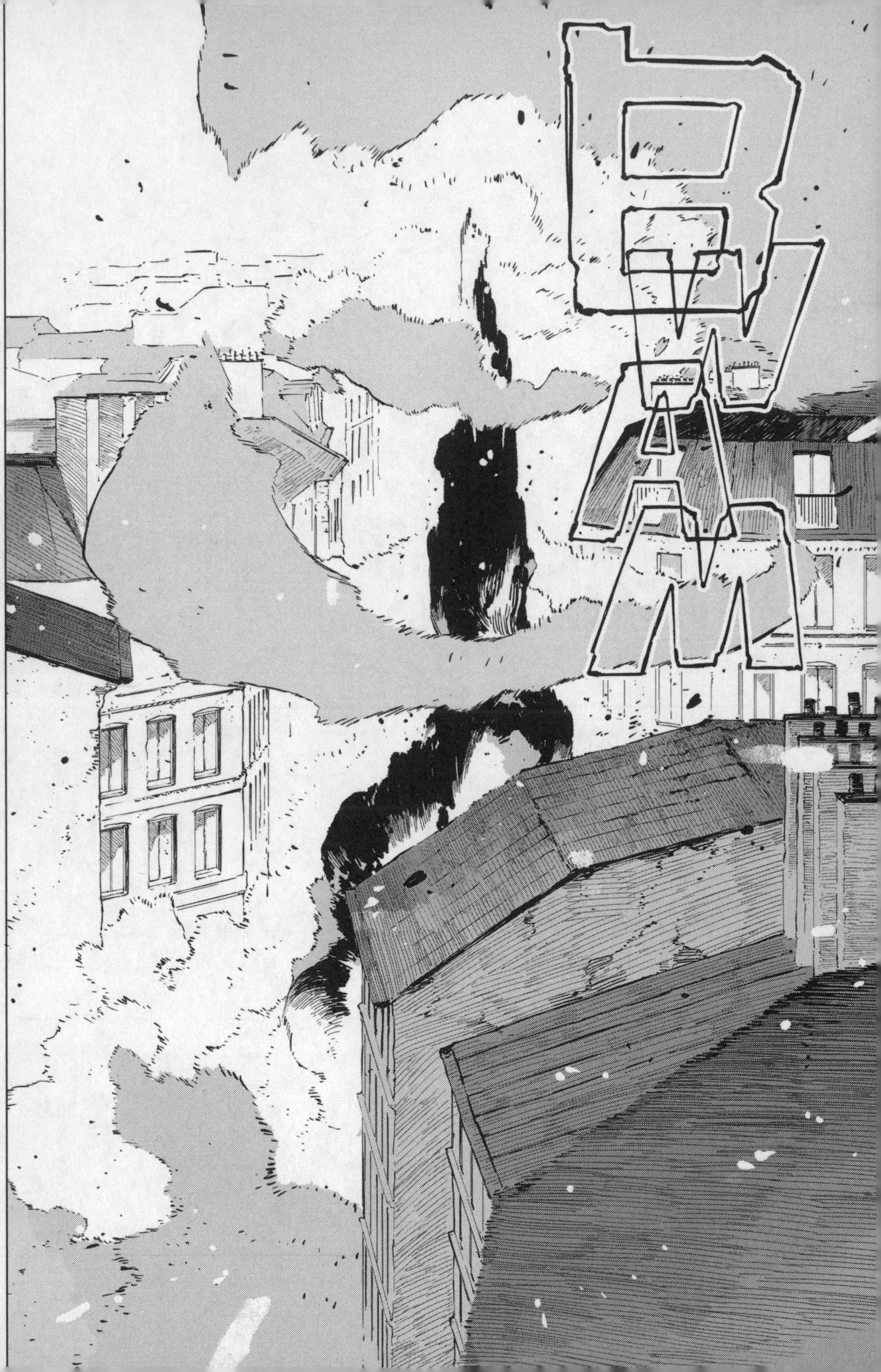
BWAM

Episode 17

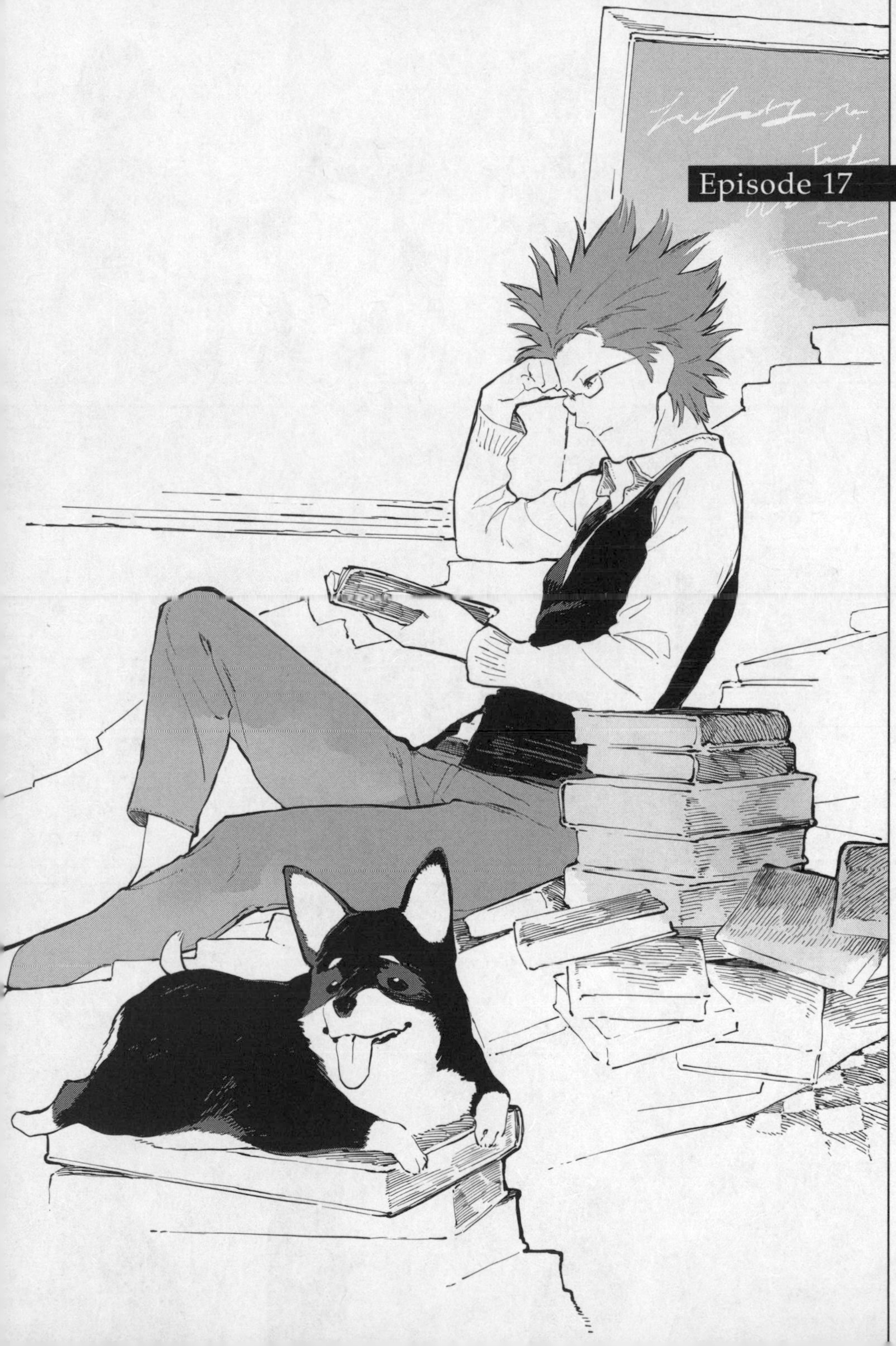

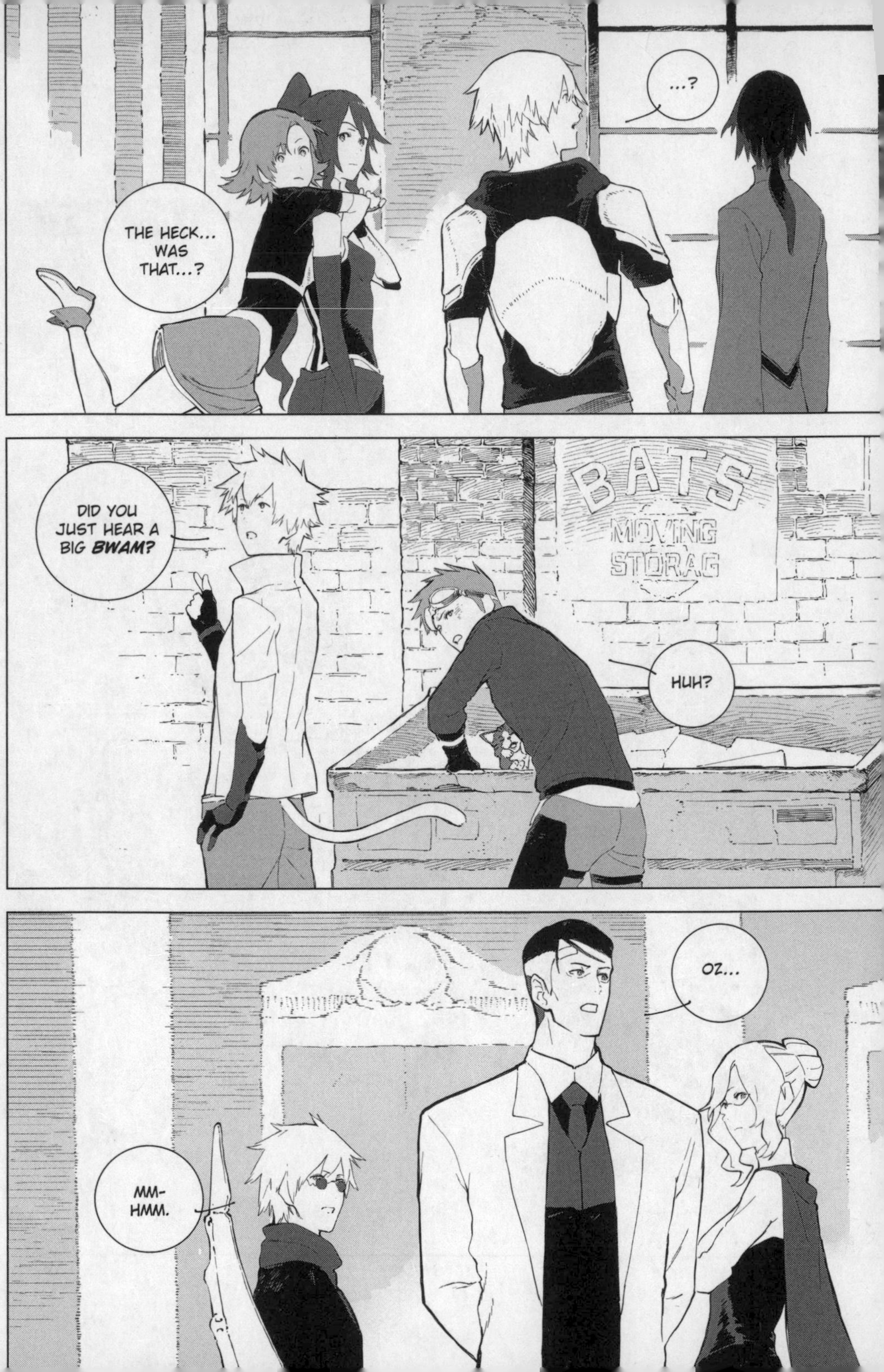
...?
THE HECK... WAS THAT...?
BATS
MOVING
STORAG
DID YOU JUST HEAR A BIG ***BWAM?***
HUH?
OZ...
MM-HMM.

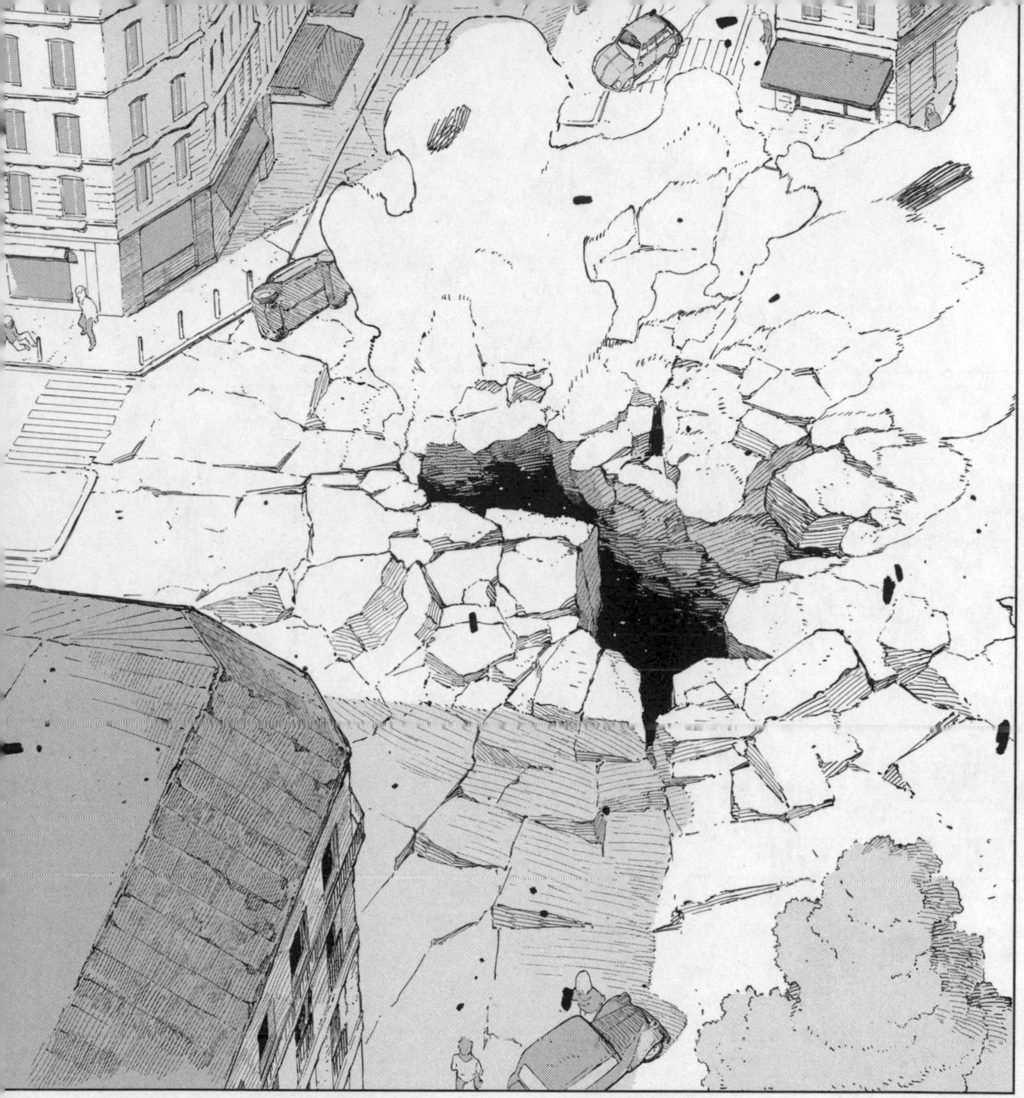
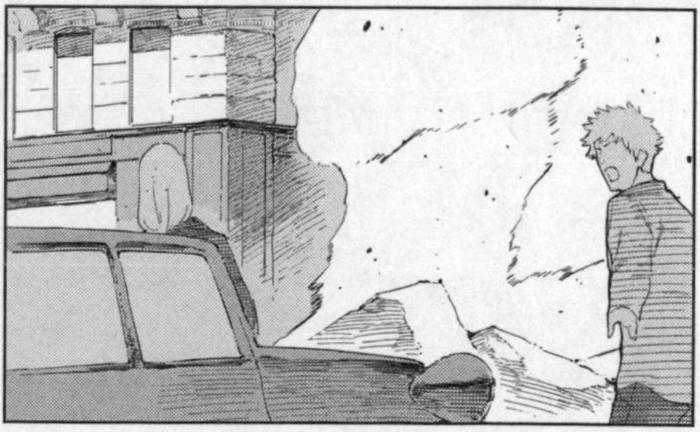
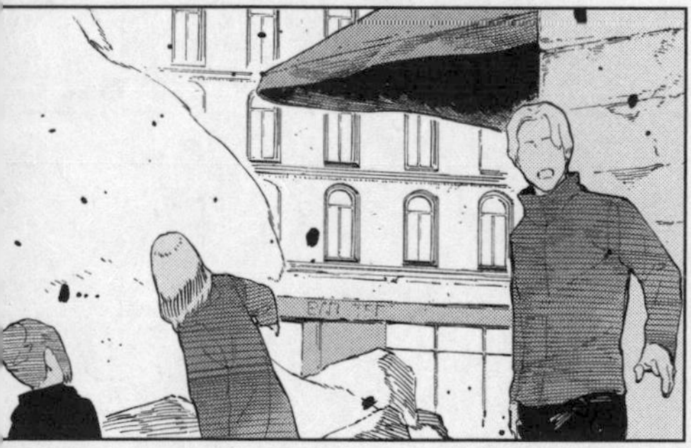

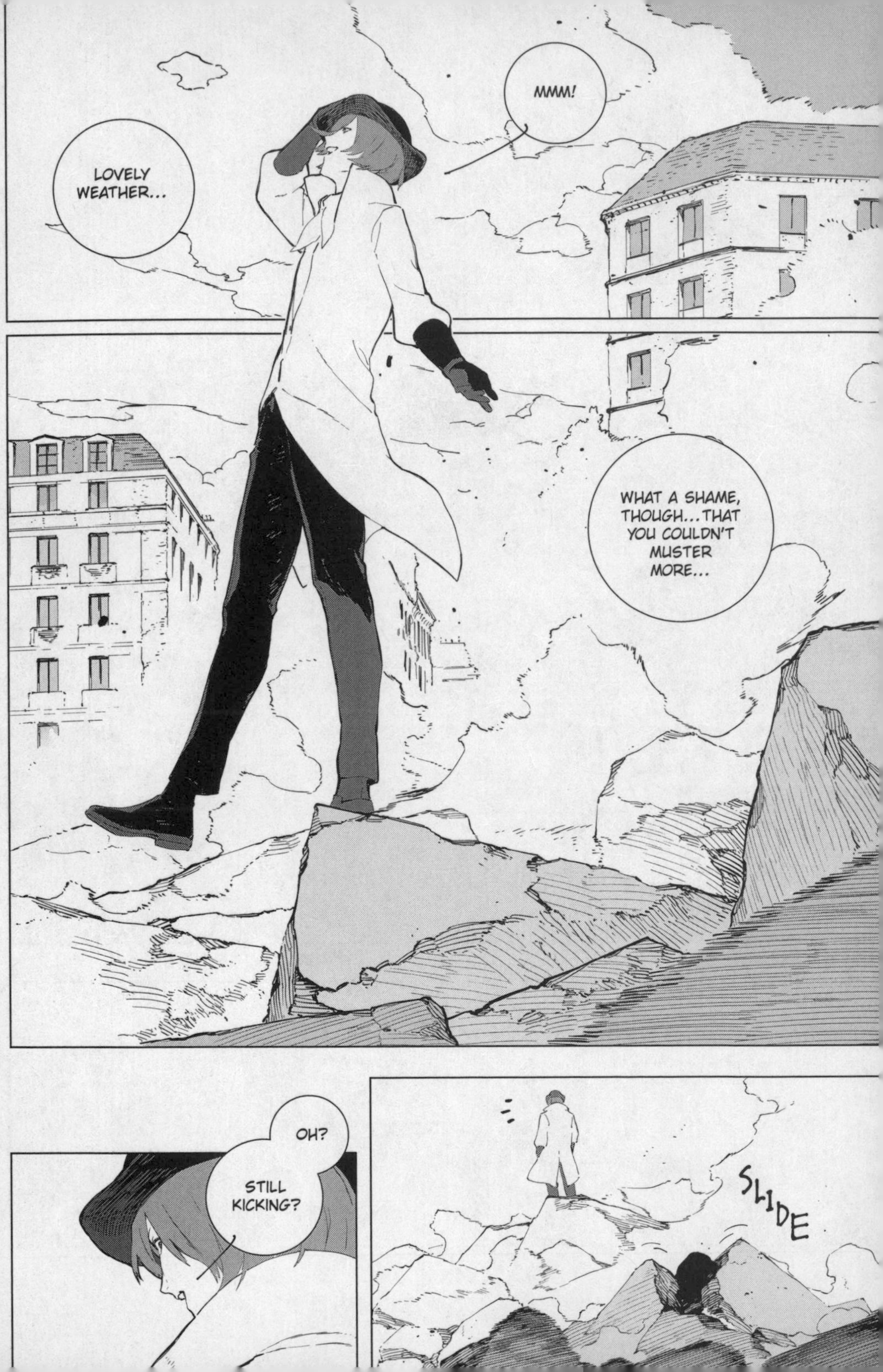
MMM!
LOVELY WEATHER...
WHAT A SHAME, THOUGH...THAT YOU COULDN'T MUSTER MORE...
SLIDE
OH?
STILL KICKING?

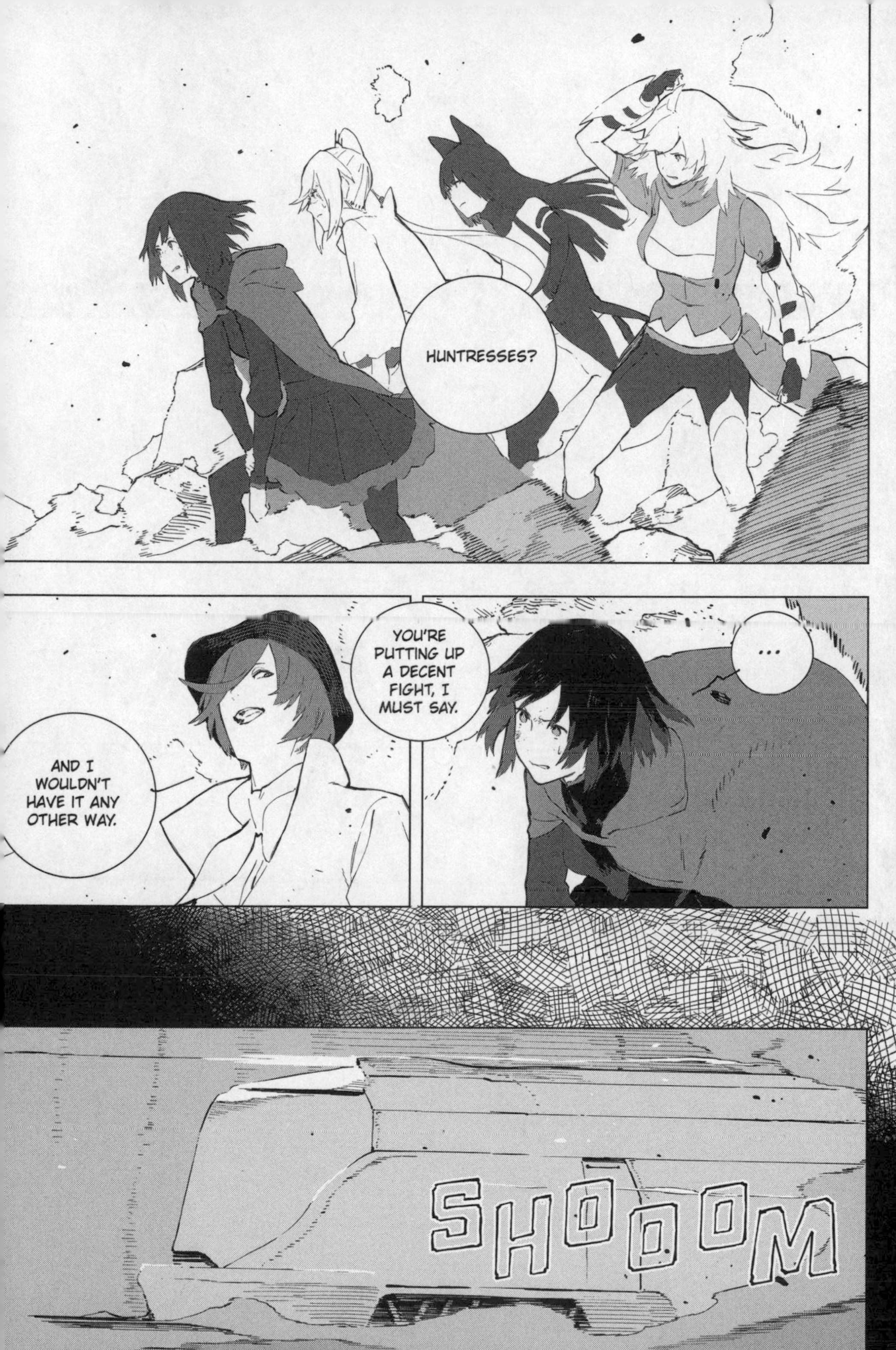
HUNTRESSES?
...
YOU'RE PUTTING UP A DECENT FIGHT, I MUST SAY.
AND I WOULDN'T HAVE IT ANY OTHER WAY.
SHOOOM

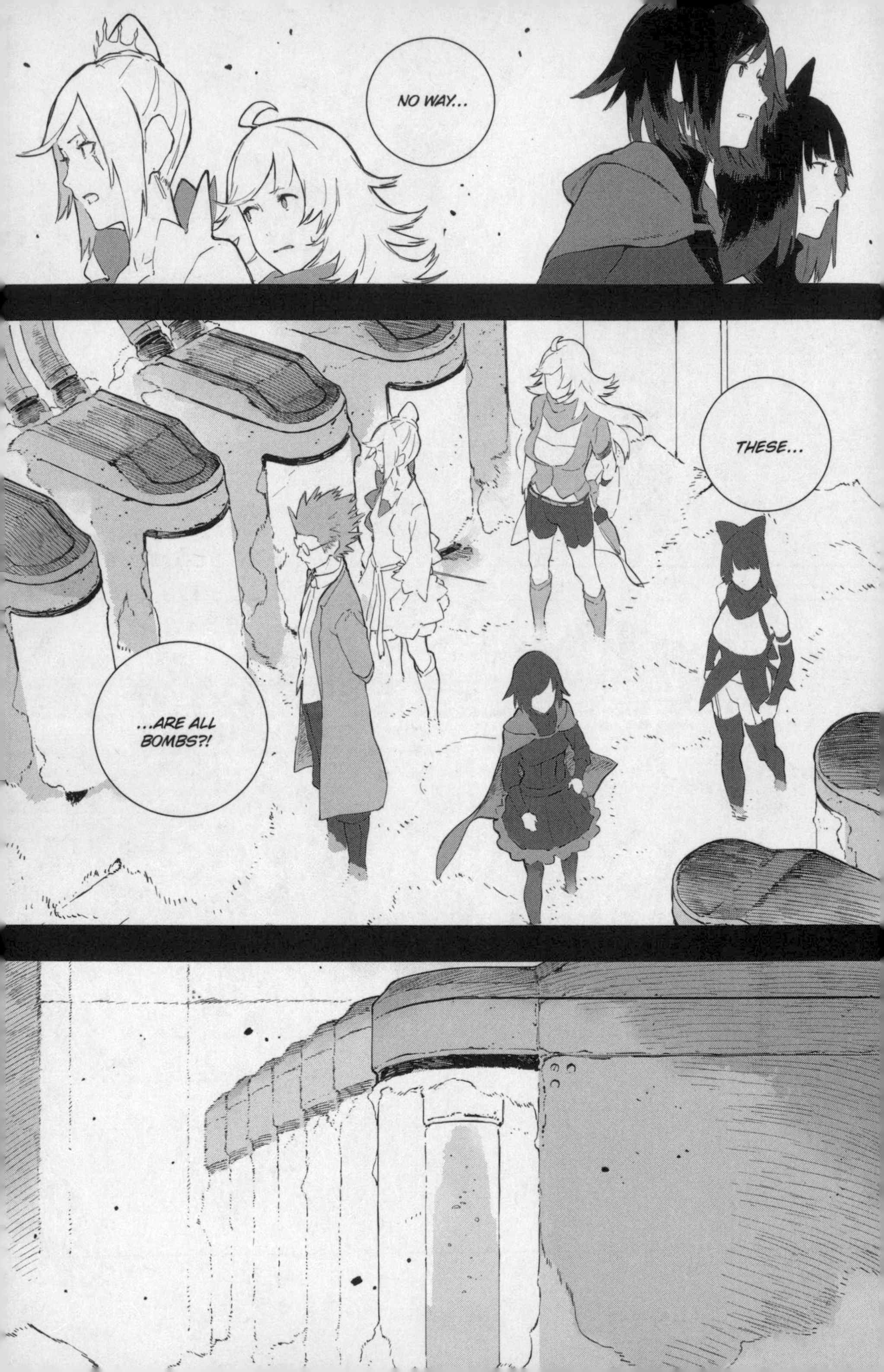
NO WAY...
THESE...
...ARE ALL BOMBS?!

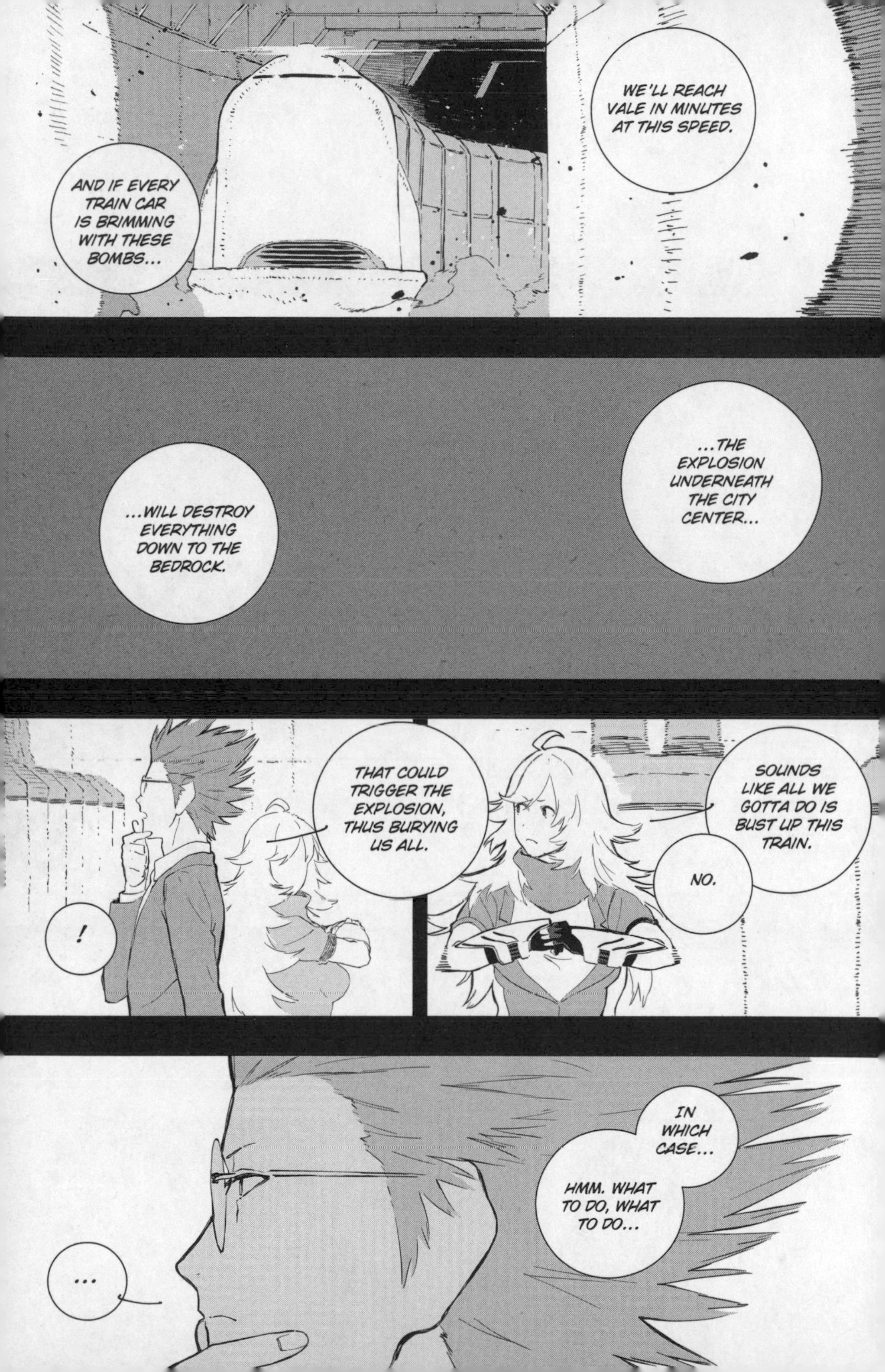
WE'LL REACH VALE IN MINUTES AT THIS SPEED.
AND IF EVERY TRAIN CAR IS BRIMMING WITH THESE BOMBS...
...THE EXPLOSION UNDERNEATH THE CITY CENTER...
...WILL DESTROY EVERYTHING DOWN TO THE BEDROCK.
SOUNDS LIKE ALL WE GOTTA DO IS BUST UP THIS TRAIN.
NO.
THAT COULD TRIGGER THE EXPLOSION, THUS BURYING US ALL.
!
IN WHICH CASE...
HMM. WHAT TO DO, WHAT TO DO...
...

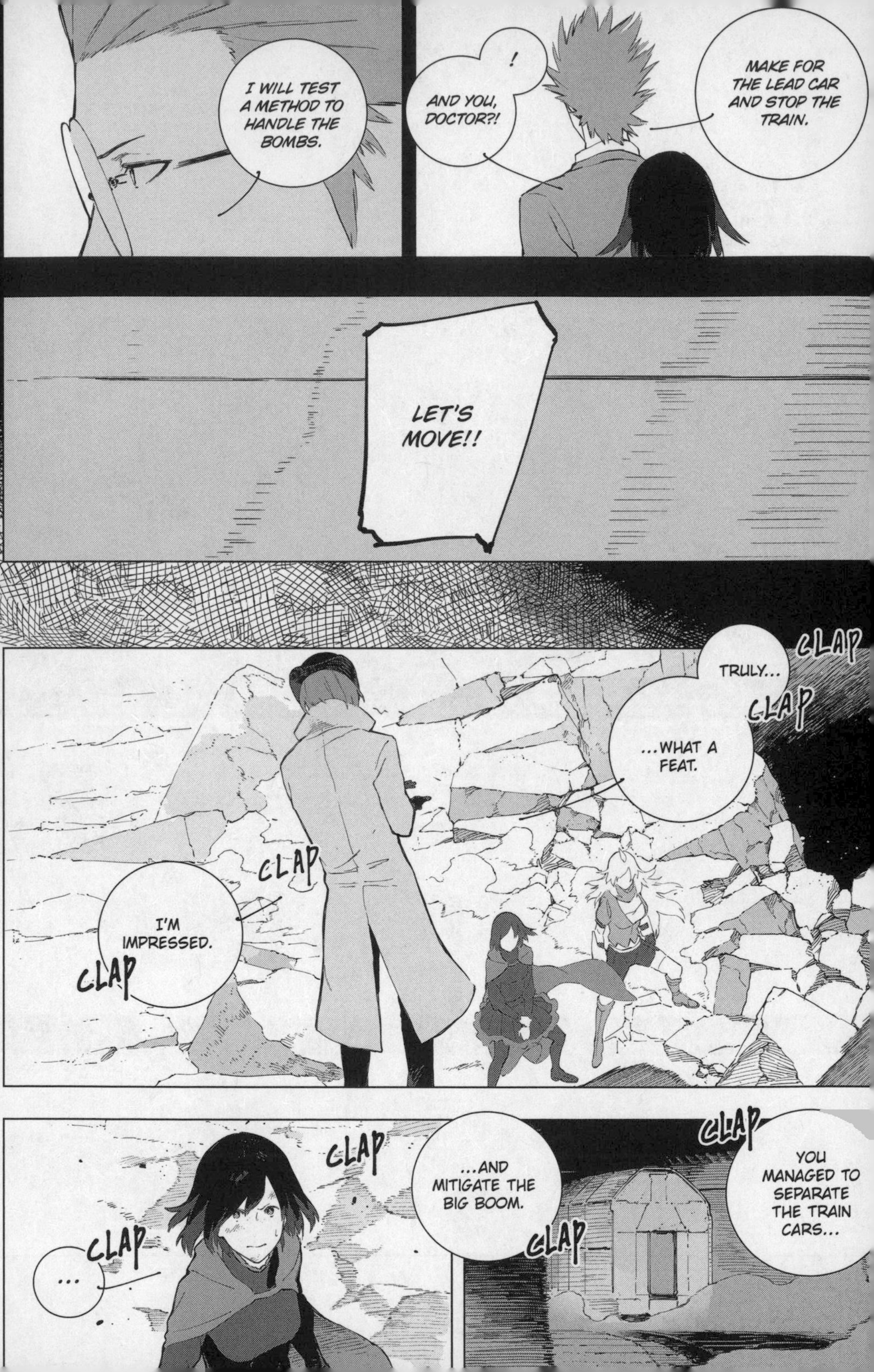
MAKE FOR THE LEAD CAR AND STOP THE TRAIN.
!
AND YOU, DOCTOR?!
I WILL TEST A METHOD TO HANDLE THE BOMBS.
LET'S MOVE!!
CLAP
TRULY...
CLAP
...WHAT A FEAT.
CLAP
I'M IMPRESSED.
CLAP
CLAP
YOU MANAGED TO SEPARATE THE TRAIN CARS...
...AND MITIGATE THE BIG BOOM.
CLAP
CLAP
CLAP
...

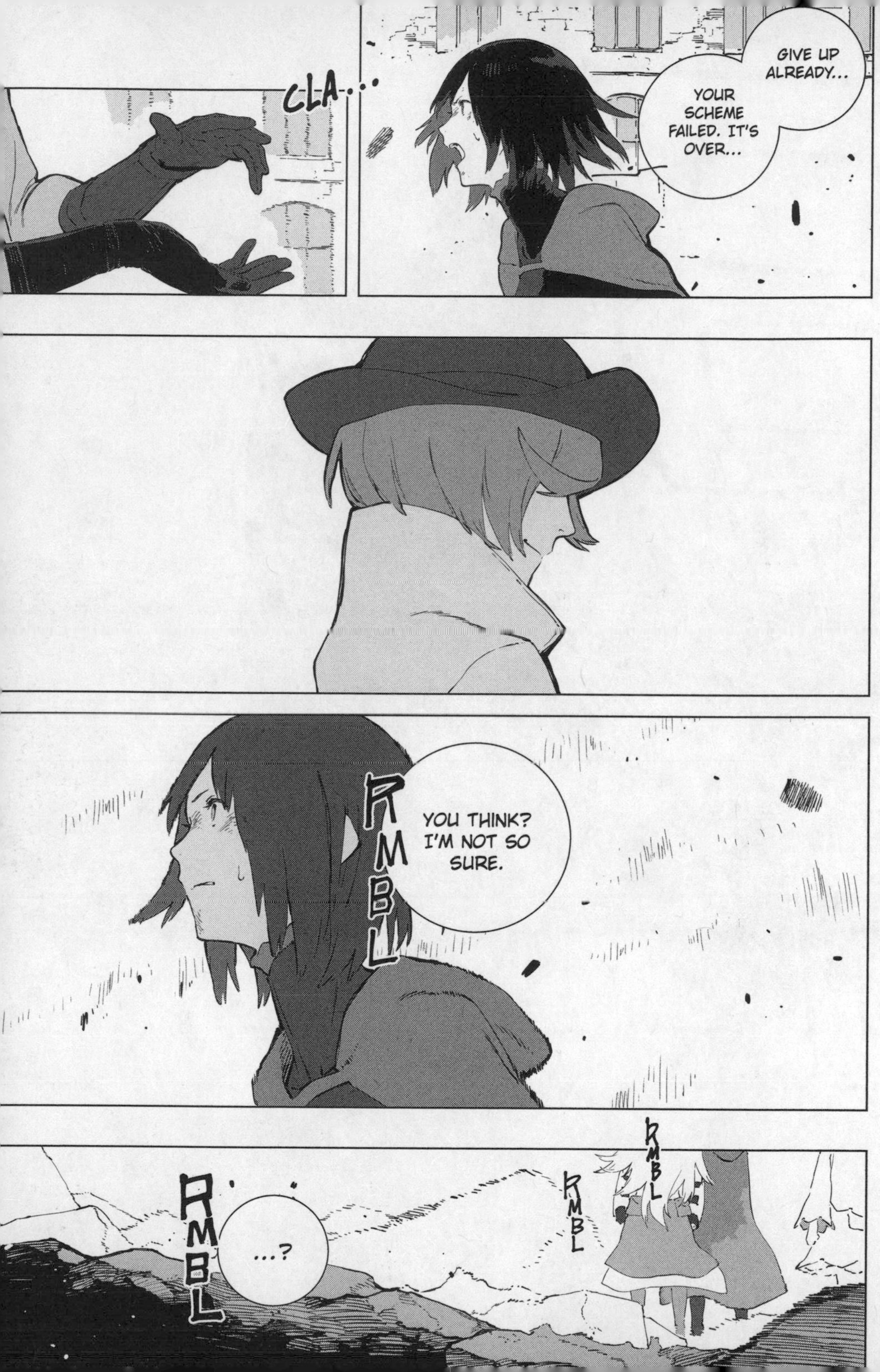
GIVE UP ALREADY...
YOUR SCHEME FAILED. IT'S OVER...
CLA...
YOU THINK? I'M NOT SO SURE.
RMBL
RMBL
RMBL
...?
RMBL

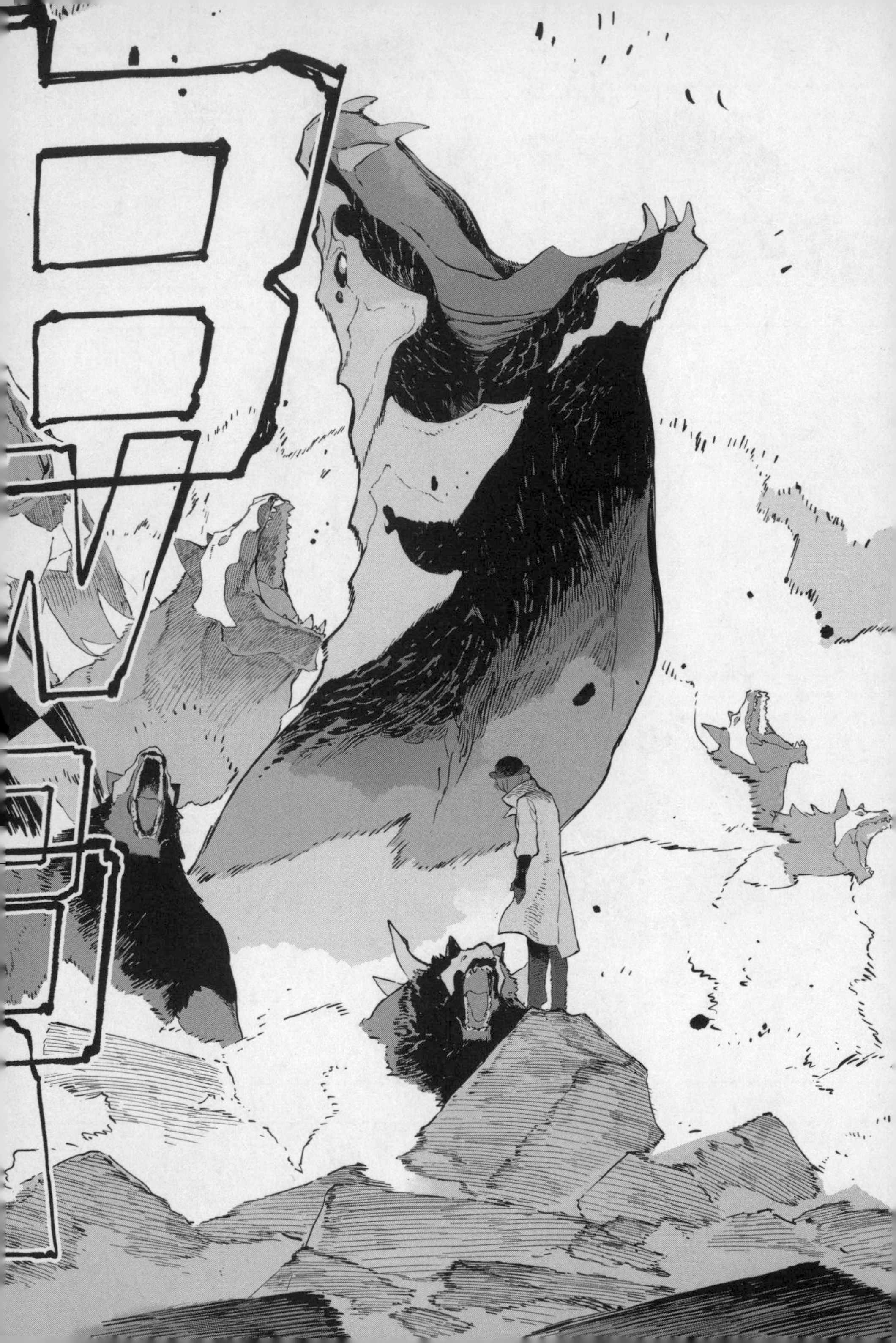

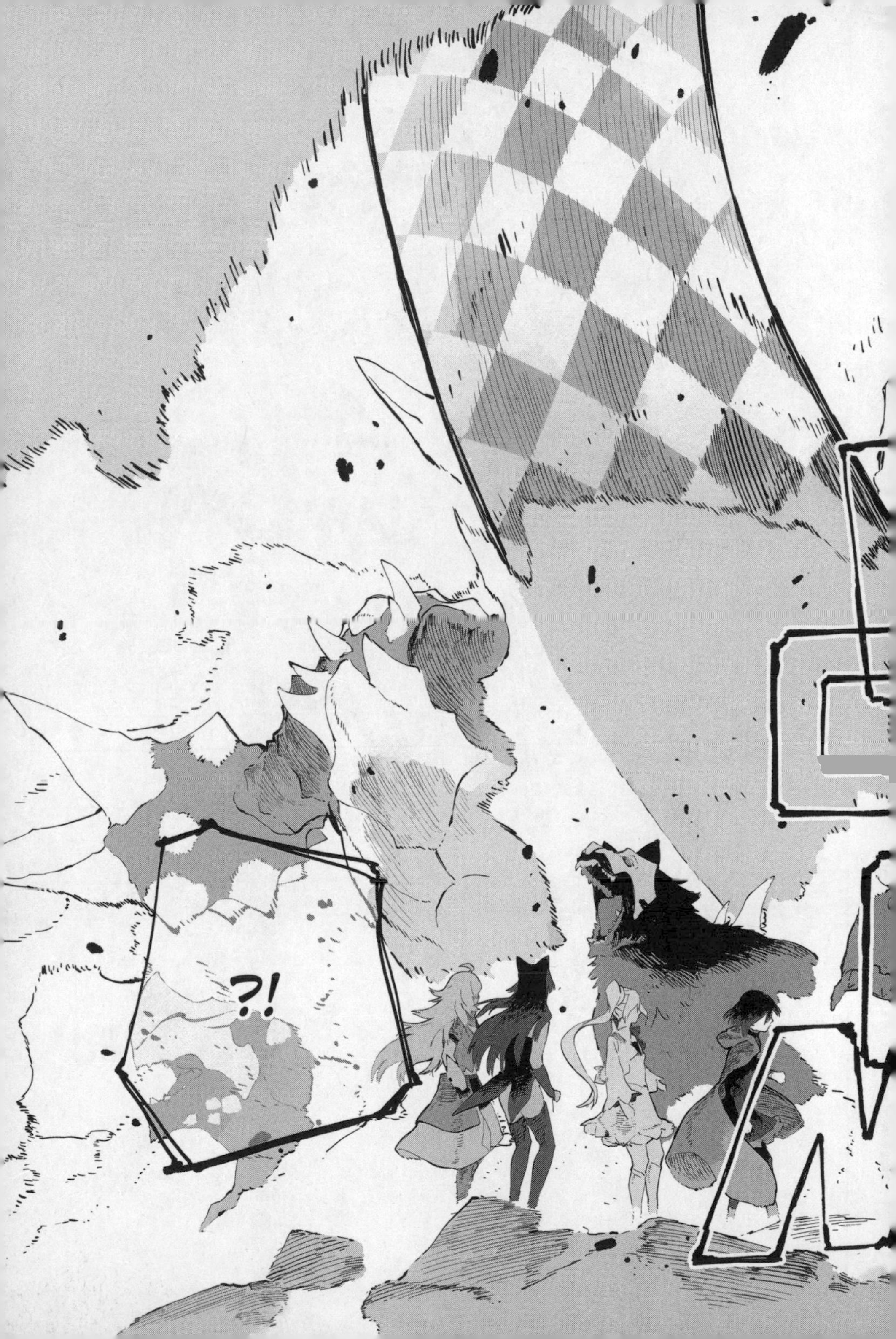
?!

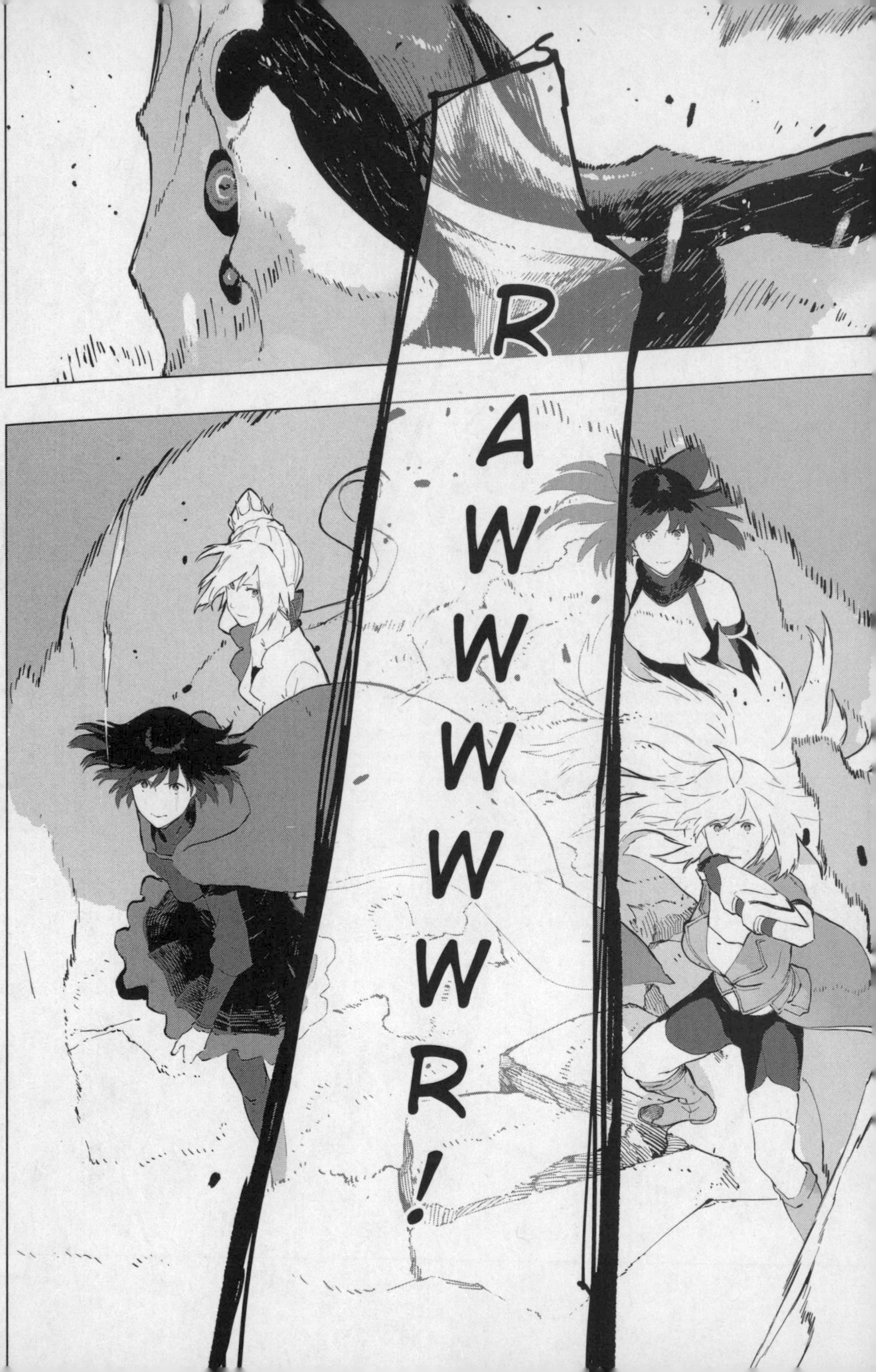
RAWWWWR!

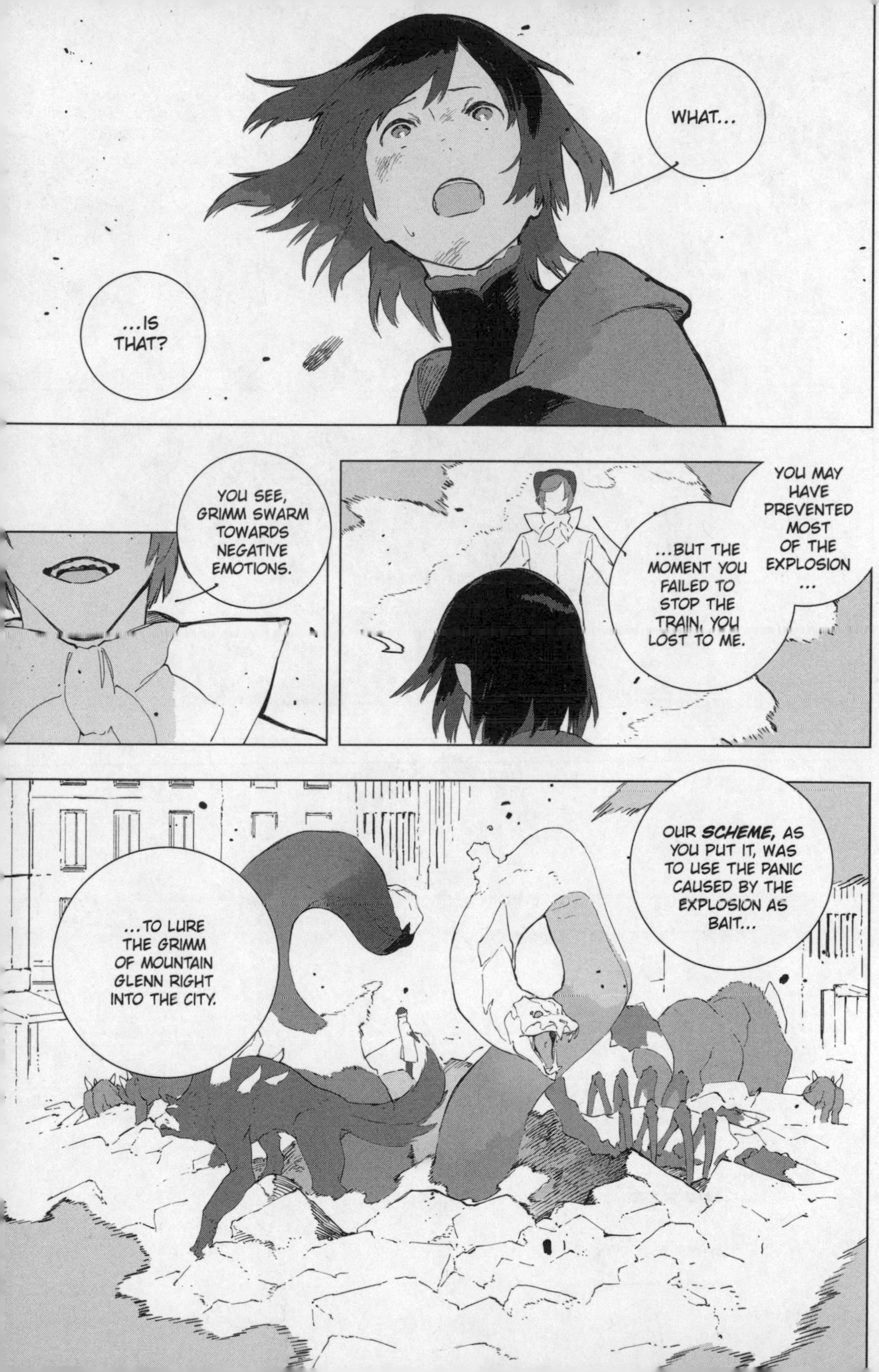
WHAT...
...IS THAT?
YOU MAY HAVE PREVENTED MOST OF THE EXPLOSION ...
...BUT THE MOMENT YOU FAILED TO STOP THE TRAIN, YOU LOST TO ME.
YOU SEE, GRIMM SWARM TOWARDS NEGATIVE EMOTIONS.
OUR ***SCHEME,*** AS YOU PUT IT, WAS TO USE THE PANIC CAUSED BY THE EXPLOSION AS BAIT...
...TO LURE THE GRIMM OF MOUNTAIN GLENN RIGHT INTO THE CITY.

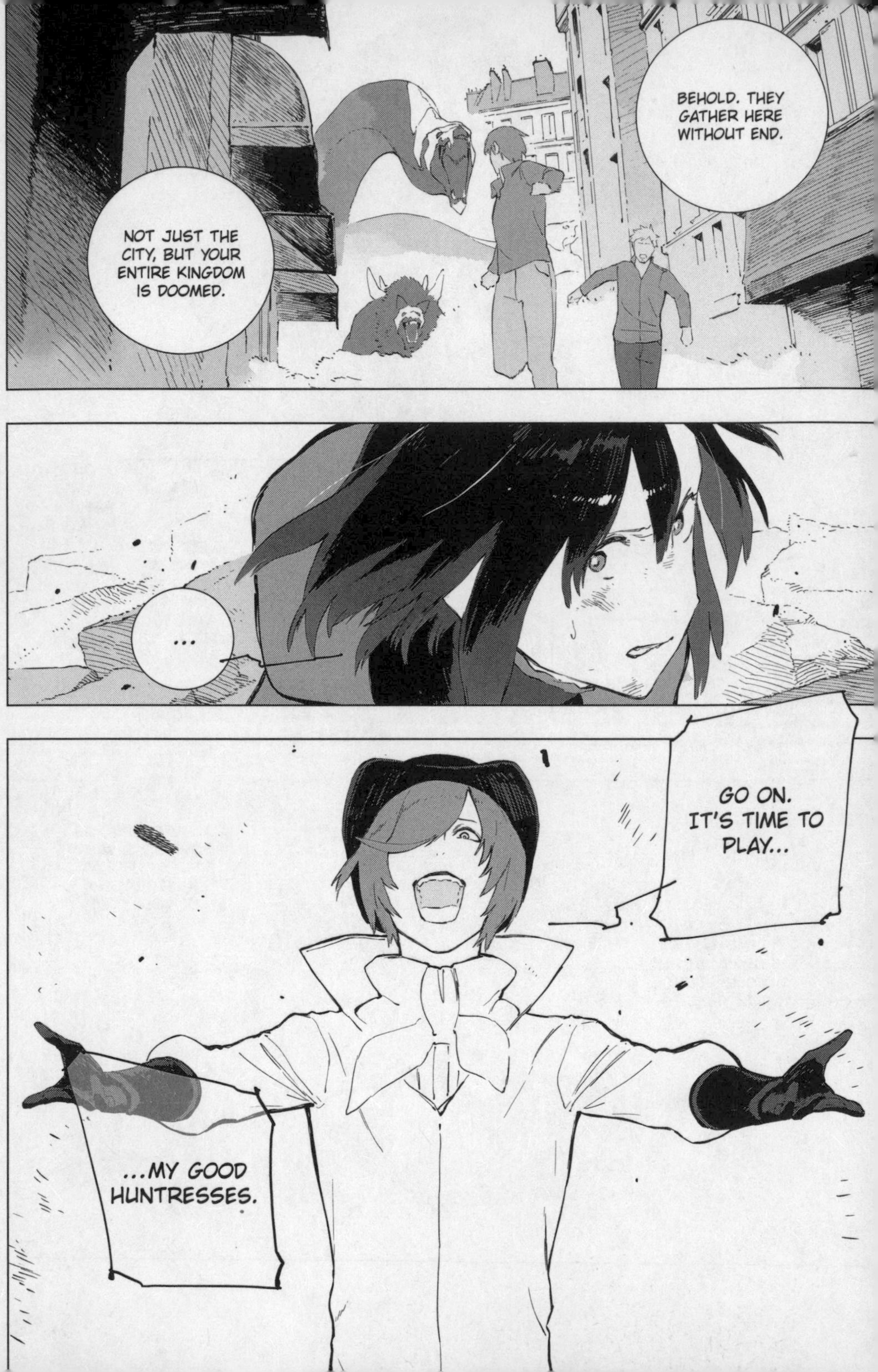
BEHOLD. THEY GATHER HERE WITHOUT END.
NOT JUST THE CITY, BUT YOUR ENTIRE KINGDOM IS DOOMED.
...
GO ON. IT'S TIME TO PLAY...
...MY GOOD HUNTRESSES.

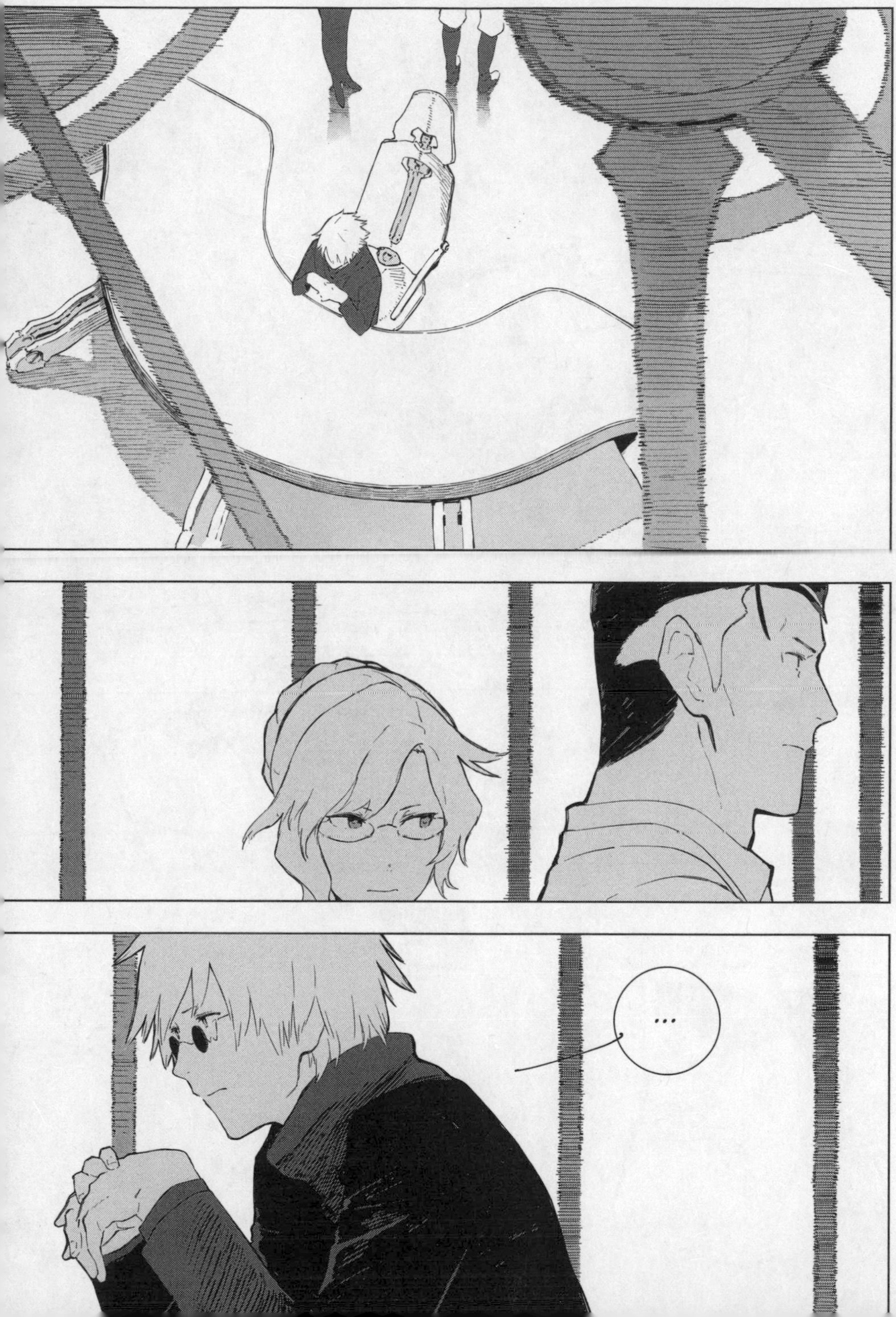
...

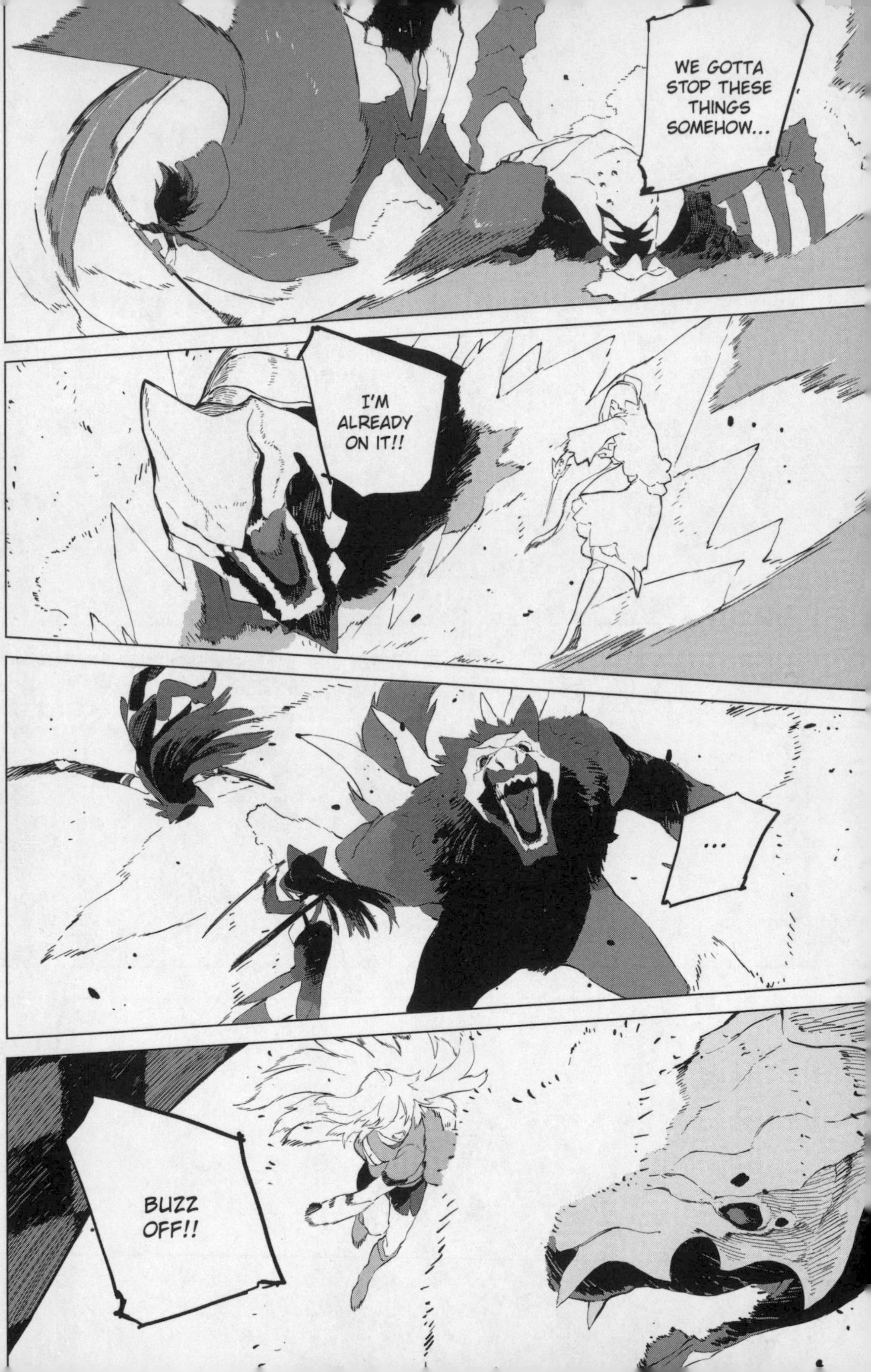
WE GOTTA STOP THESE THINGS SOMEHOW...
I'M ALREADY ON IT!!
...
BUZZ OFF!!

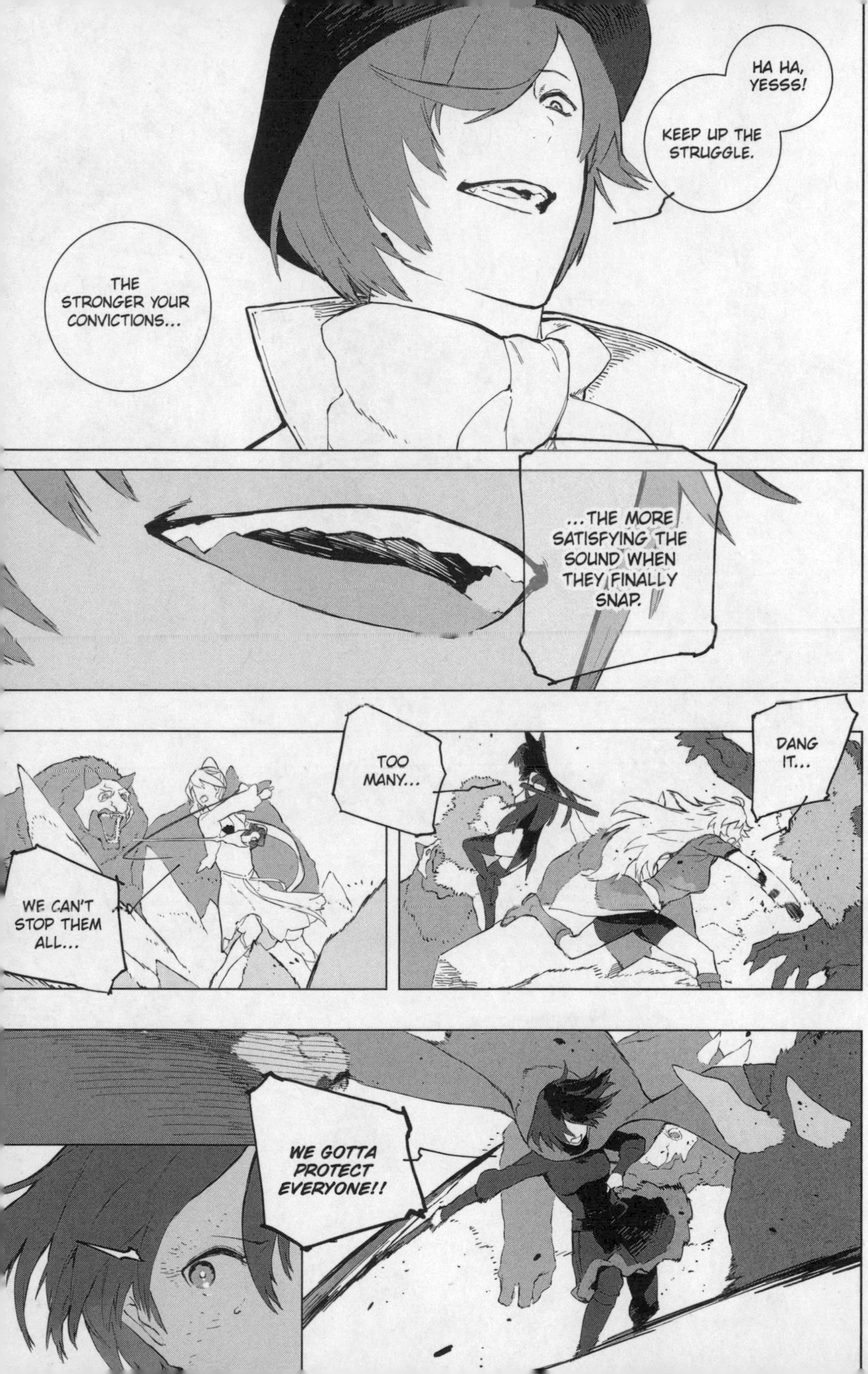
HA HA, YESSS!
KEEP UP THE STRUGGLE.
THE STRONGER YOUR CONVICTIONS...
...THE MORE SATISFYING THE SOUND WHEN THEY FINALLY SNAP.
DANG IT...
TOO MANY...
WE CAN'T STOP THEM ALL...
WE GOTTA PROTECT EVERYONE!!

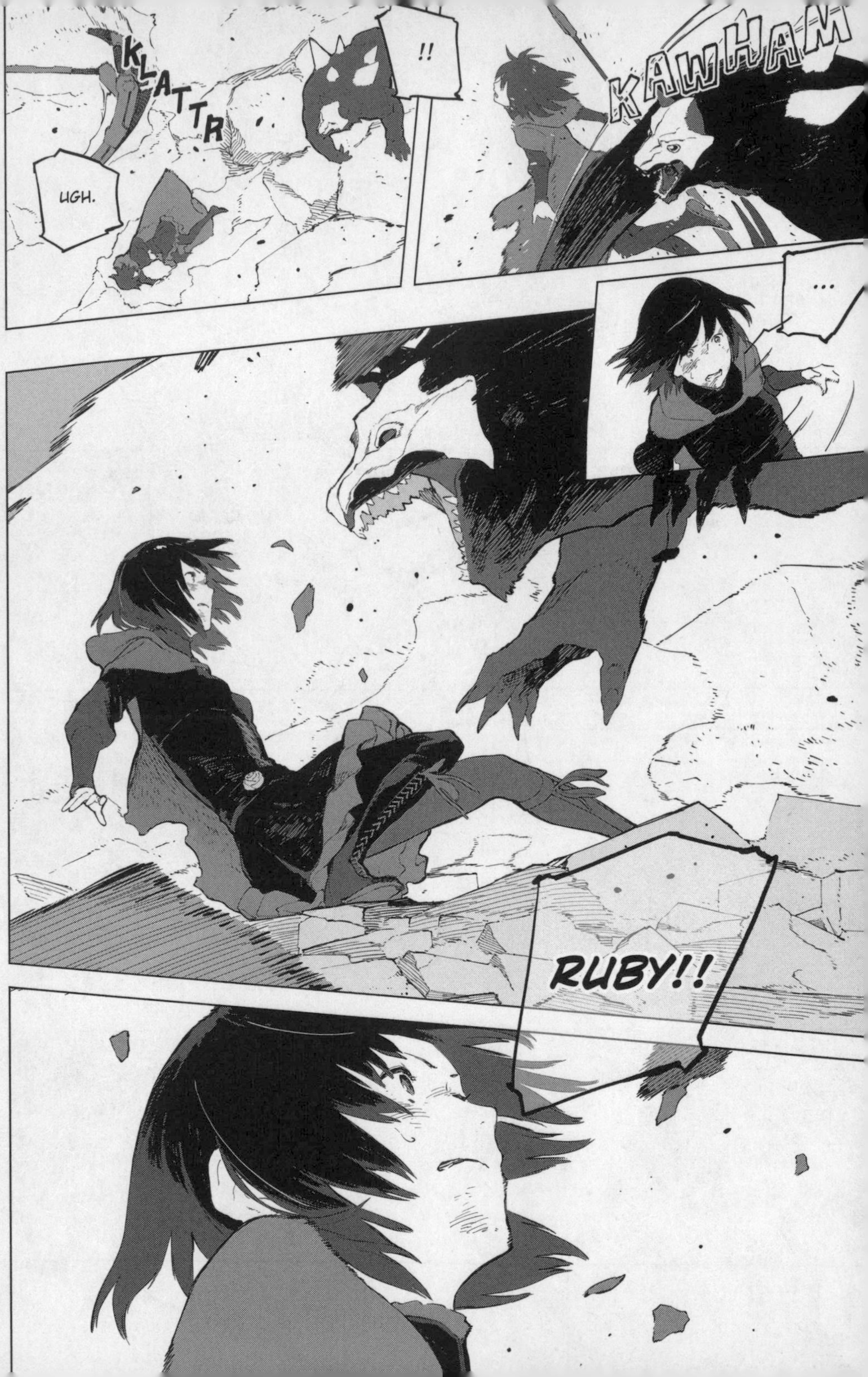
KAWHAM
!!
KLATTR
UGH.
...
RUBY!!

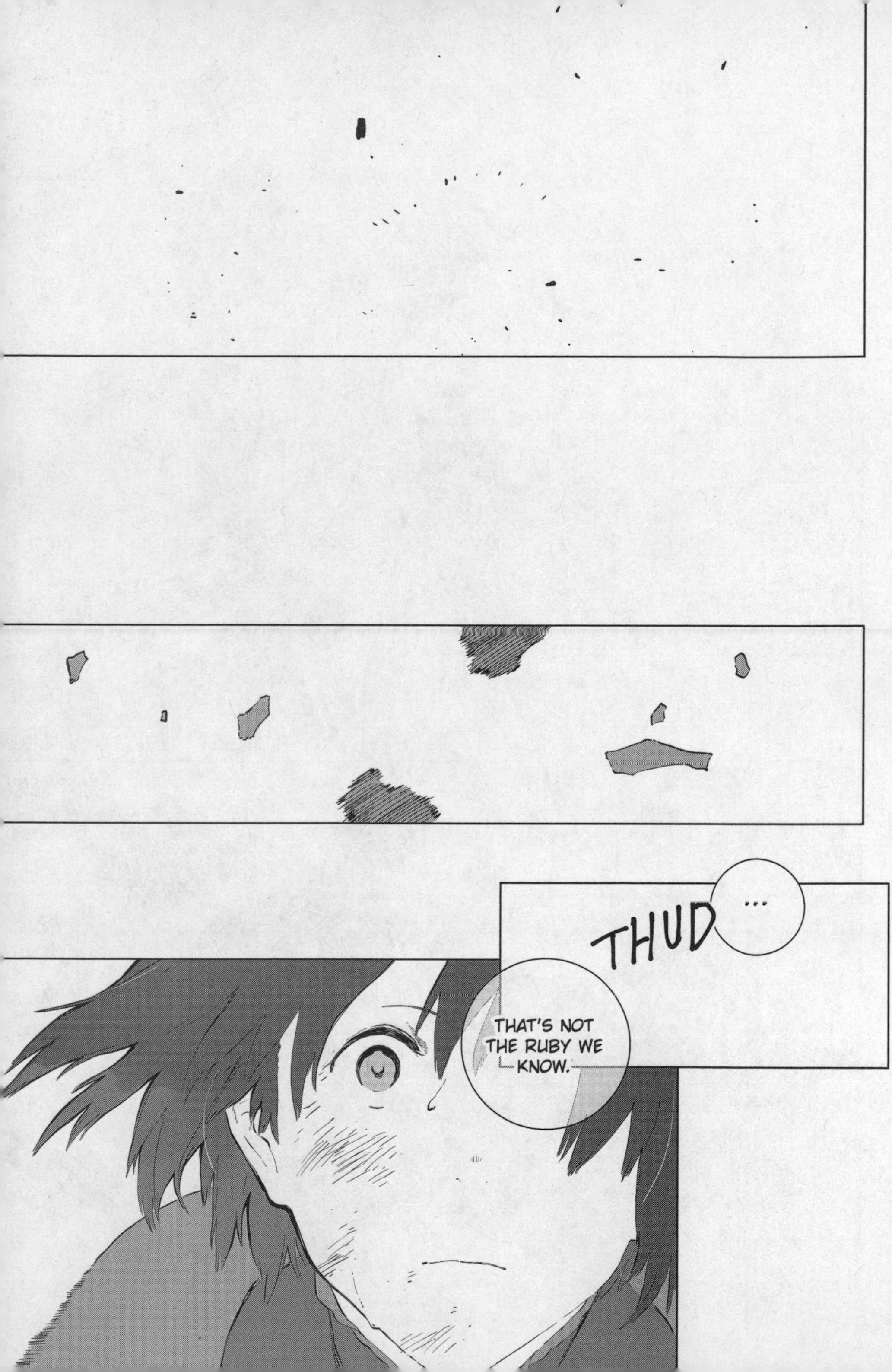
THUD
...
THAT'S NOT THE RUBY WE KNOW.

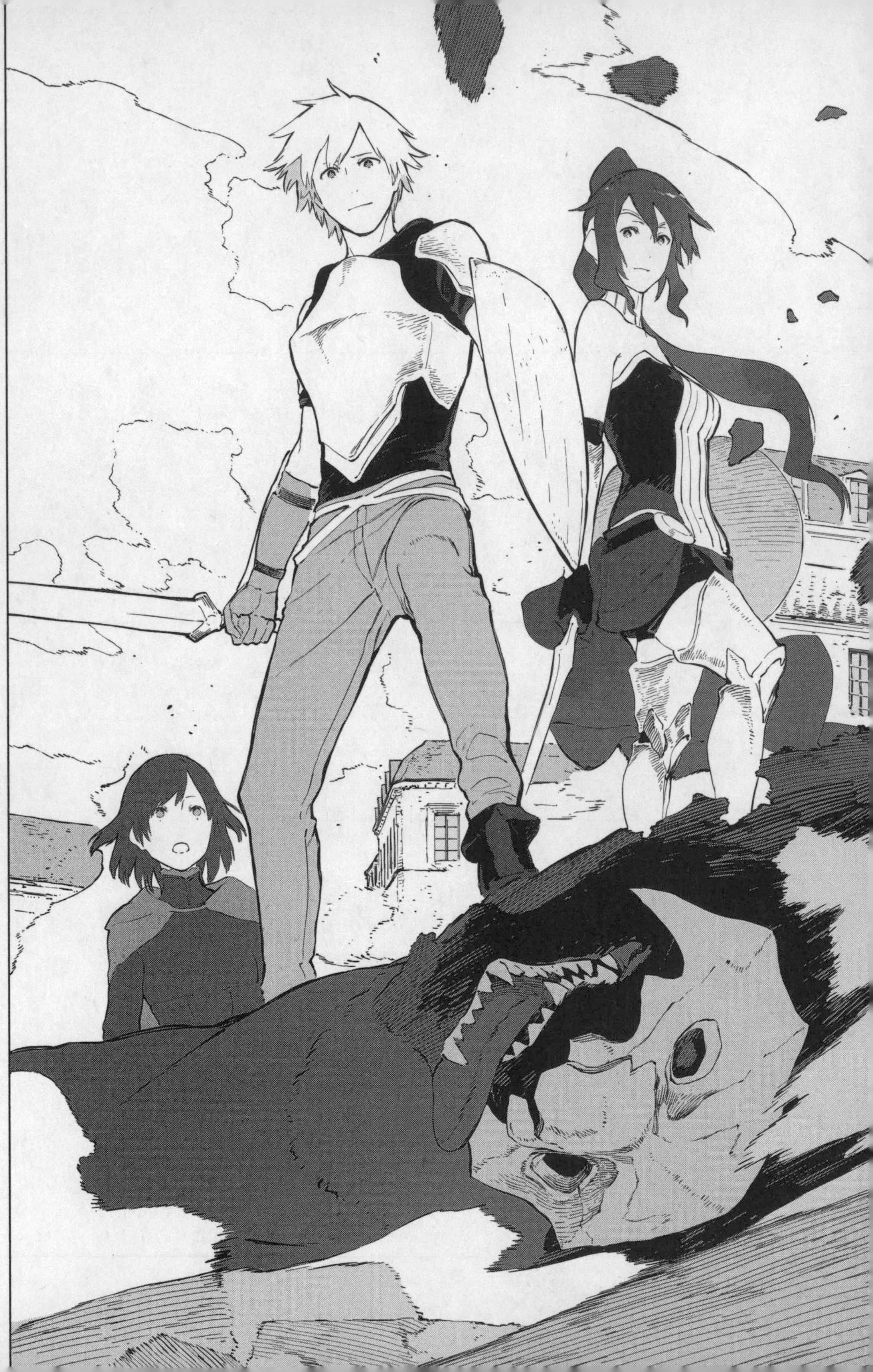

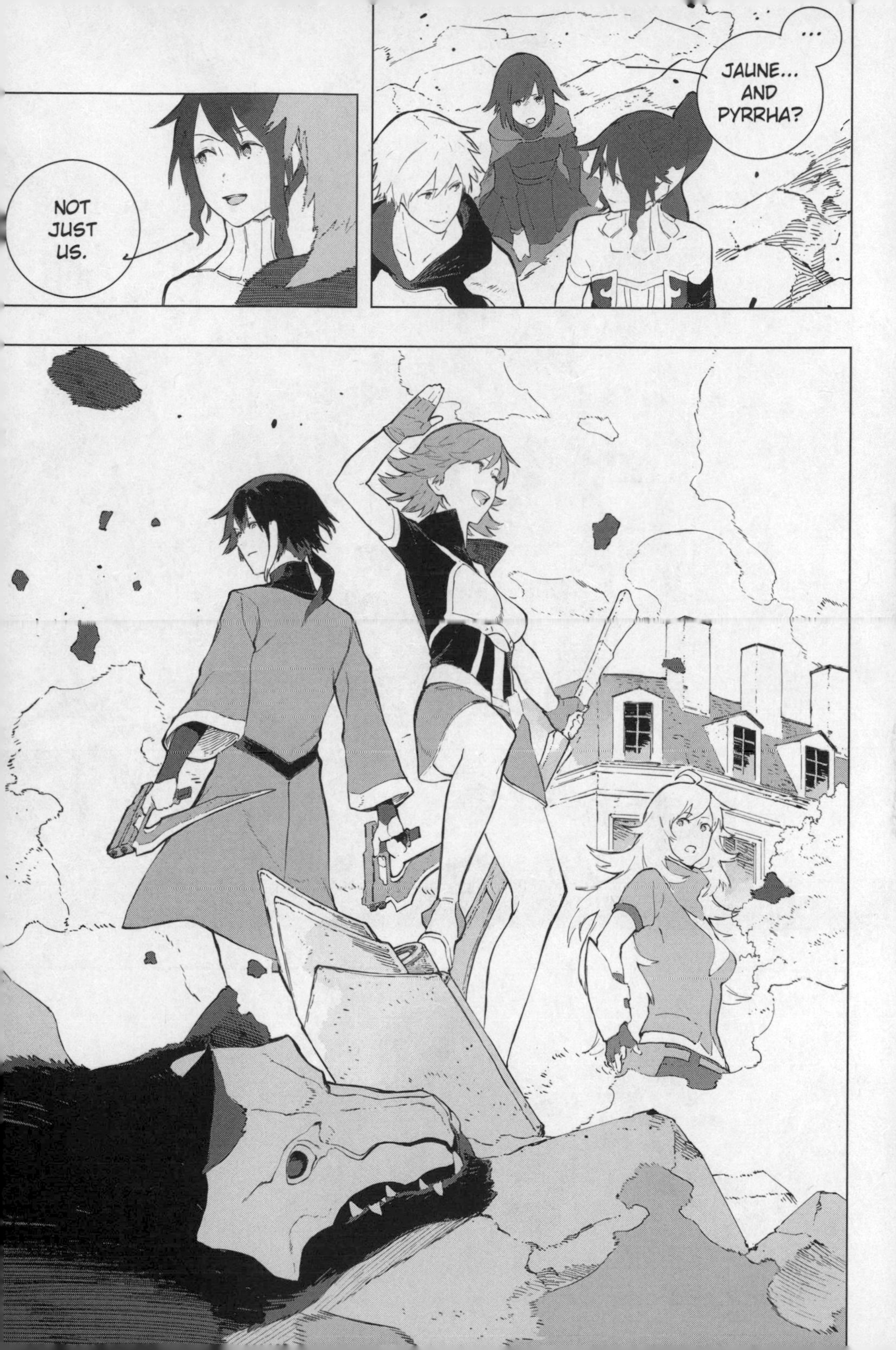
...
JAUNE... AND PYRRHA?
NOT JUST US.

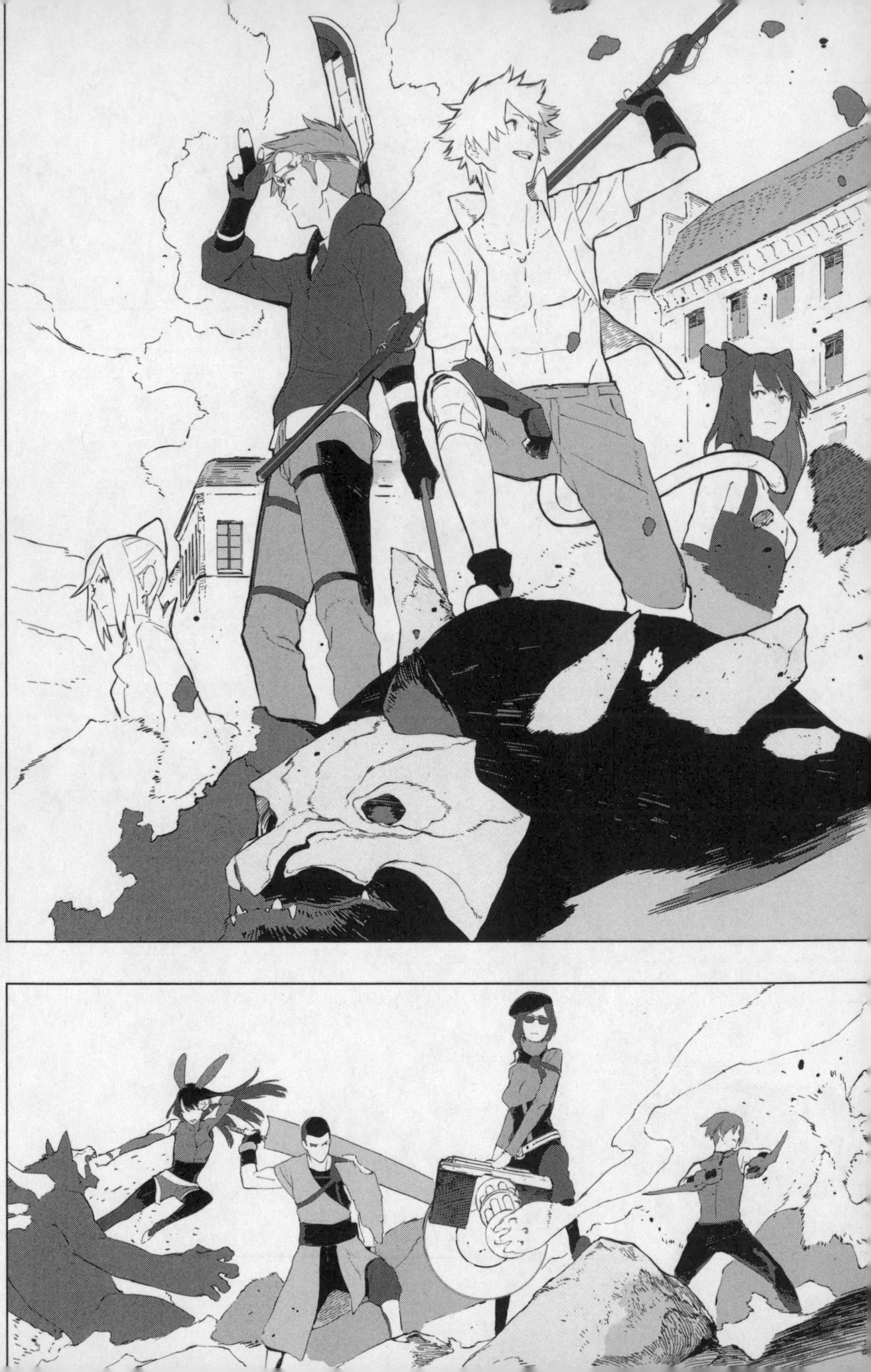

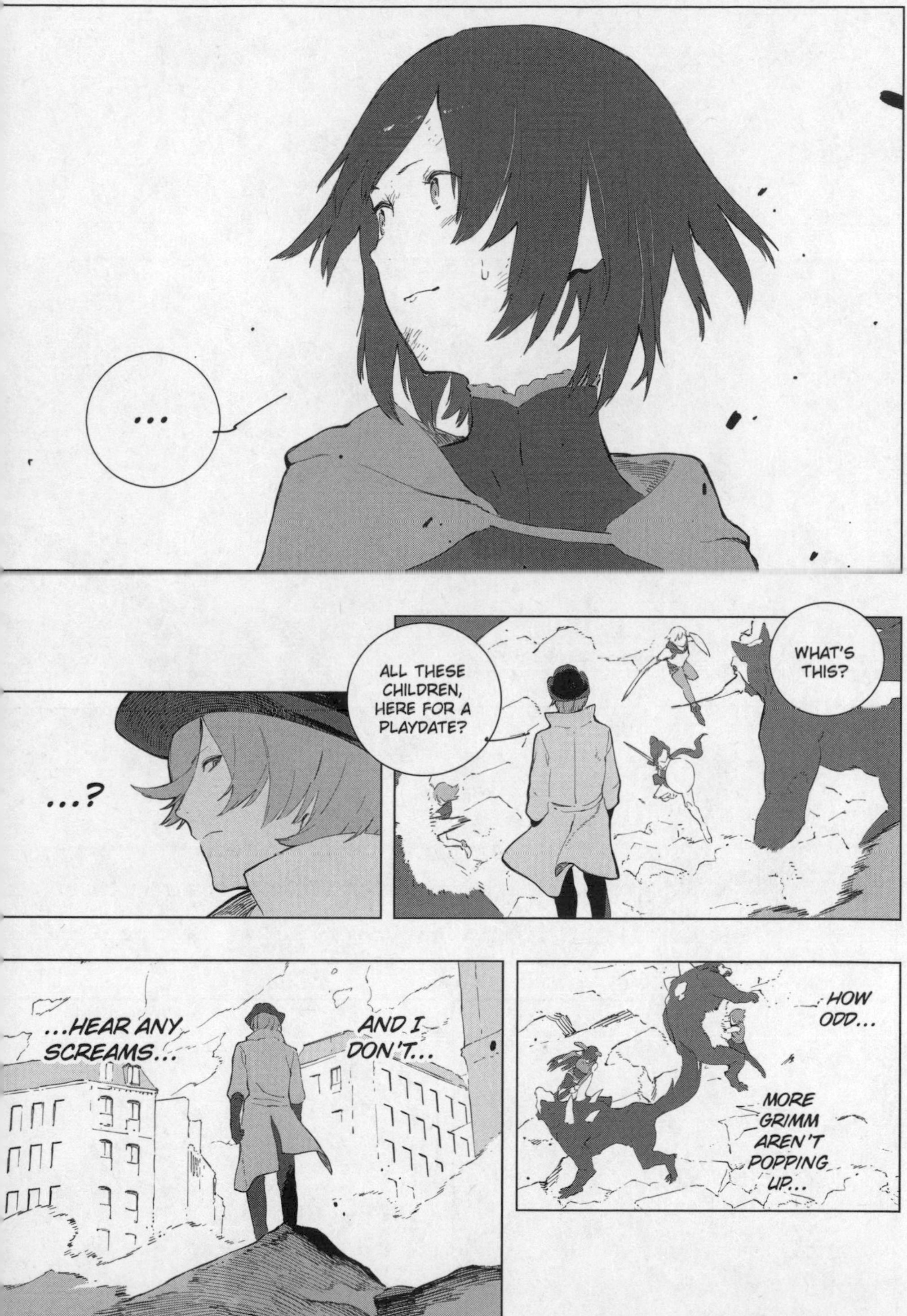
...
WHAT'S THIS?
ALL THESE CHILDREN, HERE FOR A PLAYDATE?
...?
HOW ODD...
MORE GRIMM AREN'T POPPING UP...
AND I DON'T...
...HEAR ANY SCREAMS...

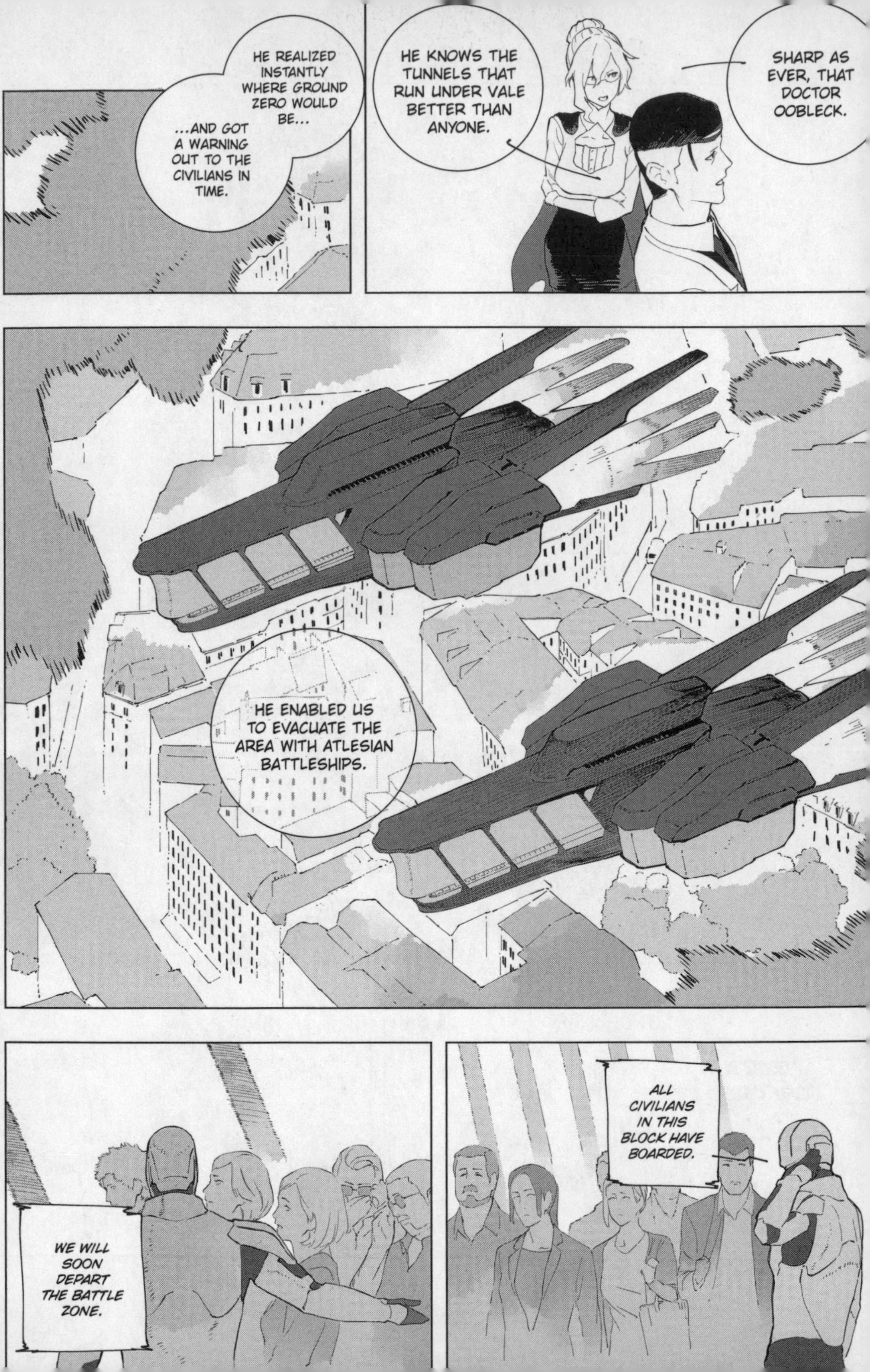
SHARP AS EVER, THAT DOCTOR OOBLECK.
HE KNOWS THE TUNNELS THAT RUN UNDER VALE BETTER THAN ANYONE.
HE REALIZED INSTANTLY WHERE GROUND ZERO WOULD BE...
...AND GOT A WARNING OUT TO THE CIVILIANS IN TIME.
HE ENABLED US TO EVACUATE THE AREA WITH ATLESIAN BATTLESHIPS.
ALL CIVILIANS IN THIS BLOCK HAVE BOARDED.
WE WILL SOON DEPART THE BATTLE ZONE.

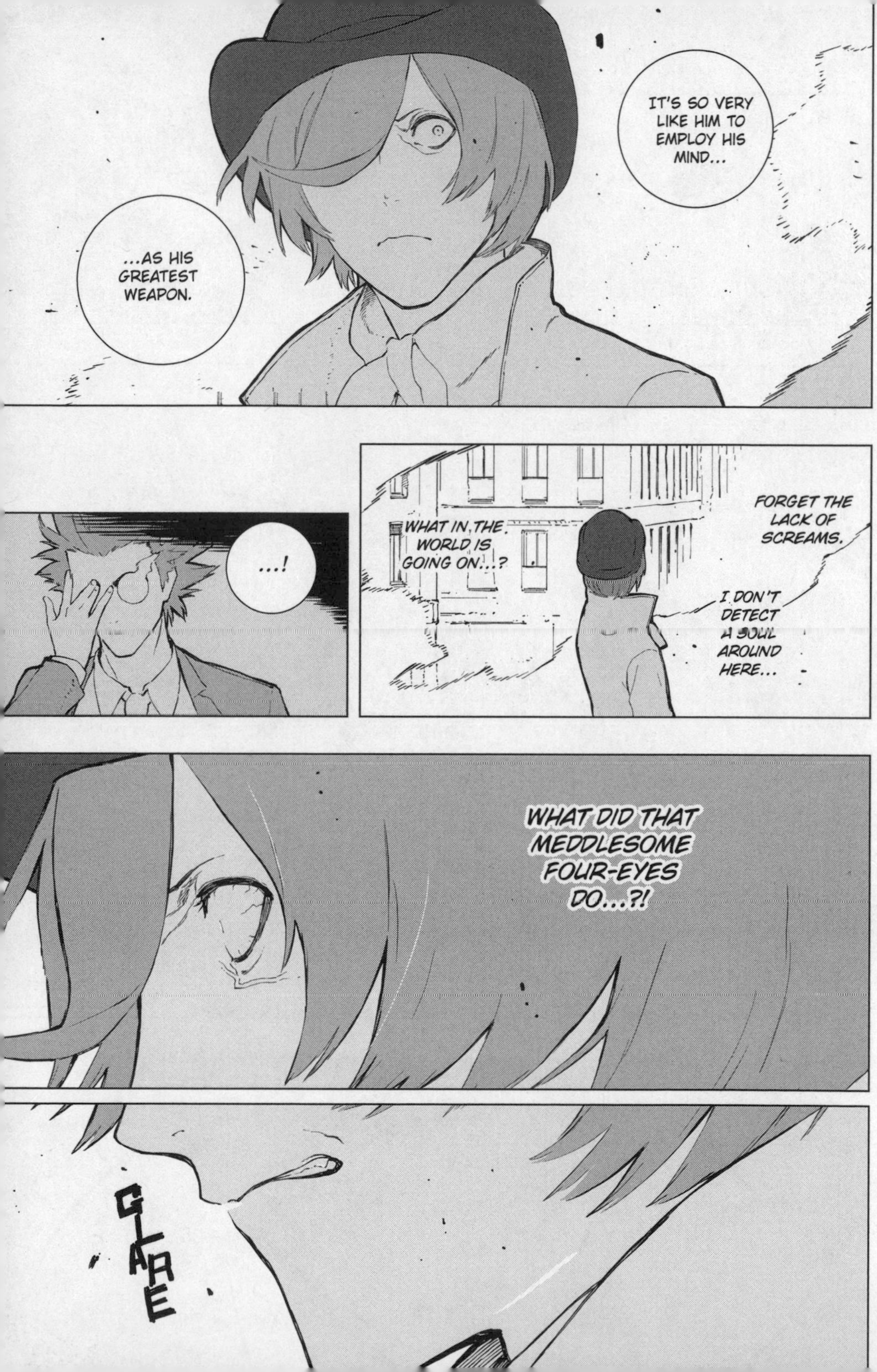
IT'S SO VERY LIKE HIM TO EMPLOY HIS MIND...
...AS HIS GREATEST WEAPON.
FORGET THE LACK OF SCREAMS.
I DON'T DETECT A SOUL AROUND HERE...
WHAT IN THE WORLD IS GOING ON...?
...!
WHAT DID THAT MEDDLESOME FOUR-EYES DO...?!
GLARE

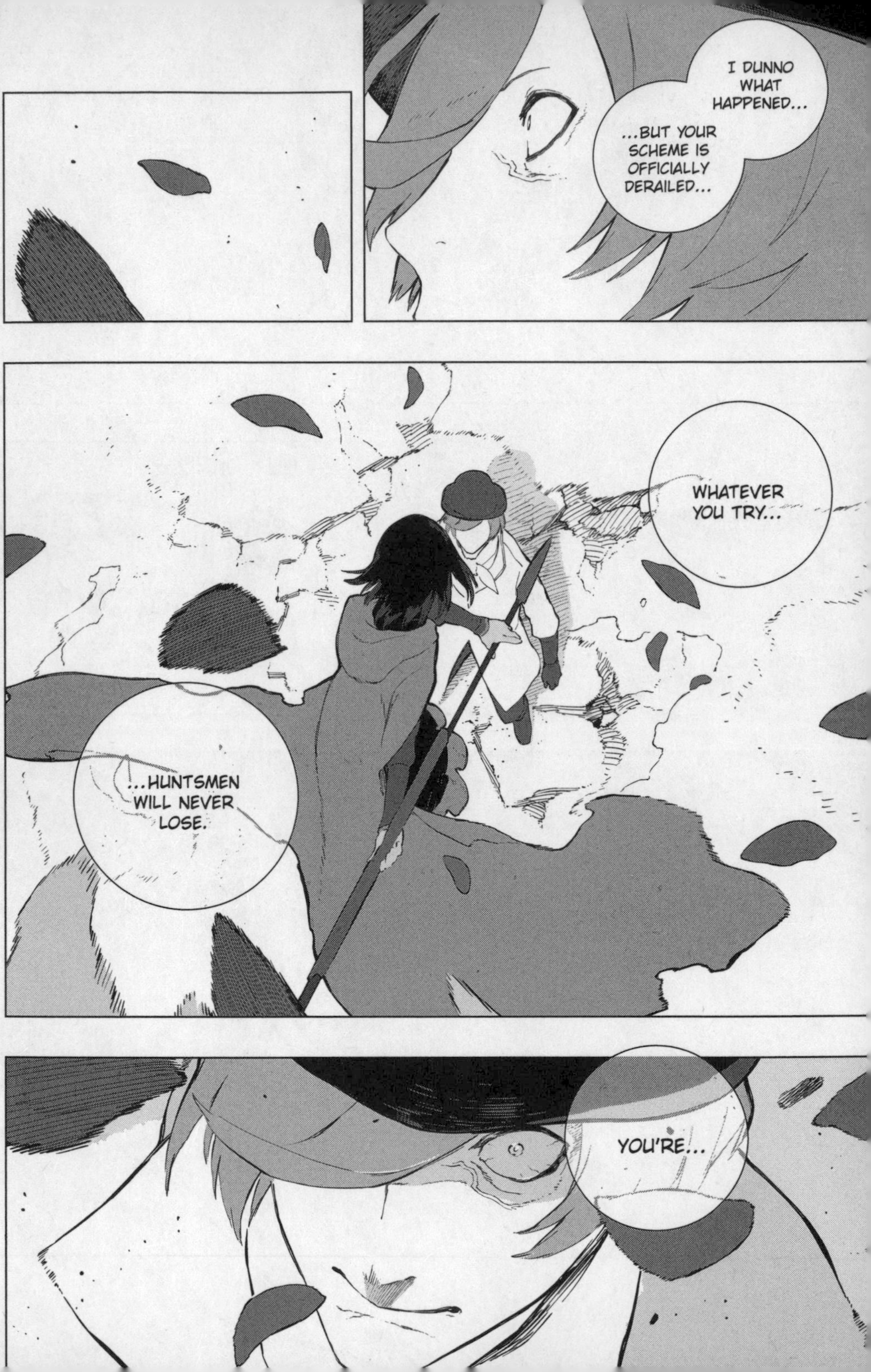
I DUNNO WHAT HAPPENED...
...BUT YOUR SCHEME IS OFFICIALLY DERAILED...
WHATEVER YOU TRY...
...HUNTSMEN WILL NEVER LOSE.
YOU'RE...

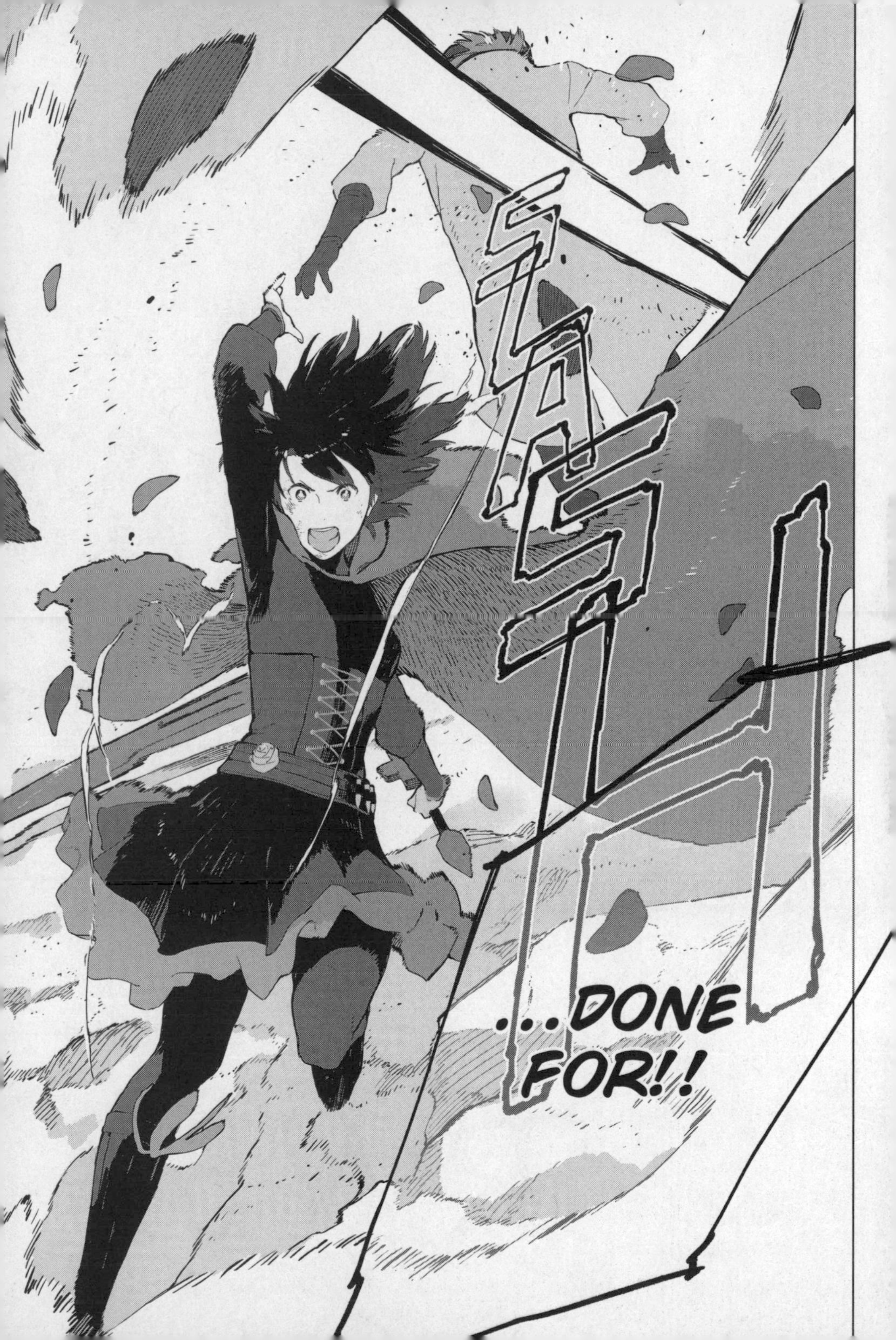

SLASH
...DONE FOR!!

RWBY

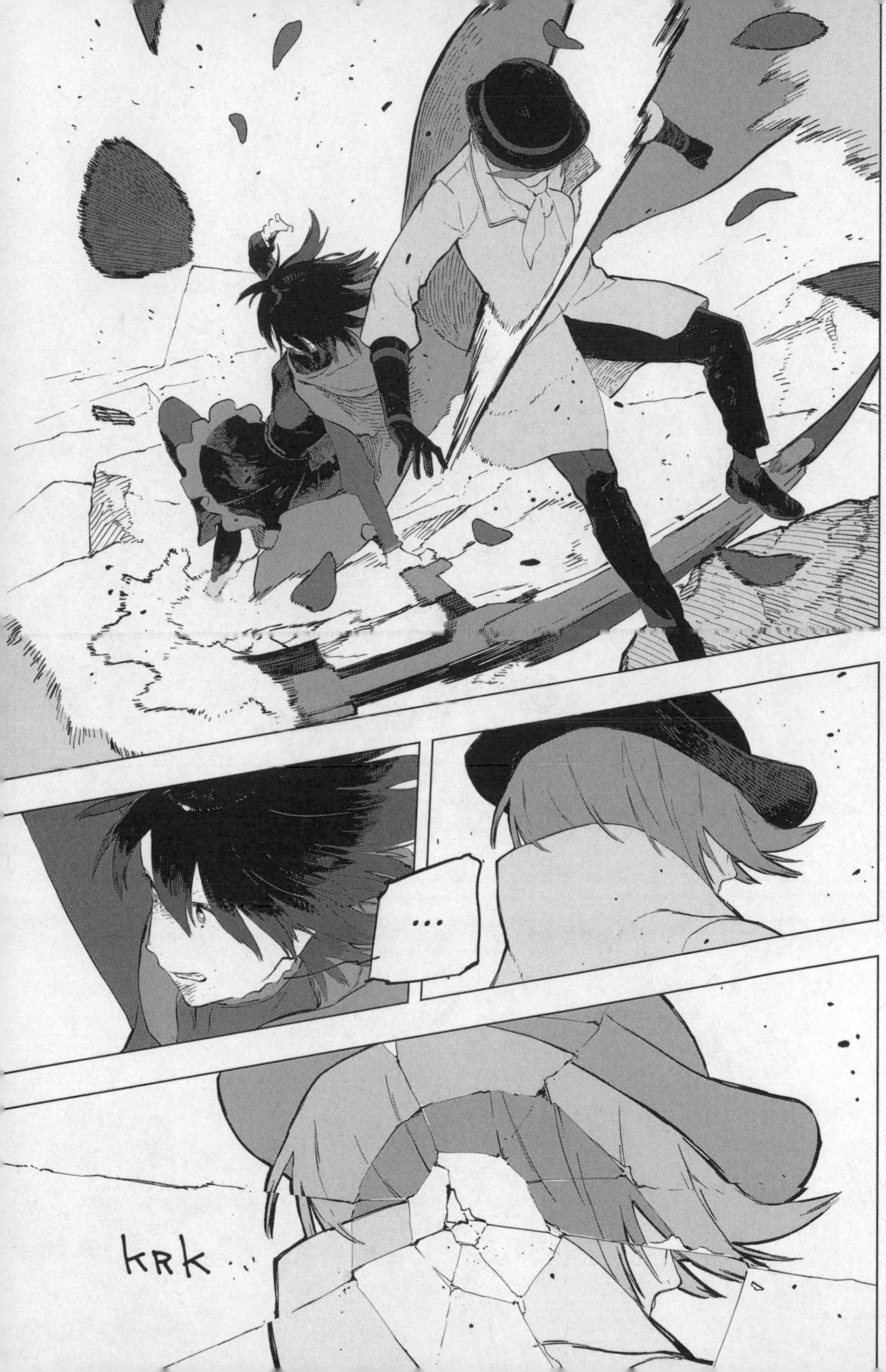
...
KRK

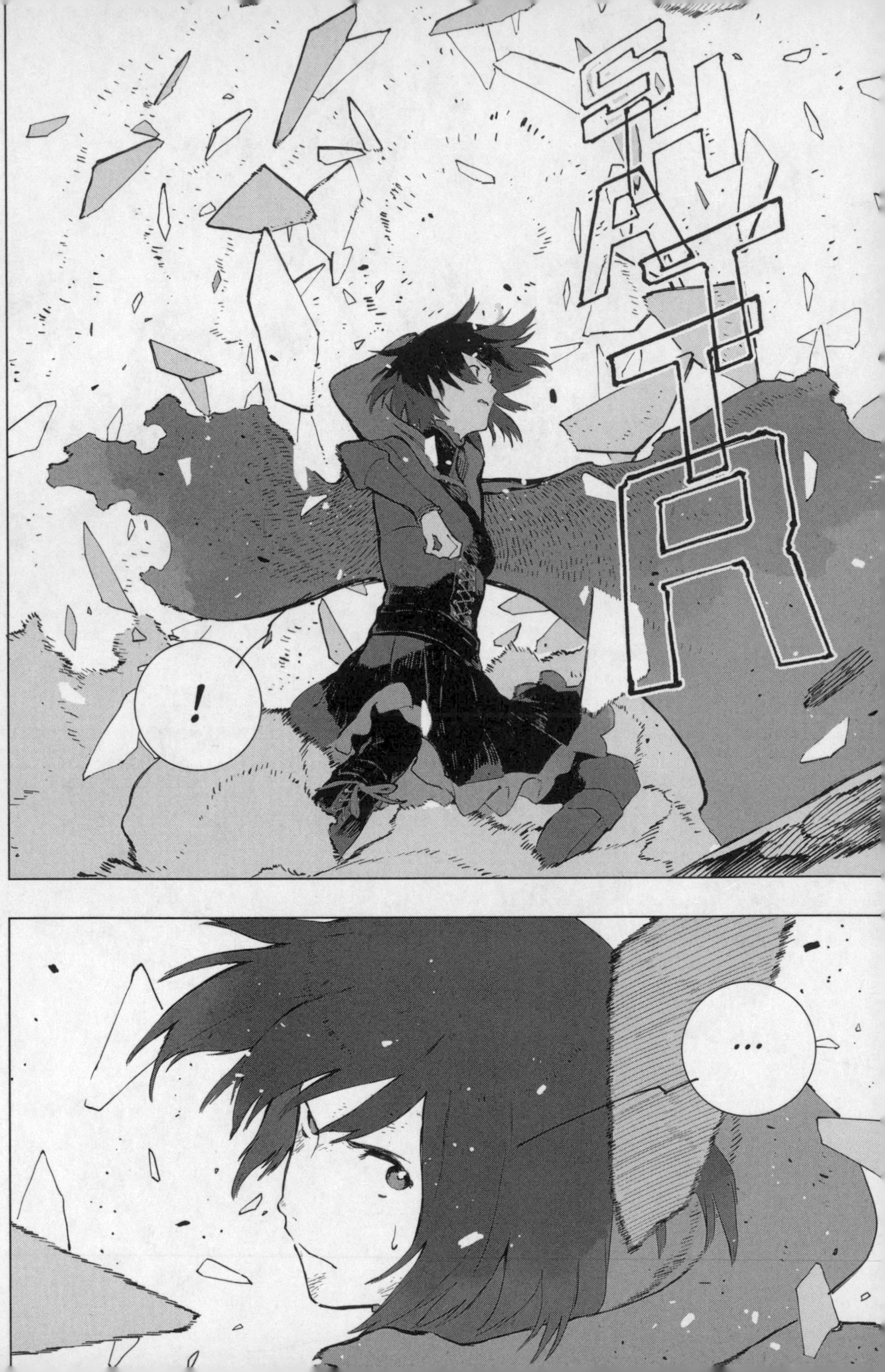
SHATTER
!
...

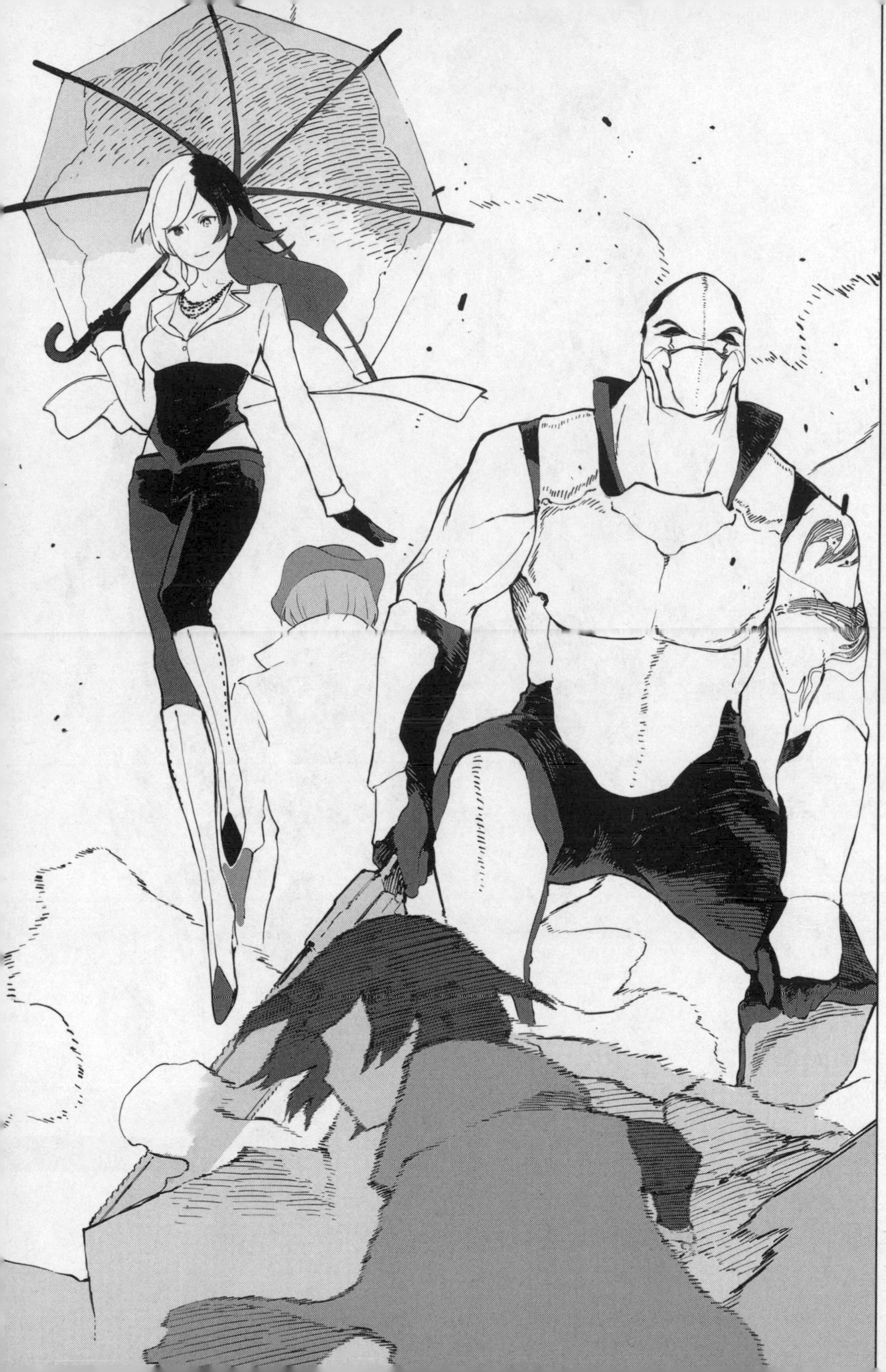

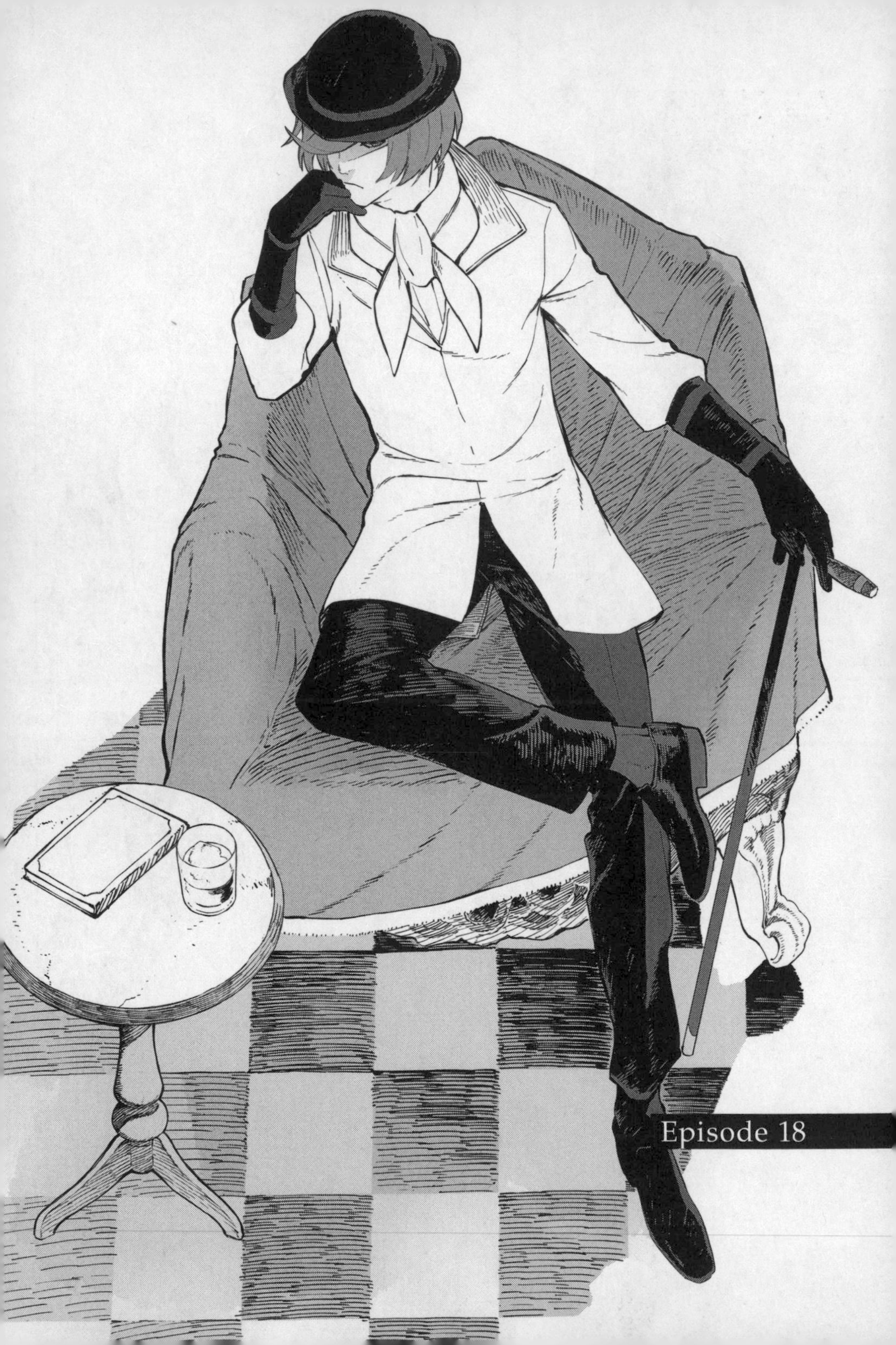
Episode 18

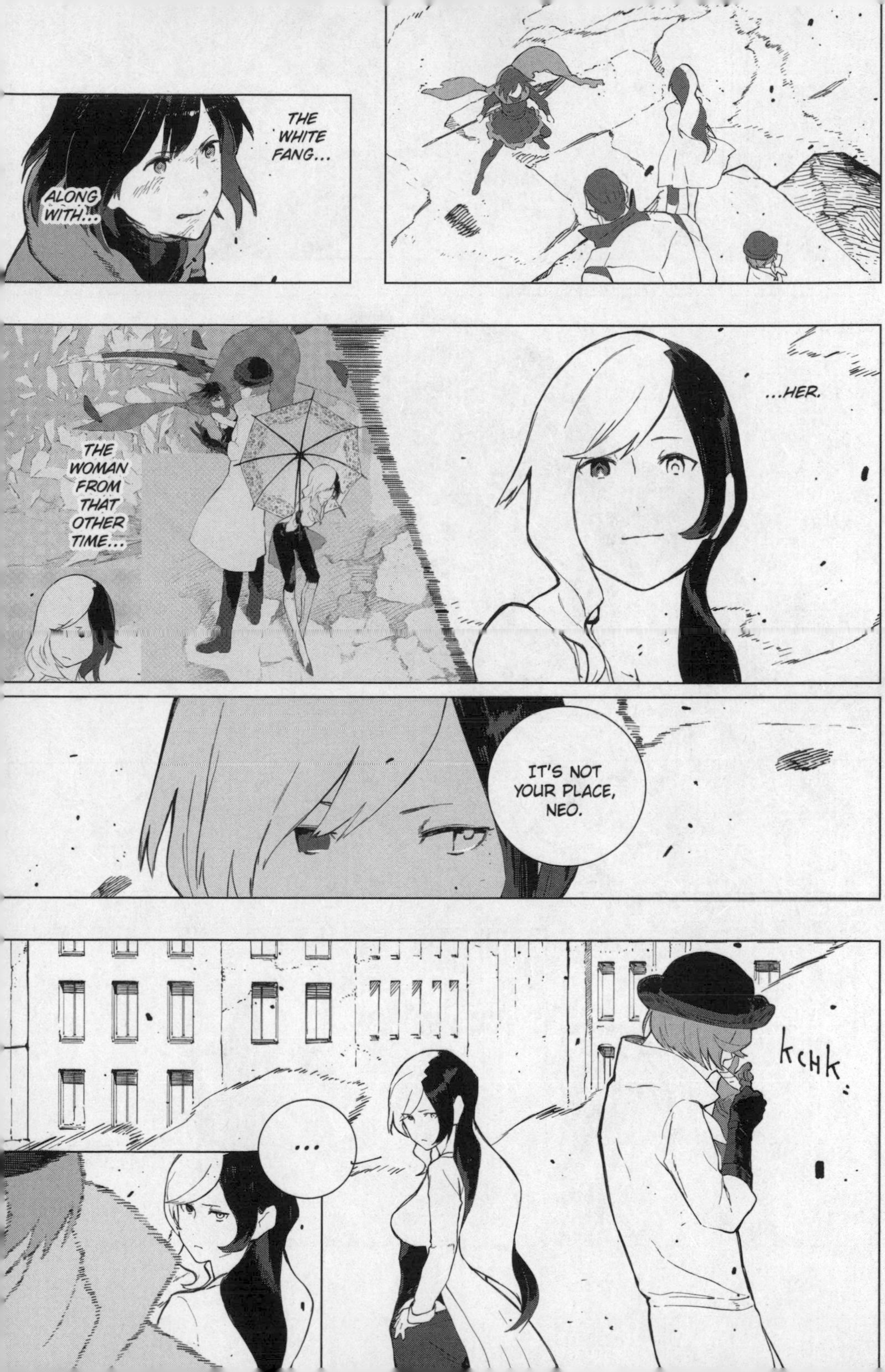
THE WHITE FANG...
ALONG WITH...
...HER.
THE WOMAN FROM THAT OTHER TIME...
IT'S NOT YOUR PLACE, NEO.
KCHK
...

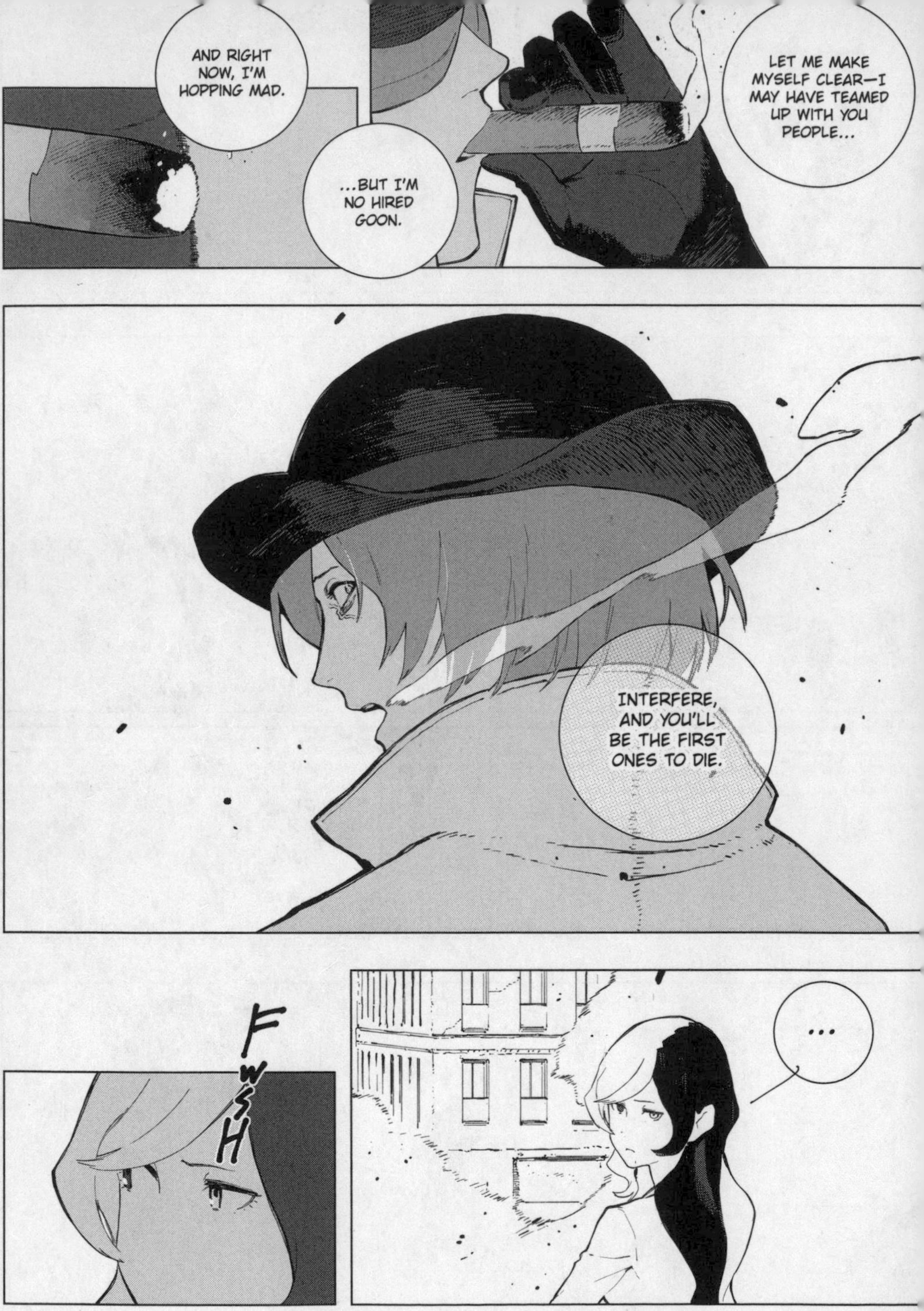
LET ME MAKE MYSELF CLEAR—I MAY HAVE TEAMED UP WITH YOU PEOPLE...
...BUT I'M NO HIRED GOON.
AND RIGHT NOW, I'M HOPPING MAD.
INTERFERE, AND YOU'LL BE THE FIRST ONES TO DIE.
...
FWSH

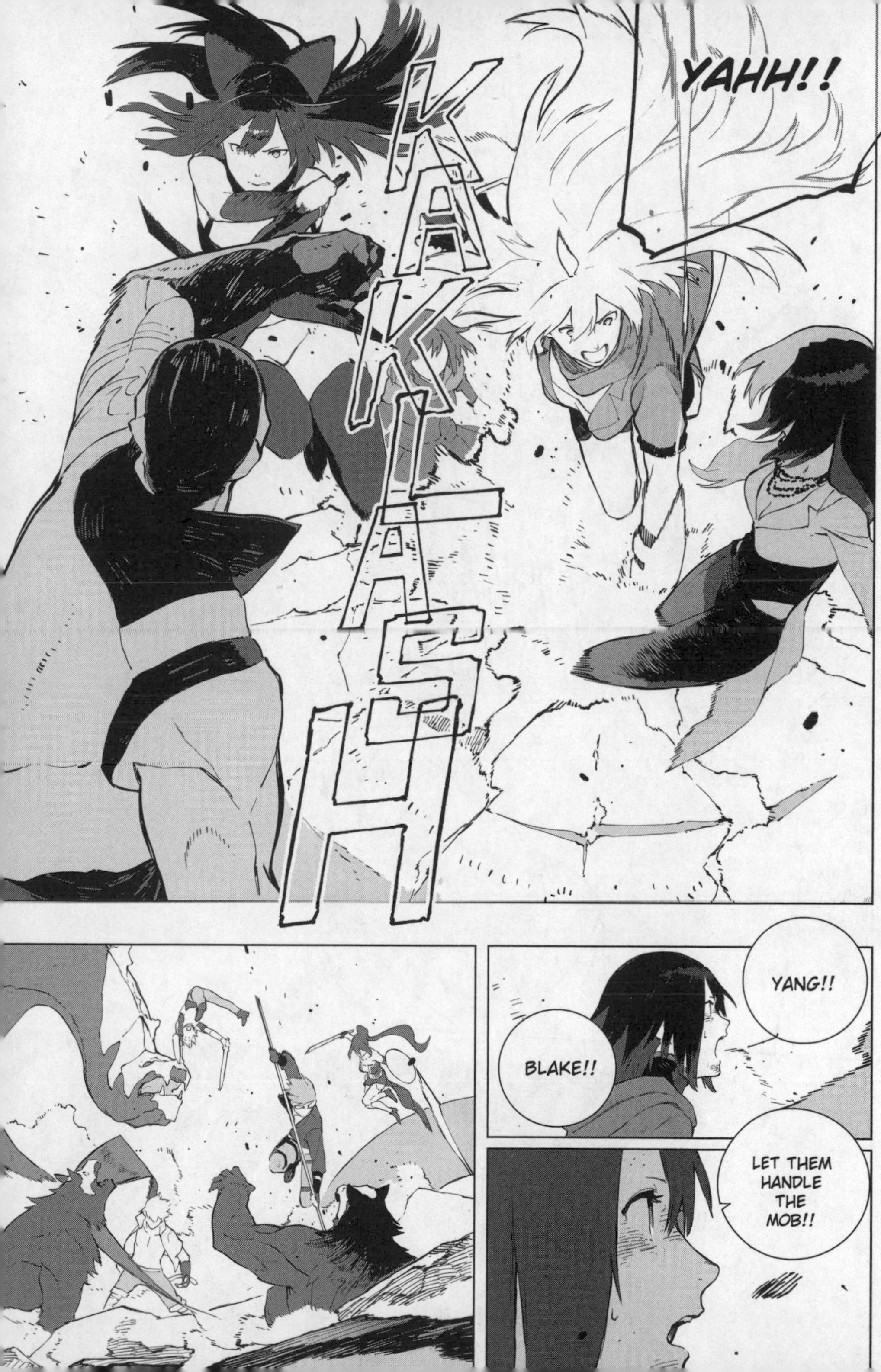
YAHH!!
KAKLASH
YANG!!
BLAKE!!
LET THEM HANDLE THE MOB!!

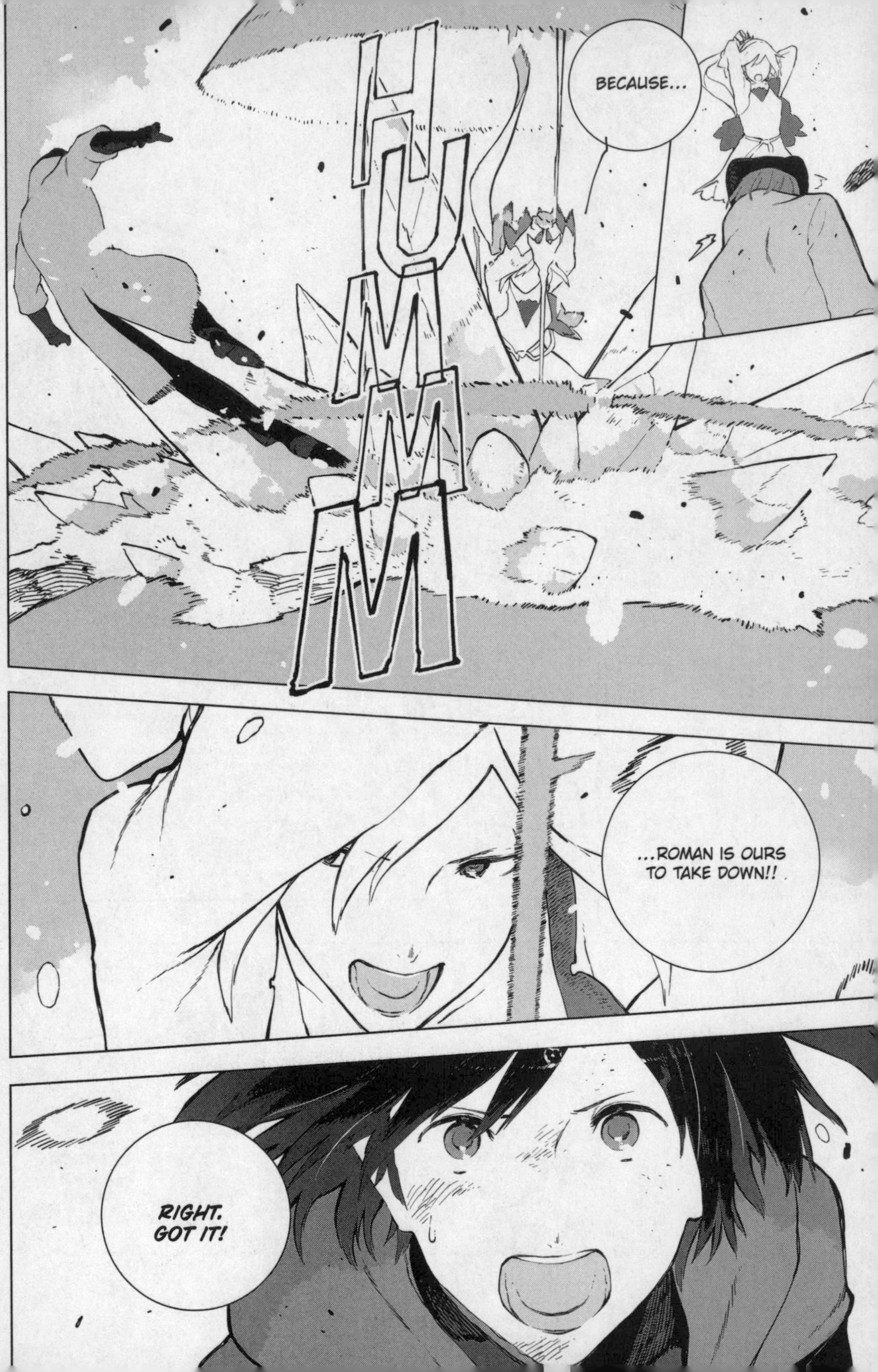
BECAUSE...
HUMMM
...ROMAN IS OURS TO TAKE DOWN!!
RIGHT. GOT IT!

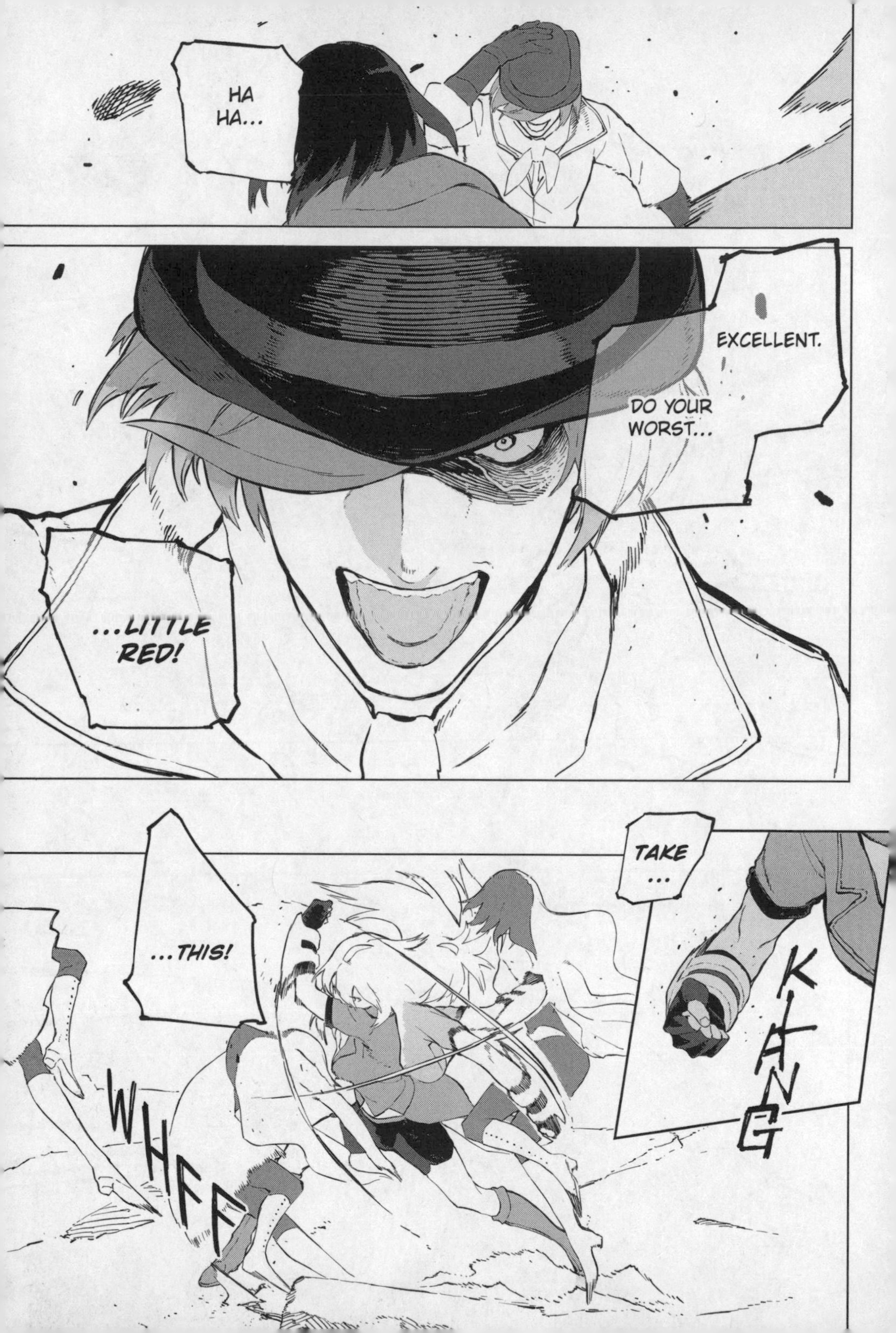
HA HA...
EXCELLENT.
DO YOUR WORST...
...LITTLE RED!
TAKE ...
KLANG
...THIS!
WHFF

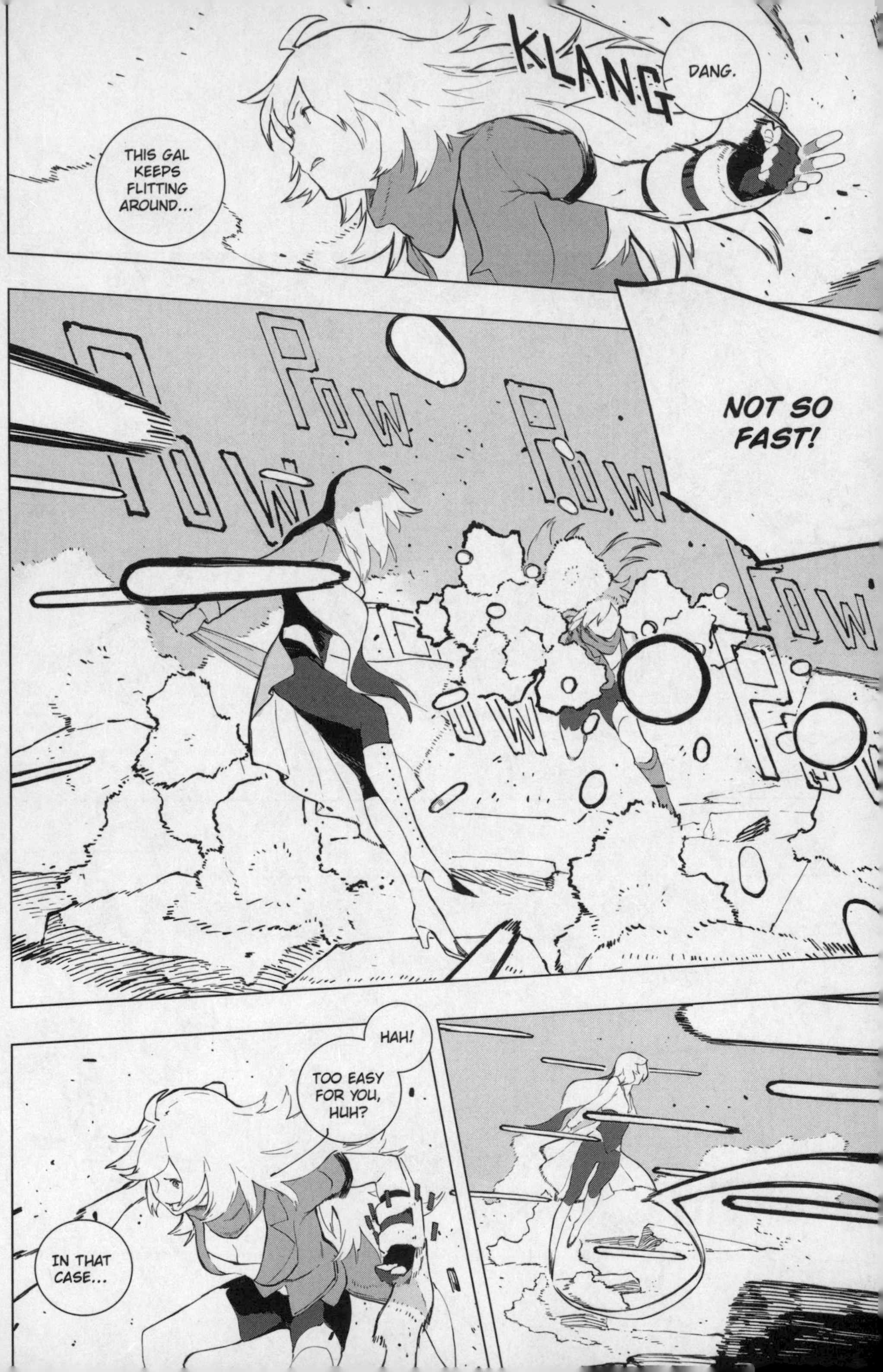
KLANG
DANG.
THIS GAL KEEPS FLITTING AROUND...
NOT SO FAST!
POW
POW
POW
POW
POW
POW
HAH!
TOO EASY FOR YOU, HUH?
IN THAT CASE...

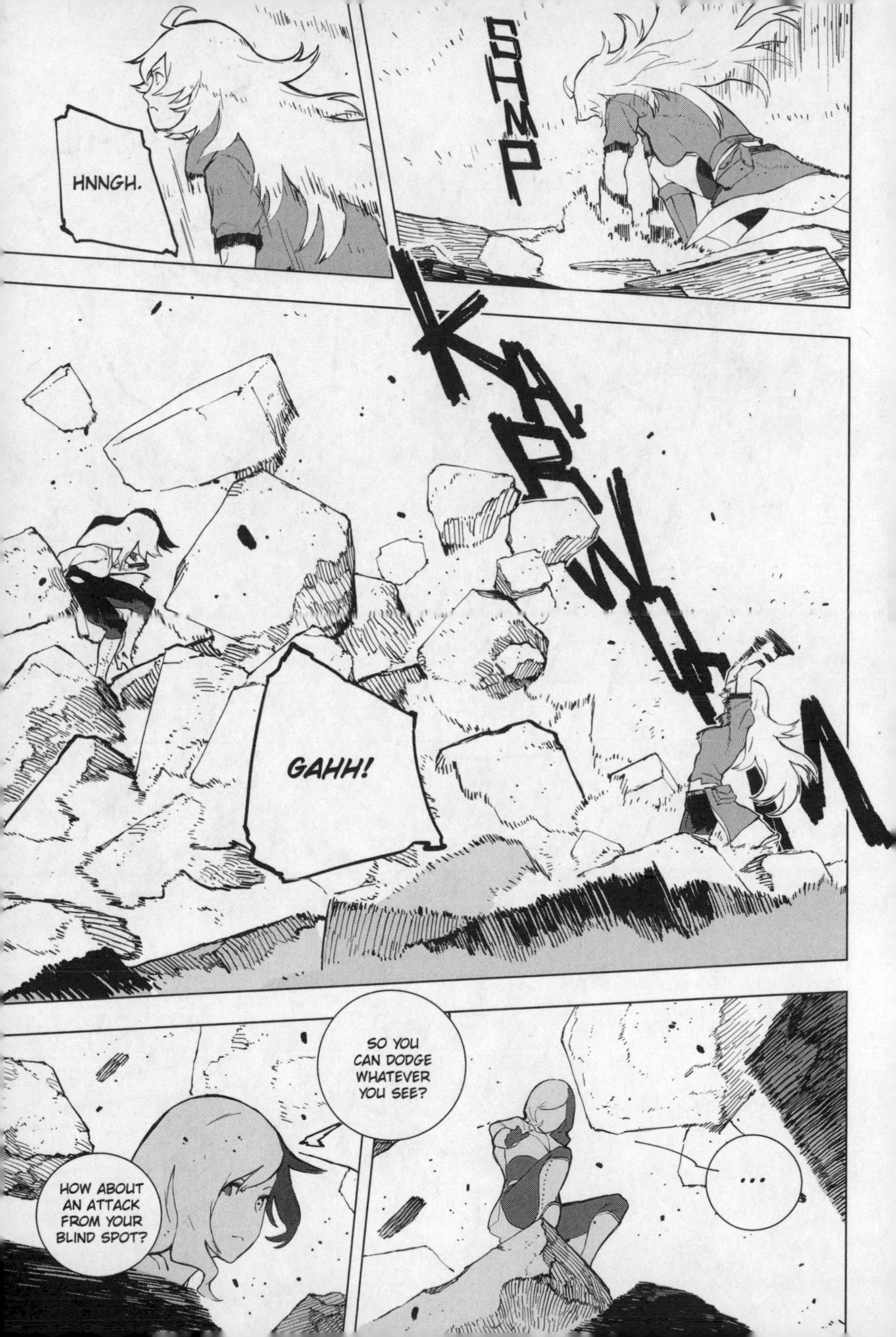
SHMP
HNNGH.
GAHH!
...
SO YOU CAN DODGE WHATEVER YOU SEE?
HOW ABOUT AN ATTACK FROM YOUR BLIND SPOT?

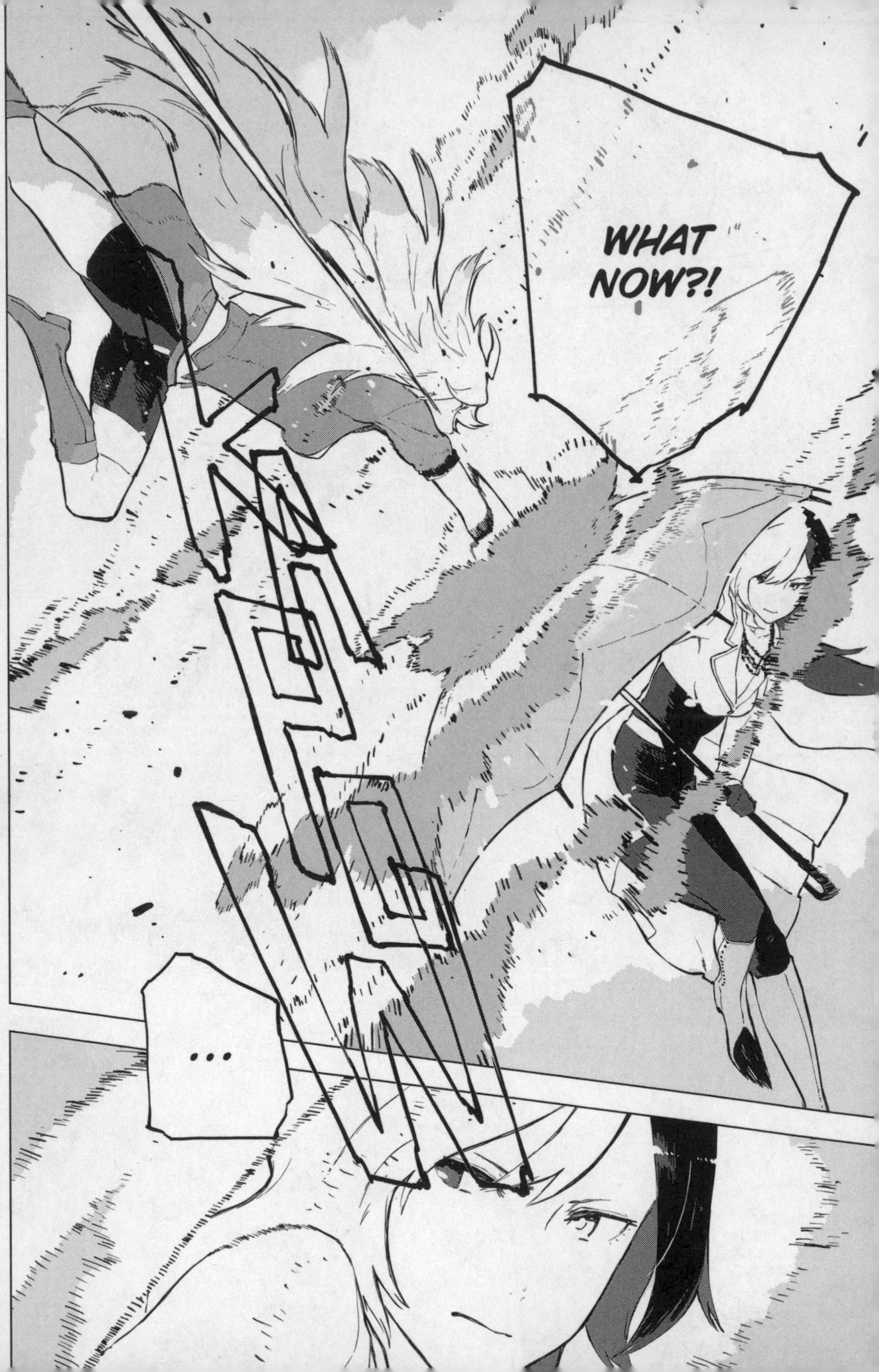
WHAT NOW?!
...

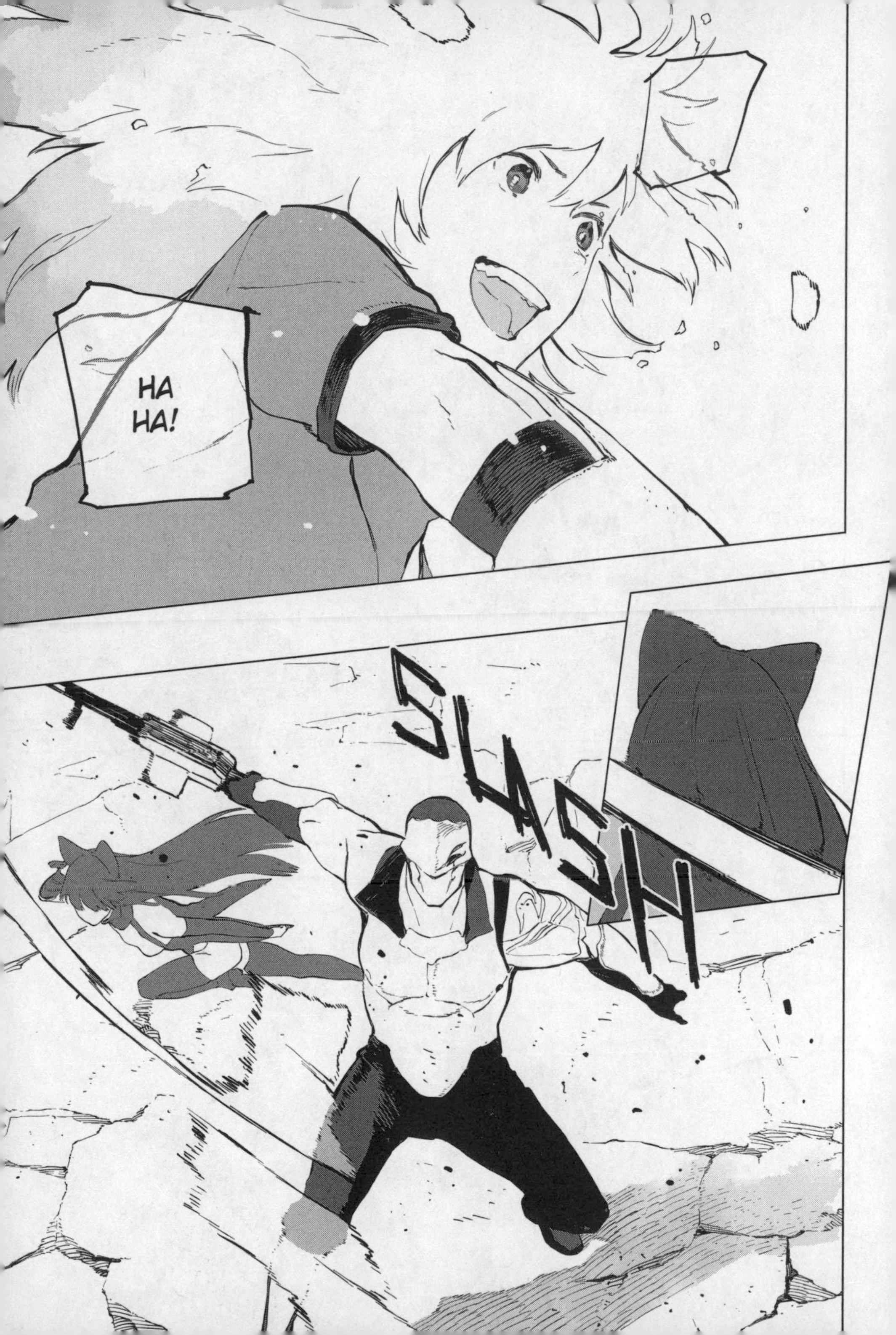
HA HA!
SLASH

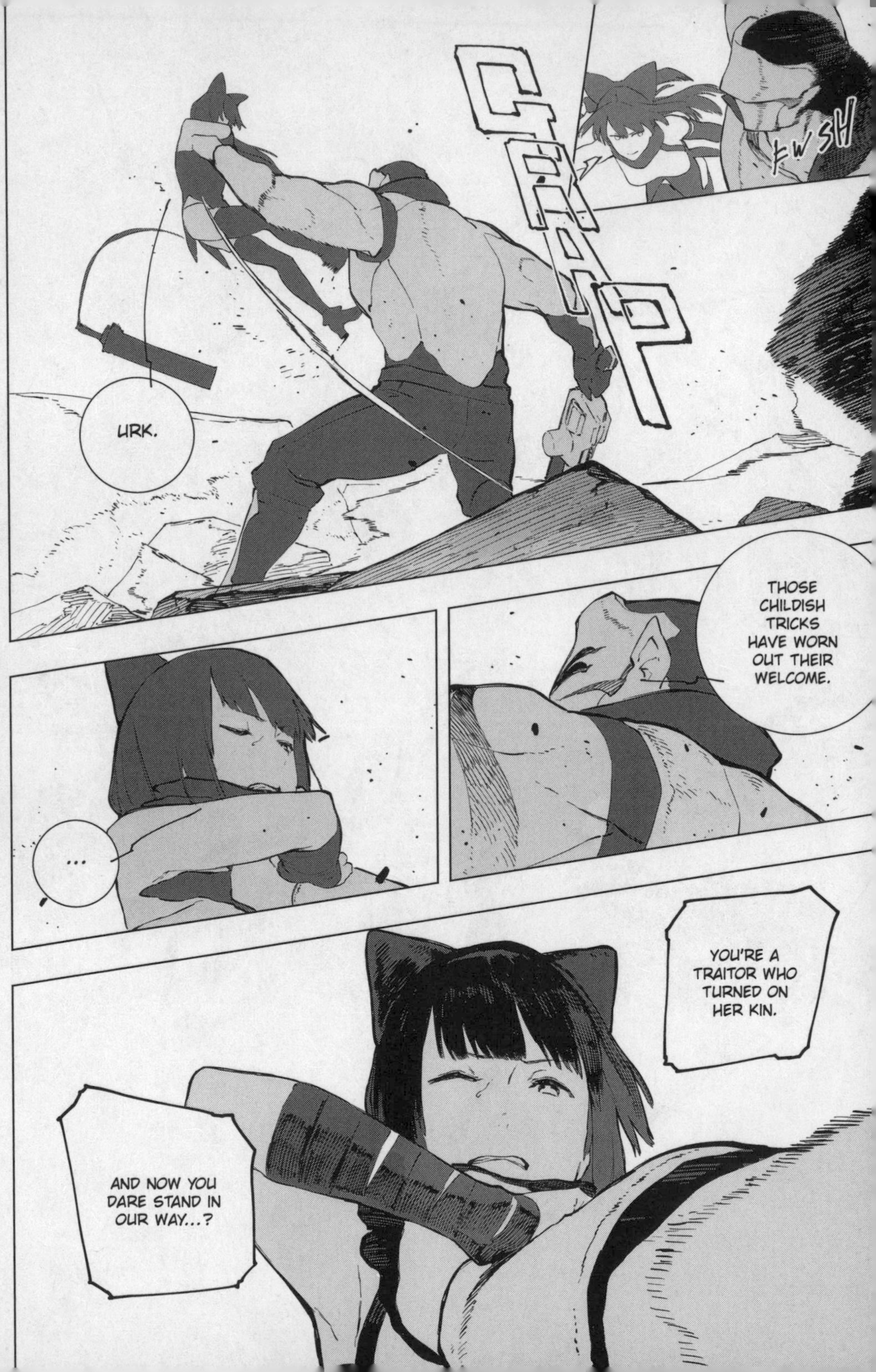
FWSH
GRAAP
URK.
THOSE CHILDISH TRICKS HAVE WORN OUT THEIR WELCOME.
...
YOU'RE A TRAITOR WHO TURNED ON HER KIN.
AND NOW YOU DARE STAND IN OUR WAY...?

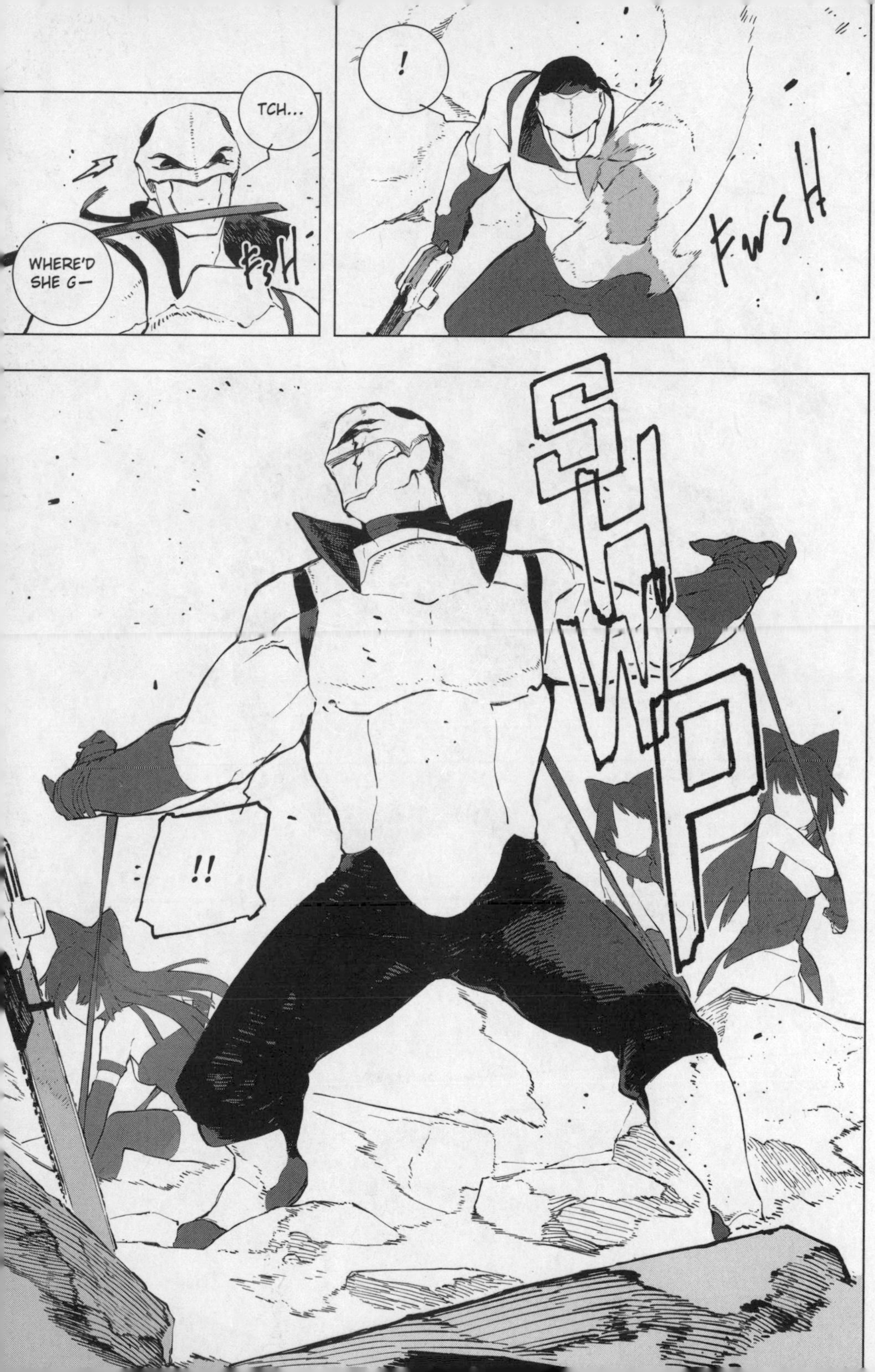
!
FWSH
TCH...
WHERE'D SHE G—
FSH
SHWP
!!

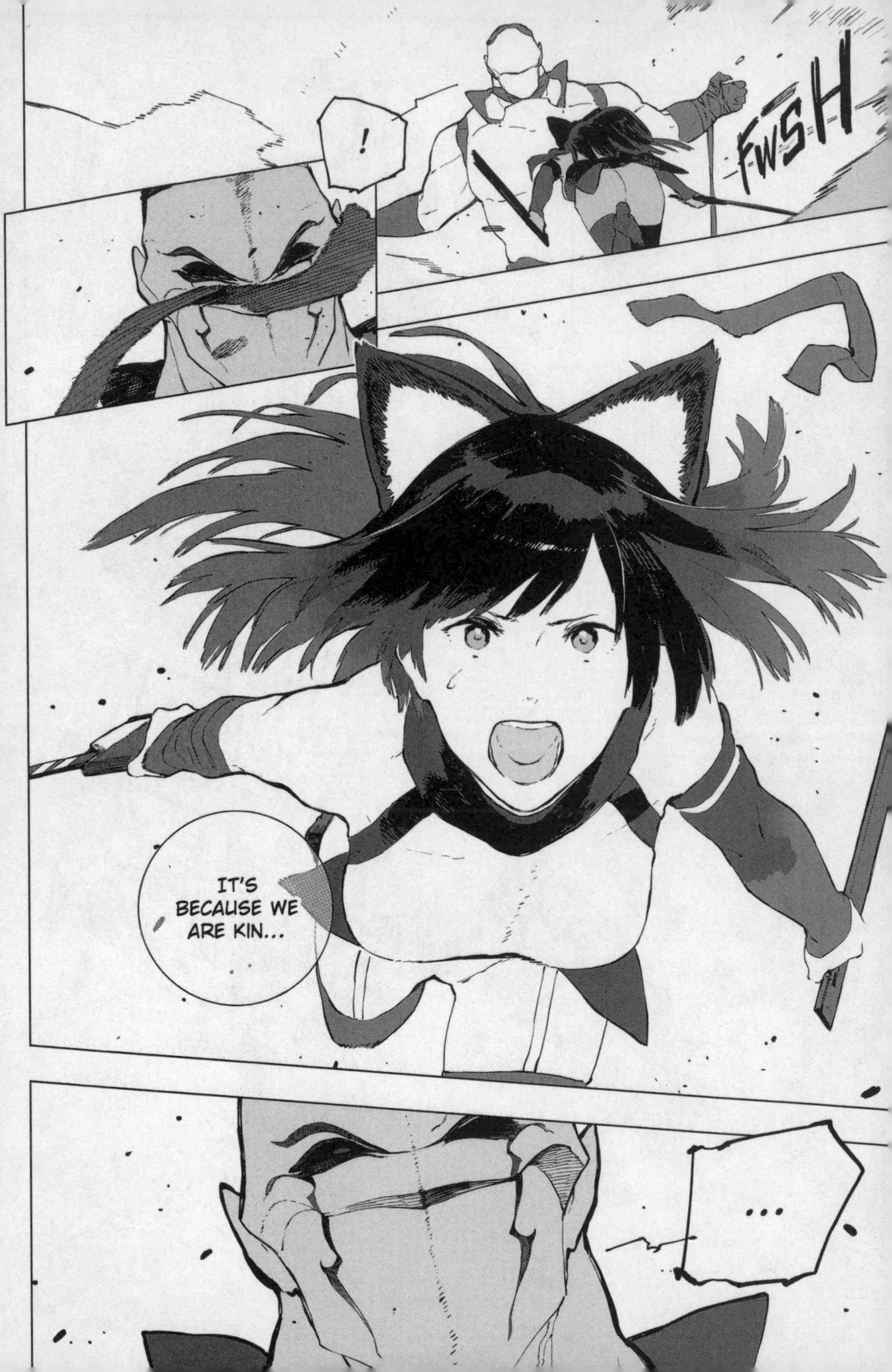
FWSH
!
IT'S BECAUSE WE ARE KIN...
...

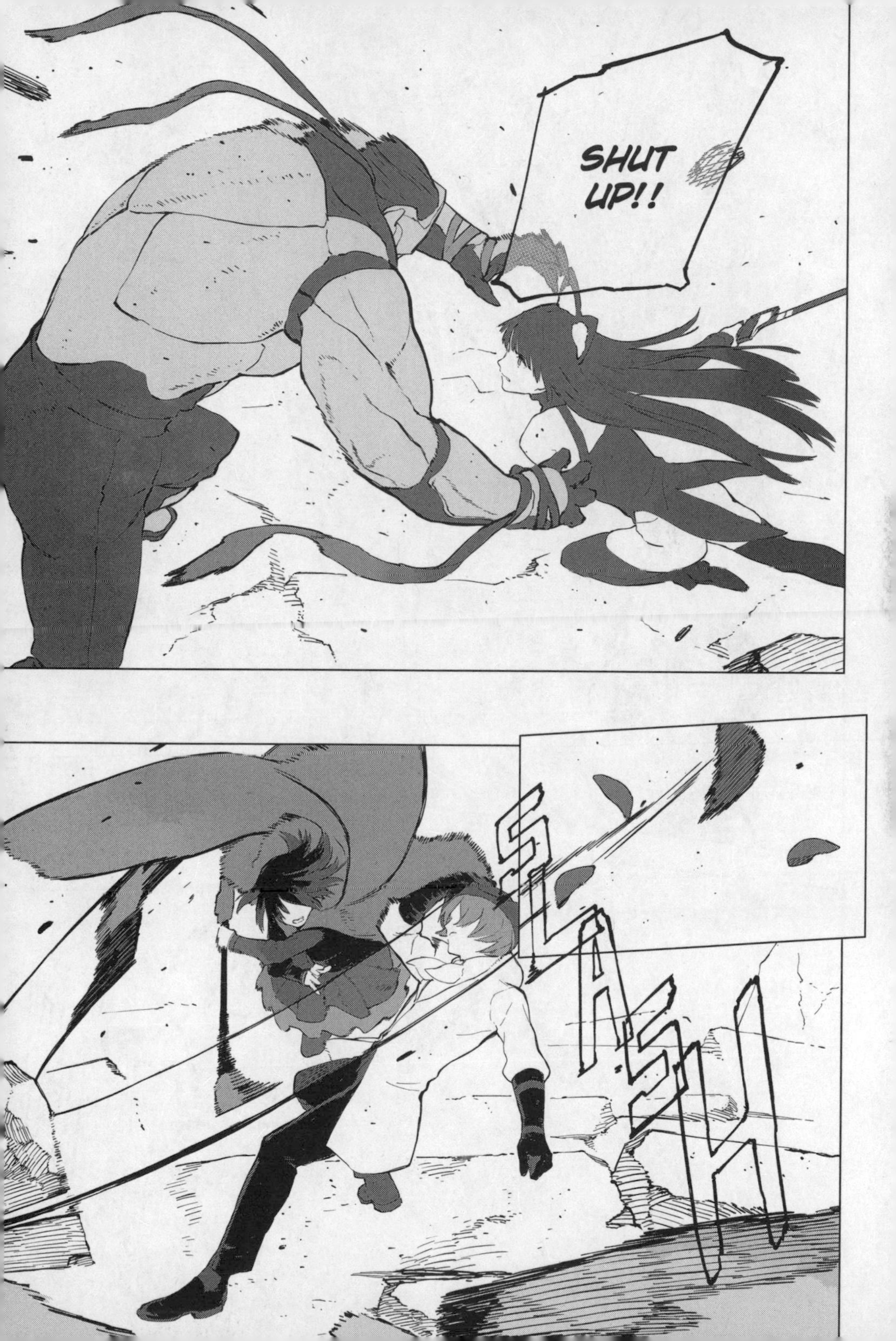
SHUT UP!!
SLASH

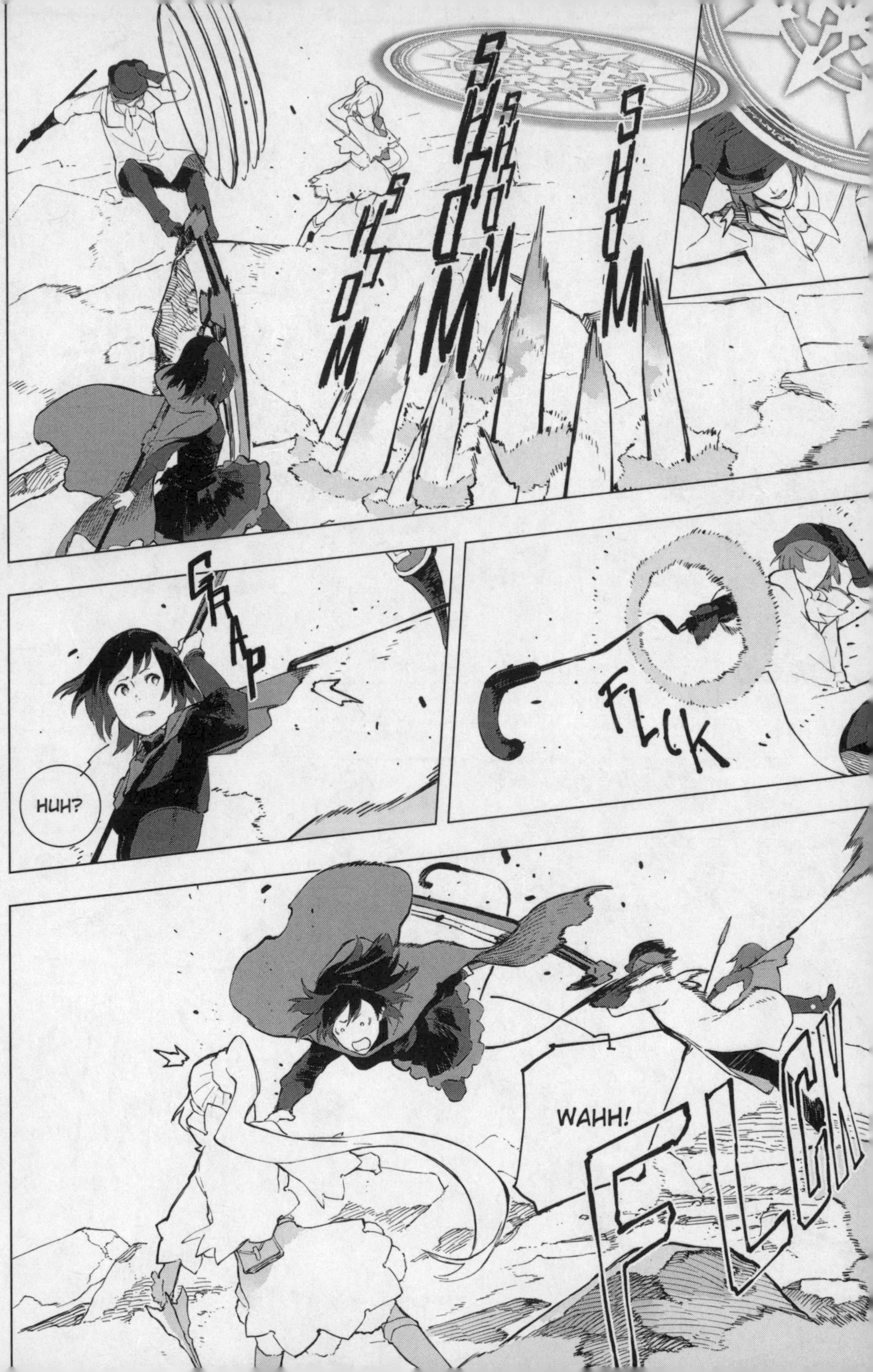
SHOOM
SHOOM
SHOOM
SHOOM
FLICK
GRAP
HUH?
WAHH!

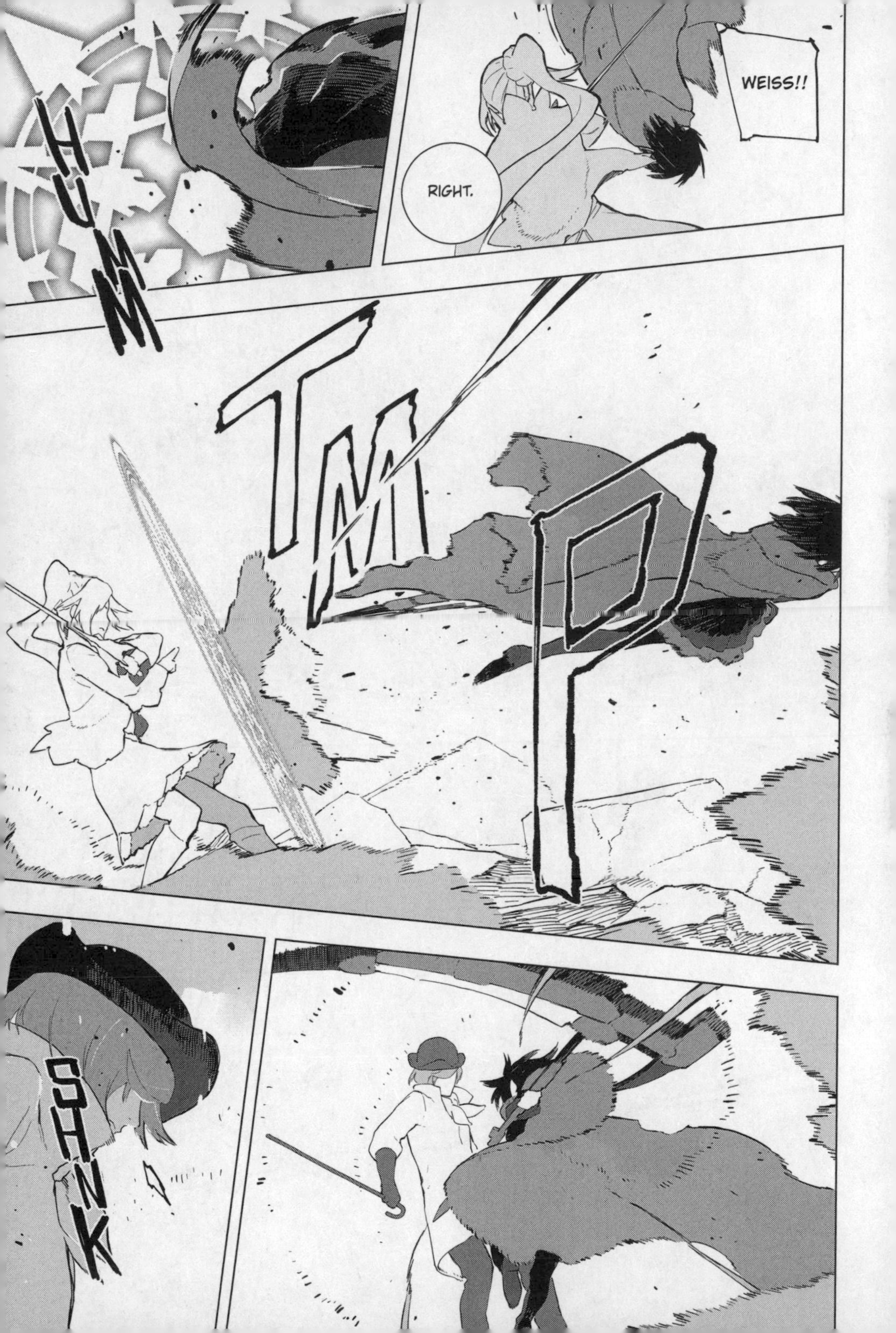
WEISS!!
RIGHT.
HUMM
TMP
SHNK

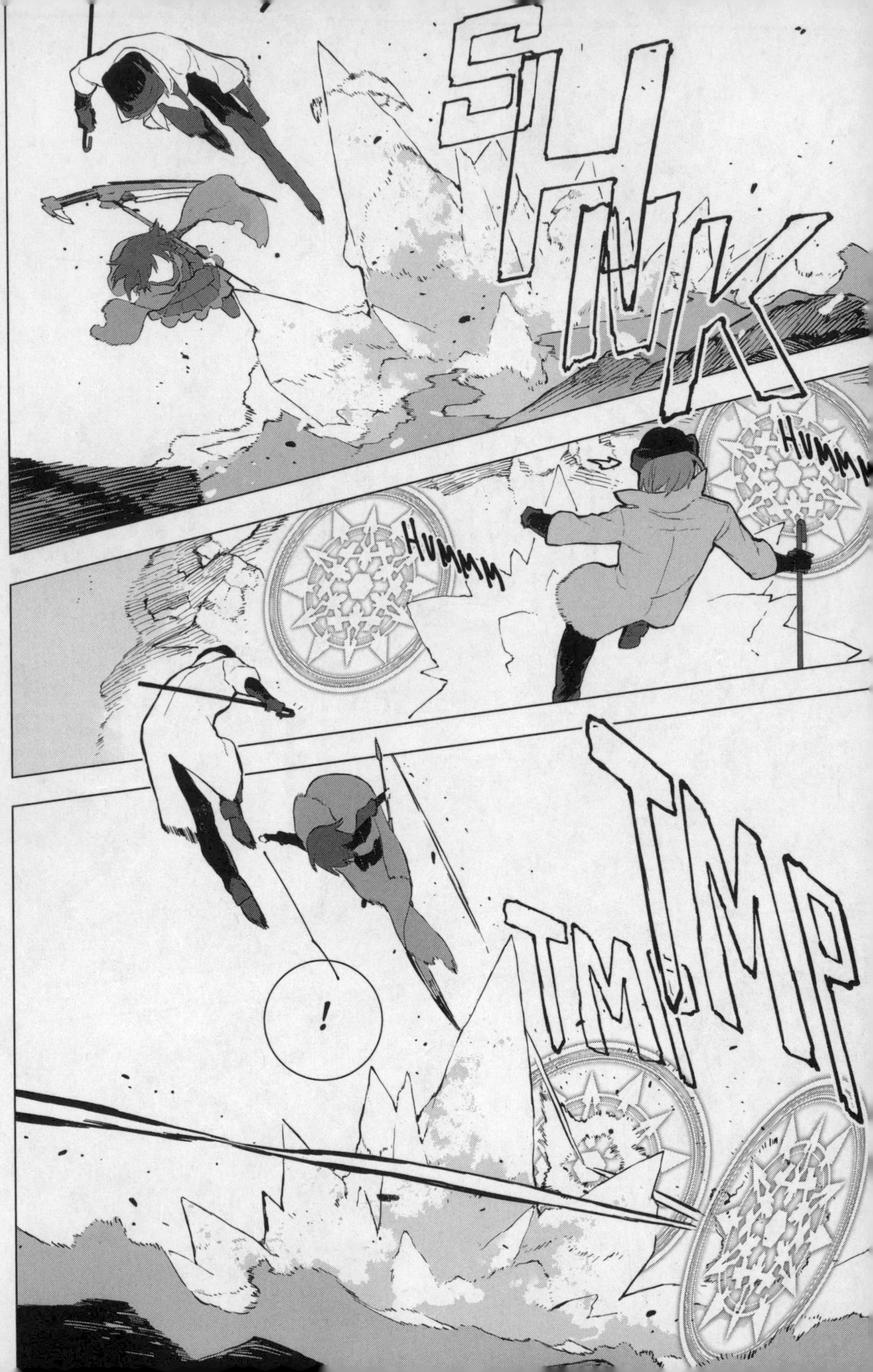
SHNK
HUMMM
HUMMMM
TMMP
TM
!

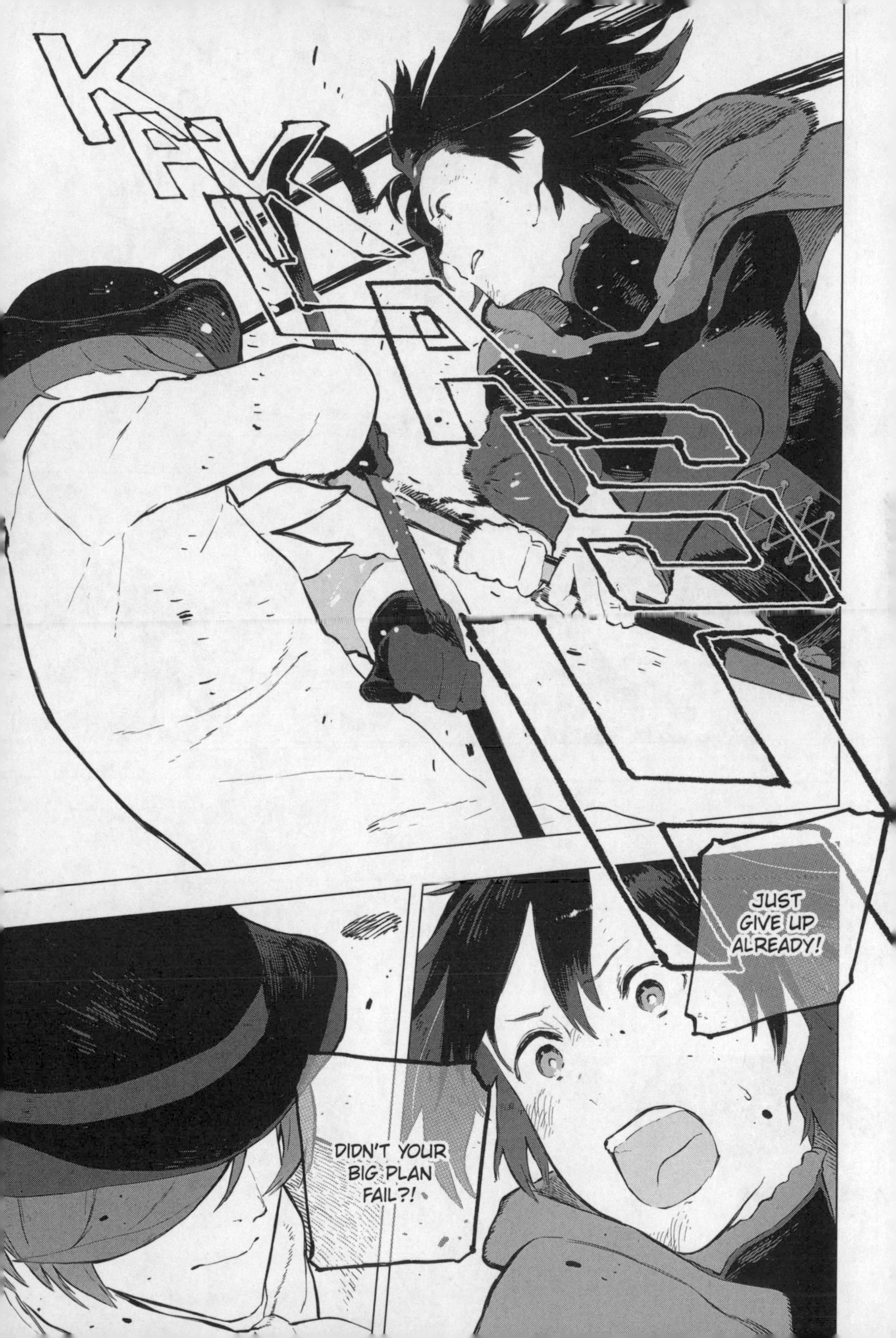
JUST GIVE UP ALREADY!
DIDN'T YOUR BIG PLAN FAIL?!

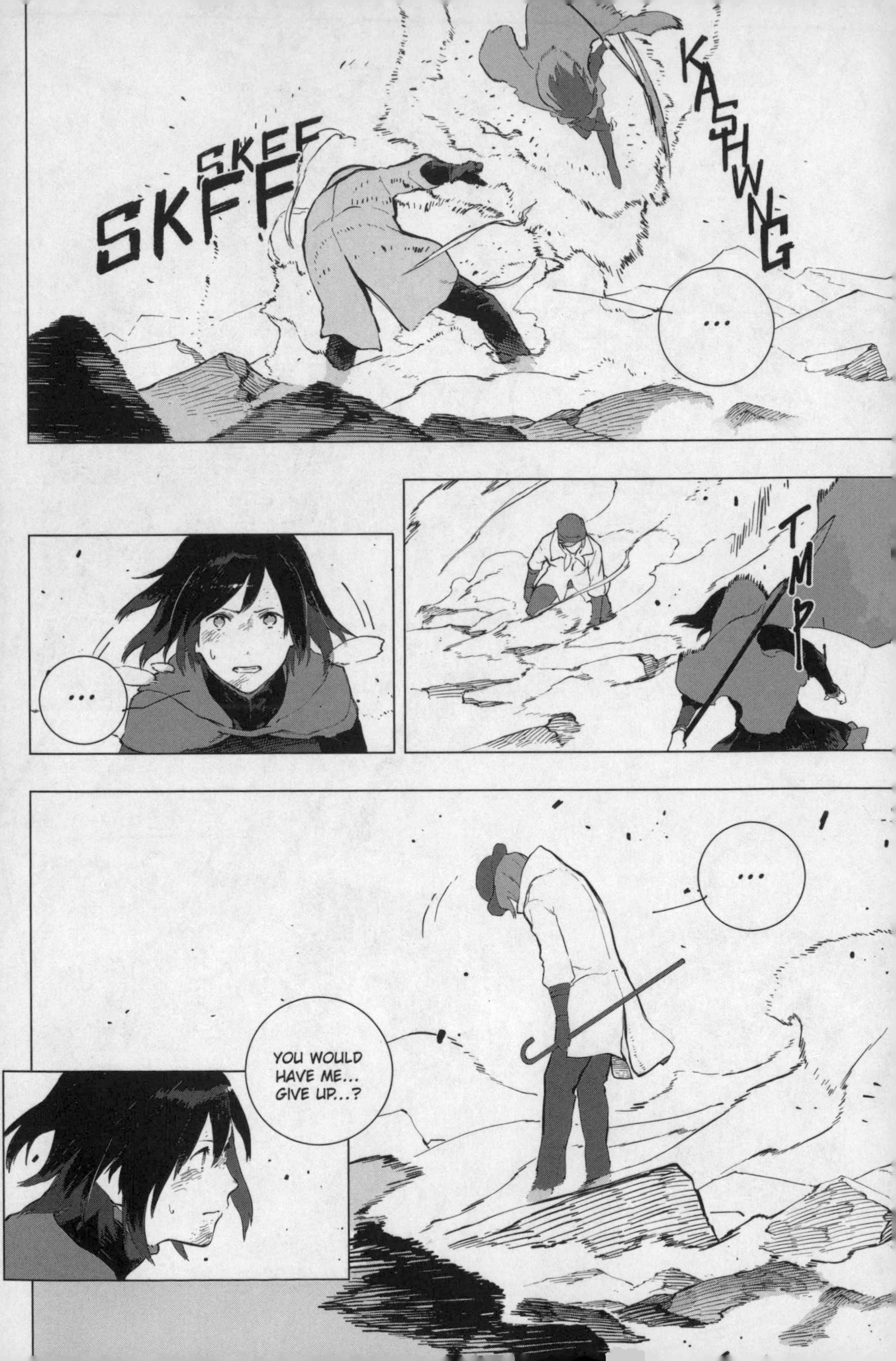
KASHWNG
SKEF
SKFF
...
TMP
...
...
YOU WOULD HAVE ME... GIVE UP...?

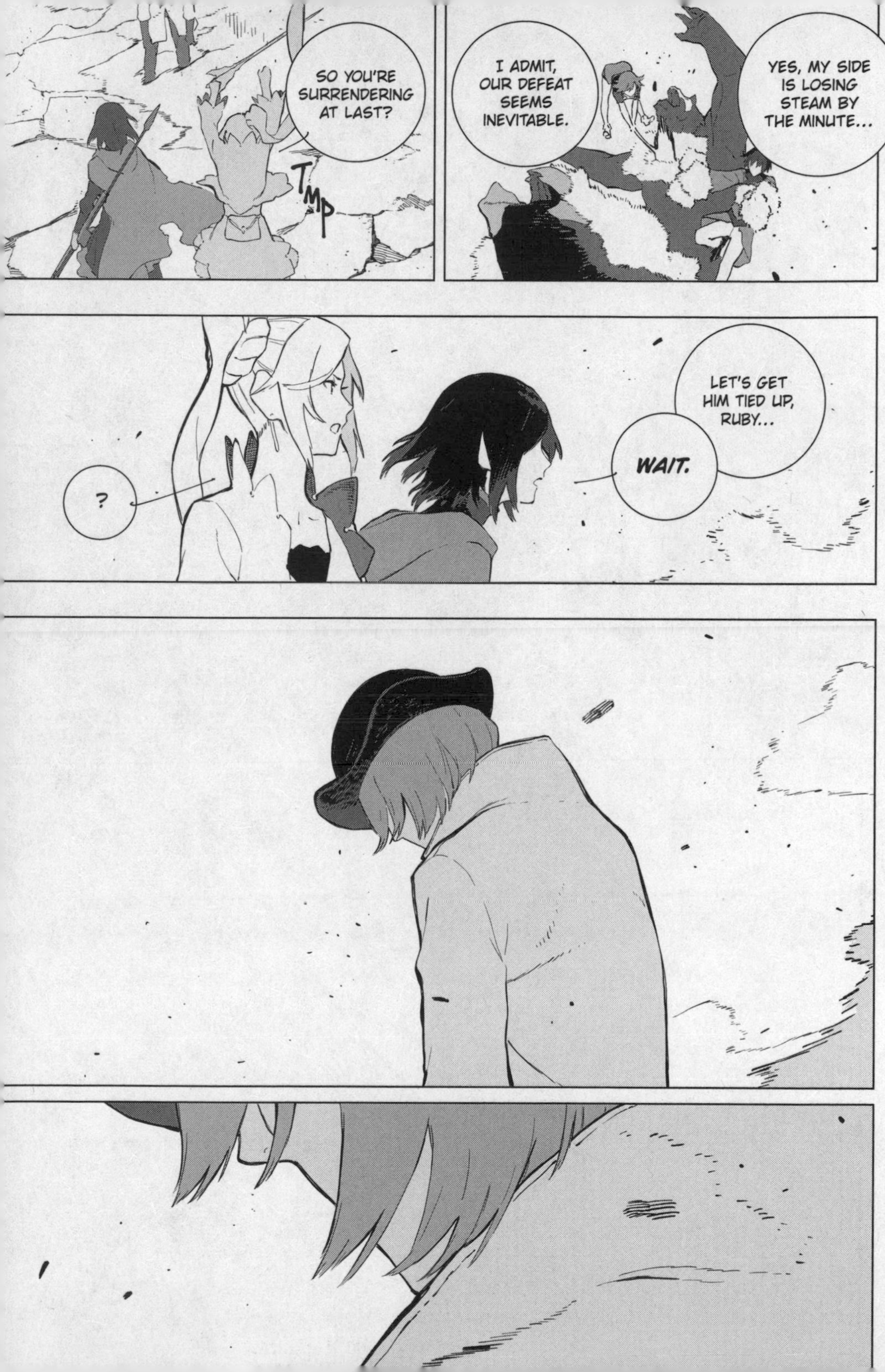
YES, MY SIDE IS LOSING STEAM BY THE MINUTE...
I ADMIT, OUR DEFEAT SEEMS INEVITABLE.
SO YOU'RE SURRENDERING AT LAST?
TMP
LET'S GET HIM TIED UP, RUBY...
WAIT.
?

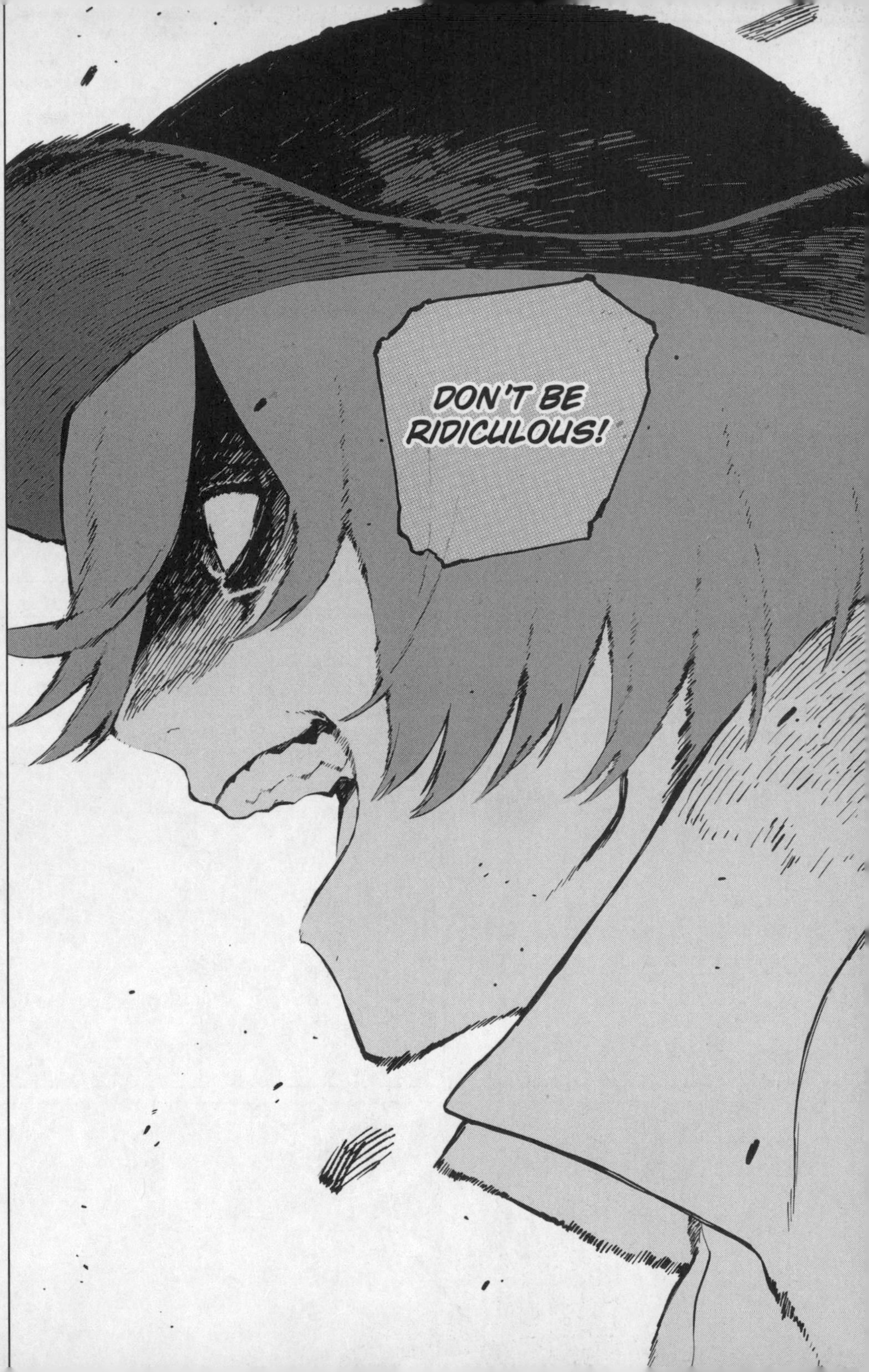
DON'T BE RIDICULOUS!

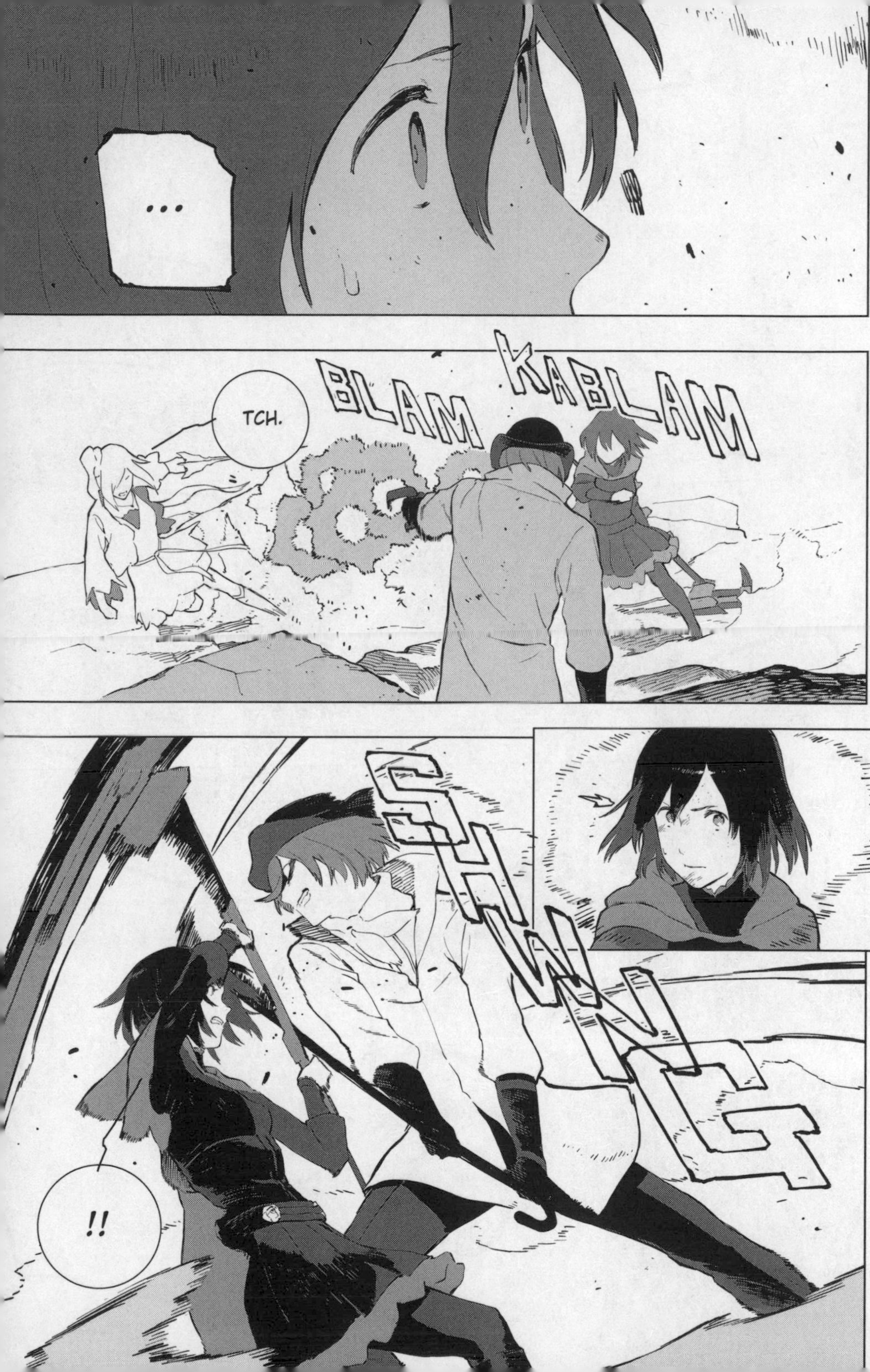
...
BLAM KABLAM
TCH.
SHWNCT
!!

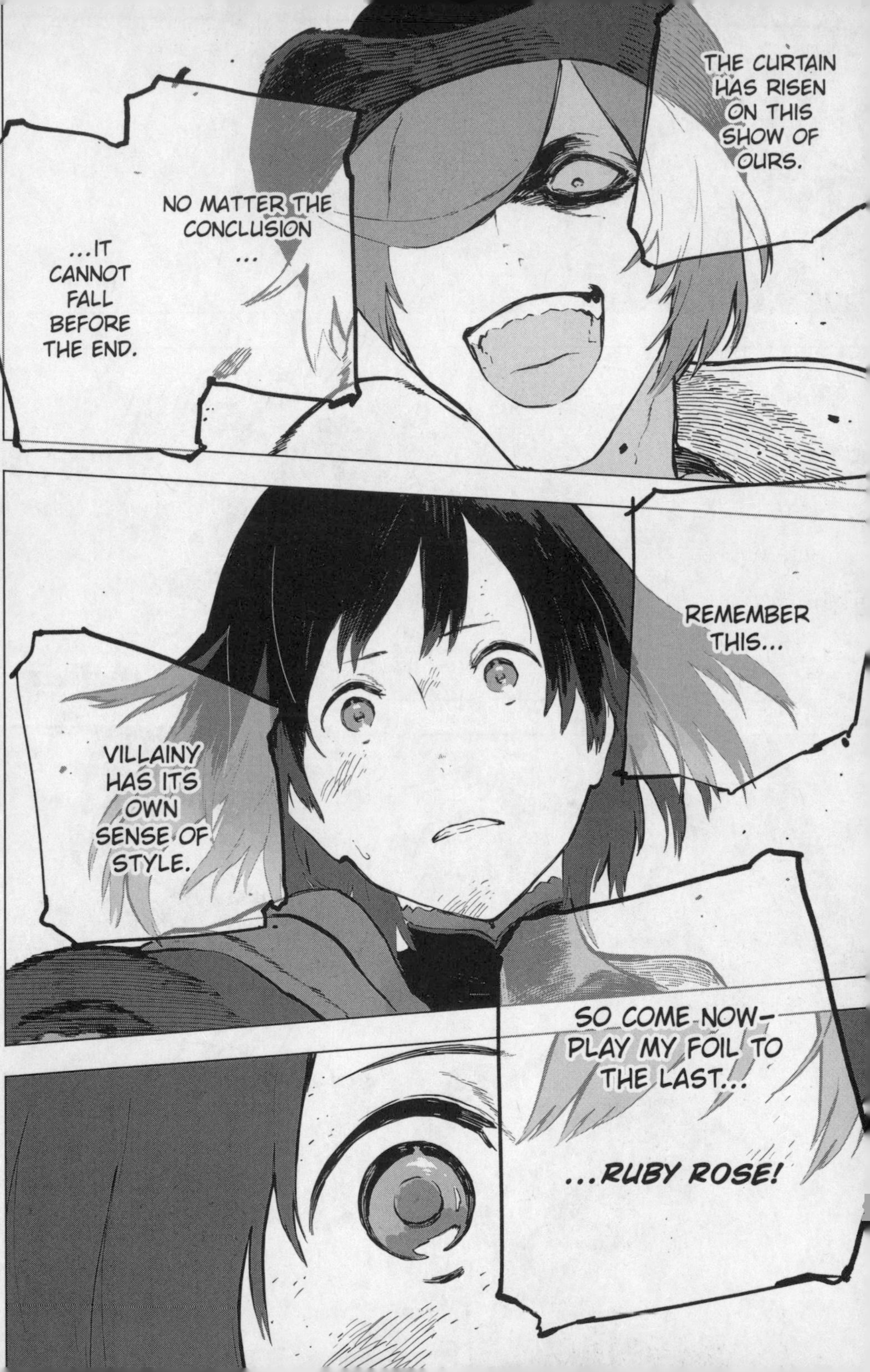
THE CURTAIN HAS RISEN ON THIS SHOW OF OURS.
NO MATTER THE CONCLUSION ...
...IT CANNOT FALL BEFORE THE END.
REMEMBER THIS...
VILLAINY HAS ITS OWN SENSE OF STYLE.
SO COME NOW— PLAY MY FOIL TO THE LAST...
...RUBY ROSE!

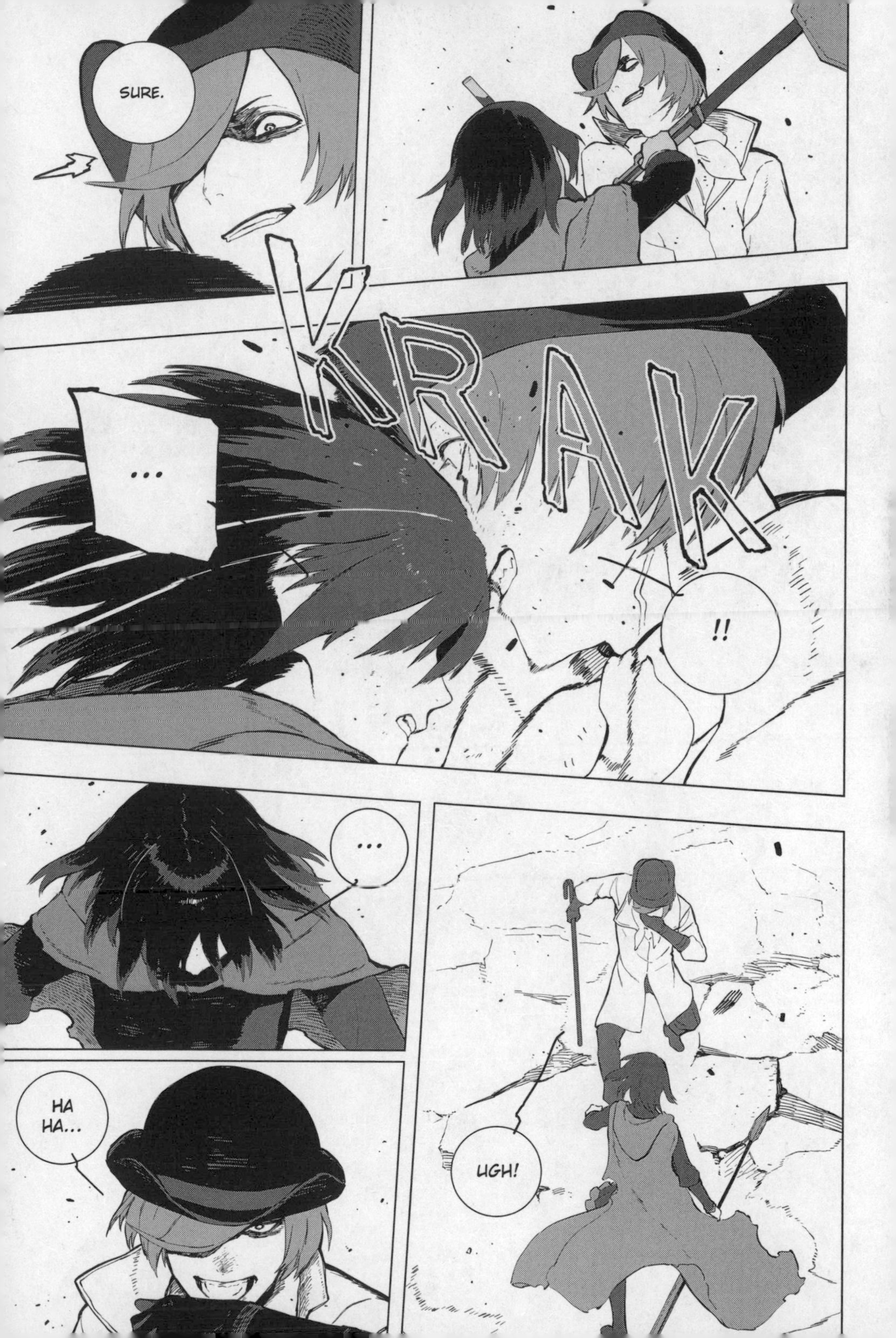
SURE.
KRAK
!!
...
UGH!
...
HA HA...

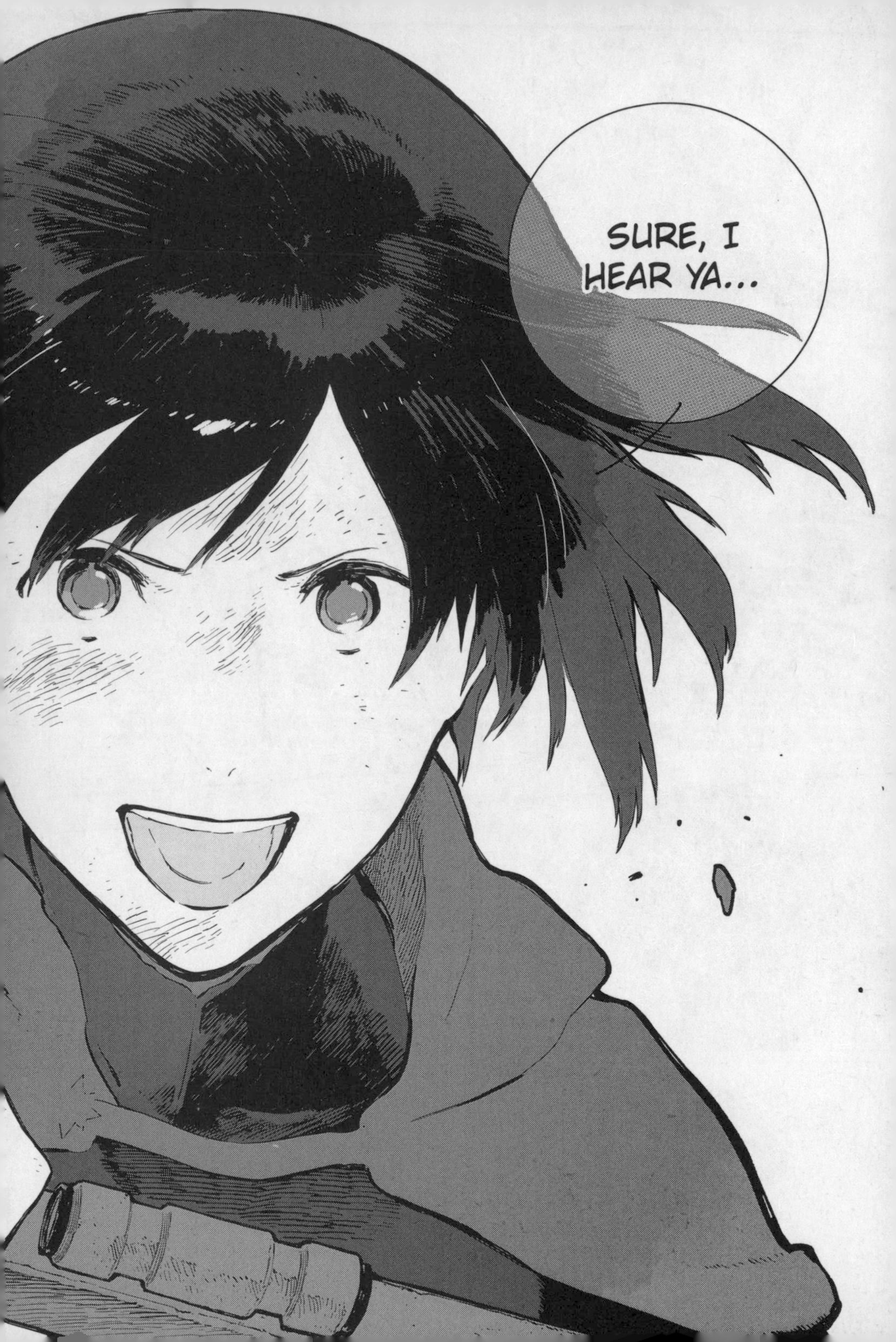
SURE, I HEAR YA...

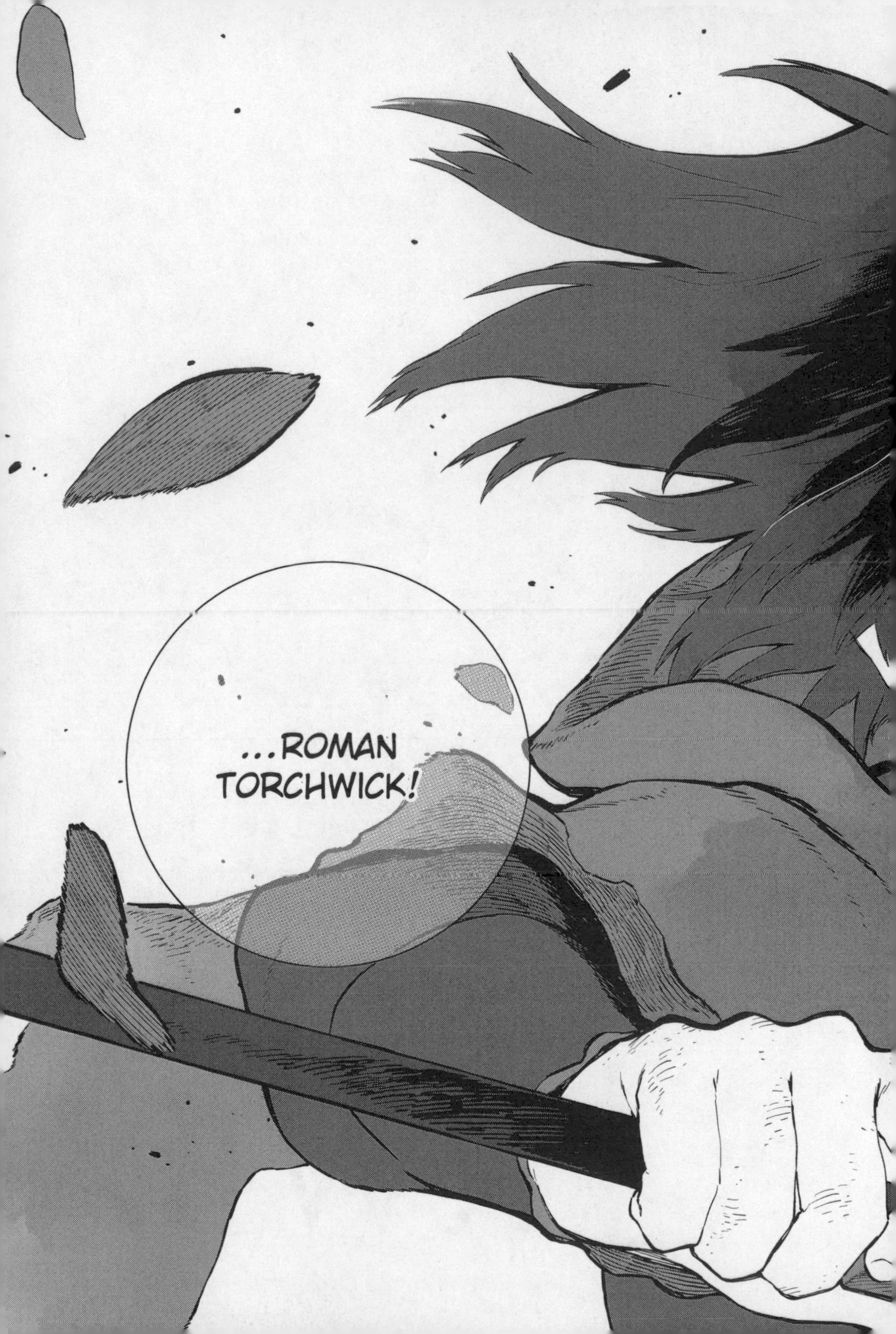
...ROMAN TORCHWICK!

RWBY

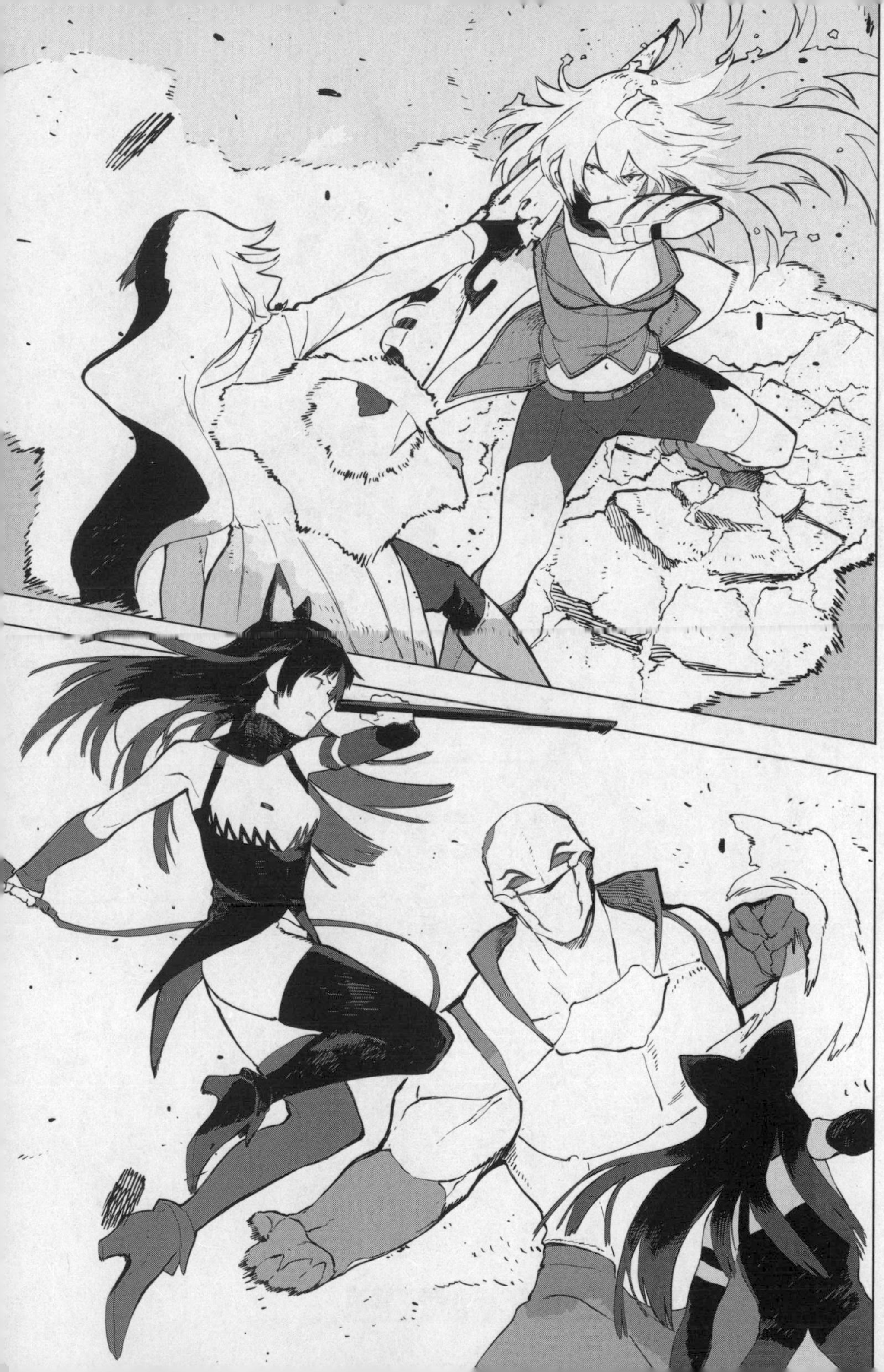

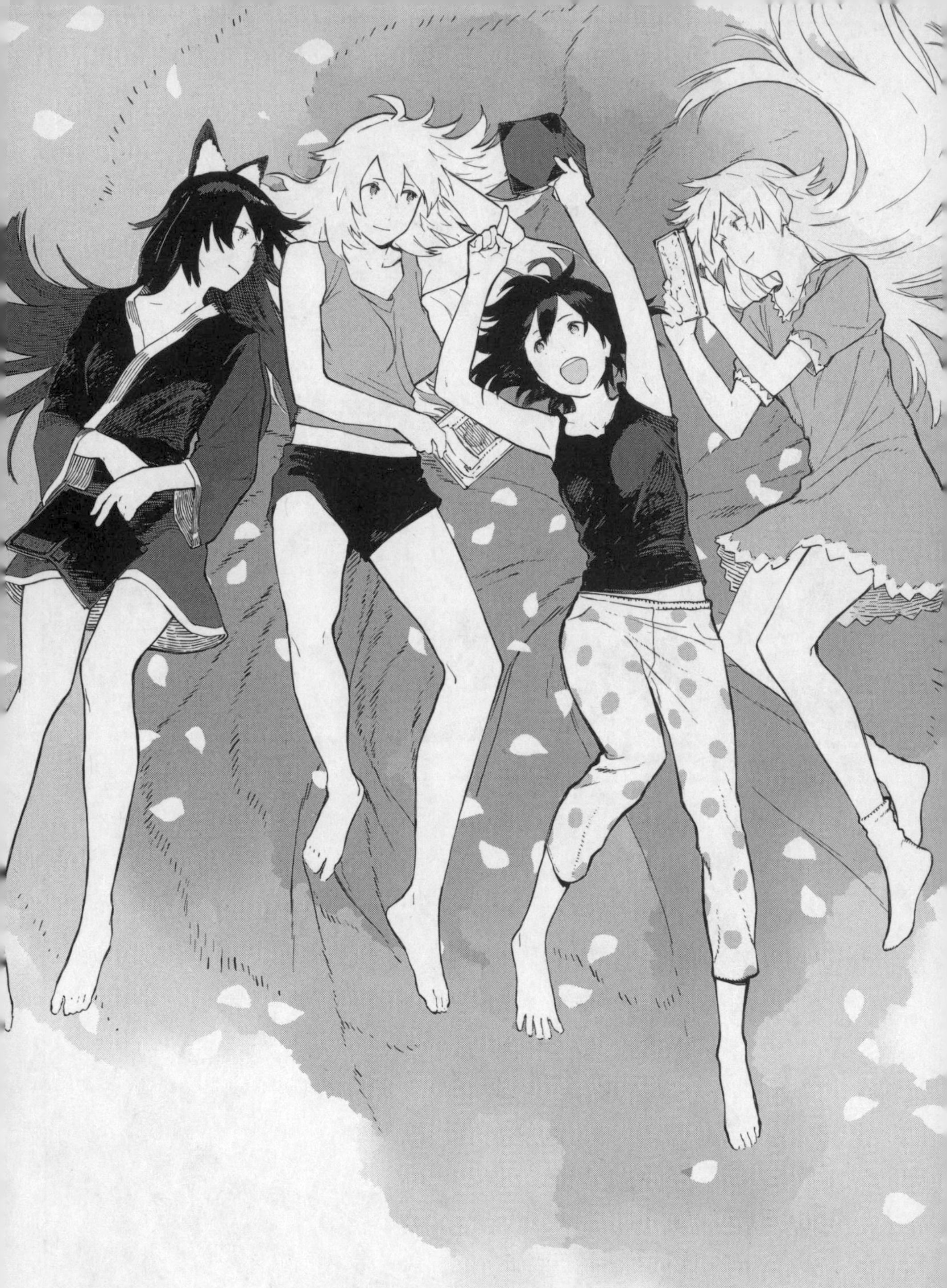

Final Episode

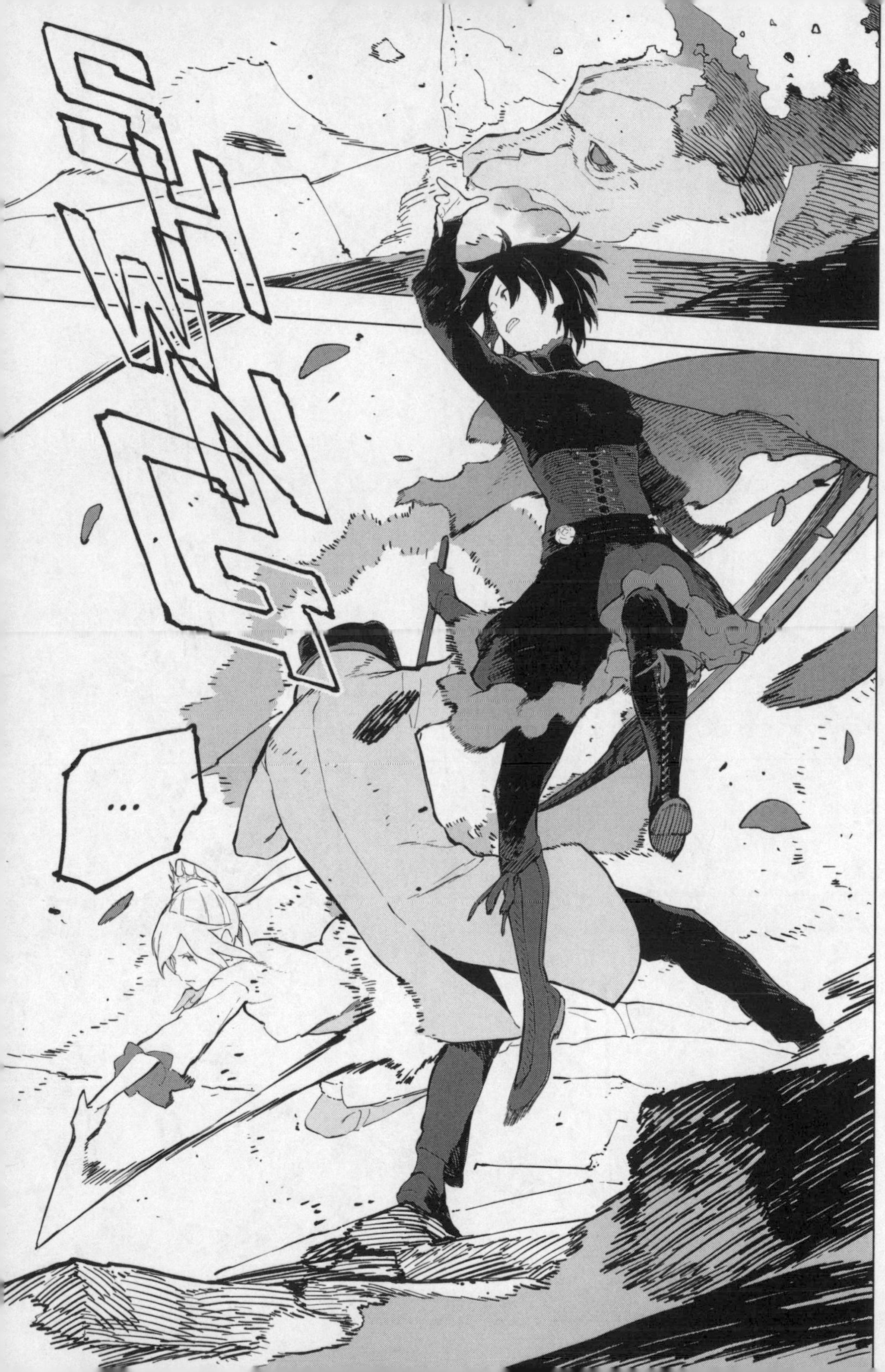
...

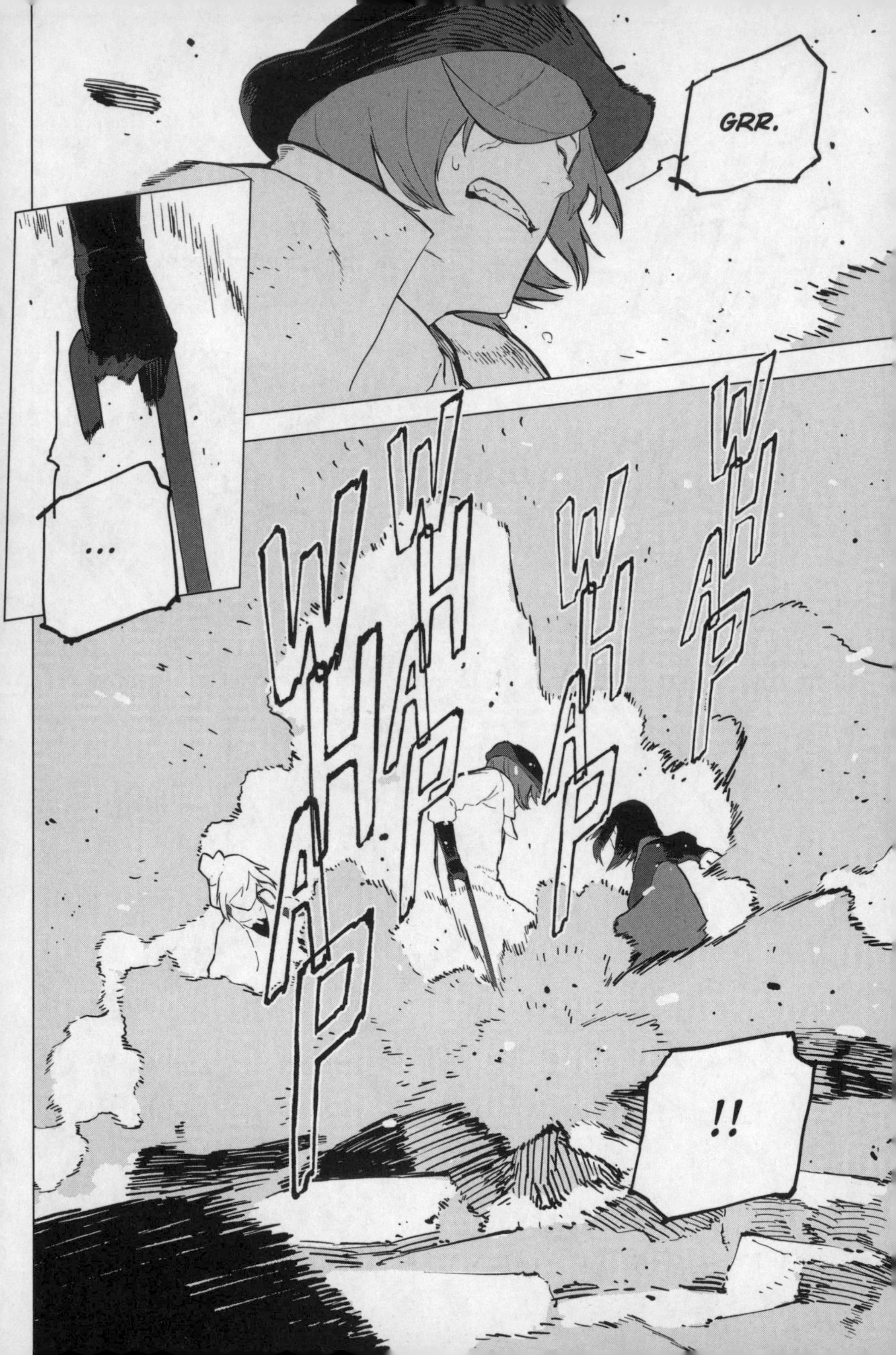
GRR.
...
WHAP
WHAP
WHAP
WHAP
!!

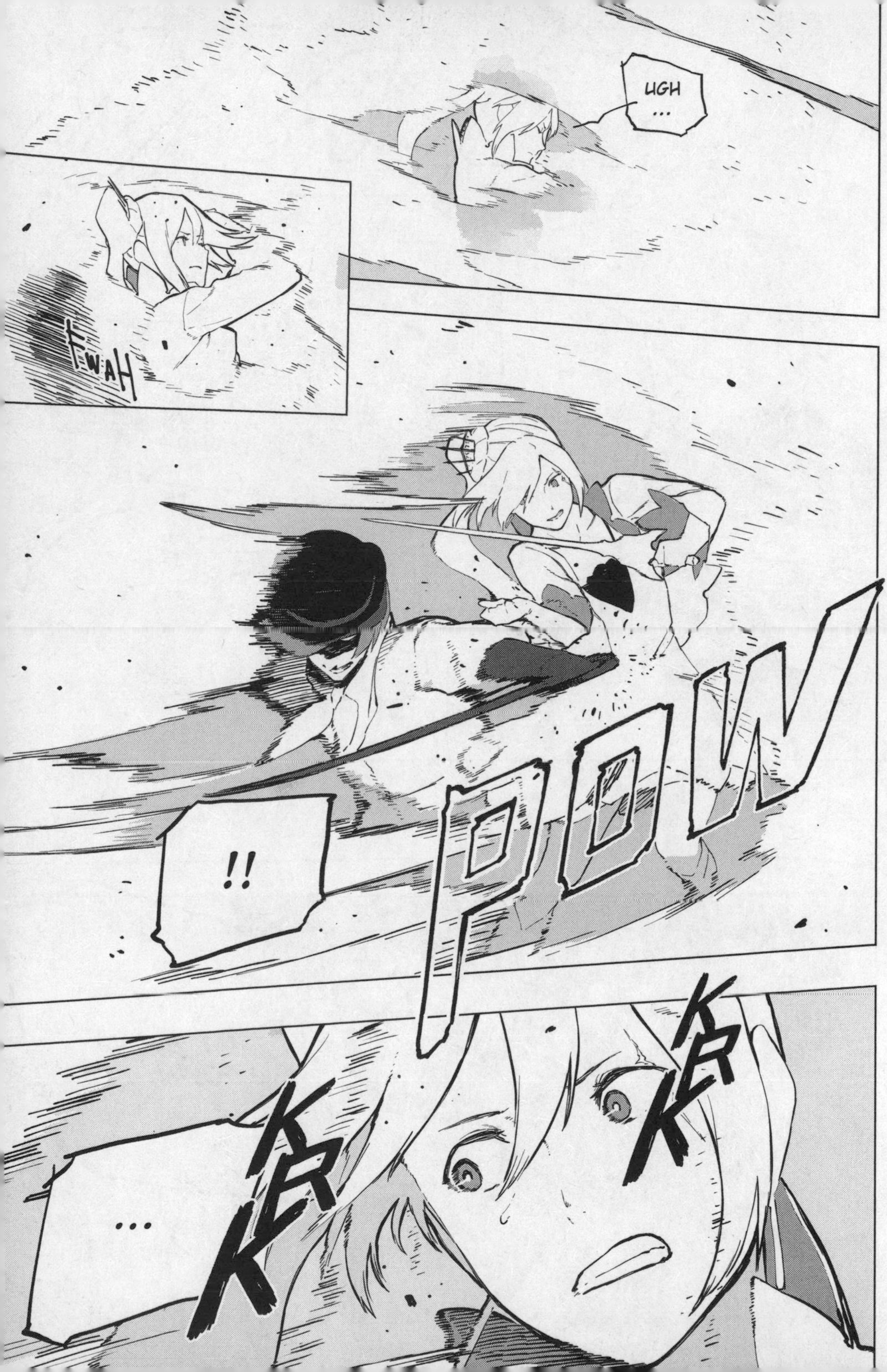
UGH
...
FWAH
POW
!!
KRK
KRK
...

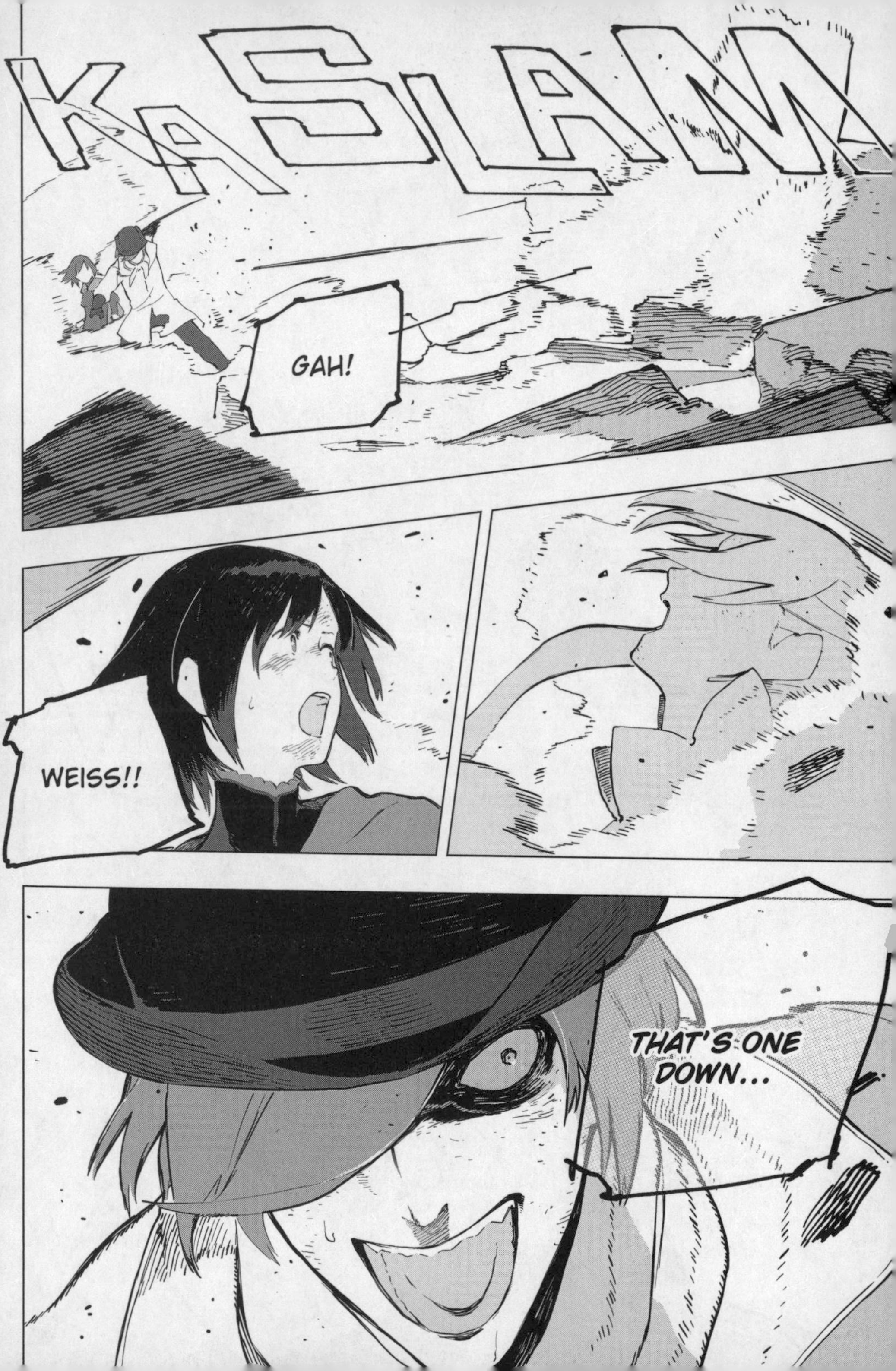
KASLAM
GAH!
WEISS!!
THAT'S ONE DOWN...

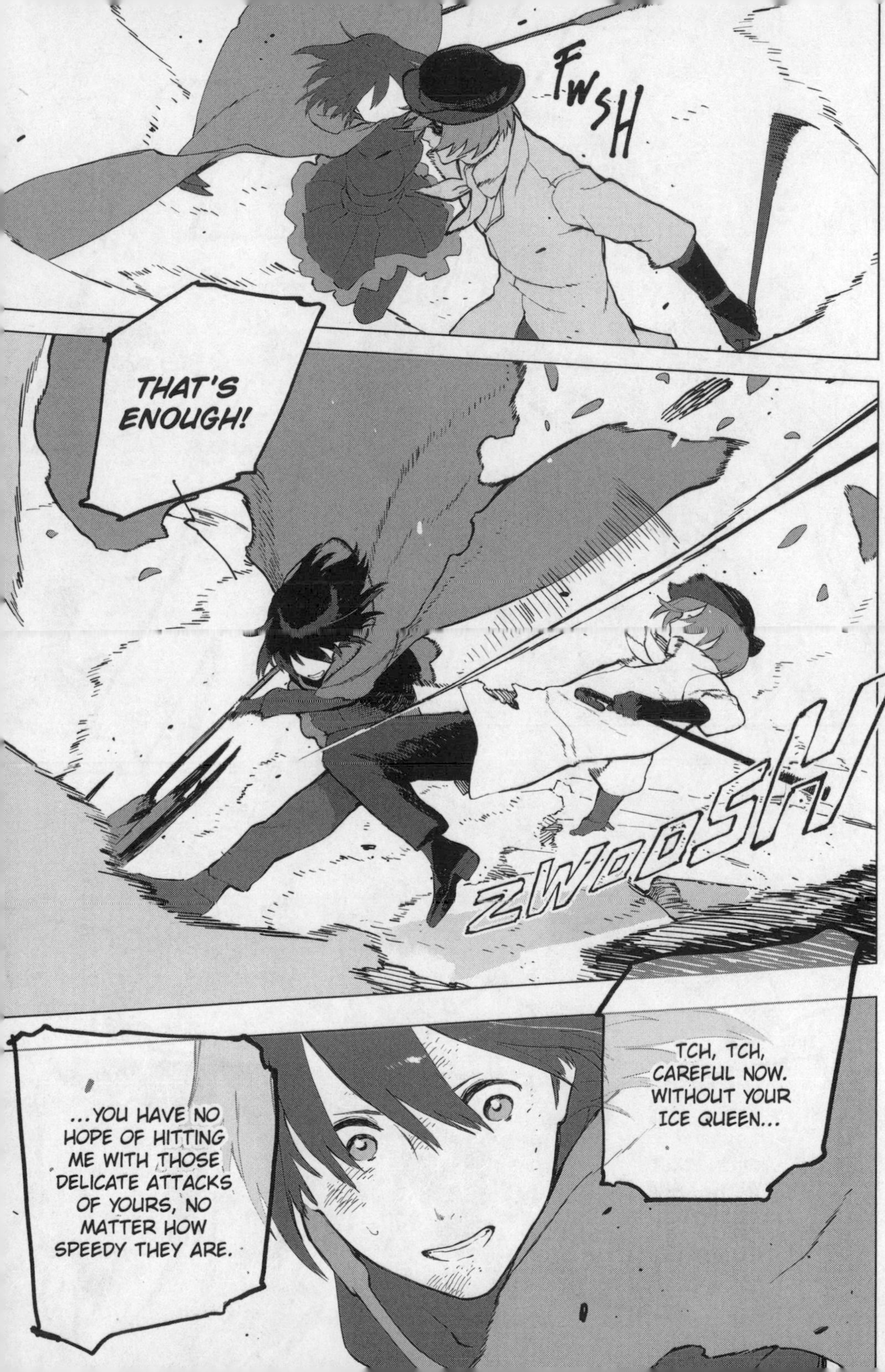
FWSH
THAT'S ENOUGH!
ZWOOSH
TCH, TCH, CAREFUL NOW. WITHOUT YOUR ICE QUEEN...
...YOU HAVE NO HOPE OF HITTING ME WITH THOSE DELICATE ATTACKS OF YOURS, NO MATTER HOW SPEEDY THEY ARE.

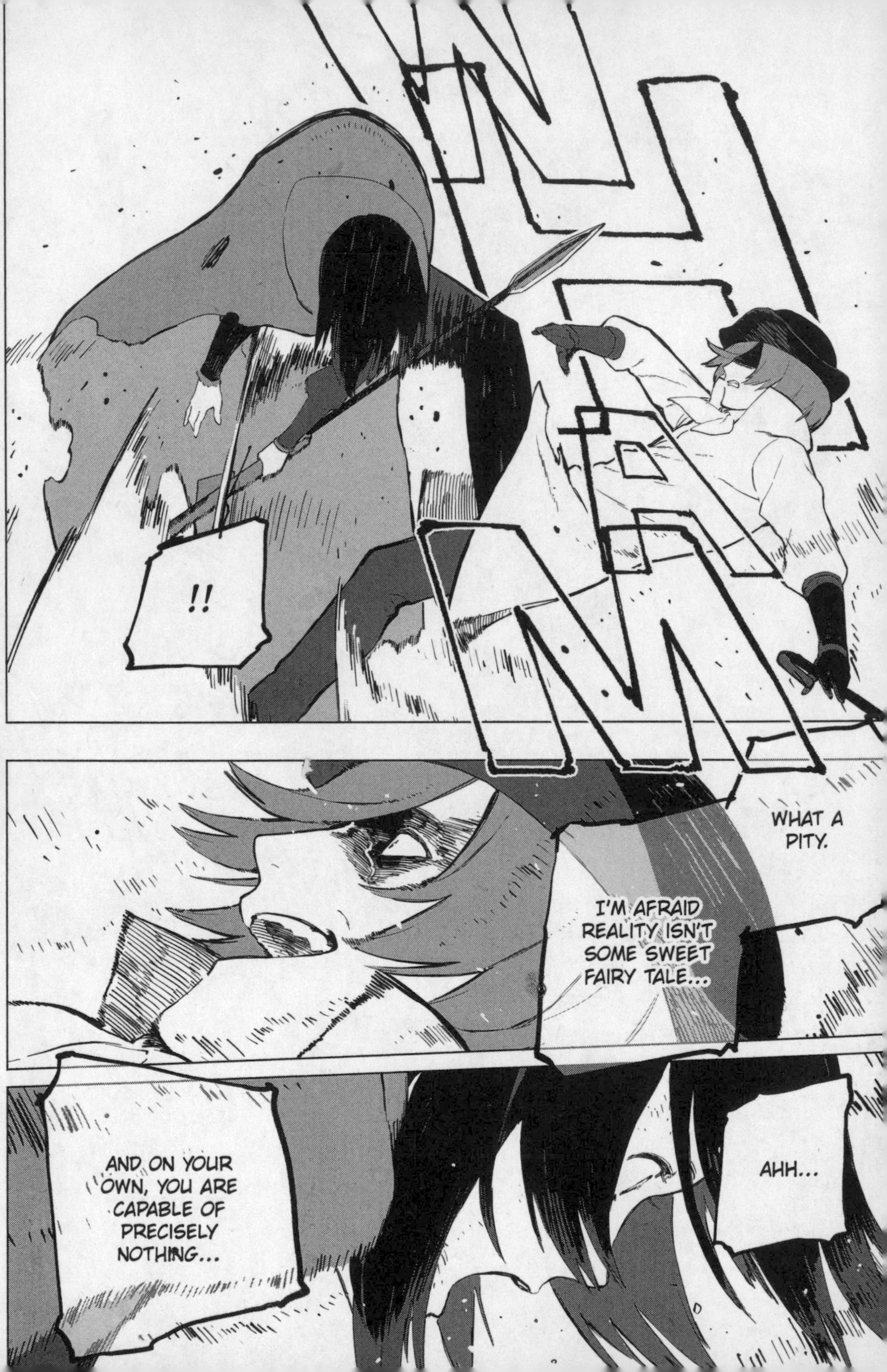
WHAM
!!
WHAT A PITY.
I'M AFRAID REALITY ISN'T SOME SWEET FAIRY TALE...
AHH...
AND ON YOUR OWN, YOU ARE CAPABLE OF PRECISELY NOTHING...

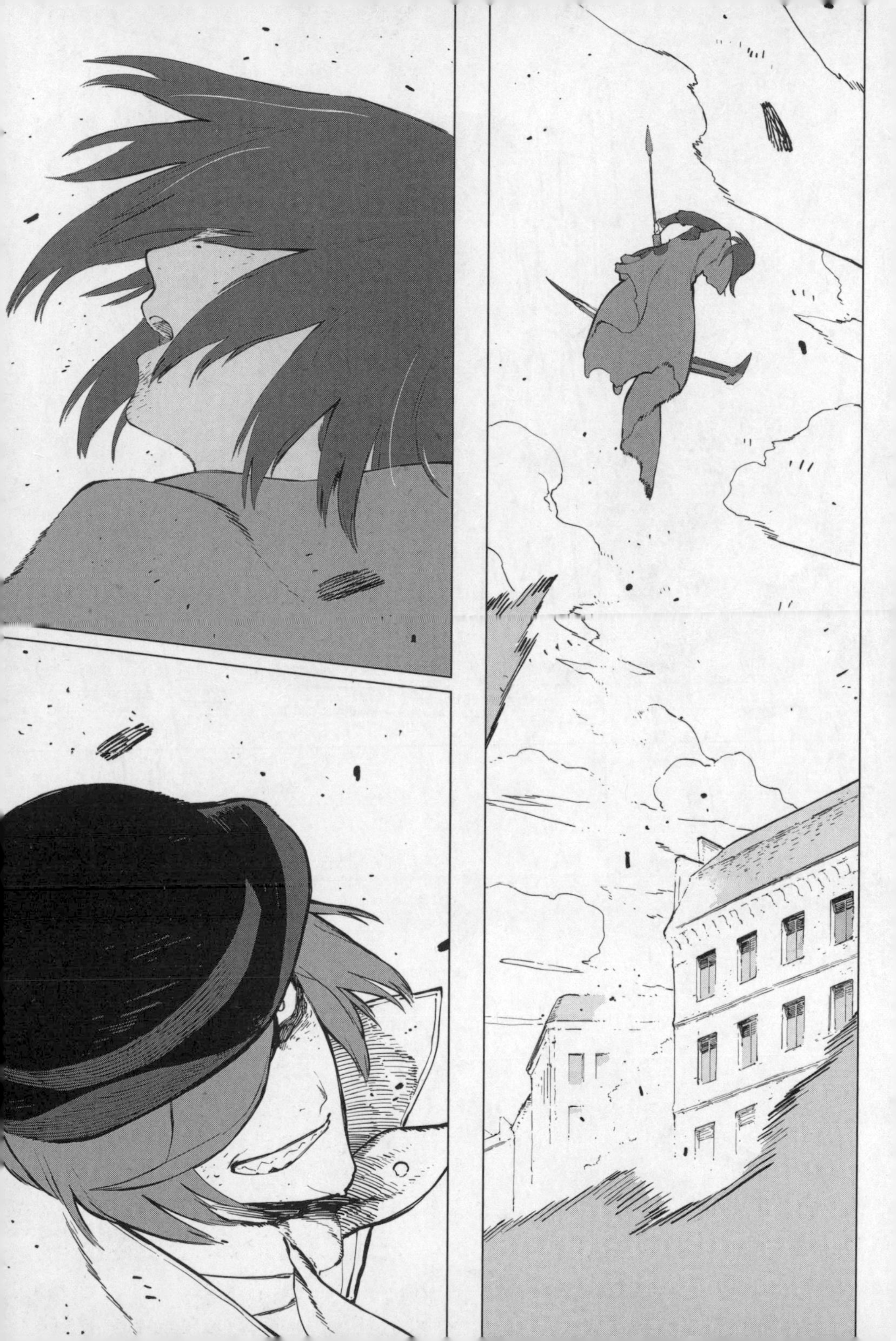

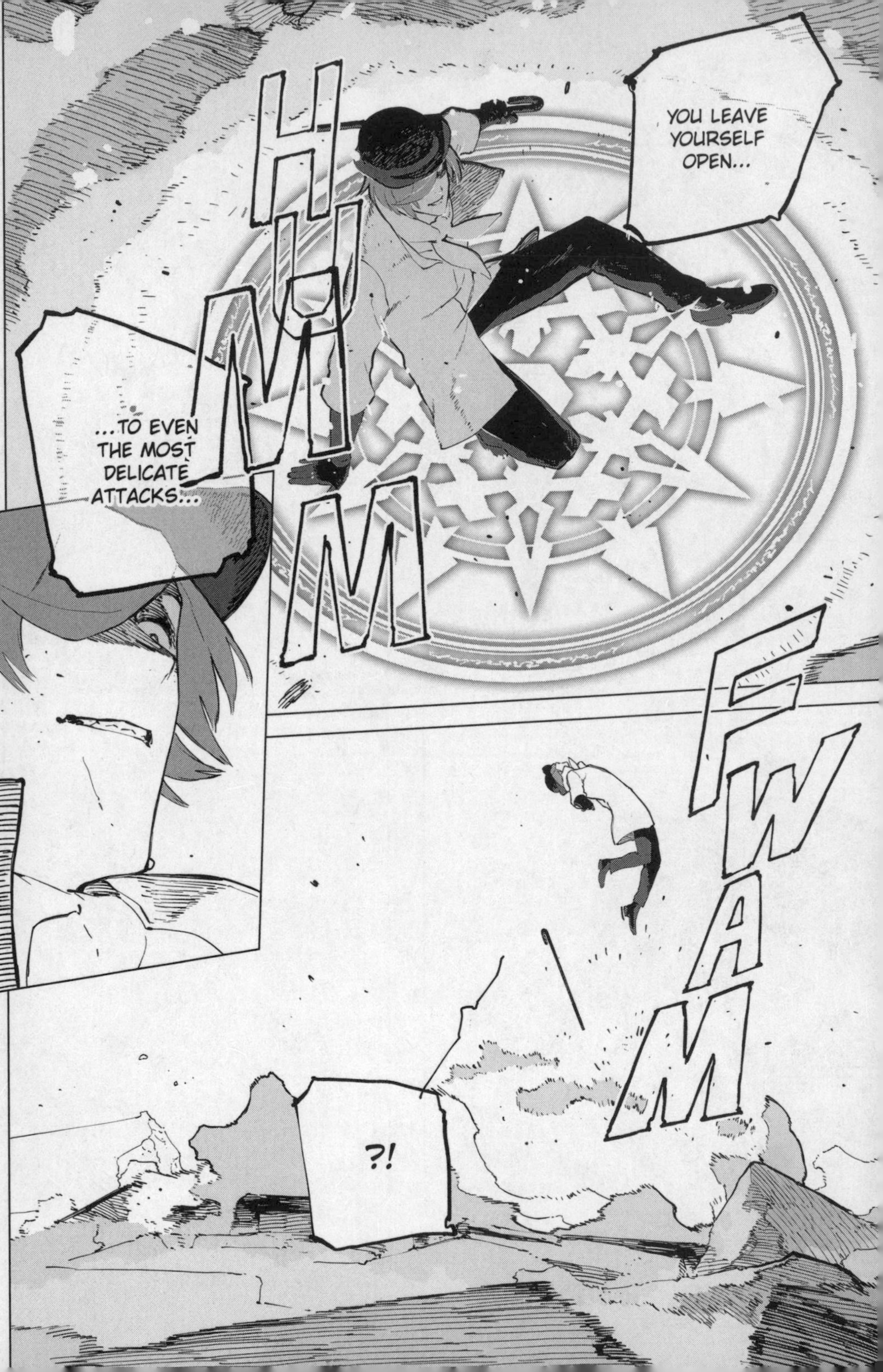
YOU LEAVE YOURSELF OPEN...
HUMMM
...TO EVEN THE MOST DELICATE ATTACKS...
FWAM
?!

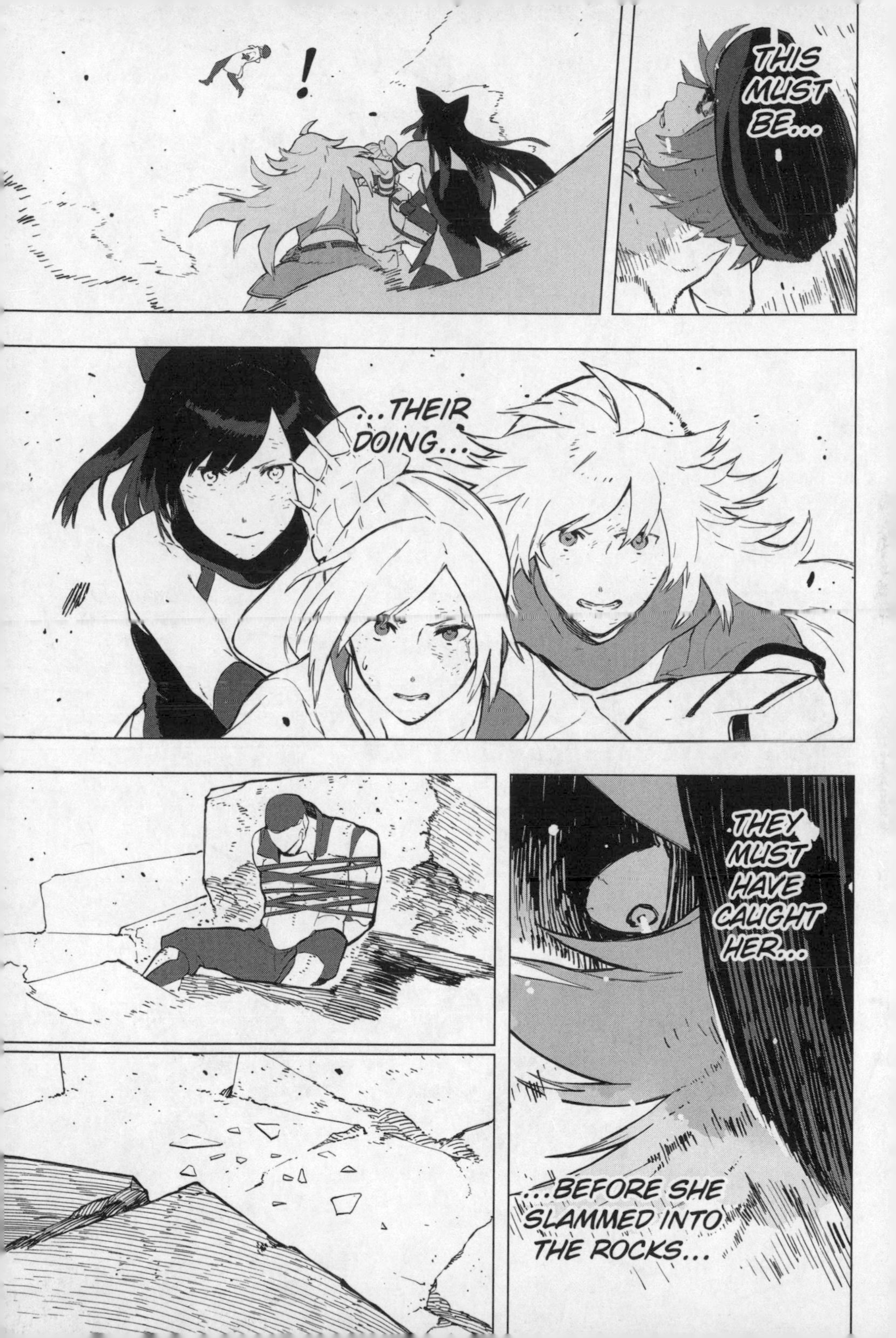
!
THIS MUST BE...
...THEIR DOING...
THEY MUST HAVE CAUGHT HER...
...BEFORE SHE SLAMMED INTO THE ROCKS...

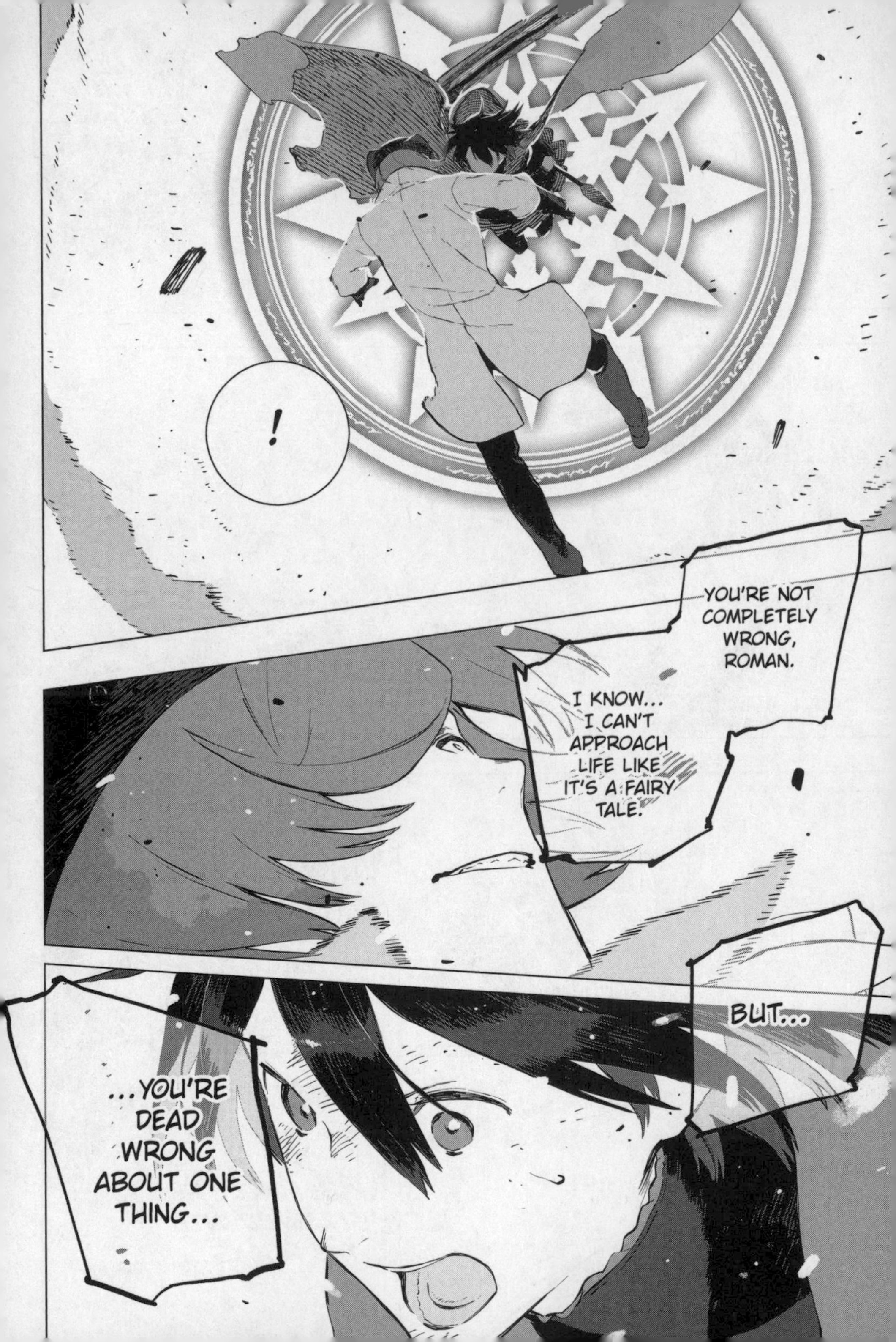
!
YOU'RE NOT COMPLETELY WRONG, ROMAN.
I KNOW... I CAN'T APPROACH LIFE LIKE IT'S A FAIRY TALE.
BUT...
...YOU'RE DEAD WRONG ABOUT ONE THING...

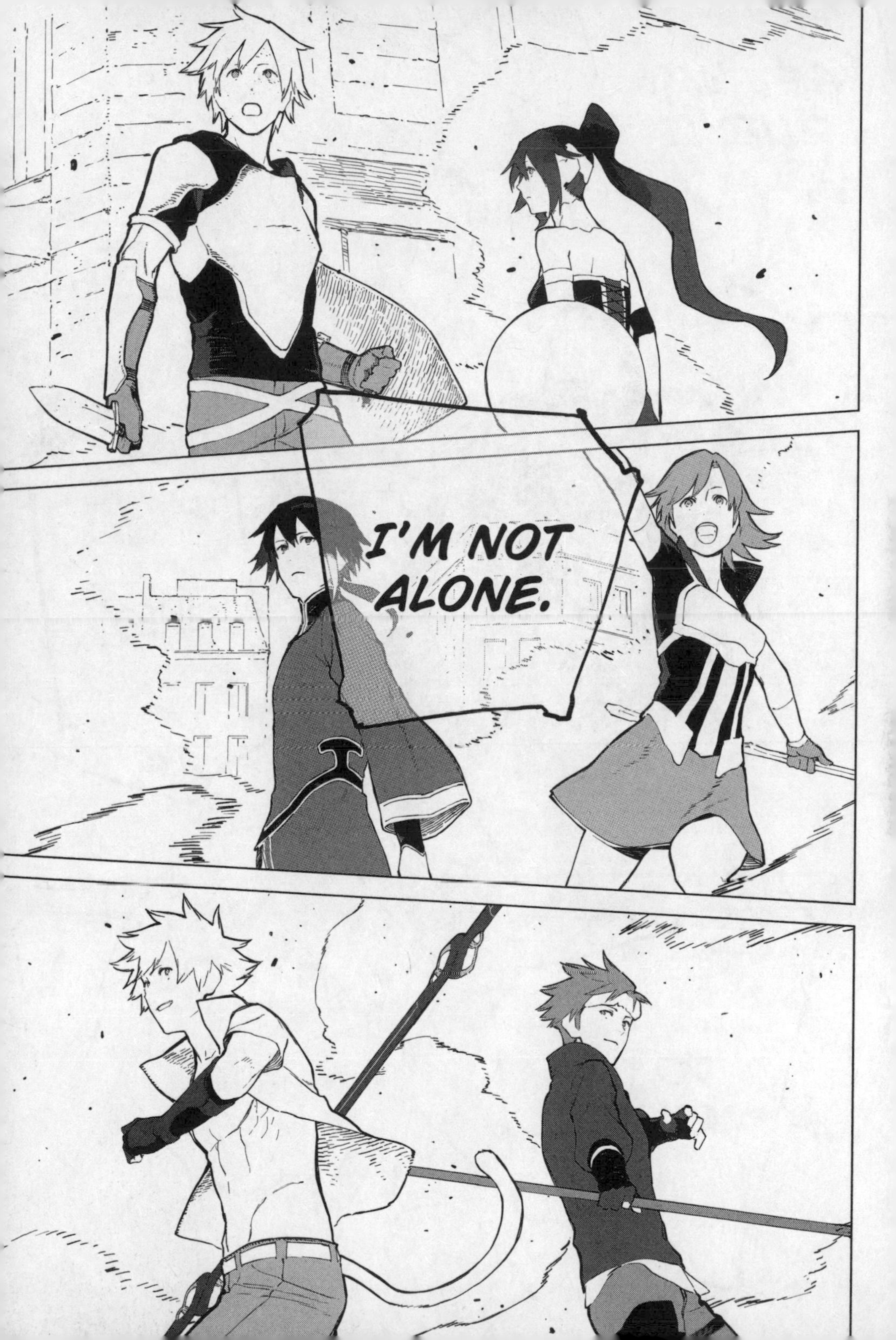
I'M NOT ALONE.

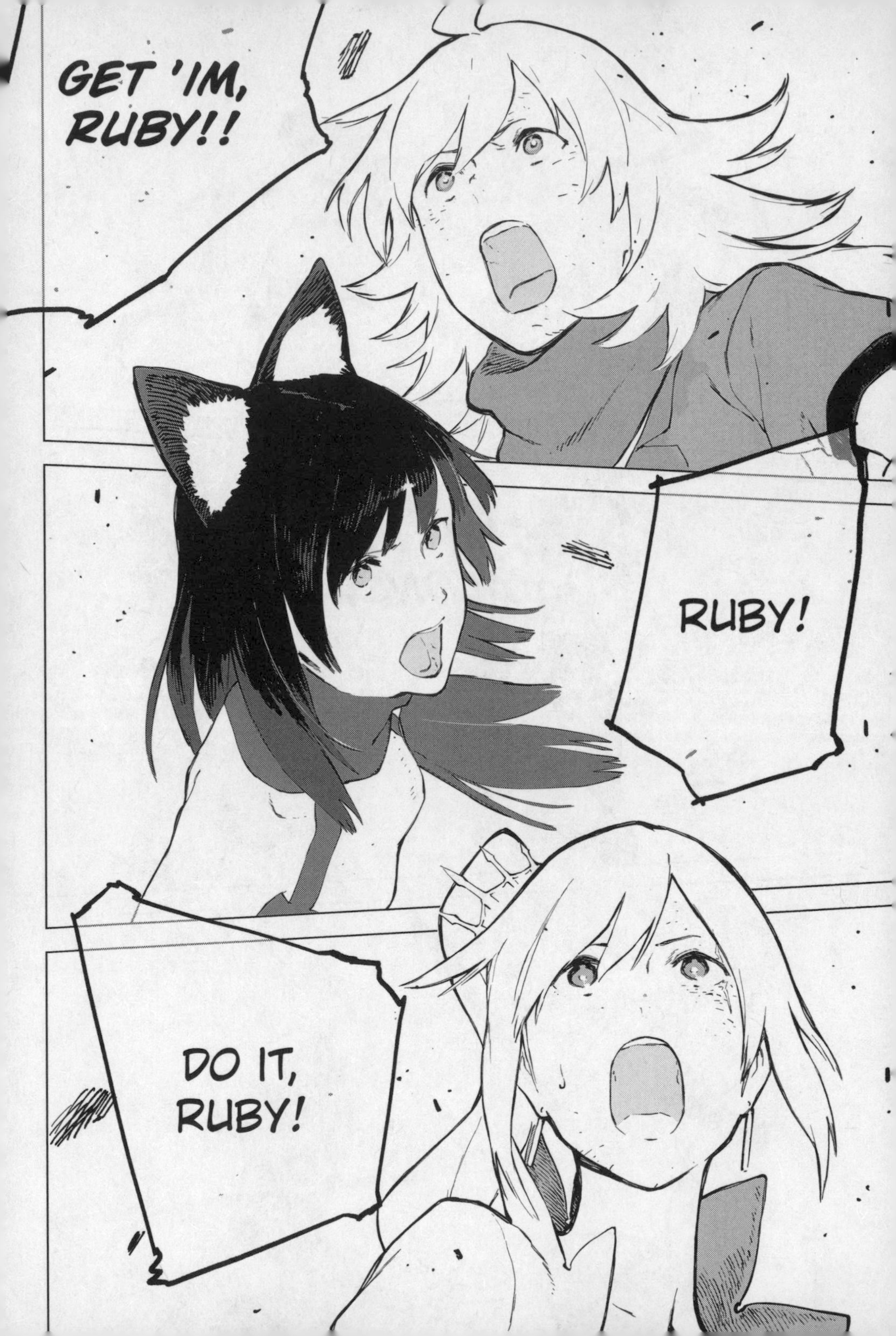
GET 'IM, RUBY!!
RUBY!
DO IT, RUBY!

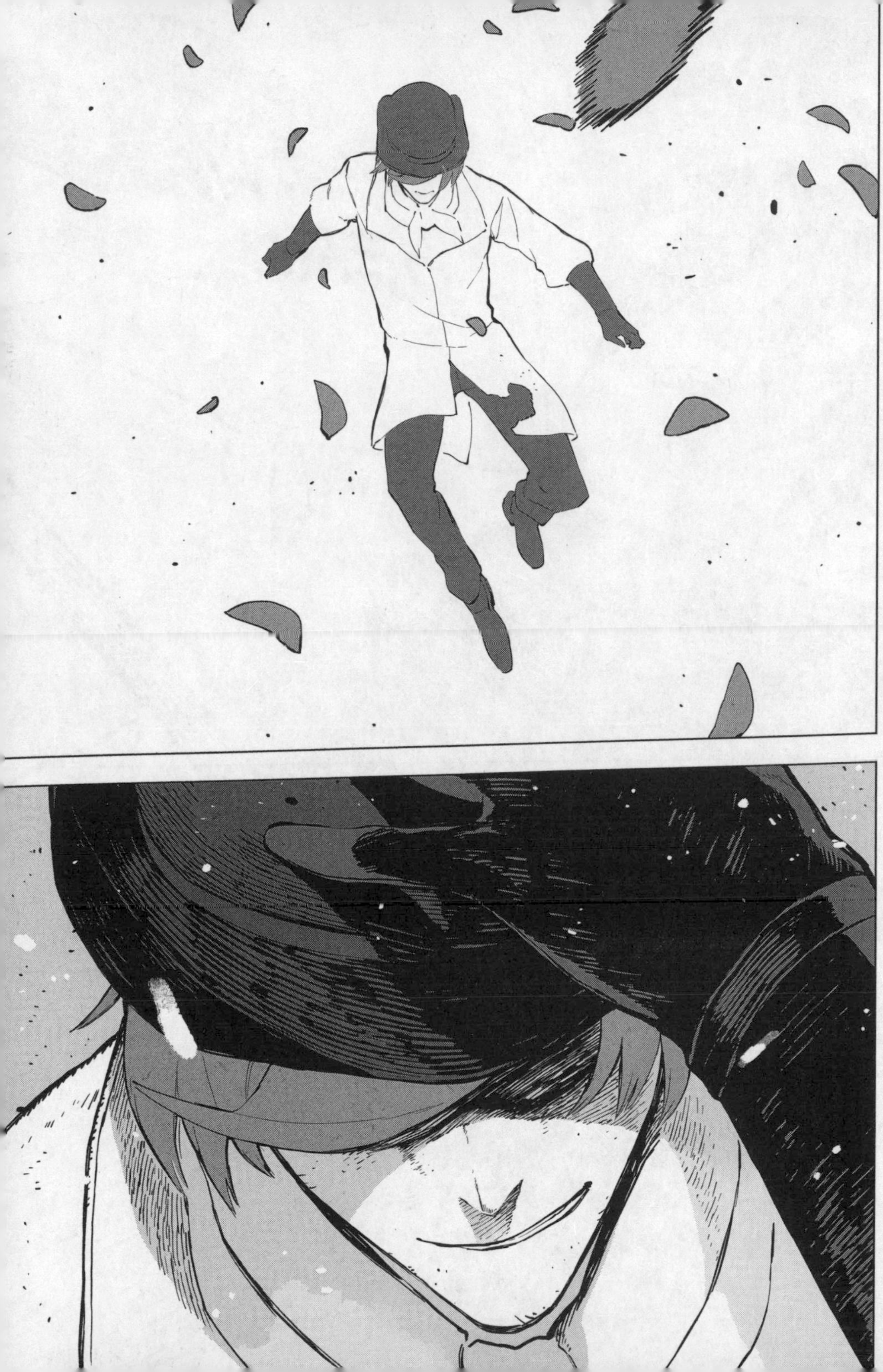

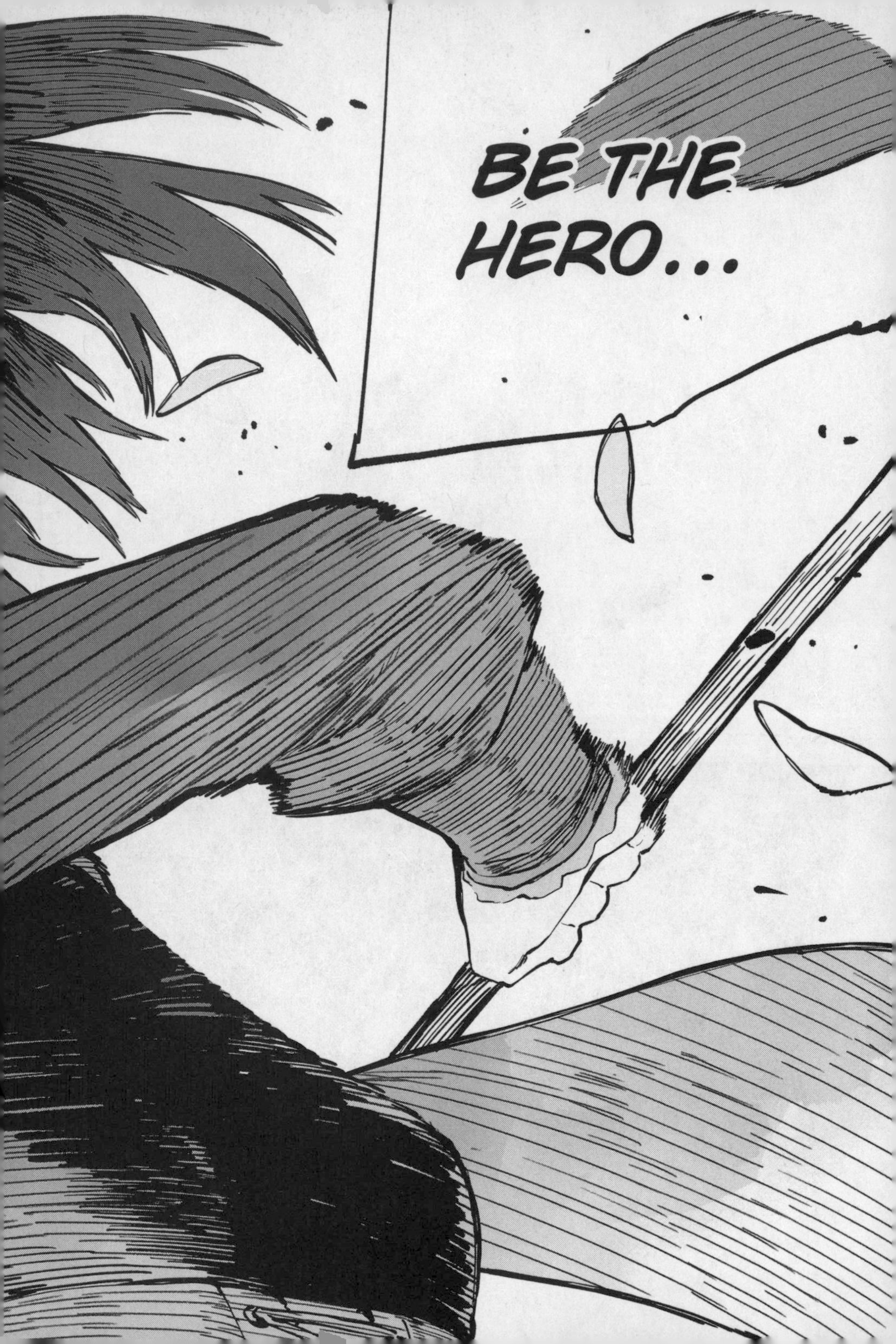
BE THE HERO...

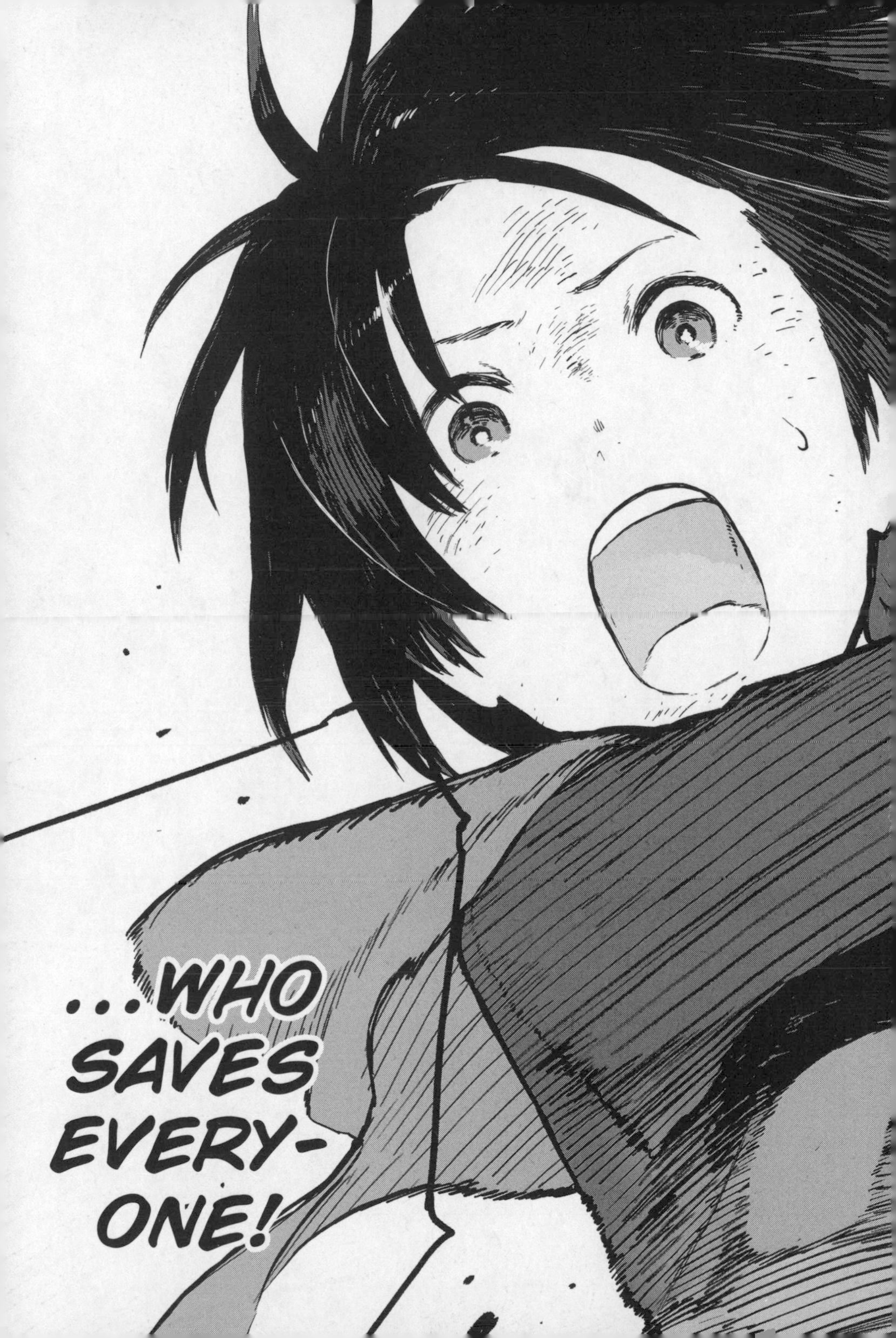
...WHO SAVES EVERY-ONE!

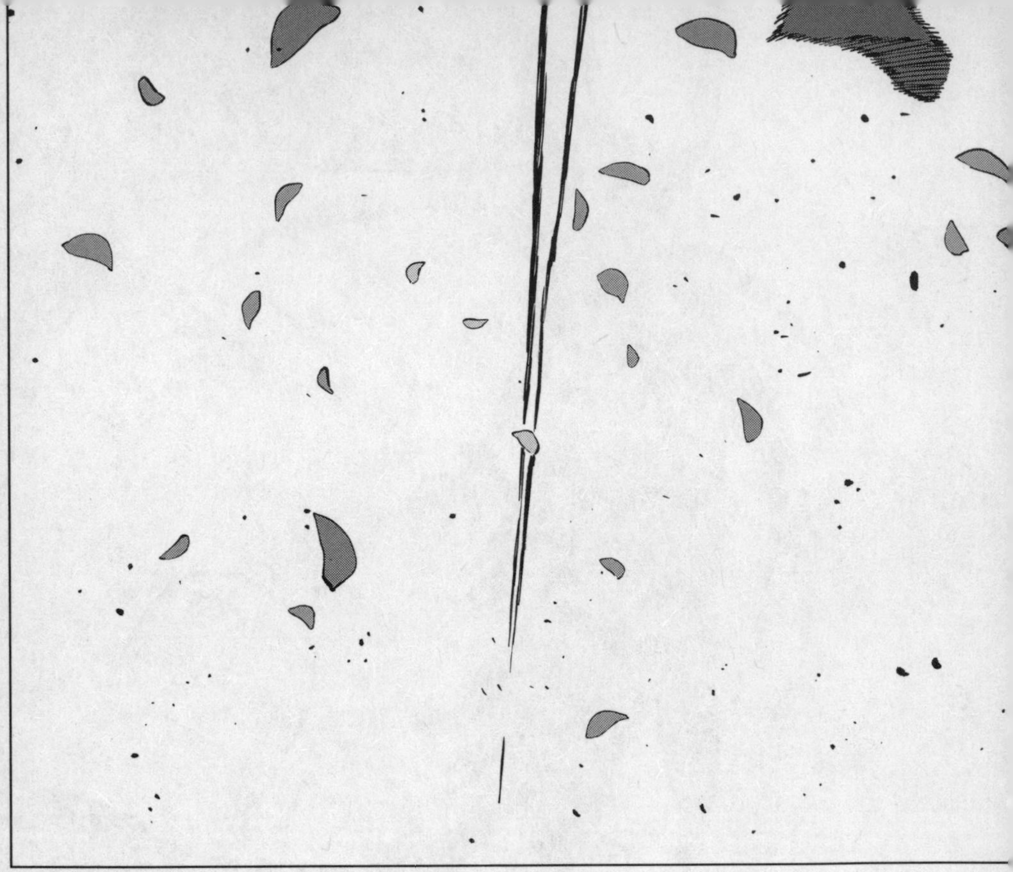
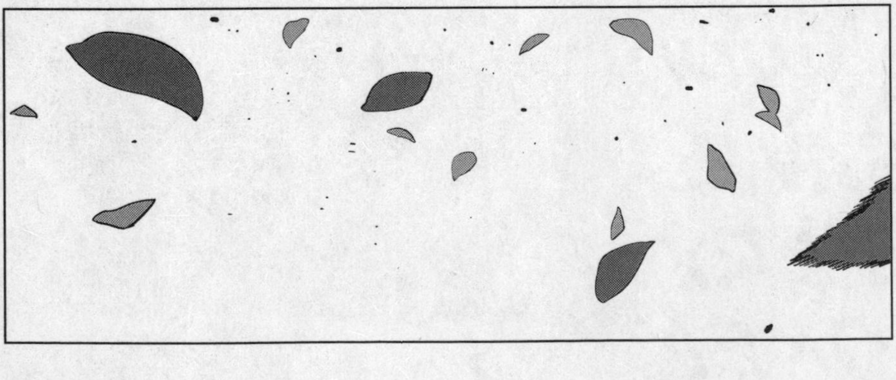

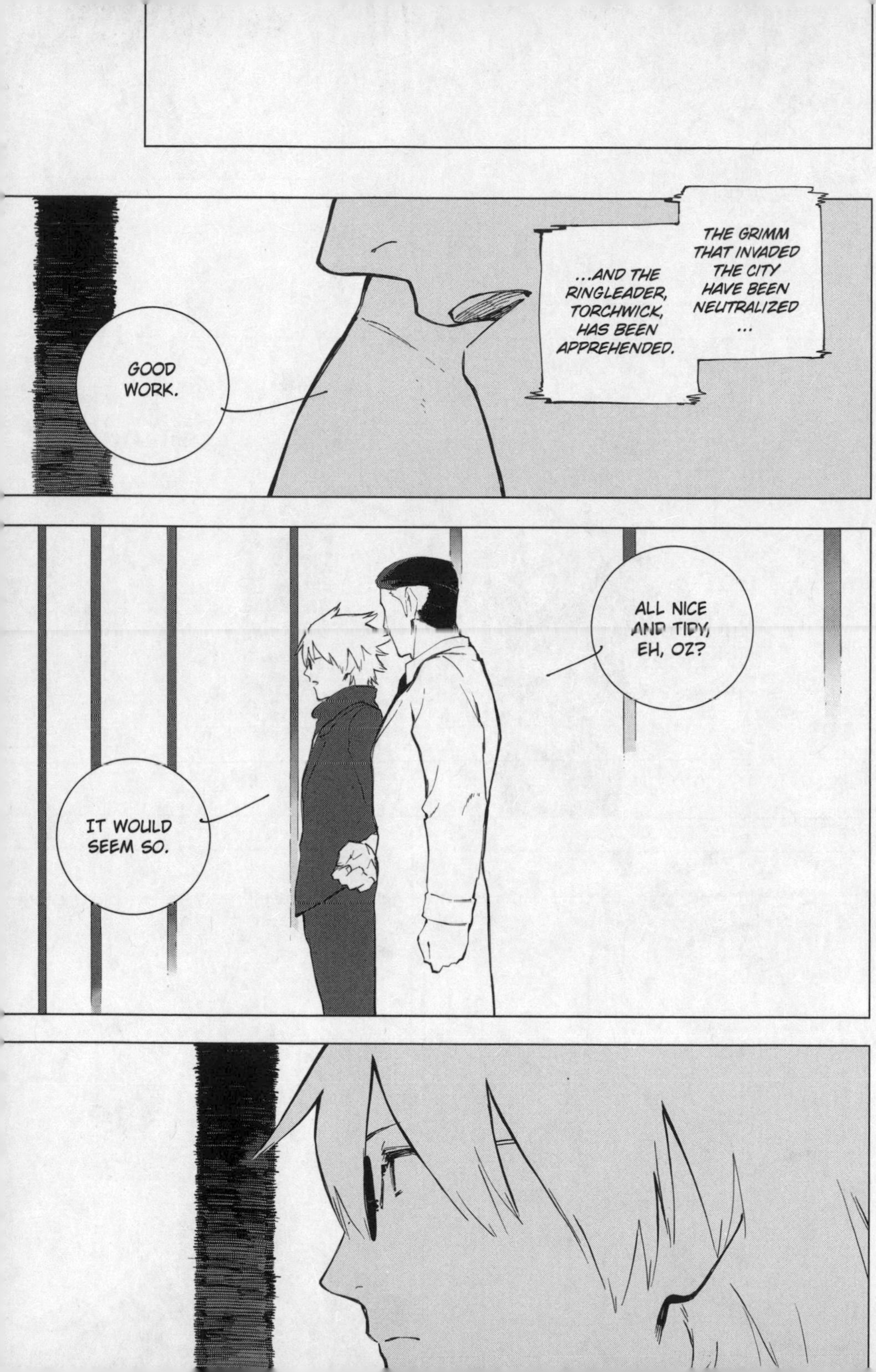
THE GRIMM THAT INVADED THE CITY HAVE BEEN NEUTRALIZED ...
...AND THE RINGLEADER, TORCHWICK, HAS BEEN APPREHENDED.
GOOD WORK.
ALL NICE AND TIDY, EH, OZ?
IT WOULD SEEM SO.

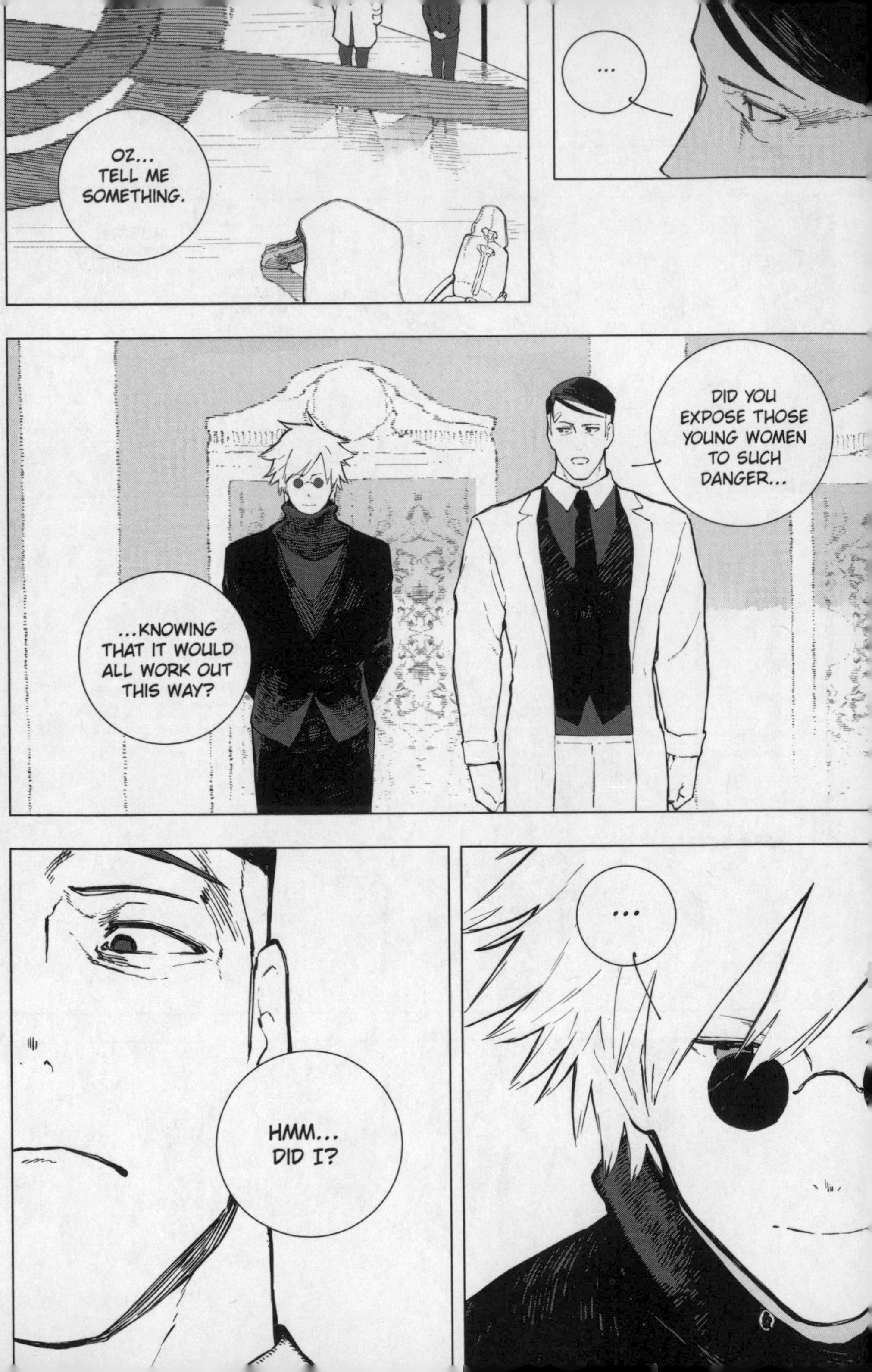
...
OZ... TELL ME SOMETHING.
DID YOU EXPOSE THOSE YOUNG WOMEN TO SUCH DANGER...
...KNOWING THAT IT WOULD ALL WORK OUT THIS WAY?
...
HMM... DID I?

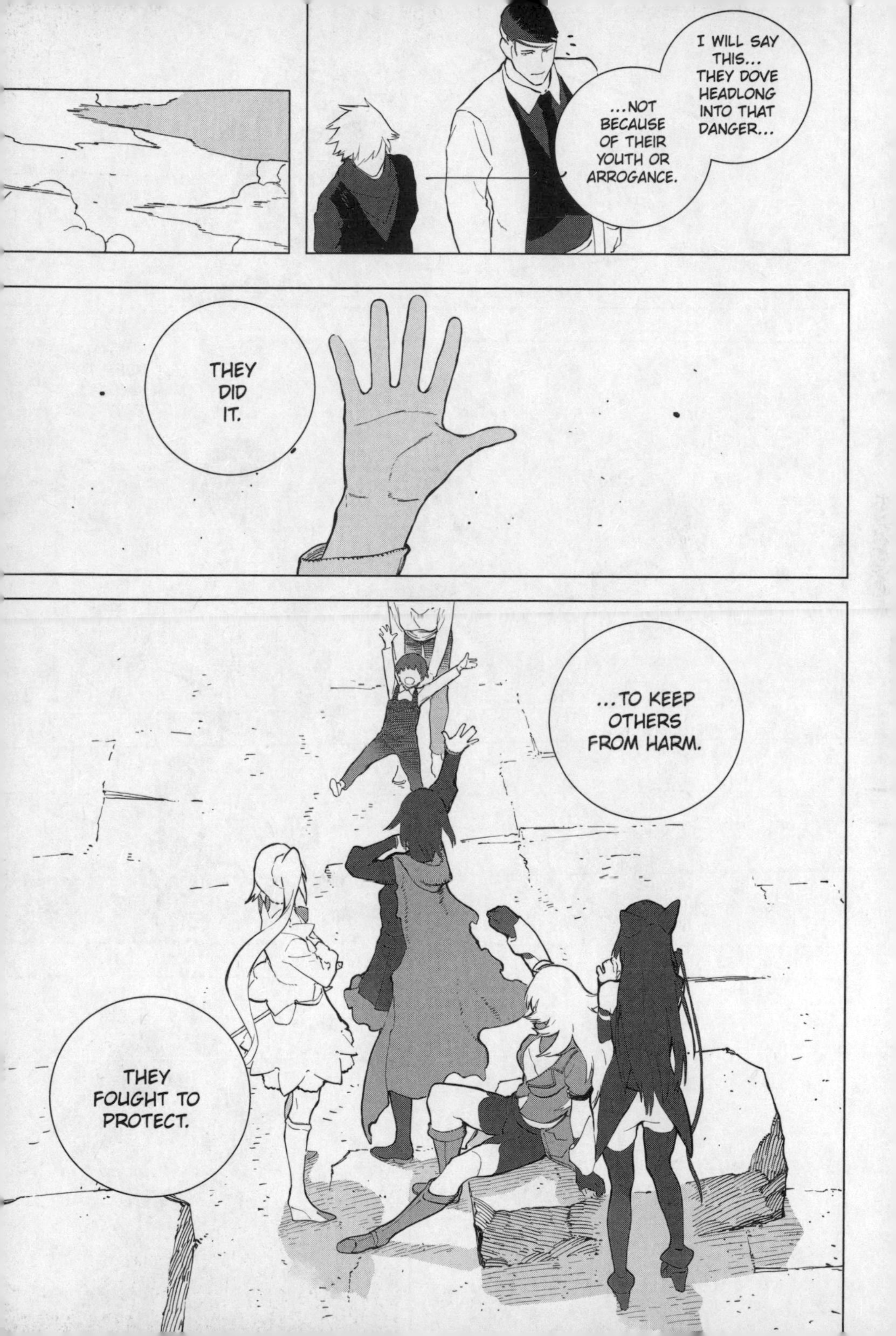
I WILL SAY THIS... THEY DOVE HEADLONG INTO THAT DANGER...
...NOT BECAUSE OF THEIR YOUTH OR ARROGANCE.
THEY DID IT.
...TO KEEP OTHERS FROM HARM.
THEY FOUGHT TO PROTECT.

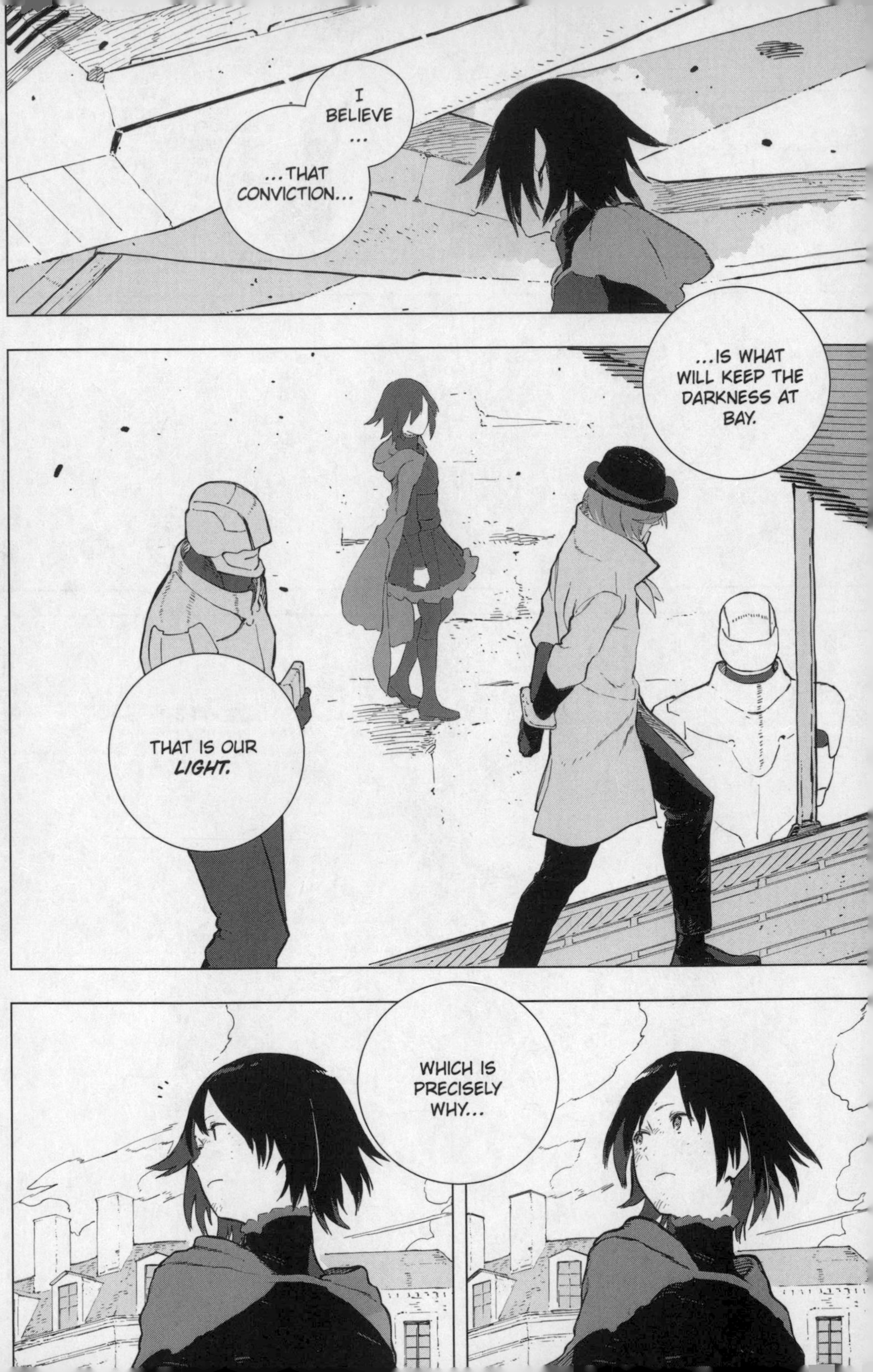
I BELIEVE ...
...THAT CONVICTION...
...IS WHAT WILL KEEP THE DARKNESS AT BAY.
THAT IS OUR *LIGHT.*
WHICH IS PRECISELY WHY...

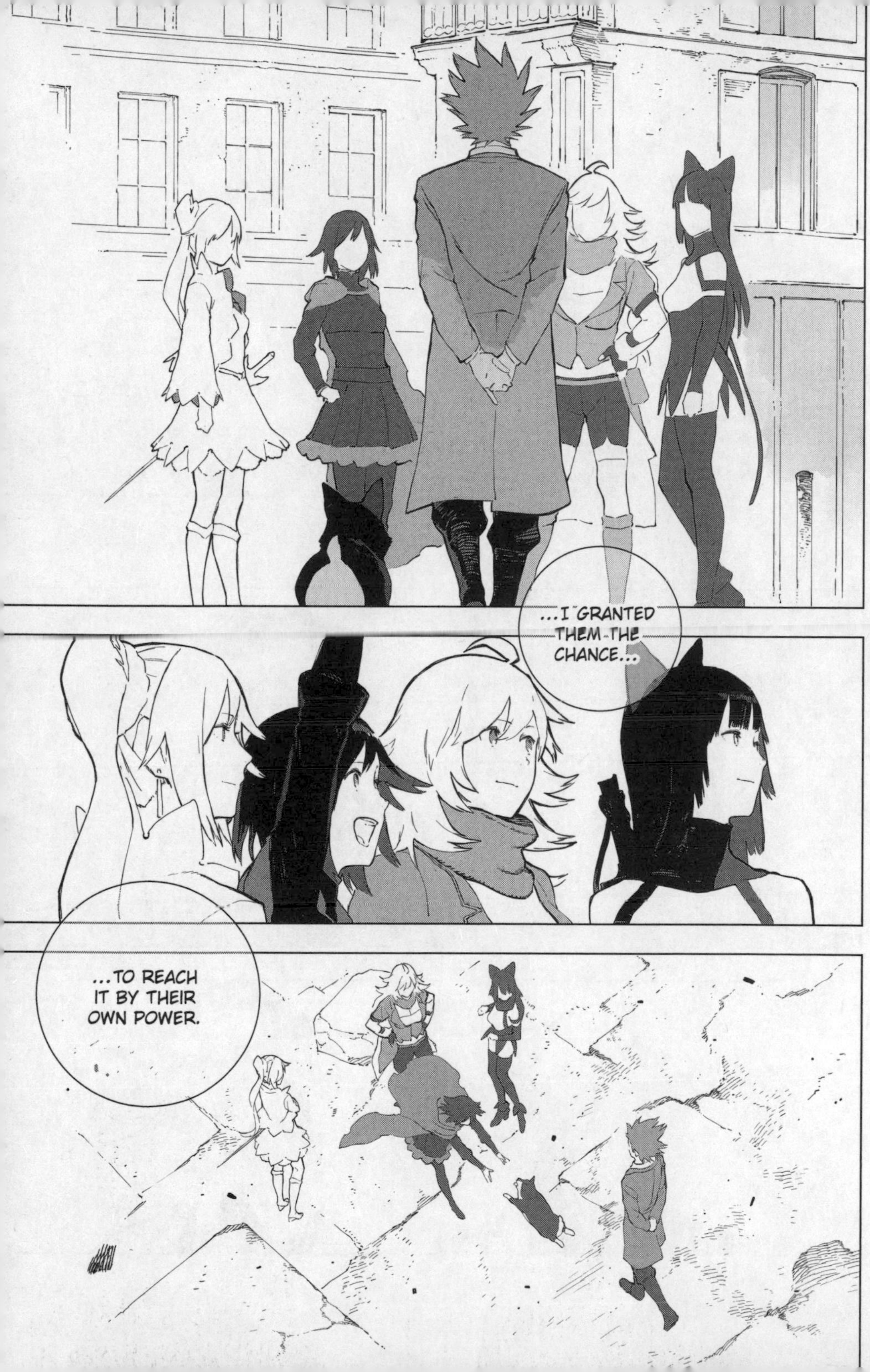
...I GRANTED THEM THE CHANCE...
...TO REACH IT BY THEIR OWN POWER.

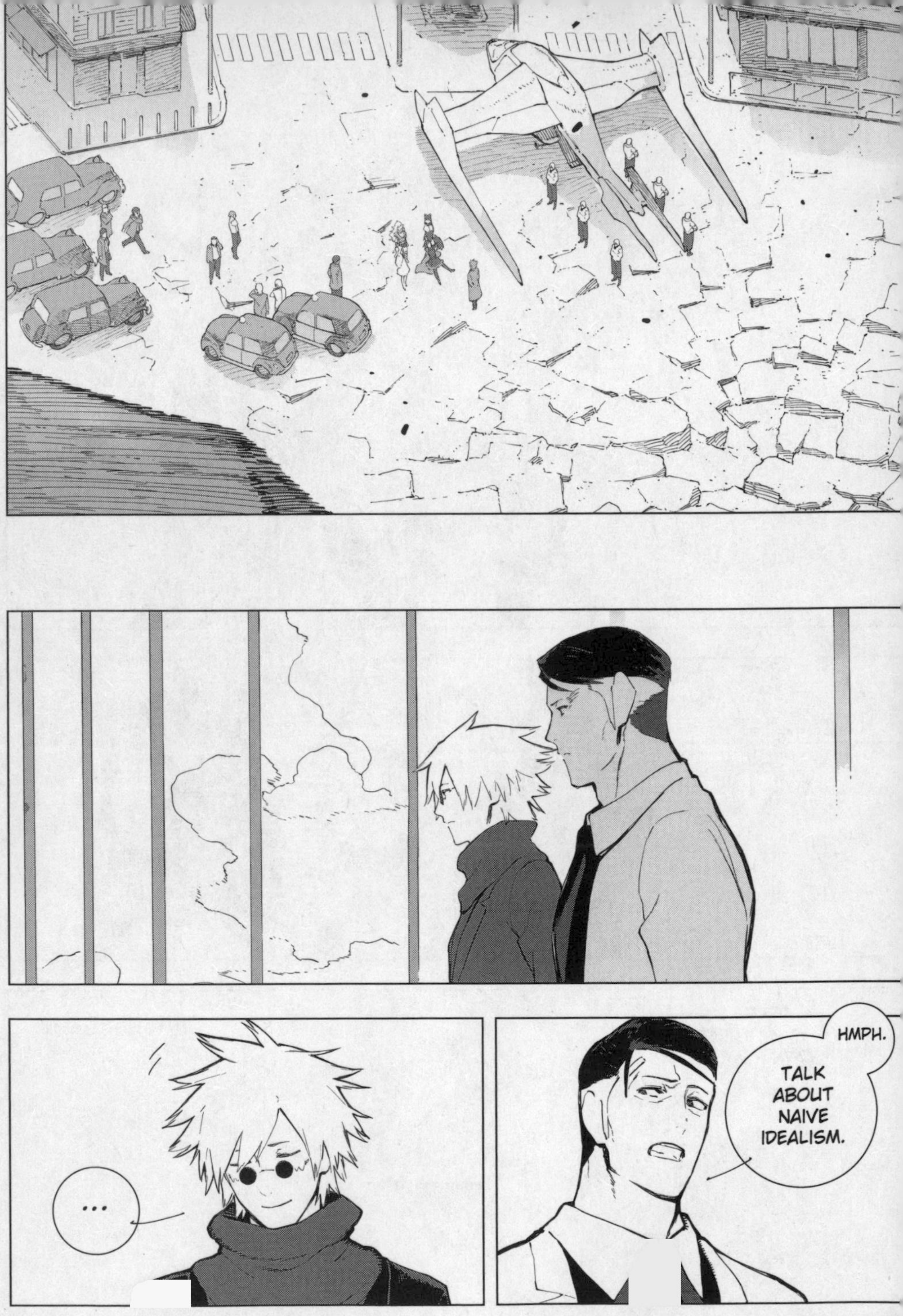
HMPH.
TALK ABOUT NAIVE IDEALISM.
...

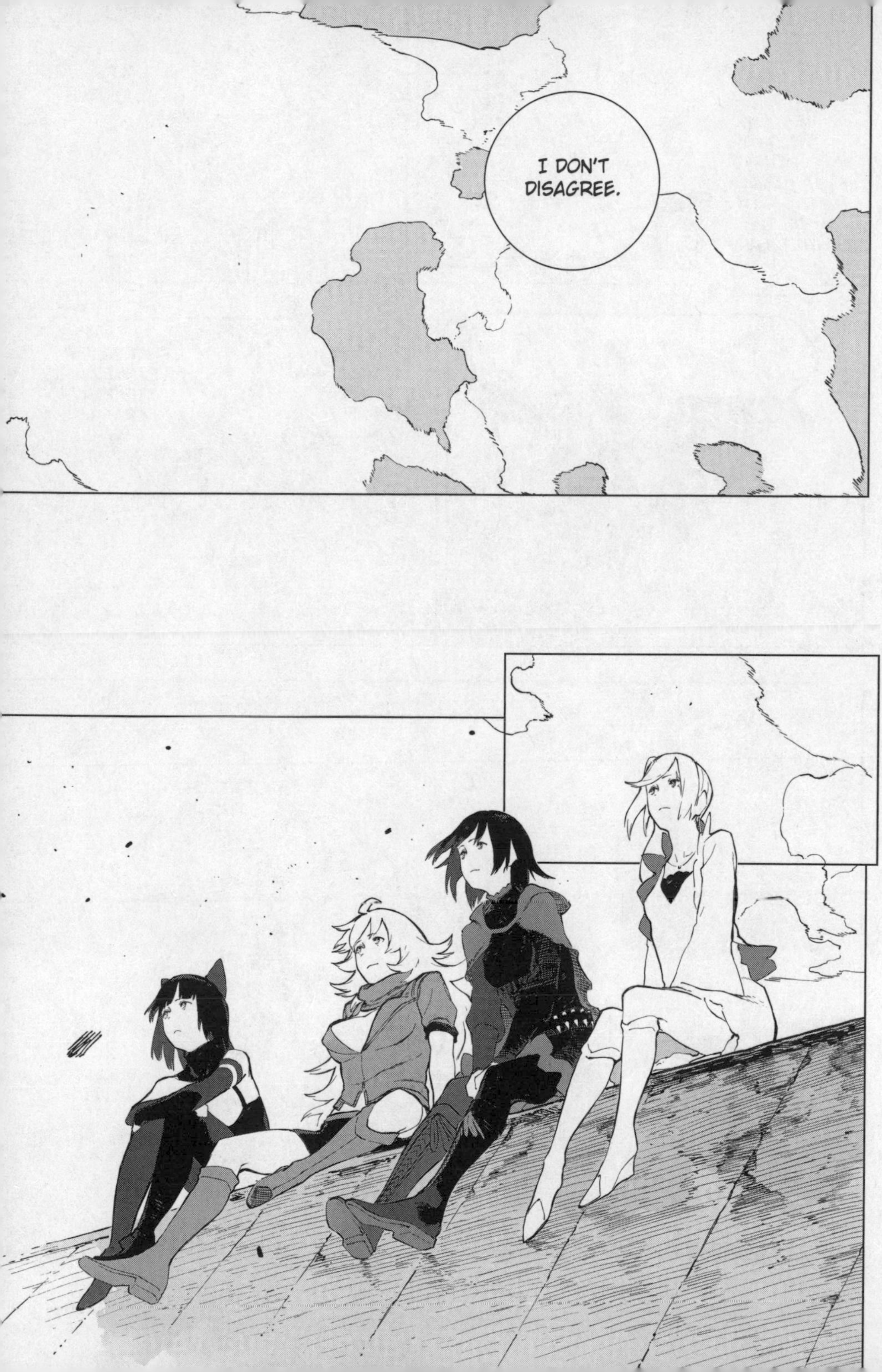
I DON'T DISAGREE.

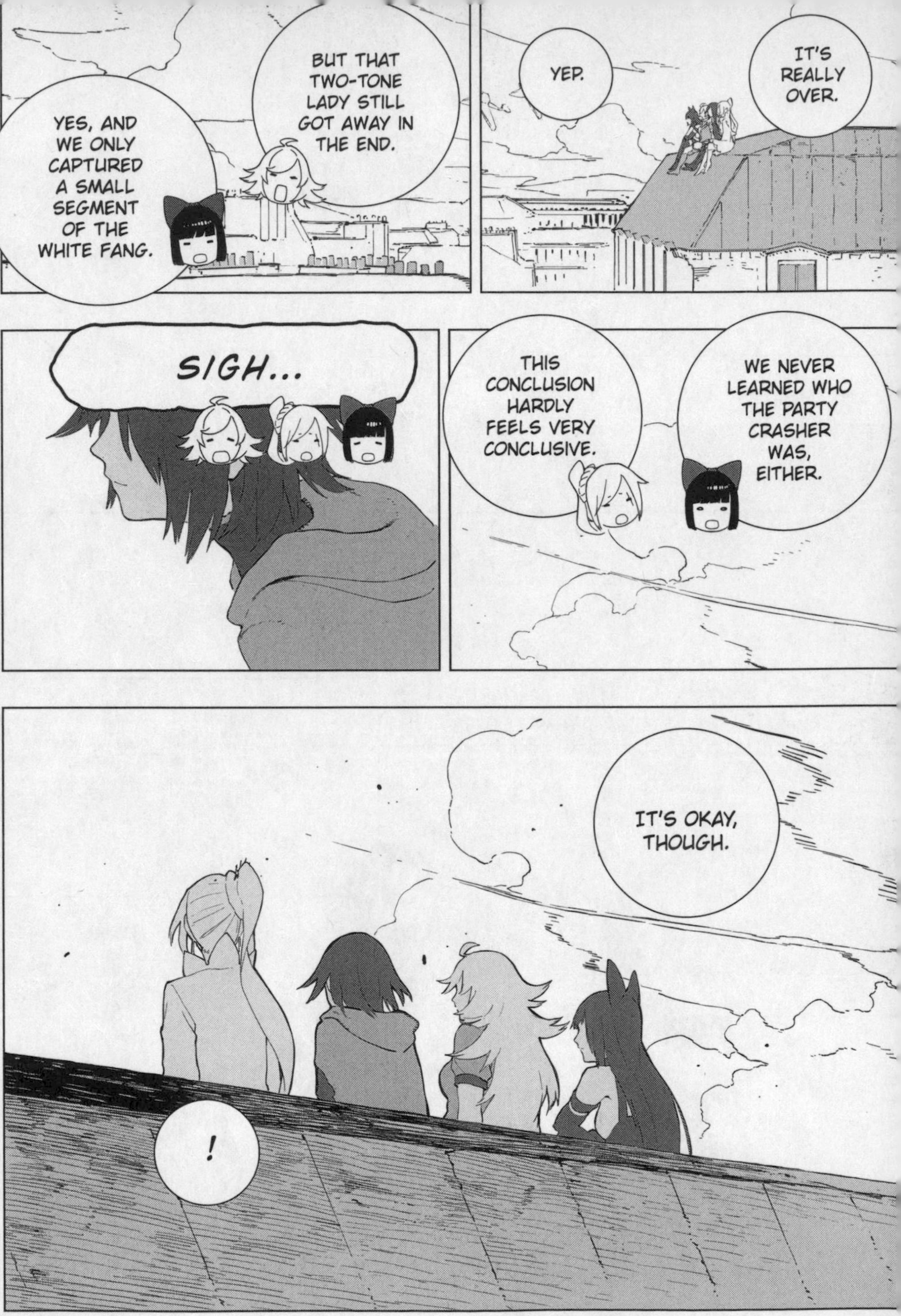
IT'S REALLY OVER.
YEP.
BUT THAT TWO-TONE LADY STILL GOT AWAY IN THE END.
YES, AND WE ONLY CAPTURED A SMALL SEGMENT OF THE WHITE FANG.
WE NEVER LEARNED WHO THE PARTY CRASHER WAS, EITHER.
THIS CONCLUSION HARDLY FEELS VERY CONCLUSIVE.
SIGH...
IT'S OKAY, THOUGH.
!

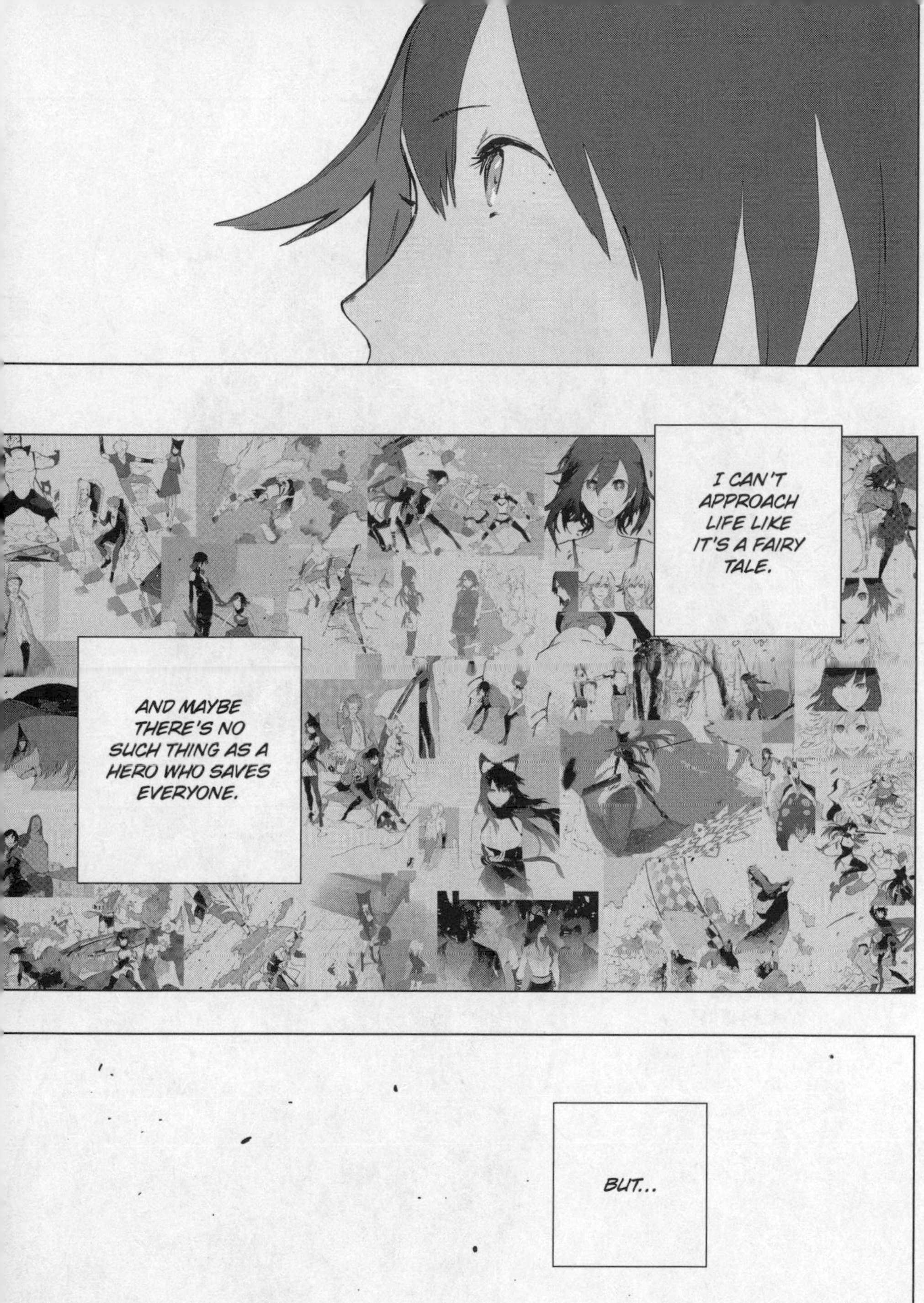
I CAN'T APPROACH LIFE LIKE IT'S A FAIRY TALE.
AND MAYBE THERE'S NO SUCH THING AS A HERO WHO SAVES EVERYONE.
BUT...

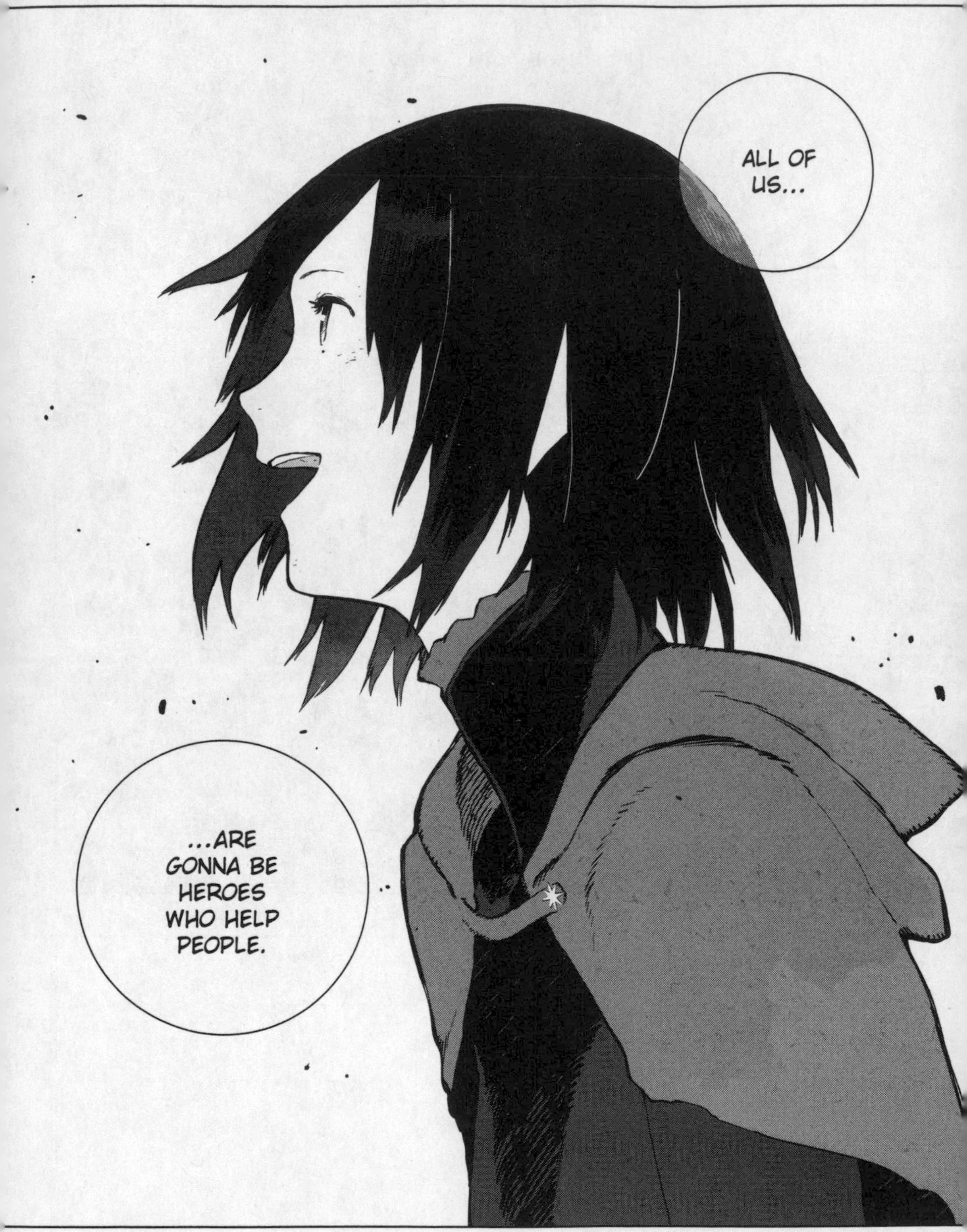
ALL OF US...
...ARE GONNA BE HEROES WHO HELP PEOPLE.

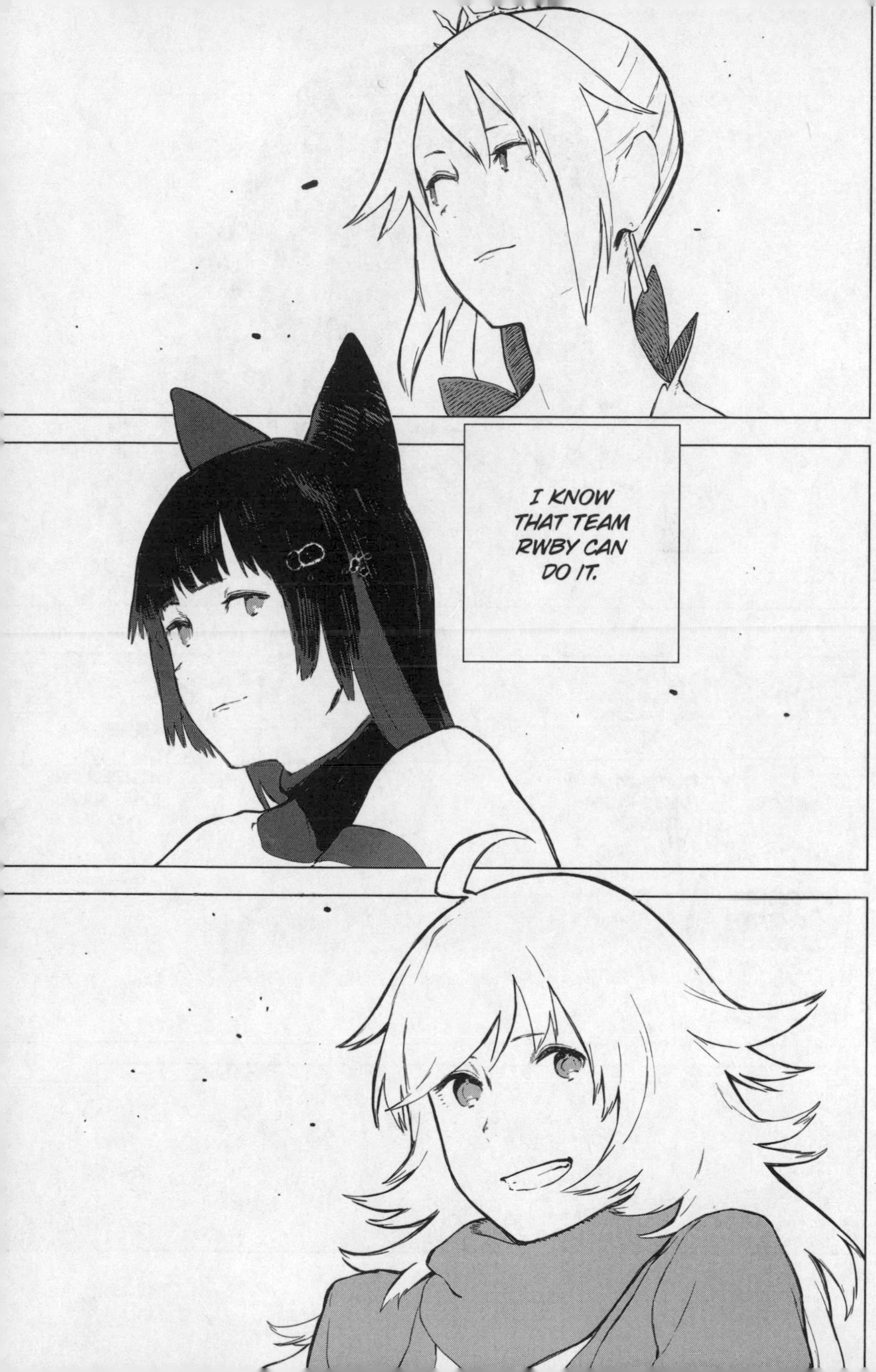
I KNOW THAT TEAM RWBY CAN DO IT.

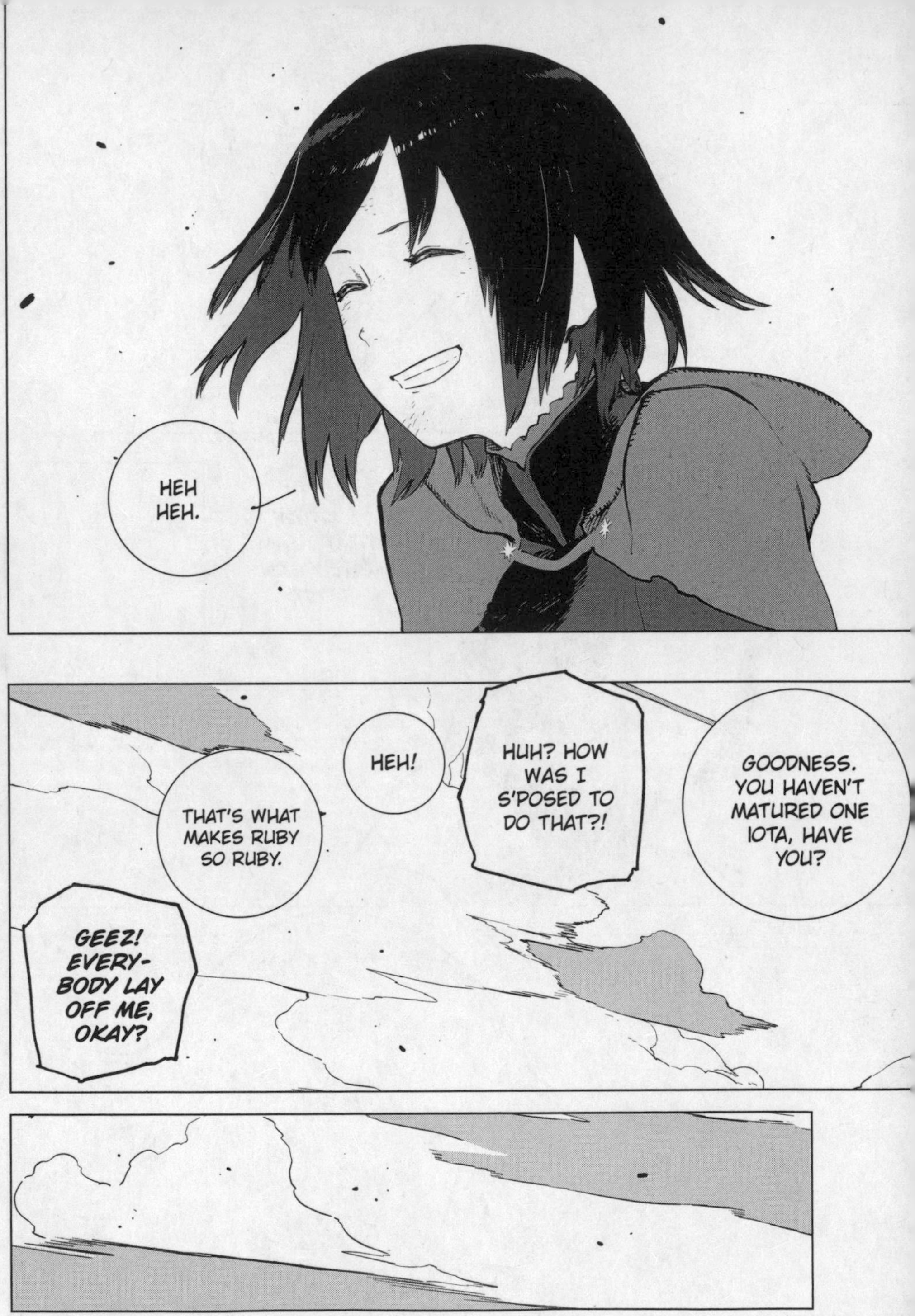
HEH HEH.
GOODNESS. YOU HAVEN'T MATURED ONE IOTA, HAVE YOU?
HUH? HOW WAS I S'POSED TO DO THAT?!
HEH!
THAT'S WHAT MAKES RUBY SO RUBY.
GEEZ! EVERY-BODY LAY OFF ME, OKAY?

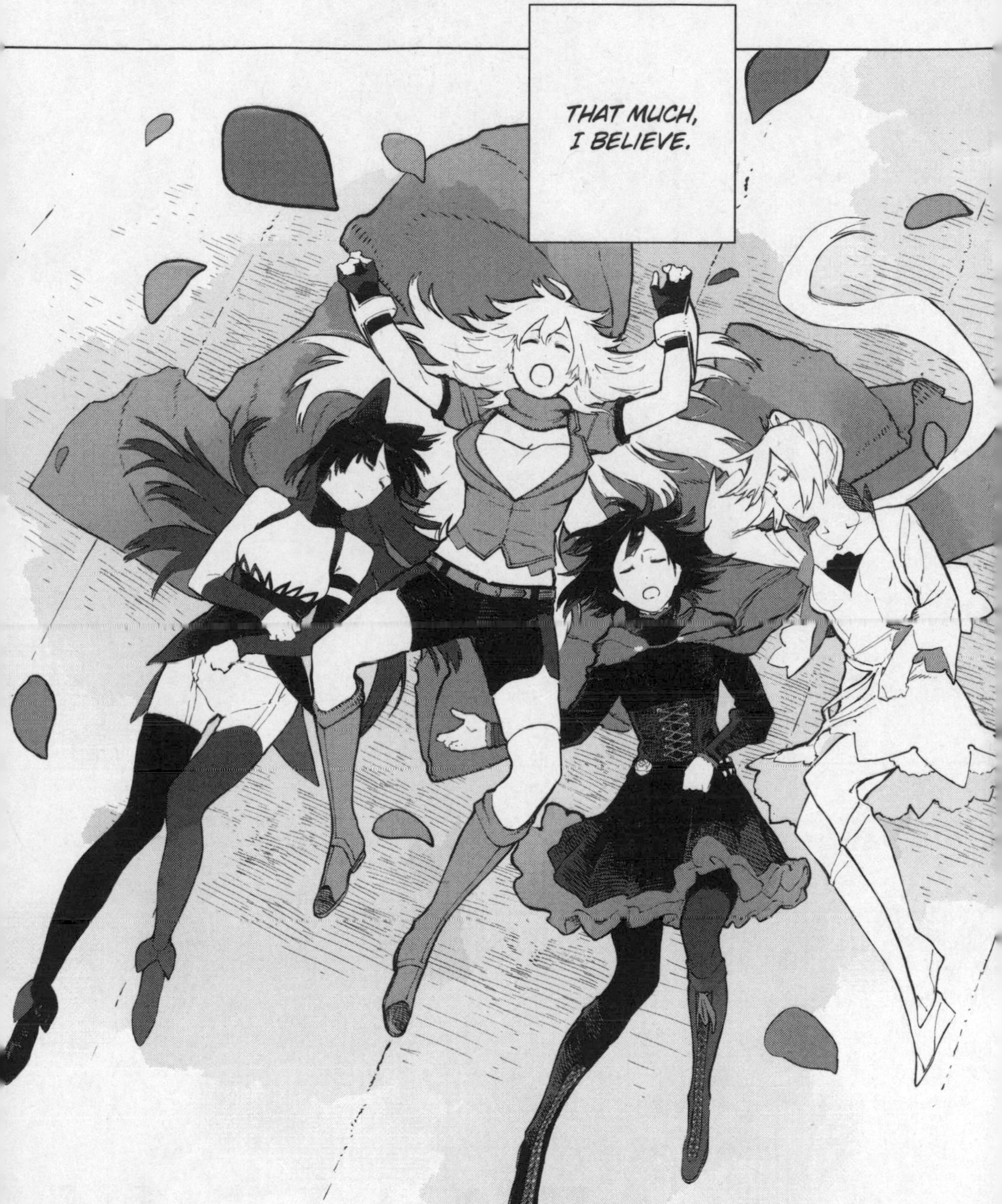
THAT MUCH, I BELIEVE.

THE END

RWBY

RWBY THE OFFICIAL MANGA

BUNTA KINAMI was born in Ibaraki Prefecture in Japan, and started drawing manga after he noticed that his friends enjoyed drawing. His favorite series include *Dogs: Bullets & Carnage* by Shirow Miwa and *Nausicaä of the Valley of the Wind* by Hayao Miyazaki. He began his professional career with *RWBY: The Official Manga*.

RWBY THE OFFICIAL MANGA

VOLUME 3
VIZ SIGNATURE EDITION

STORY AND ART BY
BUNTA KINAMI

ORIGINAL STORY BY
MONTY OUM & ROOSTER TEETH PRODUCTIONS

TRANSLATION **Caleb Cook**
LETTERING **Evan Waldinger**
DESIGN **Shawn Carrico**
EDITOR **David Brothers**

Printed in the U.S.A.

Published by VIZ Media, LLC
P.O. Box 77010
San Francisco, CA 94107

10 9 8 7 6 5 4 3 2 1
First Printing, June 2021

VIZ MEDIA
viz.com

VIZ SIGNATURE
vizsignature.com

ratings.viz.com
RATED T TEEN

PARENTAL ADVISORY
RWBY: THE OFFICIAL MANGA
is rated T for Teen and is
recommended for ages 13 and up.
This volume contains violence.

THE WORLD OF
RWBY

WRITTEN BY DANIEL WALLACE

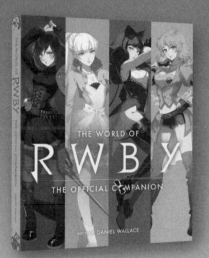

The definitive companion to the hit animated series, *The World of RWBY* is the ultimate celebration of a pop-culture phenomenon. Go behind the scenes with exclusive commentary from Rooster Teeth and explore the show's creation through In-depth interviews with the writers, animators and voice artists. With comprehensive analysis of key characters and iconic episodes, and showcasing stunning visuals from the series, this is the must-have book for RWBY fans around the world.

VIZ

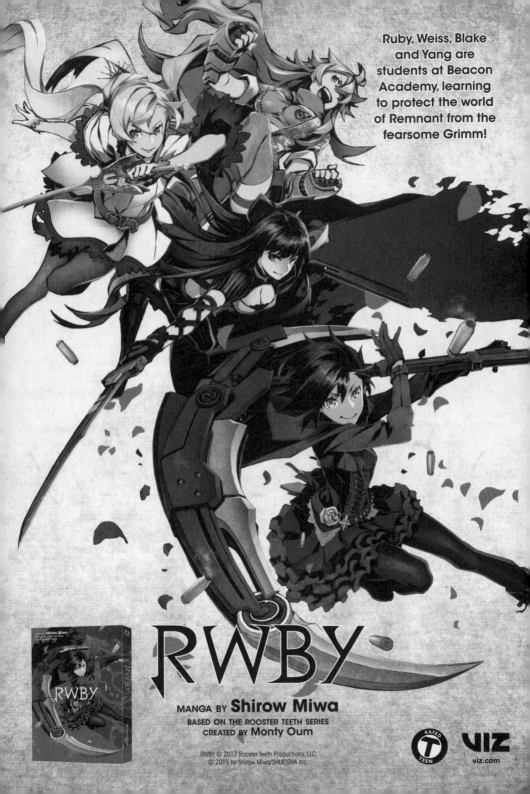

RUBY ROSE

WEISS SCHNEE

BLAKE BELLADONNA

YANG XIAO LONG

RWBY

OFFICIAL MANGA ANTHOLOGIES

Original Concept by Monty Oum & Rooster Teeth Productions, Story and Art by Various Artists

All-new stories featuring Ruby, Weiss, Blake and Yang from Rooster Teeth's hit animation series!

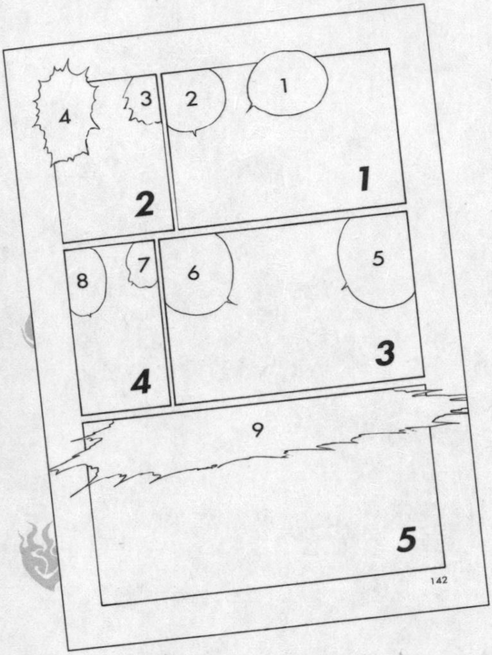
1
2
3
4
1
2
5
6
7
8
3
4
9
5
142

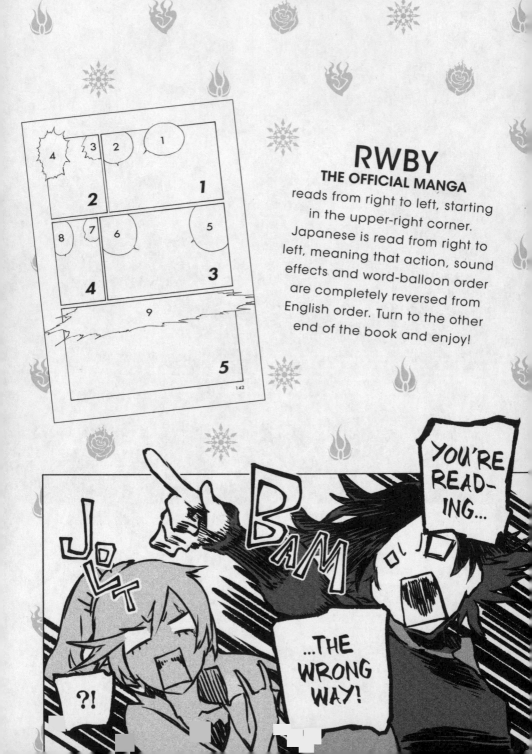

RWBY

THE OFFICIAL MANGA

reads from right to left, starting in the upper-right corner. Japanese is read from right to left, meaning that action, sound effects and word-balloon order are completely reversed from English order. Turn to the other end of the book and enjoy!

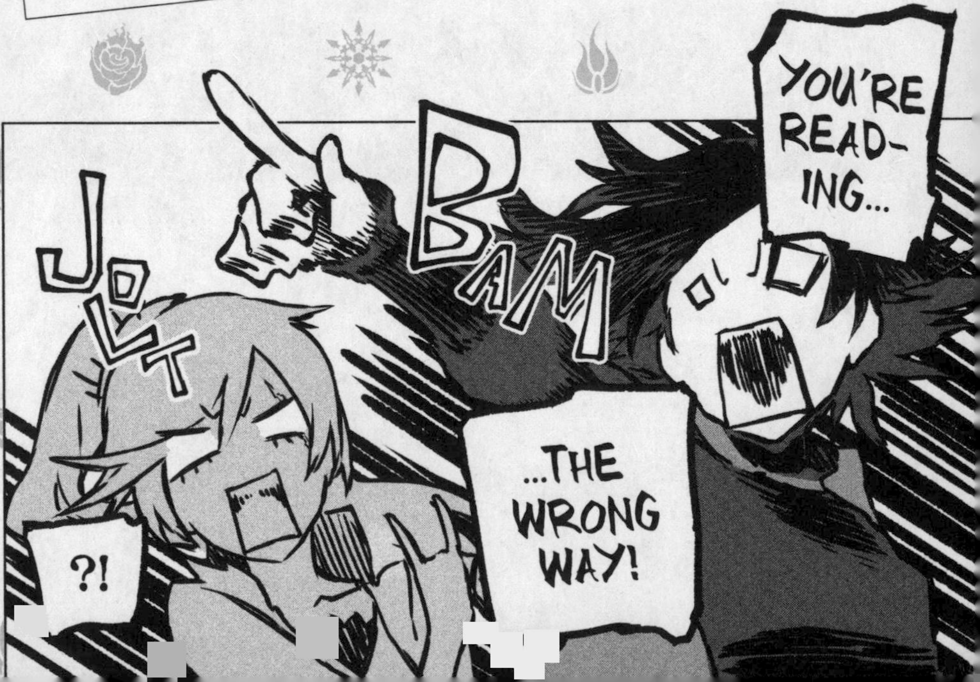
YOU'RE READING...
BAM
JOLT
...THE WRONG WAY!
?!